The Vital South

EARL BLACK
AND MERLE BLACK

THE

Vital South

HOW PRESIDENTS
ARE ELECTED

HARVARD UNIVERSITY PRESS
CAMBRIDGE, MASSACHUSETTS
LONDON, ENGLAND

This book is printed on acid-free paper, and its binding
materials have been chosen for strength and durability.

Library of Congress Cataloging in Publication Data
Black, Earl, 1942–
The vital South : how presidents are elected /
Earl Black and Merle Black.
p. cm.
Includes bibliographical references and index.
ISBN 0-674-94130-6 (alk. paper)
1. Party affiliation—Southern States—History.
2. Political parties—Southern States—History.
3. Voting—Southern States—History.
4. Presidents—United States—Election—History.
I. Black, Merle. II. Title.
JK2295.A13B583   1992
324.975—dc20   91-26725
CIP

*In memory of our mother
Dorothy Owen Black*

Contents

Acknowledgments

Many people have helped us write this book. At Harvard University Press we wish to thank Aida Donald once again for steering the enterprise and expediting publication. Kate Schmit improved the book with excellent editorial suggestions; and Carrie Curvin and Elizabeth Suttell supervised a variety of editorial tasks. We are grateful also to James L. Sundquist and John Shelton Reed for their constructive criticism and advice. David Fischer prepared the index.

At the University of South Carolina, Earl Black had the invaluable support of Sandra Hall and Lori Joye in preparing the manuscript. Mark Crislip was a superb research assistant. He produced all of the book's maps and other graphics, solving one technical problem after another with amazing skill and imagination.

Merle Black was helped by a grant from the University Research Council of the University of North Carolina at Chapel Hill and by funds from the Emory University Graduate School to the Department of Political Science, which provided summer research assistance. He has been aided by two excellent research assistants. Timothy Bovard of the University of North Carolina at Chapel Hill created most of the computer files upon which our analysis of surveys has been based. At Emory University, Dan Murphy created additional computer files and produced many of the tables on which the analysis is based. Both worked with skill and enthusiasm, and it is a pleasure to acknowledge their assistance. Additional thanks for help are due to Kenneth Hardy, Sue Dodd, Josephine Marsh, and David Sheaves of the Institute for Research in Social Science, University of North Carolina at Chapel Hill, as well as to Greg Haley, Karen Salsbury, Denise Brubaker, and Esther Nerenbaum of the Emory University Department of Political Science.

Over the years we have had the benefit of "talking politics" with a number of friends and colleagues, whose thoughts have left lasting impressions: Alan Abramowitz, Lee Atwater, Whit Ayres, Tod Baker, Thad Beyle, Ann Bowman, Courtney Brown, Charles Bullock, Jack

Fleer, Mike Giles, Blease Graham, Loch Johnson, Lee Johnston, William Keech, Harvey Klehr, Paul Luebke, Clifton McCleskey, Stuart McDonald, Bill Moore, Larry Moreland, James Peacock, George Rabinowitz, John Shelton Reed, Dick Richardson, Larry Sabato, Harold Stanley, Bob Steed, Randy Strahan, Larry Taulbee, George Tindall, and Tom Walker.

Our greatest personal debts are owed to our wives, Sena Black and Debra Larson, and to our daughters, Stacey, Claire, and Julia. All of them had ideas and suggestions—"take out the big words" was recommended more than once—that found their way into the manuscript.

In this book we have made frequent use of the National Election Studies of presidential elections from 1952 to 1988 conducted by the Center for Political Studies of the Institute for Social Research at the University of Michigan. In addition, we have used the exit polls conducted in each presidential election from 1976 to 1988 by CBS News and the New York Times, as well as exit polls of selected Senate elections conducted by these organizations during the 1980s. The National Election Studies surveys and the CBS News/New York Times Exit Polls were made available through the Inter-University Consortium for Political and Social Research. We are grateful to the consortium for the use of these data collections; neither the collector of the original data nor the consortium bears any responsibility for the analyses or interpretations presented here.

Finally, portions of Chapters 1, 11, and 13 draw upon material previously published in our chapter, "The 1988 Presidential Election and the Future of Southern Politics," in Laurence W. Moreland, Robert P. Steed, and Tod A. Baker, eds., *The 1988 Presidential Election in the South* (New York: Praeger, 1991), pp. 255–279.

All errors of fact and interpretation are our responsibility.

I

The National Setting

1

The Republican Edge

Once upon a time, so the story goes, there was a legendary southern senator who was eager to begin campaigning for another term. Reaching his campaign chairman on the phone from Washington, the senator exclaimed, "John, John, we got to announce!"

"Announce what, Senator?"

"For reelection, of course."

"But Senator, that's four years away. Don't you think it's a little early?"

"No, no, we got to get going! Now, remind me, John, how'd I do against those first fellows who ran against me?"

"Why, Senator, you beat them so bad they couldn't get elected to anything."

"That's right!," the senator replied. "Beat 'em so bad they were finished in politics. Now, how'd I do against my next opponent?"

"Well, Senator, you whipped him so bad he couldn't win a seat in the House of Representatives."

"That's right! Time I finished whipping him, he couldn't get elected to the House of Representatives. Now, remind me about that last fellow I ran against."

"Now, Senator, you remember that was ol' Buddy ——," not exactly a household name in the state.

"That's right! Knew his daddy. Tell me, what in the world happened to Buddy?"

"Ah, well, Senator, don't you recall? He got sick—and died."

"That's right! That's right!," shouted the senator. "We *killed* him!"[1]

The victorious senator was a Republican, his vanquished opponents all Democrats. Only a small leap of the imagination is required to stretch this story into a metaphor of presidential politics in the modern South. In the region where the Republican cause was once so hopeless that Republican presidential candidates never bothered to campaign, the list of thoroughly beaten Democratic presidential nominees—Hubert Humphrey in 1968, George McGovern in 1972, Walter Mondale in 1984, and Michael Dukakis in 1988—seems to grow longer with each new election.

The 1988 contest illustrates the pattern. Once again the Republicans convincingly swept the South. George Bush defeated Michael Dukakis by 58 to 42 percent, a margin of victory unapproached by the Republicans in any other region of the nation and matched or surpassed only in a few small western states. In most southern states the campaign was essentially over a month before the actual voting. The Democratic party, having nominated a politician who could be attacked in the South as the most naive sort of northeastern liberal, lacked both a convincing message and a credible messenger. Bush easily secured the overwhelming white majorities that continue to be the hallmark of Republican victories in the South.

"I can't understand the type of thinking," Bush charged in speeches across the region (and nation), "that lets first degree murderers who haven't even served enough time to be eligible for parole out on parole so they can rape and plunder again and then isn't willing to let the teachers lead the kids in the pledge of allegiance."[2] Most white southerners (including some who voted for Dukakis anyway) could not understand it, either. The shrewd Texas Republican Senator Phil Gramm captured Dukakis's predicament: "There's no one silver bullet, but you combine three or four of those issues and it induces Joe to say to Sarah across the kitchen table, 'Honey, this Dukakis guy is not our kind of person.'"[3] Perceived as someone who did not share their values, and who therefore could not be relied upon even to recognize, much less to defend and advance their interests, Dukakis was not a believable candidate to the vast majority of southern white voters.

The fall of the South as an assured stronghold of the Democratic party in presidential elections is one of the most significant developments in modern American politics. For more than six decades, from 1880 through 1944, the eleven states of the old Confederacy—Alabama, Arkansas, Florida, Georgia, Louisiana, Mississippi, North Carolina, South Carolina, Tennessee, Texas, and Virginia—regularly voted as a solid bloc in favor of the presidential candidate nominated by the Democratic party.

Over the past half-century, however, the South has shifted from an overwhelmingly Democratic area to a region characterized initially by balanced competition between the two parties (1952–1964) and, more recently, by a distinct Republican advantage.[4] Lyndon Johnson's administration (1963–1969) combined racial, economic, and cultural liberalism in pursuit of the Great Society at home with an ineffective escalation of the Vietnam War. These unpopular policies divided the southern Democratic party into antagonistic and sometimes irreconcilable factions. Once the third-party adventure of Alabama Governor George C. Wallace was exhausted, Republican strategists discovered many salient issues and themes that could be used to fashion presidential victories in the South.[5] Aside from Jimmy Carter's victory in 1976, Republican presidential candidates have now carried all or almost all of the region's electoral vote since 1972.

The Republicans have understood the dynamics of presidential politics in the South far better than the Democrats. The southern electorate—like the rest of the nation—is now splintered into Democrats, Republicans, and independents, with neither of the two parties able to attract a majority. In this broken field of partisans and independents, the basic formula for success is straightforward. Each party needs to unite the various factions that constitute its base. Even a completely united Democratic party is no longer large enough to win by itself, however, and even the most cohesive Republican party still falls short of constituting a majority of the entire electorate. In order to win, both southern parties also have to appeal to independents and even to some adherents of the rival party.

Since the end of the Great Society, Republican presidential candidates have usually beaten their Democratic rivals at both tasks, unification and outreach. Southern Republicans have rallied more cohesively than southern Democrats around their presidential nominees. Even more important, Republican nominees have run well among white independents and conservative Democrats. By contrast, all of the recent Democratic presidential candidates, with the sole exception of Carter in 1976, have fared poorly among independents. None of the Democratic nominees has generated significant support from Republicans.

Several factors have helped the Republicans secure enormous votes from white southerners in the modern era. The list begins—but hardly ends—with the parties' contrasting positions on civil rights and race relations. In the 1988 presidential election, according to the CBS News/New York Times Exit Poll, whites constituted the vast majority—83 percent—of southern voters. Much smaller shares of the region's presidential electorate were accounted for by blacks (14 percent) and Hispanics (3 percent). The Republicans have understood that, despite the successes of southern Democratic biracial coalitions in many state and local elections, it is still possible to win presidential contests without appealing directly to the region's black voters—provided that their candidate wins an overwhelming majority among the much bigger group of white voters.

From the end of Reconstruction through the last election of Franklin Roosevelt in 1944, traditional southern one-party politics rested in part on the notion that the Democratic party was the white South's chosen instrument in national politics for maintaining white supremacy. When the national Democratic party shifted decisively to a pro–civil rights position in response to the civil rights movement of the early 1960s, southern Democratic politicians correctly expected the party to lose support among white conservatives. Shortly after he signed the Civil Rights Act of 1964, President Johnson told an aide, "I think we just delivered the South to the Republican party for a long time to come."[6]

As Johnson took the Democrats to the left on civil rights, Arizona Senator Barry Goldwater led the Republicans to the right.[7] Many white southerners now regard as settled such important, permanent changes in race relations as the right to vote and equal access to places of public accommodations. Nonetheless, numerous whites remain unsympathetic to governmentally sponsored efforts to desegregate schools (particularly in metropolitan areas, where extensive busing would be required) and to monitor racial discrimination in employment.

Although majorities of both white and black southerners agree that "There would be a lot fewer problems if people were treated more equally," the issues of affirmative action and preferential treatment sharply split the races. In a spring 1988 poll conducted by the Center for Political Studies of the University of Michigan, southern whites and blacks were asked the following question: "Some people say that because of past discrimination blacks should be given preference in hiring and promotion. Others say that such preference in hiring and promotion of blacks is wrong because it gives blacks advantages they haven't earned. What about your opinion—are you for or against preferential hiring and promotion of blacks?" So salient was this controversy that few whites (less than 2 percent) or blacks (about 4 percent) had no opinions. The result was a very strong degree of racial polarization. Eighty-six percent of the southern whites were opposed to preferential treatment of blacks, while 69 percent of blacks were in favor.

Given these attitudes among whites, Republican presidential candidates have usually been seen as far more sympathetic with the views of the white majority in the South than have their Democratic opponents. Among many southern whites who think about these matters, especially since Ronald Reagan's presidency, the Republicans are generally seen as shutting the door against governmentally initiated racial change, while the Democrats are commonly perceived as opening the door.

Presidential elections still offer many ways to use racial themes to win votes. "Direct appeals to racial prejudice may no longer be acceptable in American politics," Thomas B. Edsall has observed, "but race, in an indirect and sometimes subliminal way, remains a driving force in the battle today between Republicans and Democrats."[8] Prejudicial feelings and conflicts of interest between whites and blacks can still be exploited in elections, especially when the appeal can be packaged in symbols or issues that have no explicit connection with race.

Asked in 1981 to discuss the role of race in Republican campaign strategy, an experienced official in the Reagan White House contrasted Republican strategy in the 1968 presidential campaign with its approach in the early 1980s. "As to the whole Southern strategy that Harry Dent and others put together in 1968," he stated, "opposition to the Voting Rights Act would have been a central part of keeping the South. Now [the new southern strategy] doesn't have to do that. All you have to do to keep the South is for Reagan to run in place on the issues he's campaigned on since 1964 . . . and that's fiscal conservatism, balancing the budget, cut taxes, you know, the whole cluster." The official described the evolution of Republican thought on the race issue as follows:

> You start off in 1954 by saying "Nigger, nigger, nigger." By 1968 you can't say "nigger"—that hurts you. Backfires. So you say stuff like forced busing, states' rights, and all that stuff. You're getting so abstract [that] you're talking about cutting taxes, and all these things you're talking about are totally economic things and a by-product of them is [that] blacks get hurt worse than whites. And subconsciously maybe that is part of it. I'm not saying that. But I'm saying that if it is getting that abstract, and that coded, that we are doing away with the racial problem one way or the other. You follow me—because obviously sitting around

saying, "We want to cut this," is much more abstract than even the busing thing *and* a hell of a lot more abstract than "Nigger, nigger."[9]

While the Republicans' advantage in presidential politics stems in part from taking positions on racial questions that run with the main currents of white opinion, the contemporary appeal of the party among southern whites goes far beyond concerns about race. The perennial issue of fostering prosperity has usually worked in favor of the GOP. Jimmy Carter, the sole Democratic president since 1969, stood for reelection in a year that combined high interest rates with high inflation; in the experience of many white southerners, the Democratic party became associated with bad economic times. In contrast, economic recovery since the recession of 1982–83 has prompted millions of southerners to view the Republican party positively as an instrument of economic opportunity and upward mobility. The Reagan tax cuts have allowed Republican strategists to claim that the GOP wants to let Americans keep more of what they make and that the Democrats would let the federal government tax away their earnings.

These perceptions concerning economic well-being are correlated with support for Republican presidential candidates. In the 1988 CBS News/New York Times Exit Poll, a majority (56 percent) of southern white voters said they were better off financially in 1988 than they had been in 1981. Bush won 88 percent from this group. By comparison, Bush won only 29 percent of the vote among the one-quarter of southern whites who said their economic situation was worse in 1988 than when Reagan took office. There is no reason to think the state of the economy will always work to the Republicans' advantage, and Republicans someday may have to test their candidate's appeal during an economic downturn. In 1984 and 1988, Republican presidential candidates benefited from favorable economic conditions among majorities of white southern voters.

Recent Republican presidential candidates and presidents have also benefited from the perception that they will better defend the nation's international interests. Again the comparison between the Carter and Reagan years is instructive. Whether rightly or wrongly, President Carter came to be viewed as too irresolute to stand up to the Iranians, much less to the Soviet Union. Although the Reagan record on national security was hardly a string of unbroken victories, the president did succeed in reviving national pride. President Reagan sharply increased military expenditures and concluded an arms reduction treaty with the Russians only months before the 1988 election, allowing Vice-President Bush to claim that the Reagan approach of bargaining through enhanced military strength had actually worked.

Beyond providing peace and prosperity, the Republicans have emphasized the importance of symbolic conservative values, including the preservation of traditional family values, the importance of religion, support for capital punishment, and opposition to gun control. The rhetoric of the Reagan administration was warmly received by many conservative and moderate southern whites who agreed with much of Reagan's cultural conservatism.

Finally, the Republicans have greatly benefited in the South from the popularity of Ronald Reagan. The former movie star and California governor had long been a favorite among Republican activists, and Reagan's thoughts and deeds generally ran with the grain of received white opinion. Southern Republicans discovered an authentic folk hero to personify their beliefs and goals. According to the CBS News/New York Times Exit Poll, in 1988 72 percent of southern white voters approved of Reagan's presidency, considerably more than the 60 percent of white voters outside the South. Reagan's popularity was his greatest gift to Bush, who received 89 percent of the vote among southern whites who approved of Reagan while winning only 15 percent among the 28 percent who disapproved of Reagan.

Thus recent Republican presidents have been viewed by many white southerners as more committed than their Democratic rivals to protecting their values and advancing their interests over a wide range of questions: moderating the pace of governmentally sponsored racial change, resisting tax increases, defending the nation in a dangerous world, and preserving traditional cultural values. Many factors, not a single grand factor, account for the Republicans' southern advantage in presidential politics.[10]

These momentous changes within the South have had enormous consequences for American politics. Although the fact is not always fully appreciated, the eleven states of the old Confederacy now constitute the largest region in the United States. Beginning in 1992 the South alone will contain 54 percent of the electoral votes needed to elect a president. The transformation of the South from a sturdy Democratic base into a prominent Republican stronghold has shaken the foundations of modern presidential politics.

With the collapse of the Democrats' traditional southern base, the

Democratic party has been left without an assured starting point for winning presidential elections. Reduced to basics, the Democrats have failed to develop fresh support outside the South to compensate for their loss of the region that once automatically gave them about half of the electoral votes needed to win the White House. The Republicans, meanwhile, seized the opportunity to attract southern whites and thereby successfully executed the Sun Belt strategy that Kevin Phillips had mapped out in the late 1960s in *The Emerging Republican Majority*. By combining Republican votes in the West with new Republican strength in the South, the Republicans have been able to create a much larger base of fairly reliable support than have the Democrats.

The partisan transformation of the South in presidential elections is an absorbing story. Much of this book will discuss the conditions, candidates, and outcomes of presidential politics in the region over the past half-century. What has happened—and continues to happen—in the South has profound implications for the control of the world's most important political office. The Republicans had already developed extensive and durable support among the western states in the 1950s, and the addition of the South gave them a huge area from which to mount presidential campaigns.

Politics is about interests, emotions, and aspirations. Nowhere in the nation have the interests of various groups been more conflictual, the emotions more abrasive, the aspirations more noble or despicable, or the competition among rival politicians more fierce and relentless than in the South. The South has been crucial, if not indispensable, to the renewed success of the Republicans in modern presidential politics. Nowhere have Republican victories been larger, the changes more fundamental, and the outcomes more significant for winning the presidency.

The South's allegiance in presidential elections is important not simply for the millions who live in the region but also for the much larger number of Americans who live elsewhere. The addition of the South to the Republican party's presidential base has given the GOP a striking advantage over the Democrats. The Democrats' inability thus far to devise an effective countervailing electoral strategy, one which would either emphasize states outside the South to compensate for its southern losses or reclaim part of the Republicans' southern base, has left the party poorly situated to recapture the presidency unless the Republicans stumble so egregiously that they throw an election away or are simply overwhelmed by adverse circumstances.

An image of the South as trendsetter for national politics should be kept in mind as we review the factors that have usually assisted the Republicans, and typically damaged the Democrats, in presidential campaigns in the South. Much of what we say about the South can be said of the rest of the country. Precisely. That is the point. Republicans know it and have profited handsomely from that knowledge; Democrats have yet to learn it.

Presidential Elections after the Great Society

Because presidential elections are won by carrying states, all of which adhere to the norm of "winner takes all" in assigning electoral votes to the winning party, the state is the critical political unit in presidential politics. Just as Democrats enjoyed a decisive advantage among the states in the New Deal presidential elections, since 1968 Republicans have been much better situated than Democrats to win the presidency. The magnitude of the GOP's current advantage can be illustrated by analyzing state voting histories in presidential elections since Johnson left office.

Because our goals are to understand the regional structure of the Republican edge in recent presidential elections and to lay the foundation for comparisons with other historical periods, we have separated states that have usually supported a single party from states that tend to shift back and forth from one party to another. Three types of states, which we will term *Usually Democratic, Swing,* or *Usually Republican,* will be distinguished. Partisan states, whether Democratic or Republican, are defined as those in which the same party carries a state in three-fourths or more of the elections. A partisan state may thus deviate occasionally from its support for a particular party, but by definition it typically awards its electoral votes to one party. To avoid needless repetition the modifier *Usually* will normally be omitted in the text from references to Republican or Democratic states, but it should be kept in mind that perfection is not required to be classified as a partisan state. All states not qualifying as partisan are considered Swing.

Knowledge of the relative size of each party's electoral vote base is essential if we are to understand the dynamics of majority coalition-building in presidential elections. A party which achieves a marked superiority in the size of its electoral vote base has a greater chance of surviving its own political mistakes. Compared with a party with a small base of assured electoral votes, it is less dependent on the vagaries of short-term political events and issues for success and less dependent on the nomination of a demonstrably superior presidential candidate.

In electoral college terms, winning the presidency first of all involves carrying the party's base of generally reliable states. If the base is too small to provide a majority of the electoral vote, the party must then add enough swing states to make a majority. If the party base plus the swing states fall short of an electoral college majority, winning the presidency requires capturing some states normally won by the opposition. How easy or how difficult it is for a major party to construct a winning coalition of states depends in part on the electoral votes found in the Usually Democratic, Swing, and Usually Republican states.

These general considerations can be applied to presidential elections in the post–Great Society era. When the Democratic, Swing, and Republican states are identified and mapped (see Figure 1.1), a remarkable imbalance between the major parties emerges. In the aftermath of the Great Society the Republican party developed nothing less than its broadest base in history. Beginning with the 1992 presidential election, the 39 states which have usually voted Republican in recent contests will control almost three-fourths (74 percent) of the nation's electoral vote, a political fact of the utmost practical significance.

The unprecedented breadth of the Republican presidential base contrasts fundamentally with the Democrats' situation. With a national base consisting—in its totality—of Minnesota and the District of Columbia (2 percent of the 1992 electoral vote), the Democratic party after 1964 has been reduced to its weakest position in presidential politics since the disastrous period of the Civil War and Reconstruction. It is not too fanciful to picture the current battle for the presidency as a game in which the two parties compete every four years to see who can accumulate $50.01. The Democrats begin with savings of $2 and need to win $48.01; the Republicans start with $74 in the bank and can afford to lose $23.99.

Under these mismatched terms of competition, the Democratic candidate must carry the party's meager base, sweep the swing states (which contain about a quarter of the electoral vote), *and* win several states that have ordinarily gone Republican in recent times. Carter's

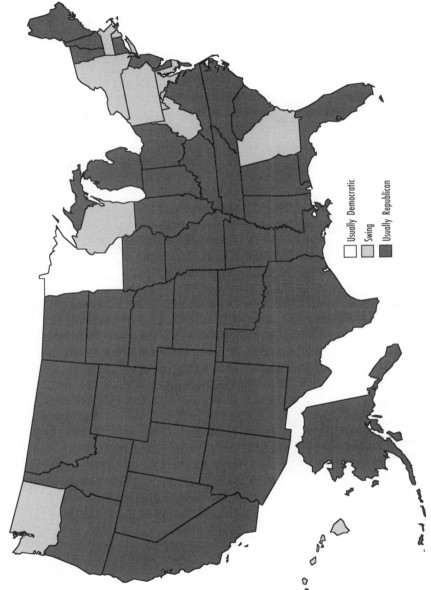

Figure 1.1 Presidential elections after the Great Society: Usually Democratic, Swing, and Usually Republican states in the 1968–1988 presidential elections. A state was classified as partisan if it was carried by the same party in at least 75 percent of the elections. Southern states were classified according to 1972–1988 elections. *Source:* Calculated by the authors from appropriate volumes of Richard M. Scammon, ed., *America Votes* (Washington, D.C.: Congressional Quarterly).

Usually Democratic

Swing

Usually Republican

performance in 1976 is a reminder that this is possible, but a Democratic victory remains improbable under current circumstances unless many factors—candidates, issues, conditions, and events—interact in state after state to discredit Republican candidates and policies while simultaneously favoring those of the Democrats.

Southern voting patterns after the Great Society need to be compared with those of other regions. Because the regional classifications of the U.S. Census Bureau are not completely suitable for our purposes, in this book we shall rearrange them slightly to distinguish five regions—South, Border, Northeast, Midwest, and West. As previously mentioned, the South consists of the 11 slave states which joined the Confederacy. Rimming the South to the north, the Border states include the remaining slave jurisdictions (Delaware, the District of Columbia, Kentucky, Maryland, Missouri, and West Virginia), as well as Oklahoma. The Northeast, which combines the Census Bureau's Mid-Atlantic and New England states, consists of Connecticut, Maine, Massachusetts, New Hampshire, New Jersey, New York, Pennsylvania, Rhode Island, and Vermont. Except for the treatment of Missouri as a Border state, the Midwest is identical to the Census Bureau's North Central region. It includes Illinois, Indiana, Iowa, Kansas, Michigan, Minnesota, Nebraska, North Dakota, Ohio, South Dakota, and Wisconsin. The West, which includes the 13 Mountain and Pacific states, is defined as Alaska, Arizona, California, Colorado, Hawaii, Idaho, Montana, Nevada, New Mexico, Oregon, Utah, Washington, and Wyoming. The term *North* will be used to indicate the United States minus the South.

At one time resentful and suspicious of the Republican party, the South has become a cornerstone of the Republican base (see Table 1.1). Aside from Georgia, which twice remained loyal to its native son Jimmy Carter and hence was mixed in its voting behavior, all of the southern states qualified as Republican in post–Great Society elections. Classifications for the southern states, it should be noted, are based on 1972–1988 elections rather than 1968–1988 elections. It is necessary, in the interest of political realism, to omit 1968 because of George Wallace's third-party campaign. Had Wallace not run in 1968, Richard Nixon would undoubtedly have defeated Hubert Humphrey in every southern state. To include 1968 for the South would severely *underestimate* the strength of Republicanism since 1972.

As the region with the largest share of electoral votes, the South has a potential leverage in presidential elections that depends on the extent to which its many electoral votes are cast for the same party.

Table 1.1 The Republican advantage in presidential politics after the Great Society: percentage of electoral vote (as apportioned by the 1990 census) cast by states classified as Usually Republican, Swing, or Usually Democratic for the 1968–1988 presidential elections, by region

	States				Region's share of electoral vote
Region	Usually Republican	Swing	Usually Democratic	R–D	
South	91	9	0	+91	27
West	87	13	0	+87	22
Midwest	82	9	8	+74	22
Border	63	31	6	+57	9
Northeast	32	68	0	+32	20
North	68	29	3	+65	73
United States	74	23	2	+72	100

Note: Southern states are classified according to the 1972–1988 elections. Regions have been ranked from highest to lowest according to the net difference *(R–D)* between the Republican and Democratic shares of the electoral votes.
Sources: Same as Figure 1.1; and *New York Times*, December 27, 1990.

In contemporary times, no region has devoted a greater share of its electoral votes to the Republicans. Although the West was almost as pro-Republican as the South, the West contains fewer electoral votes than the South. In every region except the Northeast, the Republican states contained substantial majorities of the electoral vote; in no region did the Democrats establish an impressive electoral base. The national Republican advantage of 74–2 in the size of the parties' bases was a product of a 91–0 Republican lead in the South combined with a 68–3 lead in the rest of the country. In the presidential elections after the Great Society, for the first time in American history, the South led the North as a source of dependable Republican electoral votes.

The Geography of Grassroots Presidential Elections

Although the electoral college makes individual states the central focus of presidential politics, relying solely on the state results to assess partisan tendencies could obscure important differences within states (and regions) concerning the modern party battle. By shifting to the county as a smaller political unit and then classifying the political behavior of counties as Usually Democratic, Swing, or Usually Republican using the same criteria employed for the states, we can show the Republican edge in contemporary grassroots presidential politics.

The Republicans' electoral college advantage is grounded upon an equally impressive record of repeated grassroots success (see Figure 1.2). In the post–Great Society period most of the nation's 3,100-odd counties—roughly seven in ten—have had a distinct partisan identity. Republican counties (1,183) have outnumbered Democratic counties (290) by better than six to one.

Because grassroots voting behavior has been heavily influenced by traditions dating back to the Civil War, it is not surprising to find Republican counties more common in the North (69 percent of counties outside the South usually voted Republican) than in the South (45 percent) or to discover twice as many Democratic counties in the South (14 percent) as in the North (7 percent). The imbalance between Republican and Democratic counties is especially pronounced in the West, the Midwest, and the Northeast. Many rural and small-town northern counties with small populations have traditionally supported Republicans, while central cities with substantial minority populations have been the northern areas most likely to vote Democratic. There are few northern Democratic counties, but they include the central cities of such urban giants as New York, Philadelphia, Pittsburgh, Boston, Baltimore, St. Louis, Kansas City, Chicago, Detroit, Milwaukee, Cleveland, Minneapolis, and San Francisco.

In the South, reliably Democratic settings in presidential elections have shrunk to Black Belt counties (note one cluster associated with the Mississippi River in Mississippi, Louisiana, and Arkansas and a string of Black Belt counties running from central Alabama to Southside Virginia), South Texas (heavy Hispanic population), portions of Middle Tennessee, and occasional central cities with heavy black populations (Atlanta, New Orleans, and Richmond).

Clusters of Republican counties are visible in every southern state except Georgia, where Carter's two campaigns prevented the emergence of reliable Republican bastions. Although there were three times as many Republican as Democratic counties in the South, the Republican advantage in grassroots politics was even greater since the southern Republican base included counties that contained the

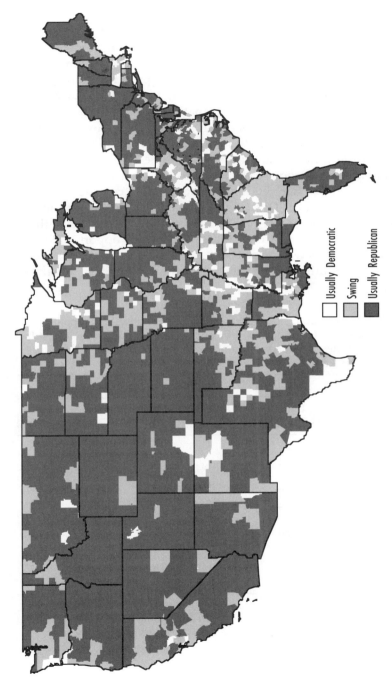

Figure 1.2 Grassroots presidential politics after the Great Society: Usually Democratic, Swing, and Usually Republican counties in the 1968–1988 presidential elections. Southern counties were classified according to 1972–1988 elections. *Source:* Same as Figure 1.1.

biggest cities and suburbs in Florida, Texas, North Carolina, Virginia, Alabama, South Carolina, and Mississippi.

Figure 1.2 specifies each party's county-level base in contemporary presidential politics but does not indicate the relative strength of grassroots Republicanism or Democracy. To appreciate fully the political significance of the county patterns, we have calculated the proportions of the popular vote emanating from counties classified as Democratic, Swing, or Republican. Across the country the vote produced by Republican counties in 1988 was three times as great as the vote cast in Democratic counties (see Table 1.2). In every region the Republican grassroots base contained at least half of the total vote, but the ratio of Republican advantage varied considerably from one region to another. Democratic bases of moderate size in the Northeast and the Midwest give Democrats fighting chances in those regions when short-term trends create Democratic opportunities.

The widest gap between the two parties' grassroots bases is found in the South. Southern counties classified as Republican generated

Table 1.2 The grassroots Republican advantage in presidential politics after the Great Society: percentage of 1988 popular vote cast by counties classified as Usually Republican, Swing, or Usually Democratic for the 1968–1988 presidential elections, by region

	Counties			
Region	Usually Republican	Swing	Usually Democratic	R/D
South	67	25	8	8.4
West	52	42	7	7.4
Border	56	28	15	3.7
Midwest	57	16	27	2.1
Northeast	50	19	31	1.6
North	54	25	21	2.6
United States	57	25	18	3.2

Note: Southern counties are classified according to the 1972–1988 elections.
Regions have been ranked from highest to lowest according to the ratio (R/D) of the share of the vote in Republican counties to the share of the vote in Democratic counties.
Source: Same as Figure 1.1.

two-thirds of the region's popular vote in 1988, while Democratic counties produced *less than a tenth* of the total southern vote. This Republican advantage of better than eight to one is another compelling indication of the South's critical importance in presidential politics.

The Modern Republican Advantage: Core and Swing Voters

Just as we have separated Usually Republican and Usually Democratic states and counties from those which display much less partisan regularity, similar distinctions need to be made about groups of voters. Which sorts of voters have generally given landslide majorities to Republican or Democratic candidates? Which groups have been more divided in their presidential voting behavior?

Drawing on the 1988 CBS News/New York Times Exit Poll, we can begin by classifying voters simultaneously according to partisanship (Democrat, Republican, or independent) and ideology (liberal, moderate, or conservative). Cross-classification produces a simple but powerful typology of voters that is very helpful in understanding how groups of voters can be combined to produce majority coalitions. It has the virtue of distinguishing voters according to concepts— "liberal Democrats," "conservative Democrats," "moderate independents," "conservative Republicans," and so on—that many individuals (politicians, strategists, journalists, and interested citizens) use daily as a sort of intellectual shorthand for making sense of the real world of American politics. The systematic categorization of voters allows us to determine the relative size of the various groups of voters, and then to see how cohesively different groups have voted in presidential elections. Because they place ideology in its partisan context (and vice versa), these categories help illuminate the dynamics of modern presidential politics, both by revealing how the Republicans have developed their advantage and by suggesting what the Democrats need to do to become competitive once again.[11]

For the moment we shall focus on white voters alone. Table 1.3 compares the percentage of southern and northern whites found in each of the nine voter types in the 1988 presidential election. Republicans outnumbered Democrats among southern white voters by 42 to 31 percent, double the lead they had in the North (38 to 33 percent). A plurality of white voters in both regions classified themselves ideologically as "moderates" (45 percent in the South versus 48 percent in the rest of the country), but substantial regional differ-

Table 1.3   Percent distribution of southern and northern white voters in the 1988 presidential election, by party and ideology

| | Party indentification | | | | | | | | | |
| | White southerners | | | | | White northerners | | | | |
Ideological identification	Dem	Ind	Rep	Tot	R/D	Dem	Ind	Rep	Tot	R/D
Liberal	8	3	2	13	0.3	12	5	2	18	0.2
Moderate	16	14	15	45	0.9	17	17	15	48	0.9
Conservative	7	10	26	43	3.7	5	7	22	34	4.4
Totals	31	27	42	100	1.4	33	29	38	100	1.2
C/L	0.9	3.3	13.0	3.3		0.4	1.4	11.0	1.9	

Note: R/D, ratio of Republicans to Democrats; C/L, ratio of conservatives to liberals. Percentages have been rounded.
Source: 1988 CBS News/New York Times Exit Poll.

ences existed in the percentages of voters who labeled themselves "liberals" or "conservatives." Conservative white southerners (43 percent) exceeded liberal white southerners (13 percent) by more than three to one. Outside the South there were only about twice as many conservatives as liberals.

While the ratio of Republicans to Democrats was essentially similar in the South and the North across all three ideological categories, the ratio of conservatives to liberals was consistently higher among southern whites than northern whites for all three partisan categories. Perhaps the most revealing comparison among the nine combinations of party and ideology is the ratio of conservative Republicans to liberal Democrats. Among both northern and southern whites, conservative Republicans were the single largest group of voters. They outnumbered liberal Democrats by three to one in the South and by two to one in the rest of the nation. The ideological orientations of white Democrats differed considerably by region, with liberals and conservatives evenly balanced in the South but liberals far outnumbering conservatives in the North.

In both the South and the North these different groups of white voters have displayed remarkable stability in the rank order of their support for Republican presidential candidates over the four Election Day Exit Polls (1976, 1980, 1984, and 1988) conducted by CBS News and the New York Times (see Figure 1.3). This analysis is based on seven rather than nine types of voters. Because of the small samples of liberal Republicans and liberal independents, each of these groups has been combined with a larger group that has similar voting patterns. Liberal independents have been placed with moderate Democrats, while the small number of liberal Republicans have been merged with moderate Republicans.

Republican nominees consistently won landslide majorities from four groups of white voters: conservative Republicans, moderate Republicans, liberal Republicans, and conservative independents. At the other extreme, liberal Democrats, moderate Democrats, and liberal independents repeatedly gave the Republican candidates their lowest votes. The remaining white vote, cast by moderate independents and conservative Democrats, gave Republican candidates medium levels of support.

Although the rankings of the seven white groups are the same in both the South and the North, in most comparisons the Republicans won larger shares in the South from similar types of voters. Among the most Republican groups, GOP presidential candidates on the

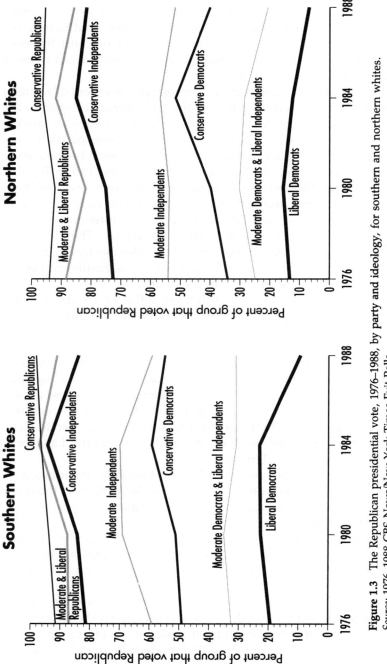

Figure 1.3 The Republican presidential vote, 1976–1988, by party and ideology, for southern and northern whites.
Source: 1976–1988 CBS News/New York Times Exit Polls.

average ran from one to seven percentage points better among southern than northern whites. Among the most Democratic groups, the Republican advantage among southern whites averaged six to seven percentage points. The most striking regional differences involve moderate independents and conservative Democrats. White southerners who were moderate independents were 11 points higher in Republican support than moderate independents elsewhere, and the South's conservative Democrats were 13 points more Republican than their northern counterparts. On the average, 54 percent of southern white conservative Democrats voted Republican over the 1976–1988 presidential elections, compared with only 41 percent Republican support among white conservative Democrats in the North.

Strategists conventionally distinguish groups that overwhelmingly support or oppose their party's candidates from groups that divide more evenly. Examination of Figure 1.3 suggests two natural dividing lines between "core" and "swing" groups of white voters. Our rule of thumb for identifying a "core," "base," "reliable," or "hip-pocket" partisan vote is a consistent advantage of two-thirds or more for the same party's candidate over a series of elections. Using this definition, the core Republican presidential vote is comprised of those groups which split two to one or greater in favor of the Republican candidate over the 1976–1988 elections, while the core Democratic presidential vote comes from those groups which provided similar levels of support for the Democratic candidate. Any group that provided neither party with a two-thirds advantage is classified as a "swing" group.

In the modern era, the most reliable Republican presidential vote has come from conservative Republicans, moderate Republicans, liberal Republicans, and independents who think of themselves as conservatives. As would be expected, conservative Republicans have been the most reliable supporters of Republican presidential candidates, dividing nineteen to one, South and North, in favor of their party's nominee. Moderate to liberal Republicans have been only slightly less supportive, usually voting nine to one for the GOP candidate. Finally, the various Republican nominees have been assisted by the sizable group of conservative independents, who have generally gone Republican by about four to one. All told, in 1988 the white Republican core group made up 53 percent of the South's total white vote and 46 percent of the northern white vote.

The white Democratic core presidential vote comes from liberal Democrats, moderate Democrats, and liberal independents. These groups constituted 27 percent of the southern white vote and 33 percent of the northern white vote, much smaller percentages than the comparable Republican core among whites. In addition, although the Democratic core groups voted overwhelmingly for Democratic presidential candidates, they were less cohesive than the Republican core groups.

Since the New Deal it has been an axiom among Republican presidential strategists that Republicans are a minority party. Precisely because the Republicans shrunk to the status of a minority party, they had to learn the hard way—their hard way was to lose five straight presidential elections—how to regain the White House even though most Americans did not—and still do not—think of themselves as Republicans. It took the Republican party two decades to regain the presidency. Since 1952, with the sole exception of Barry Goldwater's stridently inept effort in 1964, the Republicans have always been competitive in presidential campaigns and have ordinarily prevailed.

In modern presidential politics the Democrats' situation is similar to the position of the Republicans during the New Deal. The Democratic party's share of the electorate has declined from a substantial plurality to only a sizable minority of voters. Like the New Deal Republicans, the modern Democrats have experienced a long string of defeats in presidential elections. Unlike the Republicans, however, Democratic strategists have not yet learned how to be truly competitive in the unfamiliar landscape of modern presidential politics.

The types of voters we have identified are quite useful in understanding Republican successes and Democratic failures in presidential elections. A successful campaign begins with mobilizing a party's base vote. The struggle over the nomination sometimes puts different components of the base in direct competition, with the result that politicians have to secure their base. The earlier the nomination is settled, the more aggressive the outreach to losing factions, the more the losers acclimate to the likely nominee, the larger and more united is the base. In principle, the base is where presidential nominees poll landslide majorities and thus build their leads against areas of expected weakness. Generally, the larger the size of the base, and the more united the base, the more secure is the candidate in the general election.

In contemporary presidential politics mobilizing one's base—even to the hilt—never provides enough votes to win. There are a number of states, of course, where the Republican base by itself is large enough to provide victory. In most states, and in all regions, the Republicans hold an advantage in the size and cohesion of their bases, but they still fall short of victory. The Democratic party has an assured base in the District of Columbia, but its core vote does not constitute a majority in any state.

Winning the presidency turns on the extent to which the rival parties can capture majorities among voters who are not part of their core vote. Among white voters, the targets of opportunity in presidential campaigns are composed principally of moderate independents and conservative Democrats, two distinct groups with slightly different voting tendencies. Outside the South, moderate independents usually vote Republican, though not in landslide proportions; conservative Democrats usually vote Democratic, but they ordinarily do not provide landslide votes for Democratic candidates. As we have shown, in the South both of these "swing" groups have been providing substantial support to the Republicans.

These considerations suggest a further boiling down of the presidential electorate to four groups of voters—core Republican whites, swing whites, core Democratic whites, and blacks. Table 1.4 reports the relative size of the various groups in the South and the North, as well as the extent to which the various groups voted for George Bush in 1988. It demonstrates succinctly why Bush ran better in the South than in the rest of the nation.

Consider first the sizes of the core bases of presidential support in the South versus the rest of the nation. In the South, those whites who are members of groups that typically vote overwhelmingly for Republican presidential candidates made up 44 percent of all southern voters in November 1988—six points shy of a majority. The comparable Democratic party base is determined by adding the white core Democratic group (24 percent) to the percentage of blacks among southern voters (14 percent). The Democratic presidential core was thus 38 percent—12 points away from a majority. Neither core group constituted a majority, but the Republicans were much closer than the Democrats.

Outside the South the respective presidential bases of the parties were much more even. White core Republicans (41 percent) were virtually matched in the North by the combination of white core Democrats (30 percent) plus blacks (10 percent). In neither the South nor the North did a party's core voters constitute a majority of the

Table 1.4 Creating a larger Republican presidential majority in the South: percent of popular vote won by George Bush in 1988

Voter groups	Southern electorate Size × Unity = Yield			Cum total	Northern electorate Size × Unity = Yield			Cum total
White Republican base	44 ×	93	= 41	41	41 ×	90	= 37	37
White swing vote	18 ×	58	= 10	51	20 ×	49	= 10	47
White Democratic base	24 ×	24	= 6	57	30 ×	15	= 5	52
Blacks	14 ×	13	= 2	59	10 ×	11	= 1	53

Note: Size is the proportion of the vote cast by each group of voters in 1988; unity is the share of that group's vote won by George Bush; yield is the product of size times unity. For example, the white Republican base in the South constituted 44 percent of the region's voters, and Bush won 93 percent among this group; he therefore won 41 percent of the total vote cast in the South from this group. *Cum total* is the cumulative total of the popular vote received by Bush. All figures are rounded to the nearest whole number.

Source: Calculated by authors from the 1988 CBS News/New York Times Exit Poll.

entire presidential electorate. Presidential outcomes depend upon a party's ability to mobilize its base, prevail among swing voters, and take votes away from the other party's core.

In the South the 44 percent of the electorate who were core white Republican voters voted for Bush at the rate of 93 percent, thus yielding him 41 percent of the total southern vote—nine points away from a regional victory. Among the white swing groups, who made up 18 percent of the presidential electorate, Bush took 58 percent to generate another 10 points in the total vote. By this stage, without any votes from the core white Democrats or blacks, Bush had carried the South's popular vote. His southern cushion came from extracting votes from the two Democratic core groups. From the white Democratic core Bush won almost one-fourth to give him another 6 percentage points. Two more points came from the 13 percent of black voters who cast Republican ballots. The cumulative outcome in the South was a massive popular victory for the Republican candidate.

The table reveals why the 1988 election was very close outside the South. In the North the white Republican core was somewhat smaller (41 versus 44 percent) than in the South. Bush won 90 percent of the northern core vote, slightly less than in the South, for a yield of 37 percent of the total northern vote—13 points short of victory. The white swing groups made up 20 percent of the northern presidential electorate, a bit higher than in the South, but Bush narrowly lost (49 percent) this swing vote. His yield of 10 points from the white swing groups left him three points short of a majority. Bush's northern victory came from winning 15 percent among the white Democratic core groups, for an additional five points. He won an additional point by securing 11 percent of the northern black vote. Ultimately, Bush won 53 percent of the northern popular vote—a very close election.

The 1988 Republican victory in the South was no isolated event. Since 1972, for the first time in American history, a Solid Republican South has emerged in the battle for the White House. Whether the Republicans can sustain their southern advantage constitutes one of the most consequential questions in American politics. It is worth emphasizing, however, that in several respects the new Solid Republican South differs from the old Solid Democratic South. In presidential elections, as Carter's victory in 1976 indicates, the Republicans cannot take the South for granted, nor do the Democrats automatically concede it. Moreover, the size of the landslide vote producing the Solid Republican South is considerably smaller than the level of support for the Solid Democratic South at its peak. Franklin Roosevelt averaged 78 percent of the southern vote in the four New Deal elections from 1936 to 1944. By contrast, Republican presidential candidates have averaged only 57 percent of the southern popular vote in the five contests from 1972 to 1988. Accordingly, the modern Republican advantage, formidable as it is, still falls short of constituting an insuperable barrier for a Democratic candidate.

What happens in the South is extraordinarily pertinent to presidential elections. Southern size and southern unity, magnified by a method of selecting the president which allows regions to award all or virtually all of their electoral votes to one party, are the keys to the South's political leverage. Whether we examine the electoral college, grassroots voting behavior in presidential elections, or the parties' core voter groups, the South is critical in gaining or keeping control of the White House.

Because the South has more electoral votes than any other region and because it has tended to support Republican candidates with enormous electoral vote majorities, a Republican nominee who can keep the South is in excellent position to win the presidency. But the Republican advantage flowing from the South does not stop with the electoral college. In no other region (including the West) do the Republicans have such a large grassroots surplus and the Democrats such an enormous grassroots deficit. All other factors being equal, the Republicans are well situated to win the South with a minimum expenditure of campaign resources, thus allowing them to divert their resources (money and the candidate's personal appearances) to crucial northern states, such as California, Ohio, and Illinois, where the outcome might be in greater doubt. Democratic candidates with modest prospects for victory in the South are left with the immense challenge of winning the presidency on northern votes alone. With their larger southern core Republican base and their greater capacity to attract white support among partisan and swing groups, the Republicans have transformed the South into a region with a substantial Republican edge.

2

The South and the Electoral College

During much of American history the South has been the prime example of a politically distinct region.[1] For many decades after the Civil War, the South's commitment to Democratic presidential nominees was a great "given," an enduring certainty that guided strategists in both political parties. In turn, the emergence of the South since the middle of the twentieth century as a region that could go either way and, more recently, as a Republican stronghold has helped to reshape the outcomes of presidential elections.

An exploration of historical trends in presidential voting in the South and in the rest of the nation will help clarify the underlying structure of the modern struggle between Democrats and Republicans for control of the White House. The collapse of the Democrats' traditional southern base, without the development of new electoral support elsewhere in the nation, has placed the Democratic party squarely on the defensive in presidential elections. Democratic problems have been Republican opportunities. The rise of a South now favorably disposed toward the Republicans has helped give GOP presidential candidates their broadest geographical base in the history of the Republican party.

When the new nation began, there were southern states but there was not a cohesive, united "South." General recognition of a region with common problems, concerns, and interests emerged only gradually. The growth of a distinct regional identification, "a sense of the South as an entity over and above the states and localities that make it up, and some sense of patriotism toward it," observed John Shelton Reed, "had its origins in the sectional conflict of the early nineteenth century, primarily among whites from those parts of the region where slavery and the plantation system were well-established. As agriculturalists, they often found their interests to be different from those of the Northeast; as residents of a biracial region with a slave system, their interests were not those of the agricultural Midwest."[2]

In addition to the clash of interests among the different regions, the belief that the South would always constitute a minority within the nation was a crucial component of the outlook southern whites formed toward national political institutions. "The essential political fact about the South," wrote David M. Potter in 1972, "is that it has been a minority section—and, we may add, a conscious minority—for about a century and a half." Before the Civil War the principal sectional interests of this minority were the perpetuation of slavery and, to its eventual downfall, the expansion of slavery into new territories and states. When northern victory in the Civil War obliterated those goals, white southerners for more than a century sought to control race relations within the South. As a conscious minority, the enduring problem for the white South was "to maintain its sectional objectives despite adverse majorities in the nation."[3]

Historically, one of the southerners' priorities was to control the presidency. Politicians from southern states preferred to have one of their own in the office, but they were amenable to northern politicians who were sympathetic to southern goals. What they could not abide in the White House was a politician hostile to their ultimate concerns. To control the presidency southerners sought to take advantage of the rules and traditions under which Presidents are elected. Although the southern states have always been a minority within the electoral college, a fully cohesive South has usually been large enough to provide a candidate with about half of the electoral votes necessary for victory.

The Size of the South

In presidential politics the potential impact of any region in determining the winner depends on many things, but among the most important are how big it is and how completely it favors one party or another. From James Madison, Thomas Jefferson, and John C. Calhoun to Richard Russell, Harry F. Byrd, and Strom Thurmond, white southerners who represented the region in national politics have been acutely sensitive to the South's "size" problem.[4] Potter expressed the fundamental strategic situation as follows:

> historically the remarkable fact is that, for a century and a half after the South began to pass perceptibly into a minority position in terms of

population and for a century after it suffered smashing defeat in the Civil War, the region was still able to maintain an entrenched position in the American political system from which it could fight on equal terms against political adversaries who outnumbered it more than three to one.[5]

The size of any region in presidential politics is the percentage of electoral votes it controls. Over the course of the past two centuries the ebb and flow of population shifts have dramatically changed the sizes of the South, Border, Northeast, Midwest, and West (see Figure 2.1). Originally, the Northeast constituted a majority of the electoral college, although these states seldom coalesced behind a candidate from that part of the nation. After the election of 1816 no single region ever contained enough electoral votes to win a presidential election through its votes alone. Even the most united regions have needed political allies from other parts of the nation to elect presidents.

During the early decades of the Republic the southern states controlled roughly a third of the electoral college vote, but the population of the slave states (the South plus the Border states) did not grow as fast as that of the free states. In the decades leading up to the war, the slave states never controlled a majority of electoral votes. Any presidential election that completely polarized the nation between slave states and free states would have resulted in the defeat of the slave states. On the eve of the Civil War, the eleven states that were to secede accounted for only 28 percent of the electoral college vote. And among many white southerners, the belief had taken hold that the longer they remained within the Union, the weaker their minority position would become.

From the Civil War through 1960, the combined votes of the Northeast and the Midwest constituted majorities in the electoral college, while the South accounted for about one-quarter of the electoral vote. Over time, however, population movements have shifted political power away from the Northeast and the Midwest. After 1870 the Midwest displaced the Northeast as the nation's largest region. The Northeast dropped behind the South after 1960 and fell below the West after the 1990 Census. Northeastern voters now control one-fifth of the nation's electoral vote, their lowest share in American history.

The Midwest, the region with the most dramatic growth prior to the Civil War, reached its peak in the late nineteenth and early twentieth centuries. Although the Midwest was America's largest region through most of the twentieth century, its paramount status

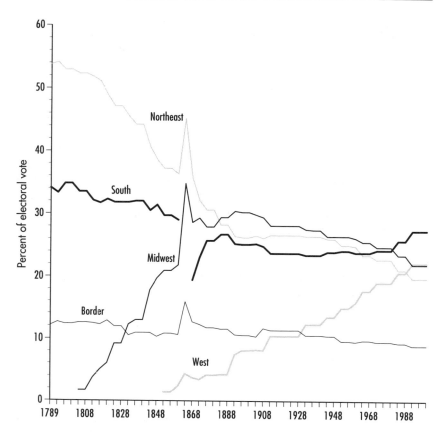

Figure 2.1 Presidential politics in regional context: percentage of electoral vote contributed by different regions, 1789–2000. *Sources:* Calculated by the authors from Congressional Quarterly, *Guide to U.S. Elections* (Washington, D.C.: Congressional Quarterly, 1975); and appropriate volumes of Richard M. Scammon, ed., *America Votes* (Washington, D.C.: Congressional Quarterly).

has gradually eroded. The Midwest fell below the South after 1980, and slightly behind the West in 1990. In the presidential elections from 1992 to 2000, the Midwest will have about 22 percent of the electoral votes.

Recent population movements have benefited the West and the South. The country's smallest region throughout the nineteenth century, the West has steadily increased its share of electoral votes in this century. Having already passed the Northeast and drawn even with the Midwest, it appears poised for additional growth during the 1990s. California, of course, dominates the West. With 54 electoral votes, California possesses one-fifth of the minimum needed to win the presidency.

In the 1980 census the South emerged as the nation's biggest region. The region had begun to attract white migrants in the 1960s; and after federal civil rights legislation eliminated the starkest differences in laws affecting race relations, the South no longer lost millions of blacks to better opportunities in other parts of the country. The 1990 census increased the South's electoral votes from 138 to 147. Beginning in 1992, the eleven states of the old Confederacy will control 27 percent of the electoral vote.

A united South is the greatest regional prize in modern presidential politics. Sweeping the region provides a candidate with more than half—54 percent—of the minimum electoral votes necessary for victory. Conversely, the failure to win any southern electoral votes imposes an awesome burden on a candidate, who would then need to capture almost seven-tenths (69 percent) of the electoral vote in the rest of the nation. While the South cannot determine the outcome of a presidential election by itself, a "cohesive" South is large enough to have a considerable impact on presidential politics.

The Unity of the South

Minorities can attempt to exert influence by concentrating their resources within a single party or by dispersing their resources among competing parties. There are advantages and risks in both approaches, but either way, the minority seeks to influence the policies of the larger entity. Even though a minority, a fully cohesive South can go a long way toward providing a party with a victory in a presidential contest. Over the long sweep of American history, southerners have often solidified their electoral votes behind particular candidates (see Figure 2.2). In the 48 presidential elections between 1796 and 1988, the South gave four-fifths or more of its electoral vote to 33 candidates (29 Democrats and 4 Republicans). In 15 contests the region split its electoral vote.

Since mid-century, however, new patterns have emerged. In all of the six contests from 1948 to 1968, the South divided its scarce electoral votes between two (sometimes among three) candidates. In the five contests from 1972 to 1988, the South has given lopsided electoral college votes four times to the Republicans, but only once to the

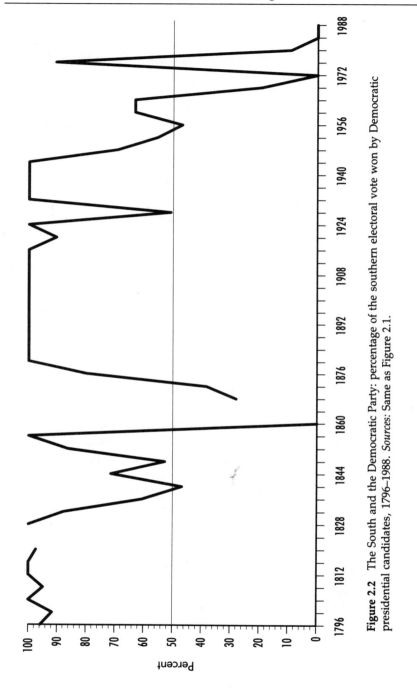

Figure 2.2 The South and the Democratic Party: percentage of the southern electoral vote won by Democratic presidential candidates, 1796–1988. *Sources:* Same as Figure 2.1.

Democrats. The Republicans have usually been the beneficiaries of a growing but still cohesive South.

To appreciate the novelty of voting tendencies in the modern South, we must explore the historical roots of Democratic strength in the South. Setting aside the uncontested elections of George Washington, a Solid South first emerged in support of candidates of the Jeffersonian Republicans, a party that had been created by and was led by southerners. This party (at that time often referred to as the Republican party but later known as the Democratic party) was organized in the 1790s by two southern planters, Thomas Jefferson and James Madison, in opposition to Alexander Hamilton and the Federalist party. Its presidential candidates were selected in the party's congressional caucus, and from 1796 through 1820 these nominations were always given to Virginia politicians—Jefferson, Madison, and James Monroe. Yet the new party was not an exclusively regional institution, for the southerners turned to allies in the northern states, chiefly New York and Pennsylvania, to supply the additional votes necessary for victory. Through 1820 the Virginia Dynasty won practically all of the South's electoral votes.

Virginia's string of leaders ran out in 1824, however, and the congressional caucus disintegrated as a means of nominating the party's presidential candidates. Andrew Jackson of Tennessee emerged as a popular hero for many southern whites, and he received an overwhelming southern electoral vote in 1828 and 1832. Nonetheless, Jackson's policies proved to be controversial within the South as well as in the rest of the nation.

A newly organized political party, the Whigs, began to campaign in the South as the more authentic champion of the interests of white southerners. Many southerners no longer saw any need to concentrate all of their political resources within a single party, and two-party competition momentarily flourished in the region. Southern politicians now tried to establish positions of influence within both major parties, the Democrats and the Whigs. "Recognizing that they lived in a nation but came from a section that had particular concerns," William J. Cooper argues, "the party men grounded their strategy for protecting the South and slavery on gaining national power through cooperation with northerners." In practice, the southerners in both Whig and Democratic parties had created a Calhounian "concurrent majority," in which both the minority and majority factions had to agree upon policies. The basis for cooperation between northern and southern politicians in both parties was widely recognized. As Cooper puts it, "To northerners the price demanded by southerners for political alliance seemed reasonable: southern control of a sectional or southern question in turn for assistance in the quest for national power."[6]

With southerners controlling racial policies in both parties, it was possible for the white voters of the South to split their support. From 1836 through 1852 the once cohesive "South" reverted again to a collection of "southern states." Democratic presidential candidates commonly won majorities of the South's electoral vote, but they never swept the region as long as the Whigs were perceived as a legitimate "southern" party. Seven southern states usually voted Democratic, but Tennessee, North Carolina, Georgia, and Florida did not. Outside the South, both parties had allies in different states. During most of the antebellum period, Indiana, Illinois, and Pennsylvania were Democratic strongholds. Democratic presidential candidates generally ran least successfully in the Border states, which frequently followed the leadership of Henry Clay of Kentucky.

Yet the position of the southern whites remained precarious, since they were outnumbered. John C. Calhoun's justified fear was that eventually the North would attack the South on the slavery issue. Indeed, as the question of slavery shifted from its existence in the South to its possible expansion to other parts of the nation, southern whites were thrown on the defensive. Northern politicians strongly resisted the expansion of slavery, and they "became increasingly unwilling either to let the South set the tone of the slavery discussion or even to allow the South to go its own way. Instead they began demanding that the South follow where they led."[7] The southern wings of both parties were resolutely pro-slavery, and the two-party system functioned to their satisfaction only when the slavery question was ignored or finessed. In the 1850s the northern and southern wings of the Whig party disintegrated over the issue of the expansion of slavery.[8] In 1860 the Democrats broke apart over the issue of slavery, when the southern and northern wings were unable to agree on a presidential candidate.

The presidential election of 1860 dramatically recorded the power shifts in American politics. "In the balloting, a national shift of historic proportions took place," Robert Kelley has concluded. "Since 1800 enough Middle Atlantic and Middle Western states in the region of the Lower North had voted for Southern-supported candidates to give them the victory in most elections. Now, however, the Lower

North moved to the other side, giving the Republican party, within six years of its founding, control of the national government."[9]

In the 1860 election the South was completely isolated from the North. Neither the feared Republican Abraham Lincoln nor the despised Democrat Stephen Douglas received any electoral votes from the South. The white South appeared to be united in its electoral vote, but this was an artifact of the "winner-take-all" rules of electoral college voting. The popular vote in the South was split. Most supported John C. Breckenridge, the candidate of the "southern" Democratic party, but a substantial minority voted for John Bell, the candidate of the Constitutional Union party. Once again, the "South" had disintegrated into "southern states."

As a disorganized minority, the southerners assuredly were impotent in national politics. Facing the prospects of the presidency in the hands of a new majority party that had united the North and West and was totally hostile to the interests of the slaveholders, the southerners were in their weakest position since the founding of the nation. Led by the "fire-eaters," a generation of younger southerners inspired by the memory and thought of Calhoun, they believed that the new government would neither respect their honor nor safeguard their interests. Over a period of months, eleven states seceded from the Union and established the Confederate States of America, a new government in which they hoped the institution of slavery would be made secure. What followed instead was civil war, defeat, northern occupation, and forced readmission into the Union.

The Civil War, one of the most destructive wars of the nineteenth century, left an indelible scar on presidential politics. For generations after, the Democratic Solid South was a constant reminder of the partisan legacy of Civil War and Reconstruction. Between 1880 and 1944, Democratic presidential candidates captured the South's *entire* electoral vote in 15 out of 17 elections, a record of electoral college solidarity unmatched by any other region in American history. Through 1944, excepting only 1920 and 1928, the South automatically provided any Democratic nominee with a substantial political base. The South's traditional contribution to Democratic presidential candidates—its large size compounded by its total unity—amounted to about a quarter of the nation's electoral votes, or approximately half that needed for victory. In return for their regular contribution to the Democratic party's meager presidential base, the southerners controlled the party's racial policies. The national Democratic party was dedicated to the strict construction of the Constitution and the rights of states to police their own affairs.

Sectional differences continued to plague the party. The Democratic party "has never been a homogeneous body," according to Potter, "but has always been a coalition. From the time when Jefferson and Madison went on their famous 'botanizing expedition' to New York in 1791, Southern Democrats and Northern Democrats have seldom had much real affinity. Jefferson and Burr hated each other more than they hated the Federalists. Stephen A. Douglas and the Southern Fire-eaters were poles apart. Grover Cleveland and William Jennings Bryan might well have agreed that there was no rational basis for both of them to be in the same party."[10] For the northern wing of the party, the southerners were a mixed blessing. Many northerners viewed southern whites as backward, violent, lazy, and ignorant people who had precipitated the worst disaster in American history. The southern wing cloaked the northern Democrats with the shroud of southernism, repelling many northern voters.

Southerners in their turn held grievances against northern Democrats. The extraordinary cohesion of the South for decades after the Civil War resulted from necessity, not choice. Republican presidential candidates were not a genuine option for most southern white voters. The Democratic party was the only institution in which they could have any influence on national policy, and here their desires were largely restricted to racial policy in the South.

While the southerners remained loyal to the Democratic party's presidential candidates, they were also restive in the party of their fathers but unwilling to pay any attention to the hated Republicans. They were caught in the predicament that applies to any minority that concentrates its resources in a single institution because it has no other realistic option. C. Vann Woodward put it this way about the situation of white southerners and the Democratic party in the early twentieth century: "It was clear that the very solidarity of the South was one important source of its political impotence. Not only did it stake all its political fortunes upon the chances of a single party but those of a consistently losing party at that. Neither of the major parties was obliged to consult seriously the needs and wishes of the South: one found it unnecessary, the other useless. The indifference of its own party was the more maddening, for nothing was expected of the other."[11]

During the New Deal the southerners' potential vulnerability became apparent. Northern Democrats historically needed the South because Democratic presidential candidates ran so poorly above the Mason-Dixon Line. From the Civil War until the Great Depression the Democratic party never won a majority of the northern popular vote in a presidential election. Beginning in 1932 and continuing through 1944, however, Franklin D. Roosevelt ran so effectively in northern states that he could have been elected without any electoral votes from the South. The South had apparently become expendable. In reality, it was not at all clear that the Democrats could regularly win the presidency without any significant contribution from its traditional southern base. The New Deal experience was based on singular circumstances—the combination of the worst depression in the nation's history, a thoroughly discredited Republican party, and a Democratic president with unique leadership skills.

In 1948 Democratic party leaders, motivated by a combination of idealism and practical politics, began to construct a party platform in which the interests of the new constituent groups of the party in northern states—members of labor unions, big city dwellers, and, most important of all, blacks—would be given primacy over the traditional interests associated with southern whites. This transformation of the Democratic party, which we shall examine in more detail in later chapters, was based on the strategic assumption that liberalizing the party's policies on a variety of matters, including civil rights, would allow the Democrats to remain strong in key northern states while retaining its historic base in the South. The assumption was not unrealistic in the short run, for President Harry Truman carried most of the southern states in 1948.

It has been an entirely different story, however, in the fullness of time. The demise of the Democratic Solid South in presidential politics began in 1948. Only once since then has a Democratic candidate again polled the type of landslide electoral vote that was commonplace during the heyday of Democratic solidarity. The Solid Democratic South gave way initially to a competitive period, 1948 to 1968, in which the region's electoral votes were divided among Democrats, Republicans, and regional third-party candidates. Since 1968 there has been a resurgence of southern cohesion, but generally on behalf of Republican presidential candidates. The decline and fall of the Solid Democratic South in presidential politics, its replacement by a Solid Republican South, and the national implications of these developments are the main themes of this book.

The Geography of the Presidential Battle since the Civil War

The enormous Republican advantage in modern presidential elections can be readily demonstrated by comparing today's geography of the party battle with the patterns of previous political eras. We will limit our attention to the elections from 1860 onwards and distinguish six political eras in this period. During the Civil War and Reconstruction (1860–1872) the Republican party ultimately established itself as the party of the victorious North. In the post-Reconstruction era (1876–1892) there was greater two-party competition for the presidency. From 1896 through 1928 the Republican party dominated the presidency almost as completely as did the Democrats during the shorter New Deal period (1932–1948). Presidential politics after the New Deal may be usefully divided into the elections which preceded (1952–1964) and followed (1968–1988) the Great Society. These six eras provide a convenient means to trace the parties' historical struggle to control the presidency.

In all of the maps we shall examine, partisan states are defined in exactly the same manner as they were for the 1968–1988 elections discussed in the previous chapter. States which were carried by the same party in three-quarters or more of the elections held within a designated period have been classified as Usually Republican or Usually Democratic. All other states are labeled Swing. Comparison of the maps in sequence gives an immediate visual sense of the shifts and continuities in the parties' state-level bases since the Civil War.

During the first era (1860–1872) Democratic support fell to exceedingly modest levels (see Figure 2.3). Republican control of many southern states during Reconstruction precluded Democratic majorities there, and in much of the North the Democratic party was effectively discredited as the party of rebellion. In the Border states, where slaves had been freed after the war and where much of the bitterest fighting had taken place, hostility to the Republicans allowed Democrats to be competitive in presidential elections. The Republicans' base in the Midwest and Northeast gave them three-fifths of the nation's electoral votes, for an overall advantage of ten to one over the Democrats.

At the end of Reconstruction, former Whigs and traditional Democrats consolidated their political resources.[12] The presidential elections of 1876–1892 witnessed the rise of the "Greater South," the South plus the Border states, as a reliable base for Democratic party nominees (see Figure 2.4). Because the Greater South typically cast

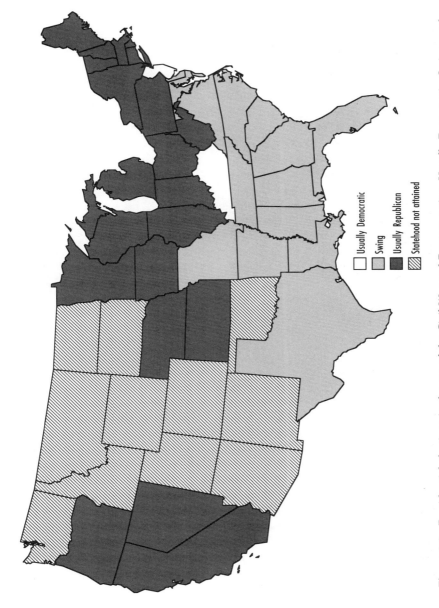

Figure 2.3 Presidential elections in the era of the Civil War and Reconstruction: Usually Democratic, Swing, and Usually Republican states in the 1860–1872 presidential elections. A state was classified as partisan if it was carried by the same party in at least 75 percent of the elections. *Source:* Calculated by the authors from Congressional Quarterly, *Guide to U.S. Elections* (Washington, D.C.: Congressional Quarterly, 1975).

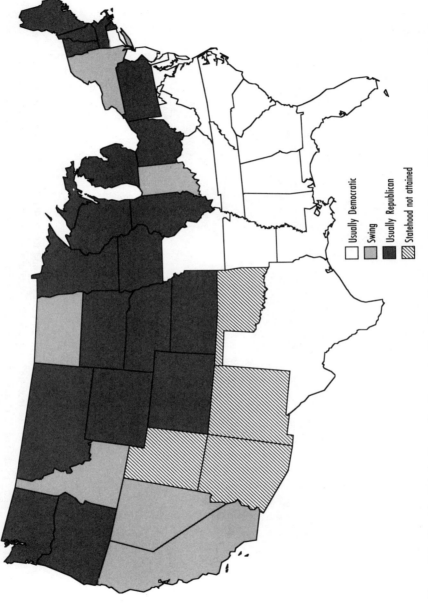

Figure 2.4 Presidential elections after Reconstruction: Usually Democratic, Swing, and Usually Republican states in the 1876–1892 presidential elections. *Source:* Same as Figure 2.3.

Usually Democratic
Swing
Usually Republican
Statehood not attained

its entire electoral vote—36 to 38 percent of the total—in favor of the Democrats, the party could win the presidency with only one-fifth of the electoral vote from the rest of the nation. As a result, Democratic tickets headed by New York politicians like Grover Cleveland had fighting chances when downturns in the business cycle (as in 1884 and 1892) damaged the Republicans. In those campaigns the Democrats combined their Greater South base with considerable strength in the Northeast (chiefly by carrying New York, New Jersey, and Connecticut). They were weakest in the Midwest and West. Partisan alignments in the 1876–1892 era were acutely sectional, commonly arraying the former slave states against most of the rest of the nation.

The critical election of 1896 initiated an extended period of Republican supremacy in presidential elections.[13] After the capture of the Democratic party by Populist and Free Silver forces headed by William Jennings Byran, the Democratic party suffered massive declines throughout the Northeast. New York, New Jersey, and Connecticut switched to the Republicans to create a northeastern stronghold for the GOP. The newly cohesive Republican Northeast, when combined with the traditionally Republican Midwest, gave the Republicans the landslide majority of northern electoral votes the party needed to win presidential elections. Border states ceased to be reliable southern allies, and the West, while neither safely Republican nor securely Democratic, commanded too few electoral votes to affect the outcome of any but the closest two-party contests (see Figure 2.5).

From the late nineteenth century until the Great Depression, the South was the single assured regional base for Democratic presidential candidates. In this lopsided sectional conflict national Democratic victories required spectacular Republican blunders. Woodrow Wilson's 1912 victory was due to irreconcilable divisions within the Republican party over the rival candidacies of William Howard Taft and Theodore Roosevelt, not to inherent Democratic competitiveness.

The Great Depression humiliated the Republicans and reshaped for a generation the regional bases of presidential elections. Under Franklin Roosevelt's dynamic leadership the Democratic party successfully seized an exceptional opportunity to transcend its narrow sectional base in the South; the five presidential elections of 1932–1948 represent the broadest and longest period of Democratic victory in American history. By retaining its southern base while repeatedly

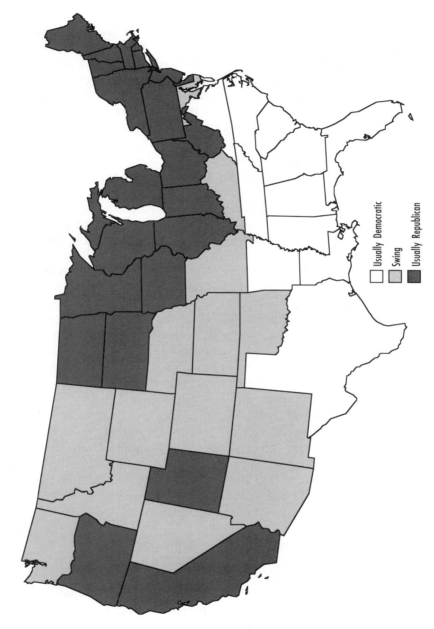

Figure 2.5 Presidential elections before the New Deal: Usually Democratic, Swing, and Usually Republican states in the 1896–1928 presidential elections. *Source:* Same as Figure 2.3.

Usually Democratic

Swing

Usually Republican

winning many northern states, the Democrats enjoyed unprecedented nationwide success in the New Deal era (see Figure 2.6).

Presidential elections in the 1950s and early 1960s shifted away from Democratic dominance (see Figure 2.7). Through 1964 the South's electoral vote was generally Democratic, but for the first time since Reconstruction the region was no longer solidly Democratic: Florida, Virginia, and Tennessee became the first southern states to vote Republican with regularity; and three more states, Texas, Louisiana, and Mississippi, ceased to be Democratic strongholds. Only Arkansas, Alabama, Georgia, South Carolina, and North Carolina usually remained Democratic. Outside the South, with Dwight Eisenhower and Richard Nixon heading the ticket in the 1952–1960 campaigns, the Republicans revived mightily. Much of the Northeast and critical midwestern states such as Illinois, Michigan, and Minnesota were swing states.

The post–Great Society presidential elections are unique in the nation's history. In the 1968–1988 era the Republicans penetrated every region, achieving in the process a breadth of support never approached by the GOP in previous eras. States that usually went Republican accounted for almost three-fourths of the nation's electoral votes, while the comparable Democratic presidential base consisted of Minnesota and the District of Columbia. The total absence of Democratic states in the South sets the contemporary era apart from every previous period in American history.

The uniqueness of the parties' 1968–1988 presidential bases deserves emphasis. For nearly three-quarters of a century, the Solid Democratic South was one of the grand realities of American politics. It was, in fact, the most significant as well as the most obvious geopolitical "given" in presidential elections. Although Republican strategists sometimes entertained illusions about regularly winning the South, through World War II the Solid Democratic South was the cardinal shared assumption of both major parties. Since 1944, however, the Democratic party has never captured all of the South's electoral votes while the Republicans have done so with increasing frequency.

Strategic Implications of Southern Solidarity

What have been the principal strategic implications of a Solid Democratic South, a Solid Republican South, or something in between for the outcomes of presidential elections? Specifically, given the fact

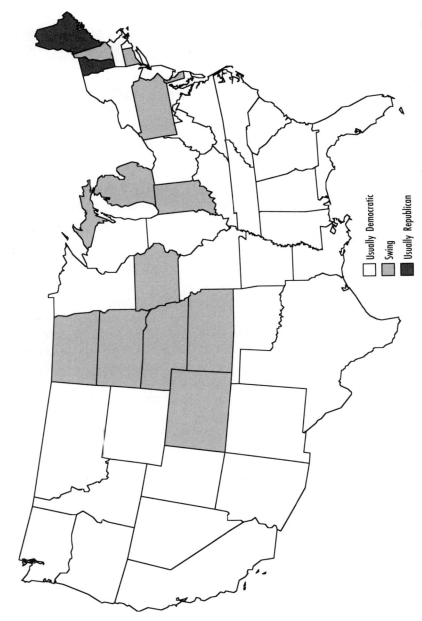

Figure 2.6 Presidential elections in the New Deal era: Usually Democratic, Swing, and Usually Republican states in the 1932–1948 presidential elections. *Source:* Same as Figure 2.3.

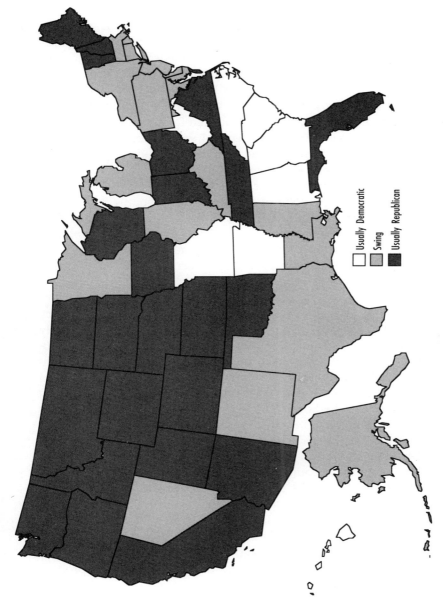

Figure 2.7 Presidential elections after the New Deal: Usually Democratic, Swing, and Usually Republican states in the 1952–1964 presidential elections. *Source:* Same as Figure 2.3.

that the South has possessed about one-fourth of the electoral college vote and historically awarded all of it to the Democratic nominee, what have been the minimum percentages of the much larger electoral college vote in the rest of the nation needed for a Democratic majority? The answer to that vital question may be calculated by subtracting the South's contribution to a Democratic victory (the number of southern electoral votes won by Democrats) from the minimum number of electoral votes needed for a majority and dividing the result by the number of electoral votes found in the North. The result is the Democratic target outside the South—the bare minimum share of the total northern vote necessary to produce a Democratic majority in the electoral college.

Figure 2.8 charts the political consequences of southern sectionalism (or its absence) for the outcomes of presidential campaigns. The graph contrasts the minimum share of the northern electoral vote needed for a Democratic victory with the actual percentage of the northern electoral vote won by each Democratic presidential candidate. Beginning in 1880, the first presidential election year after the Civil War in which conservative white Democrats controlled every ex-Confederate state, the Democratic party could win the presidency by combining the South's entire electoral vote with approximately one-third of the electoral vote in the rest of the nation. Since Republicans counted on nothing from the South, their presidential candidates needed to accumulate around two-thirds of the nonsouthern electoral vote. Because the North possessed three times as many electoral votes as the South, the Republicans did not need a totally solid Republican North in order to elect presidents.

Such were the intensity and durability of partisan attachments established or reenforced by the Civil War and its aftermath that the Republicans normally could sweep two-thirds or more of the North's electoral votes. During the half-century between 1876 and the Great Depression, the Democrats met their modest northern targets only four times, winning the presidency in 1884 and 1892 with Cleveland and in 1912 and 1916 with Wilson. The New Deal era stands alone as the sole period in American history in which the Solid Democratic South coexisted with sustained majorities in the North, thus producing national Democratic landslides.

As the Democrats' electoral vote in the South has eroded, the northern targets for Democratic presidential candidates have correspondingly increased. Only once since 1948—in Jimmy Carter's 1976 campaign—has a Democratic candidate been sufficiently successful

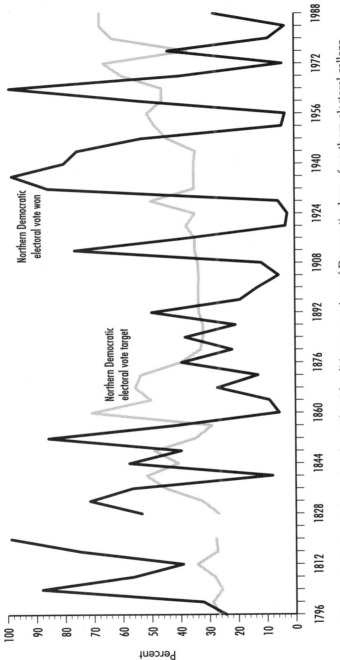

Figure 2.8 Regional dynamics of presidential politics: comparison of Democratic share of northern electoral college vote needed for victory with actual share of northern electoral college vote won by Democrats. *Sources:* Same as Figure 2.1.

in the South to require no more than a small minority (37 percent) of the northern electoral vote for victory. Democratic nominees in ten elections between 1948 and 1988 faced the prospect of winning only a portion or nothing at all of the South's electoral vote; the targets they had to meet ranged from 44 to 67 percent of the northern electoral college vote. In five out of six post–Great Society presidential campaigns the Democrats have run so poorly in the South that northern majorities on the order of three-fifths to two-thirds would have been needed to win the presidency. As the chart plainly shows, these northern targets were never approached, much less achieved.

The political consequences of the South's change of allegiance have been profound. Table 2.1 illustrates the Democratic dilemma and the Republican advantage in contemporary presidential elections by comparing the relative sizes of the Democratic and Republican presidential bases in the South and the North over time. Since the Great Society the Republicans have enjoyed an advantage over the Democrats that is almost an exact mirror image of the Democrats' national superiority during the New Deal era. The electoral components of the Republicans' current advantage—combining nine-tenths of the

Table 2.1 Constructing electoral college majorities: the regional structure of Republican and Democratic presidential bases, by electoral eras

Electoral era	Percent of electoral votes in Usually Republican states					Percent of electoral votes in Usually Democratic states					R–D
	South	+	North	=	Nation	South	+	North	=	Nation	
1860–1872	0	+	83	=	61	0	+	8	=	6	+56
1876–1892	0	+	60	=	45	100	+	19	=	39	+6
1896–1928	0	+	75	=	57	100	+	0	=	24	+33
1932–1948	0	+	2	=	2	100	+	68	=	76	−74
1952–1964	29	+	44	=	40	38	+	6	=	14	+26
1968–1988[a]	91	+	68	=	74	0	+	3	=	2	+72

a. Southern states have been classified on the basis of the 1972–1988 elections. Calculations for the 1968–1988 elections are expressed as percentages of the electoral vote as apportioned by the 1990 census. For example, southern states classified as Usually Republican will cast 91 percent of the South's electoral votes in the 1992–2000 presidential elections.

Sources: Same as Figure 2.1.

South's electoral votes with two-thirds of the North's electoral votes—have no parallels in the history of the Republican party. In modern presidential politics the Republicans have stood history on its head and in effect have become the party of the South *and* most of the North. The closest parallel to the Democrats' dismal contemporary situation—no sizable base of electoral votes in either the South or the North—is the Democrats' showing during the era of Civil War and Reconstruction.

The Parties' Bedrock Presidential Bases

Although the Republican advantage in recent presidential elections is manifest, it is conceivable that the huge GOP lead in the shares of the electoral votes might exaggerate Republican strength. If the Republicans have been winning many states by narrow margins, relatively modest changes in the popular vote might produce much closer races in the electoral college. A more rigorous test of the relative strength of the parties' bases is a comparison of their shares of the popular vote. To identify states in which the parties not only win but frequently win by substantial margins, we shall define the Bedrock Republican or Bedrock Democratic electoral vote as the percentage of the national electoral vote found in Usually Republican or Usually Democratic states in which the median party vote for a given era is 55.0 percent or greater.

This test reaffirms the uniqueness of the Republican party's commanding position after 1964 (see Table 2.2). The Republicans' initial advantage during the period of Civil War and Reconstruction gave way to a more competitive environment in the 1876–1892 sequence of elections, in which the Republicans had a smaller bedrock electoral vote than the Democrats but still managed—with some imaginative counting of the 1876 returns—to inaugurate more presidents. Republican dominance in the 1896–1928 era rested upon their second largest bedrock electoral vote (37 percent). Comparative analysis of the six periods reveals the remarkable character of the New Deal elections. Usually Democratic states with median Democratic votes of at least 55 percent controlled almost half (46 percent) of the nation's electoral vote, a display of strength unmatched by either party before or after the New Deal. However, the Democrats' enormous head start did not carry over into the 1952–1964 elections.

Presidential elections after the Great Society have been characterized by the Republicans' greatest *net advantage* ever (37 points) in

Table 2.2 Comparative head starts in presidential politics: Bedrock Republican and Democratic electoral vote bases since the Civil War, by political era

| Electoral era | Size of Bedrock Republican electoral vote | | Size of Bedrock Democratic electoral vote | | R–D | Percentage of Republican victories |
	Total	South	Total	South		
1860–1872	28	0	3	0	+25	100
1876–1892	9	0	23	84	−14	60
1896–1928	37	0	22	100	+15	78
1932–1948	2	0	46	52	−44	0
1952–1964	21	0	5	76	+16	50
1968–1988[a]	38	68	1	0	+37	83

Note: The total Bedrock Republican (Bedrock Democratic) electoral vote is the percentage of the national electoral vote contained in Usually Republican (Usually Democratic) states with median Republican (Democratic) votes of 55.0 percent or more for a given political era. Also reported are the percentage of the Bedrock Republican (Bedrock Democratic) electoral vote contributed by the South. For example, in the 1896–1928 period, 100 percent of the Bedrock Democratic Electoral Vote came from the South.

a. Southern states have been classified on the basis of the 1972–1988 elections. The figures for the 1968–1988 elections were calculated according to the redistribution of electoral votes arising from the 1990 census. In 1992, for example, Bedrock Republican states will control 38 percent of the nation's electoral votes, and 68 percent of those votes will be contributed by the South.

Sources: Same as Figure 2.1.

bedrock electoral votes. Only during the New Deal did the Democrats enjoy a greater advantage in securing a majority of the electoral vote than the Republicans currently possess. Moreover, the regional structure of the 1968–1988 core electoral votes is radically different from that of previous eras. For the four political periods from the end of Reconstruction to the mid-1960s, southern states contributed disproportionately to the bedrock Democratic electoral vote while supplying nothing to the core Republican electoral vote. In post–Great Society politics, for the first time in American history, two-thirds of the bedrock Republican electoral vote originated in the South. Under these circumstances it is no wonder that the Republicans have won a higher percentage of elections (83) after 1964 than in any other era since the end of Reconstruction.

A comparison of the median Republican votes in 1952–1964 and 1968–1988 for all 50 states confirms that the Republicans' extraordinary electoral vote advantage in the latter period is anchored in a large share of the popular vote (see Figure 2.9). Using 55 percent as a cutoff point to distinguish the most pro-Republican states, the scatter plot identifies nine northern states that were highly Republican in both periods and thirteen more states, including ten in the South, in which Republican medians exceeded 55 percent in the post–Great Society era. These new pro-Republican states more than offset Republican declines among seven northern states whose medians had exceeded 55 percent in the earlier period. Many of the states whose Republican medians failed to reach 55 percent in either period nonetheless were highly competitive. California, Illinois, Pennsylvania, New Jersey, and Michigan, for example, recorded Republican medians in the 50–54 percent range before and after the Great Society.

As of 1992 the states whose Republican medians for 1968–1988 exceed 55 percent contain 203 electoral votes, or 38 percent of the nation's total. If the Republicans can continue to carry these states, the GOP can control the presidency simply by winning 67 more electoral votes out of the 225 found in states with 1968–1988 Republican medians of 50–54 percent. Under current circumstances the Republicans have numerous opportunities to secure electoral majorities simply by concentrating on states where they have an established record of success.

When the Republican medians in Figure 2.9 are contrasted with the Democratic medians shown in Figure 2.10, it is obvious that vastly different political tasks confront Democratic and Republican presidential candidates. The Democrats begin presidential campaigns without a single bedrock state. The District of Columbia, resolutely Democratic in its voting habits before and after the Great Society, is the sole source of exceptionally high Democratic popular votes. And while there were 25 states in which the median Republican presidential vote for 1968–1988 ranged from 45 to 54 percent, the Democrats were similarly competitive in merely eight states. Only about a fifth of the electoral votes (101) are located in states where the Democratic median reached or exceeded 45 percent. Hence even if the Democrats can carry every jurisdiction whose median Democratic vote exceeds 45 percent, another 169 electoral votes are still needed from the other 42 states.

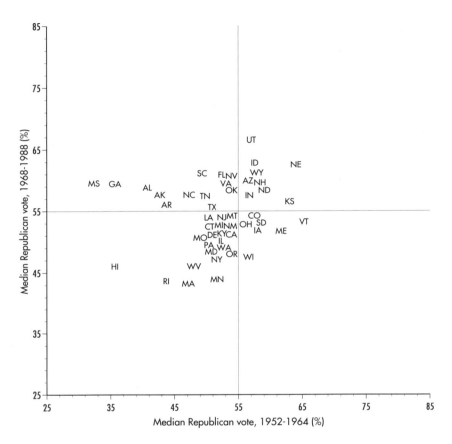

Figure 2.9   The emergence of the South as a center of substantial Republican majorities: median Republican votes in the 1952–1964 and 1968–1988 presidential elections. Southern medians for the second period were calculated according to 1972–1988 votes. *Source:* Calculated by the authors from appropriate volumes of Richard M. Scammon, ed., *America Votes* (Washington, D.C.: Congressional Quarterly).

Political Implications

In the two-party system that evolved from the climactic events of the Civil War and Reconstruction, the fundamental structure of presidential coalitions reflected tenacious regional attachments to the Republican and Democratic parties. Because the North was never as completely Republican as the South was Democratic, the central

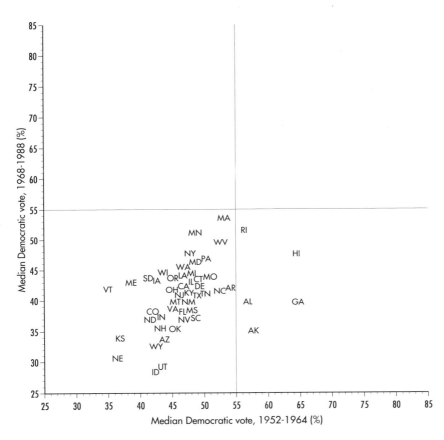

Figure 2.10 The absence of states with substantial Democratic majorities: median Democratic votes in the 1952–1964 and 1968–1988 presidential elections. Southern medians for the second period were calculated according to 1972–1988 votes. *Source:* Same as Figure 2.9.

problem of Republican strategists was to win despite the certainty that the South would support the opposition, and the fundamental task of Democratic strategists was to locate enough northern allies to secure a national majority.

As a result of the Solid Democratic South, the Republicans were compelled to run exceedingly well in the rest of the country. From roughly 1880 until the Great Depression, the formula for a Republican presidential victory was the unwritten but exceedingly important two-thirds rule: they must capture two out of every three northern electoral votes. No matter how big and how united the South might be in favor of the Democrats, it was still a political minority and as such could be outvoted. Because there were three times as many electoral votes outside the South as there were within it, a North that could unite by better than two to one in favor of the Republicans could control the White House without any southern support. The old Democratic formula for winning the presidency was to sweep the South and capture one-third of the northern electoral vote. But the same historical dynamics that produced the Solid Democratic South made it exceptionally difficult for the Democrats to meet their modest northern target.

In the aftermath of the Great Depression the Republicans temporarily went into political receivership as the party of unrelieved economic catastrophe while the Democrats became a national party for the first time since the Civil War. The Democrats' southern and northern majorities disintegrated in the elections of 1952–1964, and since then we have witnessed patterns of regional support previously unknown in presidential politics.

The conversion of the South into a Republican stronghold represents a fundamental change in the structure of presidential politics. The new southern realities—the South's propensity to go Republican by comfortable margins—amount to the repeal of the old Republican two-thirds rule and its replacement by a new one-third rule. For all presidential elections through 2000, sweeping the South would permit the Republicans to win the presidency with slightly more than three-tenths of the northern electoral vote. Conversely, the loss of southern electoral votes means that the Democratic party now must win a higher percentage of the North's electoral vote (69 percent if no electoral votes are won in the South) than the Republicans once needed when they had to write off the South.

These new regional realities need to be fully understood by all participants and observers of presidential politics. In view of the fact that—aside from the New Deal—the Democratic party has never succeeded in establishing substantial bases in the North, the party's current need for a great showing outside the South places an extraordinary burden on Democratic candidates. Thus far in American history there has never been a presidential election in which the Democratic party lost the entire South but was sufficiently successful in the North to win the election. There have been six occasions—1912, 1932, 1936, 1940, 1944, and 1964—in which the Democratic party won more than 70 percent of the northern electoral vote. However, all of these elections were national Democratic landslides. The southern electoral vote was totally Democratic in Wilson's election and in all four of Roosevelt's campaigns, and Lyndon Johnson won 63 percent of the South's electoral votes in 1964. If the Democratic party is to win the presidency while completely losing the South, a trailblazing campaign will be required.

Our exploration of electoral college politics in American history thus points to the tremendous practical significance of the loss of the South as a bastion of Democracy. To appreciate the true importance of this change one must see it in conjunction with the atypical politics of the New Deal. As we have shown, the New Deal was the only period in which the Democrats had pronounced strength in the North as well as the South. In having lost its remaining southern base without having gained an impressive group of safe northern states, the modern Democratic party now bears a strong resemblance to the Republican party during the New Deal.

3

The Changing Geography
of Presidential Elections

To this point we have analyzed the changing structure of presidential politics mainly by focusing on states, the central actors in the electoral college. While most states have generally favored one party or the other in different political eras, clearly not all parts of a state have voted in the same manner as the state as a whole. An examination of voting patterns in the more than 3,000 counties of the nation—what we call the "grassroots" level of politics—makes it possible to portray more precisely the changing fortunes of the two parties. For anyone interested in understanding the outcomes of presidential elections in the 50 states, it is important to know the geography and the relative size of the major parties' grassroots bases.

County voting returns are accessible for presidential elections from 1896 to the present.[1] We shall explore the partisan structure of presidential voting for the period preceding the New Deal (1896–1928), the New Deal era (1932–1948), the post–New Deal elections (1952–1964), and the post–Great Society campaigns of 1968–1988. Most American voters, it turns out, have lived in localities with distinct partisan orientations. In all four periods under consideration the vast majority of the popular vote cast in presidential elections—usually around three-fourths of it—came from reliably partisan counties, counties classified as Usually Republican or Usually Democratic.

Just as winning the states that constitute a party's presidential base is the first step toward securing a majority of the electoral vote, carrying the counties that constitute a party's base *within* a state is the initial goal of a nominee's strategy. The greater a party's grassroots base vis-à-vis its opposition, the greater its capacity to weather political mistakes or adverse conditions and still win. A party whose grassroots base includes a substantial majority of the vote cast is much less dependent on the quality of its candidates, for example, than one whose grassroots base includes only a small share of the popular vote. The greater a party's comparative disadvantage in the size of its grassroots base, the more it needs unusual circumstances— such as major blunders by the opposition or manifestly superior candidates—to order to be competitive.

Grassroots Sectionalism before the New Deal

Underlying the profound sectionalism previously identified for the states during the nine presidential elections of 1896–1928 was an equally vivid grassroots sectionalism. An overwhelmingly Democratic South was aligned against a predominantly Republican North (see Figure 3.1). For counties as well as for states, the Solid South was no myth. By 1896, with most blacks either purged from southern electorates or soon to be, white Democrats had solved the problem of insuring their supremacy in southern politics. Over four-fifths of the South's counties qualified as Democratic for the 1896–1928 elections, giving the Democrats an advantage of twelve to one over the Republicans in the number of partisan counties. The South's few Republican counties, which were concentrated in Tennessee, Virginia, and North Carolina, reflected traditions of Mountain Republicanism growing out of the Civil War. Elsewhere Republican counties, such as Gillespie in Texas and Winston in Alabama, were few and far between.

During this lengthy period of Republican dominance of the presidency, the Border states served as a buffer zone dividing the mainly Democratic South from the heavily Republican Northeast and Midwest and the less Republican (but not Democratic) West. Outside the former Confederate states there were only 209 Democratic counties, and about three-fourths of them were concentrated in Border states like Missouri, Kentucky, Oklahoma, and West Virginia. In the pre–Civil War free states (the Northeast, Midwest, and West combined), the Republicans enjoyed an advantage of fifteen to one over the Democrats at the county level.

The Northeast, the nation's center of industry and finance, provided the sharpest possible contrast with the South. In terms of the number of counties, the Northeast was 43 times more Republican (87 percent) than Democratic (2 percent). Only four Democratic counties in Pennsylvania prevented the Democrats from being completely deprived of a grassroots base in the Northeast. Nor did the Demo-

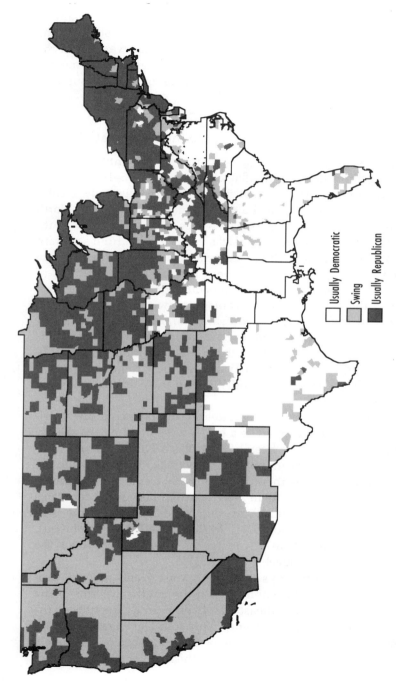

Figure 3.1 Grassroots presidential politics before the New Deal: Usually Democratic, Swing, and Usually Republican counties in the 1896–1928 presidential elections. A county was classified as partisan if it was carried by the same party in at least 75 percent of the elections. *Sources:* Calculated by the authors from Edgar E. Robinson, *The Presidential Vote: 1896–1932* (Stanford, Calif.: Stanford University Press, 1934); and Richard M. Scammon, ed., *America at the Polls* (Pittsburgh: University of Pittsburgh Press, 1965).

crats make a significantly stronger showing in the Midwest, although many of the rural counties of the Great Plains states failed to qualify as Republican. In the underpopulated West, where three-fifths of the counties had no distinct partisan orientation, Republican counties (37 percent) were still far more common than Democratic counties (3 percent).

The profound sectionalism of the grassroots party battle between 1896 and 1928 is also apparent in Table 3.1, which reports the percentage of the 1928 vote from Usually Republican, Swing, and Usually Democratic counties. Fundamentally different attachments to the major parties characterized the South and the North. Reliably Democratic counties supplied almost four-fifths of the South's popular vote, while comparably loyal Republican counties cast two-thirds of the northern vote. Within the North, the Northeast and the Midwest both exhibited net Republican advantages similar to the Democratic advantages found in the South.

Because the North possessed three times as many electoral votes as the South during this period, the Republicans had an enormous advantage. The Republicans' grassroots base alone—three-fifths of the national popular vote—normally provided a surplus, whereas the Democrats' grassroots base of one-tenth of the popular vote was so small that the party's main hope of victory lay in exploiting irreconcilable Republican divisions in specific elections. Woodrow Wilson's 1912 victory over President William Howard Taft and ex-President Theodore Roosevelt resulted from a combination of the Solid Democratic South with three-quarters of the northern electoral vote, the latter made possible only because Republicans split between Taft and Roosevelt. So pronounced was the Republican grassroots advantage in many large northern states that they could win the presidency during this period simply by carrying all states where the vote in the reliably Republican counties exceeded the vote in the reliably Democratic counties by at least 55 percentage points. With an advantage of this magnitude, Republicans had to work hard to *lose* the presidency.

Democratic Recovery in the New Deal

The Great Depression—and particularly the image of Republican President Herbert Hoover and his party generally as inactive, inept, or indifferent to prolonged economic misery—transformed the landscape of presidential politics for a generation. The grassroots political

Table 3.1 The changing regional structure of grassroots presidential politics: percentage of popular vote cast by Usually Republican, Swing, and Usually Democratic counties, by political era

Region	1896–1928				1932–1948				1952–1964			
	UR	S	UD	R-D	UR	S	UD	R-D	UR	S	UD	R-D
South	10	12	78	-68	3	4	92	-89	40	21	38	+2
West	53	46	1	+52	2	13	85	-83	49	38	14	+35
Border	41	38	21	+20	9	21	70	-61	44	21	36	+8
Midwest	71	26	3	+68	15	34	51	-36	61	24	15	+46
Northeast	74	26	0	+74	35	10	55	-20	41	30	28	+13
North	66	30	4	+62	20	20	60	-40	50	29	21	+29
United States	61	28	11	+50	18	19	64	-46	48	27	24	+24

Note: Each entry is the percentage of the total vote cast by Usually Republican (*UR*), Swing (*S*), or Usually Democratic (*UD*) counties classified as Usually Democratic for the period 1896–1928 cast in the final election of each electoral era. For example, southern counties classified as Usually Democratic for the period 1896–1928 cast 78 percent of the South's total vote in the 1928 presidential election. For ease of comparison with Table 1.2, regions have been ranked from highest to lowest according to the net difference (*R–D*) between the Republican and Democratic shares of the popular vote cast in 1988.

Sources: Same as Figure 3.1; and appropriate volumes of Richard M. Scammon, ed., *America Votes* (Washington, D.C.: Congressional Quarterly).

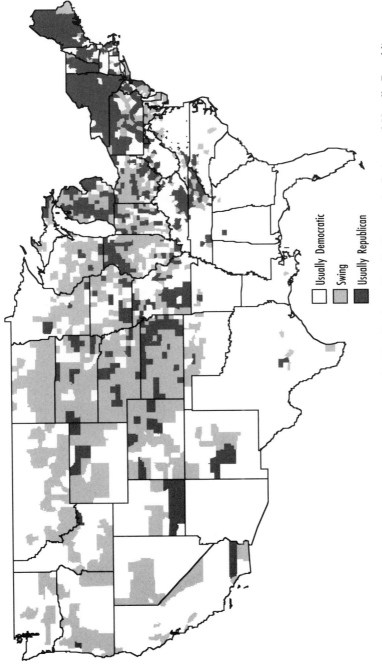

Figure 3.2 Grassroots presidential politics in the New Deal era: Usually Democratic, Swing, and Usually Republican counties in the 1932–1948 presidential elections. *Sources*: Same as Figure 3.1.

costs to the Republican party were enormous (see Figure 3.2). Under Franklin Roosevelt's skillful leadership the Democratic party strengthened its southern base while establishing itself for the first time as the dominant political force in the North. Although the Republican party in the Northeast enjoyed continued grassroots success outside the central cities and although a majority of the midwestern counties were swing rather than partisan during the 1932–1948 elections, the Democratic party won broad grassroots appeal in the New Deal era. Roosevelt's popularity with big-city workers helped the Democrats win northern central cities previously integral to Republican success. From New York, Boston, Philadelphia, and Pittsburgh in the Northeast to Chicago, Detroit, Cleveland, Minneapolis, and Milwaukee in the Midwest and to Los Angeles and San Francisco in the West, voters in many of the North's principal cities gravitated to the Democratic party.

In the South the Great Depression seemed to confirm the worst nightmares of many white Democrats about the Republican party, and the immediate political result was an intensification and strengthening of Democratic voting tendencies. During the New Deal elections the Democrats retained 99 percent of their base counties and added the vast majority of the counties previously ranked competitive as well as a quarter of the pre-Depression Republican counties. As a result the Democratic grassroots advantage was almost total.

The Republican party, whose 1896–1928 grassroots base included a slight majority of all northern counties, witnessed a decline during the New Deal to a quarter of the nonsouthern counties. The New Deal is the only period since the Civil War in which Democratic counties outnumbered Republican counties (39 to 24 percent) in the North.

As Table 3.1 shows, the relative sizes of the votes produced by Democratic and Republican counties favored the Democrats in every region during the New Deal. In the South, the West, and the Border, the Democrats had huge net advantages in their grassroots bases. While the Republicans were more competitive in the Northeast and Midwest, here too over half the regional vote came from Democratic counties.

Because the Democrats maintained a net grassroots advantage of three to one in the North and thirty to one in the South, during the New Deal the Republicans were as hostage to Democratic errors as the Democrats had been in the previous era. With the South routinely generating about half the electoral votes necessary for a Democratic victory, the Republicans' collapse in the North easily enabled the Democrats to surpass their northern electoral vote targets. The Democratic party could elect presidents merely by carrying every state in which the net Democratic advantage in the size of the parties' grassroots bases was 51 percentage points or greater.

The northern and southern Democratic alliance worked to perfection during Roosevelt's four campaigns and survived its only hard test in 1948. In that campaign Harry Truman overcame Deep South defections over civil rights (Truman won 69 percent of the southern electoral vote rather than the normal 100 percent) by capturing 53 percent of the northern electoral vote.

The Grassroots Republican Revival, 1952–1964

No one who carefully scrutinizies the shifting geography of presidential politics before, during, and after the New Deal can fail to be impressed by the exceptional Democratic advantage in the aftermath of the Great Depression. During the New Deal—and only during the New Deal—a party without an impressive historical northern base temporarily found itself, under a gifted president, the beneficiary of failed Republican economic policies. The New Deal marked the high tide of persistent grassroots support for Democratic presidential candidates.

Figure 3.3, which maps the party battle from the early 1950s through Lyndon Johnson's landslide in 1964, documents the Republicans' resurgence in the North and their initial advances in the South, especially in the growing southern cities. Across the nation the number of Democratic counties fell from 1,835 (59 percent) in the New Deal to 921 (30 percent) in the pre–Great Society era. Republican counties, on the other hand, increased from 502 (16 percent) to 1,728 (56 percent). In the North, Republican counties rose from 24 percent during the New Deal to 73 percent following it, while the Democratic share of northern counties declined from 39 to 15 percent. With a popular war hero heading the Republican ticket in 1952 and 1956, the Republicans even managed to run competitive races in several northern central cities (for example, Chicago, Cleveland, and Milwaukee) that usually voted Democratic.

Within the South the post–New Deal elections produced the first wave of Democratic grassroots losses in the twentieth century. Some 630 southern counties (55 percent) qualified as Democratic in the 1952–1964 elections, compared with 1,066 in the New Deal era. While

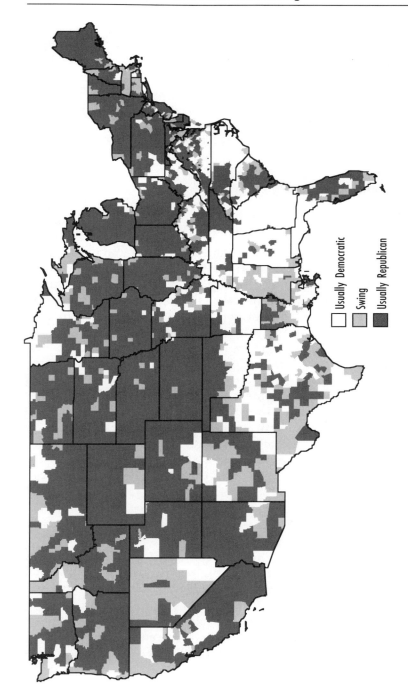

Figure 3.3 Grassroots presidential politics after the New Deal: Usually Democratic, Swing, and Usually Republican counties in the 1952–1964 presidential elections. *Source:* Calculated by the authors from appropriate volumes of Richard M. Scammon, ed., *America Votes* (Washington, D.C.: Congressional Quarterly).

Usually Democratic

Swing

Usually Republican

the Democrats retained three-fifths of their New Deal counties, a fifth of them converted to a Republican stance and the other fifth shifted to the Swing category. The proportion of Republican counties rose from 3 percent in the New Deal to 26 percent during these years.

In Tennessee, North Carolina, Virginia, and (on a smaller scale) Arkansas, the rise in grassroots Republicanism represented an extension of traditional Mountain Republicanism, but it also included advances in several urban and suburban counties. In post–New Deal presidential elections there were distinct sectional cleavages between Democratic and rural North Florida and Republican and urban South Florida; between the Republican cities and Black Belt elites in South Carolina versus the Democratic upcountry; and between Republican northern Louisiana and Democratic southern Louisiana. There were comparatively few Republican counties in Texas and Alabama, but Houston and Dallas were prominent exceptions in the former state and Birmingham and Montgomery stood out in the latter. Georgia remained the most solidly Democratic of the southern states, while Mississippi was already in revolt against the racial policies of both national parties.

In the post–New Deal era Republican advances in southern cities enabled them to establish a slightly larger grassroots base than the Democrats (see Table 3.1). Two-fifths of the South's vote in 1964 came from Republican counties, compared to 38 percent in Democratic counties and the remaining fifth in counties without a pronounced partisan orientation. With northern Republican counties controlling half of the vote outside the South and with the Democratic counties accounting for only a fifth of the northern vote, the Republican party returned to its pre–New Deal position of grassroots strength. A comparison of the grassroots bases before and after the New Deal indicates, however, that the Republicans had much less margin for error in the 1952–1964 campaigns than in the earlier period. They could secure a majority of the electoral vote by carrying every state wherein the party's net grassroots advantage over the Democrats was at least 23 points, a much narrower margin than the party had before the New Deal. The Republicans won easily enough when Eisenhower was on the ballot, but they were vulnerable when the Democrats nominated candidates (John Kennedy and Lyndon Johnson) who knew how to appeal to swing as well as to Democratic areas. And with the nomination of the inept Barry Goldwater, the Republicans contributed generously to the Democrats' landslide presidential and congressional victories in 1964.

The Republican Advantage, 1968–1988

While the New Deal was a resounding national success for the Democratic party, no comparable period of Democratic dominance in presidential campaigns was associated with the Great Society. Just the opposite occurred. Beginning with Richard Nixon's 1968 victory, unprecedented national grassroots strength for the Republican party has been the hallmark of presidential elections (see Figure 1.2 in Chapter 1).

The dynamics of grassroots political change are highlighted when we compare the partisan behavior of counties before and after the Great Society. For each party it is possible to classify every American county as either a *continuing success* (reliably Republican or Democratic in both periods), a *gain* (reliably Republican or Democratic only since 1968), a *loss* (reliably Republican or Democratic before the Great Society but not after it), or a *continuing failure* (reliably Republican or Democratic in neither period). Partisan successes thus reflect patterns of fairly stable support for the same party dating back to the early 1950s, and partisan gains indicate the geographical areas where a party added to its pre–Great Society base. Just as some counties acquired a new partisan identity in the aftermath of the Great Society, other counties lost their previous partisan orientations and became either competitive or (less frequently) reliable bases for the other party. Finally, if we are to measure a party's political performance, we must identify its grassroots failures, those counties which never provided consistent support.

The Republican party's grassroots record before and after the Great Society has included many continuing successes and many gains, but few losses and few continuing failures (see Figure 3.4). Continuing Republican successes were especially prominent in the North. While the South contained proportionately fewer successes, many of the Republican party's successful southern counties were located in rapidly growing cities or suburbs. Republican gains were most notable in the South (see especially Texas, Mississippi, Alabama, North Carolina, and Virginia) and the West (particularly Nevada and New Mexico). Aside from scattered losses in their grassroots bases (most of the Republicans' Deep South losses reflect increased black participation in Black Belt counties), the Midwest was the primary source of Republican defections. Rural counties in Iowa, Wisconsin, Minnesota, Illinois, and the Dakotas account for most of the Republican losses. There were relatively few continuing Republican grassroots

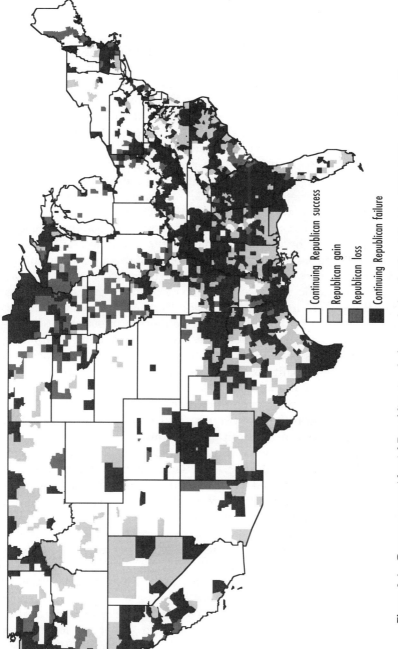

Figure 3.4 Grassroots presidential Republicanism before and after the Great Society: 1952–1964 county classifications compared with 1968–1988 (for the South, 1972–1988) county classifications. *Source:* Same as Figure 3.3.

failures, areas where the GOP did not develop consistent support either before or after the Great Society. Most Republican failures were located in the South or in the Border.

In the transition to post–Great Society politics the Republicans essentially kept the bases they developed in the South and North in the 1952–1964 elections. They then won half of the counties that were competitive before the Great Society and converted a fifth of the Democratic counties to Republicanism. The Republicans were especially successful in the South at shifting previously Swing and Democratic counties into reliably Republican counties.

The national scope of grassroots presidential Republicanism contrasts vividly with the Democrats' anemic performance before and after the Great Society (see Figure 3.5). Compared with the Republican record, there were few continuing Democratic successes or Democratic gains but many Democratic losses and continuing Democratic failures. Whereas almost half of the nation's counties were continuing Republican successes, two-thirds of them were continuing Democratic failures. In the entire nation there were only 215 continuing Democratic successes (7 percent of all counties), and over half of these were in the South. Aside from Atlanta, New Orleans, South Texas, and portions of Middle Tennessee, most of the Democratic successes were small counties in the Black Belt. Continuing Democratic successes in the North, though few in number, included such metropolitan giants as New York, Philadelphia, Pittsburgh, Boston, Detroit, and Baltimore.

Democratic gains were even rarer than continuing Democratic successes. In the South the main sources of Democratic advances were Black Belt counties in Mississippi and South Carolina; outside the South Democratic gains were widely scattered but included Chicago, Cleveland, Milwaukee, Buffalo, and San Francisco. Nine out of ten counties could be classified as Democratic losses or continuing Democratic failures. In the North there were far more Democratic losses than gains, but the most common type of county (83 percent) was the continuing Democratic failure. Southern counties were about evenly divided between Democratic losses (44 percent) and continuing Democratic failures (42 percent).

The transition from post–New Deal to post–Great Society voting patterns involved a second huge decline in the size of the Democratic grassroots base. Reliably Democratic counties fell from 55 percent of all southern counties in the earlier period to 14 percent in the later era. The Democrats retained only a fifth of their 1952–1964 base.

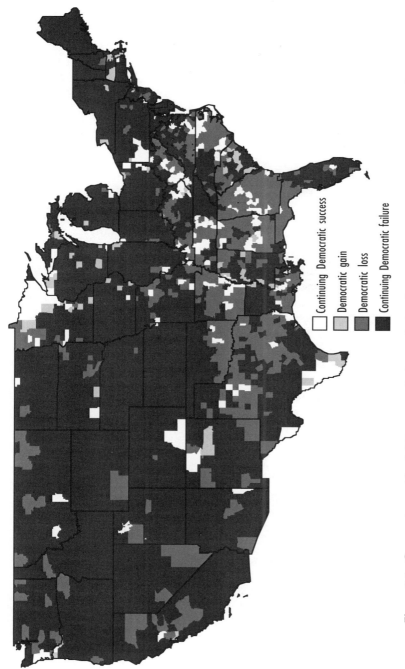

Figure 3.5 Grassroots presidential Democracy before and after the Great Society: 1952–1964 county classifications compared with 1968–1988 (for the South, 1972–1988) county classifications. *Source:* Same as Figure 3.3.

Continuing Democratic success
Democratic gain
Democratic loss
Continuing Democratic failure

Three out of every five Democratic counties shifted to a swing position and the other fifth became Republican. And since the southern
Republican counties were generally more urban and suburban than
the southern Democratic counties, the Republican advantage in the
number of partisan counties understates the political significance of
each party's grassroots base. In 1988, two-thirds of the South's popular vote was cast in Republican counties while less than a tenth
came from Democratic counties. In the North the urban-rural advantage was different. Seven percent of the northern counties were
Democratic, but these (mainly) urban areas produced a fifth of the
northern vote. Although 69 percent of the North's counties were
Republican, they cast 54 percent of the section's total vote.

Political Implications of Grassroots Change

In this chapter we have used county voting patterns to trace the
evolving anatomy of presidential politics. The comparisons plainly
demonstrate that the New Deal era, which established the modern
image of the Democrats as the nation's majority party, was unlike
any period before or since. Viewed in comparison to the rest of
American history, the New Deal stands out as the only exception in
the twentieth century to the general rule that the Republicans have
normally enjoyed a substantial grassroots advantage in presidential
elections.

The distinctive feature of contemporary presidential Republicanism
is that the GOP has finally succeeded in creating a national, rather
than a sectional, grassroots base. Transcending its historical roots as
the party of the North, the Republican party has become about as
national as the Democratic party was during the New Deal. This
development is of the utmost importance in understanding recent
presidential elections. By increasing its southern strength without
surrendering much northern support, the Republicans have returned
to a position of strength reminiscent of presidential elections before
the New Deal. By losing its remaining southern base without significantly adding new northern bases, the Democratic party has been
relegated to a position of weakness only marginally superior to its
standing before the Great Depression.

In state after state the Republican grassroots advantage translates
into a substantial head start in the race to secure a majority of the
electoral vote. We can provide a final demonstration of the Republi-

can grassroots advantage by ranking the 50 states and the District of Columbia according to the net difference in the size of the Republican and Democratic bases. Table 3.2 reports the percentages of the 1988 presidential vote cast by Usually Republican, Swing, and Usually Democratic counties. The most important fact about presidential elections after the Great Society is that, in the struggle to win 270 electoral votes, the Republicans can assemble majorities simply by carrying states in which they have a substantial grassroots advantage.

Eighty-one electoral votes are found in the 12 states (mainly small western states but also Florida and Indiana) in which the difference between the Republican and Democratic grassroots base exceeded 75 points. Another 133 electoral votes are located in the 13 states (including six southern states) where the net Republican advantage ranged between 50 and 74 points. By carrying all these states plus seven more states (through Maryland in Table 3.2), the Republicans can exceed 270 electoral votes simply by winning states where their grassroots advantage was at least 39 points.

And the Republican grassroots edge does not end with Maryland. An additional 120 electoral votes are contained in the remaining states which had Republican advantages of 25 points or more. Chief among this group is California, the greatest electoral prize of the 50 states. Although the reliable Republican counties in California control only 40 percent of the vote, the Democratic counties (primarily San Francisco and Oakland) account for only 8 percent. Presidential elections in California tend to be fairly close fights for the 52 percent of the state's vote found in the swing counties (including Los Angeles). But since the Republican base has five times as many voters as the Democratic base, California Democrats compete at a severe disadvantage.

These comparisons suggest why the Democrats have experienced so much difficulty amassing a majority of the electoral vote. Counting the District of Columbia, only five out of 51 units registered a net Democratic advantage in elections since 1968. If the Democrats are to prevail, they must find ways to win numerous states in which the Republicans begin the campaign with a superior county-level base.

Because they lack significant bases at either the county or state levels, Democrats face the recurring problem of creating an electoral majority from the personalities, issues, and events of specific campaigns. If they nominate a demonstrably superior candidate, one who can attract moderate and liberal independents as well as Dem-

Table 3.2 Grassroots presidential politics and the states: percentage of 1988 popular vote cast by counties classified as Usually Republican, Swing, or Usually Democratic for the 1968–1988 presidential elections

State	Counties			R–D	Cumulative electoral vote
	UR	S	UD		
Alaska	100	0	0	+100	3
Nebraska	99	1	0	+99	8
Utah	99	1	0	+99	13
New Hampshire	97	3	0	+97	17
Arizona	95	5	0	+95	25
Florida	93	6	0	+93	50
Idaho	93	7	0	+93	54
Wyoming	92	8	0	+92	57
North Dakota	91	7	1	+90	60
Kansas	92	3	6	+86	66
Montana	85	9	6	+79	69
Indiana	86	5	9	+77	81
Oklahoma	73	25	1	+72	89
Connecticut	71	29	0	+71	97
Vermont	69	31	0	+69	100
Texas	74	20	6	+68	132
Colorado	72	23	5	+67	140
South Dakota	66	33	1	+65	143
New Mexico	75	14	11	+64	148
North Carolina	73	16	11	+62	162
Virginia	71	17	12	+59	175
Alabama	66	26	8	+58	184
South Carolina	64	26	10	+54	192
New Jersey	62	29	9	+53	207
Mississippi	60	32	8	+52	214
Kentucky	57	32	10	+47	222
Michigan	66	12	21	+45	240
Missouri	64	16	20	+44	251

Table 3.2   (continued)

State	Counties			R–D	Cumulative electoral vote
	UR	S	UD		
Maine	44	56	0	+44	255
Nevada	44	56	0	+44	259
Louisiana	57	27	16	+41	268
Maryland	53	34	14	+39	278
Tennessee	44	49	6	+38	289
Ohio	58	21	20	+38	310
Iowa	47	43	10	+37	317
Oregon	61	15	24	+37	324
California	40	52	8	+32	378
Delaware	31	69	0	+31	381
Arkansas	39	50	10	+29	387
Washington	28	70	2	+26	398
New York	59	3	38	+21	431
Wisconsin	48	18	34	+14	442
Pennsylvania	51	11	38	+13	465
West Virginia	32	47	21	+11	470
Georgia	23	63	14	+9	483
Hawaii	0	100	0	0	487
Illinois	44	10	47	−3	509
Minnesota	15	31	54	−39	519
Massachusetts	4	44	52	−48	531
Rhode Island	0	43	57	−57	535
District of Columbia	0	0	100	−100	538

Note: A county is classified as partisan if it is carried by the same party in at least 75 percent of presidential elections (1972–1988 for southern states; 1968–1988 for all other states). All counties not classified as Usually Republican (*UR*) or Usually Democratic (*UD*) are considered Swing (*S*). States are ranked from highest to lowest according to the net difference (*R–D*) between the Republican and Democratic shares of the popular vote. The cumulative electoral vote figures are based on the 1990 census.

Source: Compiled by authors from various editions of Richard M. Scammon, ed., *America Votes* (Washington, D.C.: Congressional Quarterly).

ocrats; if the economic, social, and foreign policy issues of the day clearly place the Republicans on the defensive; and if political events lead voters to conclude that it is time for a change, the Democrats will have a much better chance to win the presidency. Otherwise the Republicans' grassroots head start will be hard to overcome.

II

Presidential Nominations in Historical Perspective

4

The South and Democratic Nominations

Historically, the Democratic party was the principal institution through which white southerners tried to influence presidential elections. For generations after the Civil War the South's political leaders concentrated their resources on behalf of the Democratic party in return for control of its racial policies. Southern Democrats could never win their party's presidential nomination, but they did not come away from national conventions empty-handed. "Within the Democratic party," V. O. Key, Jr., affirmed in 1949, southern politicians "maintained the right to veto prospective presidential nominees." Key was mightily impressed with the southerners' strategic and tactical skills: "All in all their strategy of obstruction provides an instructive illustration of the great power—at least negative power—of cohesive and determined minorities."[1]

The irony of Key's observation is that it was made after events had demonstrated conclusively that the white South had *lost* its informal veto rights in the presidential wing of the Democratic party. In 1948 the conservative white South had suffered its most embarrassing and consequential defeat in a Democratic national convention since 1860. The convention went on record in favor of civil rights and then proceeded to nominate, by an even larger vote, President Harry Truman, who many southerners thought had betrayed the South by sponsoring civil rights legislation. The southerners' defeat in 1948 was no isolated incident. Southern and northern Democrats divided in the next three conventions over the choice of the nominee, and in each instance the southerners were beaten.

Although the southerners had lost their leverage within the Democratic party, southern electoral votes were still necessary to give Democratic presidential candidates realistic chances to win the general election. Southern politicians were awarded the consolation prize of the vice-presidency. By 1960, when Lyndon Johnson joined the ticket headed by John F. Kennedy, it was clear that southern Democrats who campaigned for the White House needed to stress their national credentials. "Wherever I may go, I will never speak as a Southerner to Southerners, or as a Protestant to Protestant, or as a white to whites," Lyndon Johnson told an audience in Tennessee. "I will speak only as an American to Americans—whatever their region, their religion, or their race." It was not the sort of appeal that would have thrilled John C. Calhoun.[2]

The waning influence of southern conservatives at Democratic national conventions is crucially important in understanding the subsequent transformation of modern presidential politics. Over time the South's loss of a veto in the Democratic national convention destroyed one of the cornerstones of the Solid Democratic South. Diminished southern influence *within* the Democratic party was followed by the withdrawal of southern white support for Democratic presidential nominees, as disaffected voters turned either to third-party candidates or to Republicans.

From Dominance to Secession

The Democratic party was created by the leaders of slave states. They controlled its policies and supplied most of its early presidential candidates. Thomas Jefferson, James Madison, James Monroe, and Andrew Jackson, southerners all, dominated the "Democratic Republican" party and led the ticket. Their nominations were almost always carefully balanced with candidates from the nation's other largest region, the Northeast. Most frequently the Democrats nominated a Virginian for president and a New Yorker for vice-president.[3]

The southerners' exhalted position of leadership in the Democratic party could not be sustained. Fierce disagreement over the issue of extending slavery into the new territories undermined the appeal of southern Democratic politicians among many northern and western voters. In this new climate of public opinion, southerners could seldom expect to occupy the presidency. They turned instead to sympathetic northern politicians to lead the Democratic party and to protect the interests of the slaveholding South. Martin Van Buren, Jackson's designated successor, was amenable to the slaveholders' interests during the 1830s, and in later conventions southern Democrats backed such friendly northerners as Lewis Cass of Michigan,

Franklin Pierce of New Hampshire, and James Buchanan of Pennsylvania.[4]

Van Buren's nomination initiated a different regional pattern in which the Northeast displaced the South as the most frequent source of Democratic presidential candidates. Almost two-thirds of the Democratic presidential candidates between 1836 and 1960 came from the Northeast. The Midwest produced another fourth of the Democratic nominees, while the Border states accounted for two candidates. Only one southerner—James K. Polk of Tennessee in 1844—was chosen to lead the party.

Although the southerners were no longer at the top of the ticket, they still held a strong hand in the internal politics of the Democratic national convention. Beginning in 1832, delegates from the various state Democratic parties assembled to nominate candidates for president and vice-president. At the first convention, David M. Potter has pointed out, "the convention adopted a rule that the vote of two-thirds of the delegates would be required to make a nomination." Keenly aware of the importance of maintaining a truly national party, the Democrats agreed upon a rule that required exceptionally broad agreement within the party to select a nominee. The chairman of the rules committee argued that the two-thirds requirement "would show a more general concurrence of sentiment in favor of a particular individual, would carry with it a greater moral weight, and be more favorably received, than one made by a smaller number." Conversely, a resolute and united minority could successfully veto a candidate preferred by a majority simply by organizing a blocking coalition of one-third of the delegates. It was a rule of the Democratic nominating game that the southerners well appreciated.[5]

The basis of the South's leverage in the antebellum period can be succinctly identified. From 1844 to 1860, southerners sent an average of 29 percent of the delegates to the convention. Under the nomination rules, where one-third of the delegates could veto a potential nominee, a completely cohesive group of southerners could furnish 86 percent of the votes necessary to block an aspirant. Moreover, a cohesive South would need to attract only 7 percent of the much larger group of nonsouthern delegates to constitute a successful blocking coalition. Without any votes from southern delegates, however, a candidate would require 94 percent of the votes cast by northern and western Democrats to win the nomination. A nomination "won" with such an acute degree of regional polarization would be practically doomed in a general election.

The South's veto power colored politics within the antebellum Democratic conventions, and it persisted for decades after the rebel states had rejoined the Union. Its effectiveness was first demonstrated in 1844 against Van Buren, once a favorite of the southerners but then an outcast because he opposed annexing Texas as a slave state. The former president won only three of seventy-five southern delegates. Van Buren captured three-fourths of the votes cast by nonsouthern Democrats, but this fell short of the share needed to win two-thirds of all the delegates. Southern Democrats demonstrated their power by ending the presidential hopes of a politician who had crossed them on a matter of ultimate concern to many slaveholders. Northern Democrats took notice.[6]

Democratic presidential conventions frequently involved pitched battles between southerners and northerners in the 1840s and 1850s. Many ballots were needed to locate acceptable candidates: nine in 1844, four in 1848, forty-nine in 1852, and seventeen in 1856. In every convention from 1836 through 1856, the eventual nominee proved satisfactory to a majority of southern delegates, and the slave states were still sufficiently influential to win the vice-presidential position on the Democratic ticket. Nonetheless, by this time slaveholders were playing veto politics in the party their predecessors had dominated.

White southerners vacillated between acting as a *defensive minority*, bent mainly on preserving the institution of slavery within the South, and behaving as an *expansionist minority*, determined to uphold their "right" of taking slaves into the new territories. Northern and western Democrats were willing to humor their fellow party members in the South as long as the southerners limited their demands to the preservation of slavery within their own states. The expansion of the slave empire was an entirely different matter. Northern and western Democrats championed free labor and wanted no competition from slaves in the new territories.[7]

Sectional tensions within the Democratic party culminated in the disastrous conventions of 1860. Senator Stephen A. Douglas of Illinois, the leading candidate of northern Democrats, was totally unacceptable to the southerners. Douglas had prevented the adoption of a southern-backed, pro-slavery constitution for the state of Kansas. The southerners viewed him as yet another northern politician who had betrayed an initial sympathy for the interests of slaveholders. To complicate matters, the Democrats gathered in Charleston, South Carolina, "the worst possible place for the convention. Douglas delegates felt like aliens in a hostile land. Fire-eating orators held forth outdoors each evening," commented James M. McPherson. "Douglas's supporters were as determined to block a slave-code plank as southerners were to adopt one." When the northern majority adopted a platform position on slavery that fell short of the southerners' demands, fifty southerners walked out of the convention. Douglas received a majority but failed to amass a two-thirds vote. After fifty-seven fruitless ballots, the convention adjourned without selecting a nominee. Six weeks later, when the Democrats reconvened at Baltimore, the Douglas forces were in full control. Having lost on the single issue they cared about, many southerners were indifferent to the eventual nominee. Again, many southerners walked out. Douglas was declared the nominee by virtue of winning two-thirds of the delegates, mainly northerners, who remained in the hall.[8]

Even in 1860, the South and its allies still possessed enough votes to deny the nomination to unfriendly northerners. However, southern Democrats could not remain in a party whose platform did not guarantee their interests and whose candidate actively opposed their interests. By bolting from the party convention, they abandoned their main institution for exercising some leverage over northerners. The result was the disintegration of the Democratic party, one of the few institutions that had kept the nation together during earlier sectional disputes.[9]

Exiled from the Ticket

The Civil War produced a new balance of political power within the Democratic party. Power passed into the hands of northeastern and midwestern Democrats. The bitterly divided party, thrown on the defensive by the revolt of its southern faction, lacked able and creative leaders. As one observer put it, "When the South seceded the brains of the party went with it." After hostilities ended, the northern Democrats still floundered. The only certainty was that the southerners had lost any chance of visible national leadership for generations. Southern Democrats were an enduring burden for the national party in presidential campaigns, and there was assuredly no place for a southerner on the party's national ticket.[10]

The southerners did not immediately grasp this fundamental shift in the regional balance of power. So unrealistic were the first southern Democrats who returned to the party's national convention in 1868 that three-quarters of them voted to renominate President Andrew

Johnson, whose pro-southern policies after Abraham Lincoln's assassination had infuriated northern public opinion and brought him to the brink of removal from office. Under these circumstances, backing Johnson was a truly Confederate gesture—overwhelming support rendered on behalf of an absurdly hopeless cause. After twenty-two ballots, the southerners finally joined with nonsouthern Democrats in support of a conservative New Yorker, Horatio Seymour.[11]

During the next half-century, the southerners never again wasted their votes in a Democratic convention by supporting a regional candidate. Instead, they searched for the most attractive northern candidates to support, while the managers of northern candidates campaigned hard for votes among the southern delegations. Once the southerners regained legitimacy within the party, they exerted their veto power to block unacceptable candidates. "Negative power is the power of obstruction, not the power of accomplishment," Potter has stressed. "It would never have sufficed for a New Deal, a Square Deal, or a Great Society. But that kind of power, the power of veto, the power of the concurrent voice, was the power which ruling elements in the South sought for a century after the Civil War."[12]

With the two-thirds rule unchanged, a cohesive South still exercised considerable leverage over the potential nominees of the Democratic party. The South averaged 24 percent of the membership of the Democratic convention between 1868 and 1932, the last convention that used the rule. A fully cohesive but slightly smaller South in this period constituted 73 percent, rather than 86 percent, of the votes needed to block a nomination. A South at full strength, however, still went a long way toward a successful blocking coalition, for the southerners needed only the help of 12 percent of the nonsouthern delegates. Any Democratic hopeful who took positions unacceptable to the South needed to mobilize 88 percent of the remaining delegates, a threshold sufficiently high under ordinary circumstances to prompt most realistic candidates to come to terms with southern leaders.

The South's influence in the Democratic national convention was tolerated for several reasons. The southerners behaved essentially as a defensive minority. Having regained control of the party's racial policies, they limited their demands on other issues and acquiesced to northern leadership. For decades after the Civil War southerners did not seriously contend for the party's presidential nomination. In addition, the northerners needed to allow the southerners some say in party matters because they had to sweep the southern states to be competitive for the presidency. It would do them no good to wrest total control from the southerners if that manuever destroyed their only secure base in the electoral college.

There was little doubt about the strength of Democratic presidential candidates in the South once federal troops had been withdrawn. After 1876 white Democrats increasingly consolidated their control of elections, and the Solid Democratic South became one of the great certainties of presidential politics. The Republicans were not completely eliminated as an alternative, but in every southern state Democrats either had the votes or, if necessary, could simply report the votes required to win presidential elections. Because of the Democratic party's assured southern base, no southerner was needed on the ticket to make it palatable to southern voters.[13]

The Democrats' far more compelling need was to make their tickets attractive to voters in the northern swing states. Most nineteenth-century Democratic presidential candidates came from the Northeast, especially New York, and they looked mainly to midwestern states, such as Indiana, Illinois, and Ohio, to broaden their appeal in presidential elections. When the presidential nominee came from a midwestern state, the ticket was usually balanced by a northeastern politician.[14]

Southerners were the junior partners in two different types of presidential coalitions. Most frequently, they aligned with conservative eastern Democrats, the "right fork" coalition. Seymour was the first of a long line of conservative New Yorkers, which also included Samuel Tilden, Grover Cleveland, and Alton Parker. Northeastern Democrats generally held racist views, sympathized with home rule and states' rights, and favored the promotion of business. Their main weakness was insensitivity toward the political attitudes of debt-ridden farmers, which cost them dearly in the 1890s and early 1900s. In times of economic stress the southerners generally turned away from the East toward a political alliance with the farming West. In three of the four elections from 1896 through 1908, the South favored William Jennings Bryan of Nebraska, who advocated increased circulation of silver to inflate the currency and allow farmers to pay back debts. The "left fork" alliance with the rural West constituted a popular option for rural southern Democrats, though it was much less common than the eastern alliance.[15]

Not until 1912 did a southern politician—Congressman Oscar W. Underwood of Alabama—seriously attempt to win the Democratic presidential nomination. "The contest of the Presidential nomination in 1912 was the first in half a century," C. Vann Woodward observed, "in which the South played a conspicuous and perhaps even decisive part, and it was the most heated contest of the kind in that period." Underwood had represented Birmingham and surrounding areas, salting a basic conservatism with some progressive ideas. As a racial conservative, he had led the local fight to ratify the constitution that helped eliminate black voting. His second marriage to the daughter of one of the wealthiest Birmingham steel manufacturers had reinforced his conservatism, and his reputation as an effective leader of House Democrats led him to be encouraged. Underwood was unable to unite the South (only Alabama, Georgia, Mississippi, and Florida voted as units for him), however, and he had utterly no support outside the region.[16]

The 1912 convention provided another illustration of the southerners' ability to use the two-thirds rule to veto a political opponent. Missouri Congressman Champ Clark, the Speaker of the House of Representatives, was the majority choice of the convention. Clark had little following in the South and could not manage to poll enough support outside the South to capture two-thirds of the total. Many white southerners were cheered in 1912 by the nomination and eventual election of New Jersey Governor Woodrow Wilson, a "hyphenated-Southerner." A native of Virginia, raised in Georgia, Wilson had lived most of his adult life in New Jersey. Many southerners considered Wilson a true son of the South. For northerners, however, it was Wilson's success as governor of New Jersey that made him an attractive candidate. Southern birth no long automatically disqualified a candidate, but one still needed to be properly credentialed by success achieved outside the region.[17]

Although southerners returned to prominence in the Democratic convention during the Wilson era, they faced new regional rivals within the party in the 1920s. Southern defensiveness was rooted in the Democratic party's growing diversity. The Democrats who assembled in national conventions during the 1920s were "an impossible coalition," a mixture of diverse constituencies, each with its own goals and priorities. In Robert K. Murray's words, "the Democratic party was actually three parties: eastern and northern (urban and ethnic-dominated and opposed to prohibition); western (militantly farm-oriented and pro-prohibition); and southern (bone-dry, Klan-riddled, and fundamentalist inclined)."[18]

During the 1920s southern Democrats had been generally dissatisfied with the party nominees. Only half of the southern delegates supported Governor James Cox of Ohio in 1920 on the final ballot. Their preferred candidate in 1924 was William Gibbs McAdoo, another hyphenated southerner, who had been raised in Tennessee but had spent most of his adult life in New York and California. They maintained for more than 100 ballots a blocking coalition against Governor Al Smith of New York, the wet, Irish Catholic, before finally agreeing, in exhaustion, to the nomination of John W. Davis, a Wall Street lawyer.[19]

The First Collapse of the Veto

The stage was now set for the collapse of the southern veto of Democratic presidential candidates. Although Smith had lost in 1924, his supporters renewed their efforts at the next convention. "Among the Democrats," wrote Matthew and Hannah Josephson, "the Smith drive gathered irresistible momentum in the early months of 1928: the April primaries in Wisconsin and Michigan were easily won by his supporters; the large northeastern states then came into his camp and several western states followed." While many southern Democrats were wary of Smith, they were horrified at the prospect of another deadlocked convention. As one southern Democrat concluded, "It would be less embarrassing to accept Al Smith and risk loss of the election than to turn him down and alienate four million Roman Catholics in New York, Illinois, New Jersey, and Massachusetts." No southerner could have beaten Smith in a two-candidate contest, and no serious threat to Smith emerged outside the South.[20]

Convening in Houston, Texas, the Democrats promptly nominated Smith on the first ballot. The vaunted "veto" of southern Democrats against an unpopular northern candidate did not work in 1928, in part because southern delegates were not completely cohesive. Nearly one-fifth of the southerners supported the New Yorker on the first ballot. Smith captured all of the Arkansas and Louisiana delegates and picked up additional votes from Alabama, North Carolina, and Virginia. He was completely shut out in the other southern states. In part the veto failed because Smith got an overwhelming vote from delegates representing the rest of the nation. "The nomination of Al Smith in 1928 had marked the first major step in a transfer of power within the modern Democratic party," Richard L. Rubin observed, for "electoral strength within the party had moved from the agrarian states of the South and West to the major urban states of the East and the industrialized Midwest."[21]

Smith's convention victory did not mean, however, that he was likely to win the general election. Even after Smith's nomination was assured, less than a third of the southern delegates were willing to go on record in support of a Catholic politician. The New Yorker's nomination therefore put the Solid Democratic South's electoral votes at risk for the first time since the end of Reconstruction. National party leaders accordingly felt obliged to make the ticket more attractive to southern voters. As a result, the vice-presidential nomination was offered to a native white southerner, Arkansas Senator Joseph T. Robinson, a conservative Little Rock lawyer with ties to agriculture and corporations. "Robinson as a Southerner and a dry, it was hoped, would lend balance to the ticket," explained Richard O'Connor, "but at least one observer thought it was like trying to carry fire and water in the same bucket."[22]

Smith did not help his cause in the South by indicating "a personal desire to liberalize the Volstead Prohibition Act and then by selecting for national chairman John J. Raskob, Catholic, wet, General Motors executive, and at least until recently a Republican," observed George B. Tindall. "'He obviously is acting on the theory that the South is obliged to vote for him regardless of anything or everything,' Carter Glass wrote after a conference with Smith, 'and that his sole effort . . . must be directed to getting the vote of certain wringing wet Eastern states.'" Much of the Protestant South, especially Methodists and Baptists, organized against Smith, and the Ku Klux Klan vilified him. "By rumor, speech, and broadside the Roman menace was flaunted across the South," Tindall summarized, noting that "the penultimate was probably reached by Mordecai F. Ham, itinerate revivalist and pastor of Oklahoma City's First Baptist Church. 'If you vote for Al Smith you're voting against Christ and you'll all be damned,' he told his congregation."[23]

The Smith-Robinson ticket won in Arkansas and the Deep South, where majorities of whites remained loyal to the Democratic party. In the Deep South racial appeals helped the Democrats hold the traditional line. "'The campaign should be waged on the sharply-defined issue that the Democratic party is the white man's party and the Republican party is the Negro party,' a Mississippi editor advised. 'Let the thinnest trickle of independent voting . . . be permitted,' the Charleston *News and Courier* warned, 'and the torrents of independent action will sweep away the solid dam which holds the white people in the same party in South Carolina.'" Deep South whites understood and responded to these appeals. "I will support the Democratic ticket nominees because I am a white man and a Democrat," explained John Sharp Williams of Mississippi. "Generally the whites of the black belts remained most steadfast in their loyalty to the Democratic party," Key concluded, "while in the areas of few Negroes the shift to Hoover was most marked." In the Peripheral South, where whites were less fearful that a vote for Hoover would alter race relations, fundamentalists opposed to a Catholic president won the day, though in all instances by very slim margins. Herbert Hoover, the Republican presidential candidate, carried five Peripheral South states. Robinson's appearance on the ticket salvaged at least part of the South for the Democrats, while reinforcing the conventional wisdom that a Catholic could not be elected President.[24]

Thus in 1928 the Democrats returned to the sectional balancing that had often proved successful in the two decades before the Civil War: a northerner at the top of the ticket and a southerner as the vice-presidential candidate. Between 1928 and 1960, the Democrats produced such a ticket in two-thirds of their conventions. It represented a partial rehabilitation for the southerners. They were now sufficiently presentable to supplement the head of the ticket, though still not qualified to lead the party.

In 1932 southerners played a critical role in nominating Franklin Roosevelt, the governor of New York, for president, and in selecting John Nance Garner of Texas, the Speaker of the House of Representatives, as the vice-presidential candidate. In this convention the motives for putting a southerner on the ticket were quite different from the strategy of four years earlier. Roosevelt had developed close personal ties with many southern politicians, considered himself an "adopted Georgian" because of his many visits to Warm Springs, and was a genuinely popular figure in the South. He needed no help in carrying the region against the immensely unpopular Hoover. Rooosevelt *did* need Garner's help in meeting the two-thirds requirement for the party nomination. His bitterest rival was Smith, who held most of New York's convention votes, as well as those from the heavily Catholic states of the Northeast.[25]

Garner's candidacy was supported mainly by the Texas and California delegations. According to Sam Rayburn, Garner's instructions for the convention were to prevent at all costs a deadlock. "We are going to win the election this fall," Garner said, "unless we make damn fools of ourselves as we did in 1924." Garner understood that he was "not going to be nominated for President" but expressed an interest in the vice-presidency. Rayburn thought Garner would receive the vice-presidential nomination if Garner's delegates eventually shifted to Roosevelt.[26]

Roosevelt led during the early voting, but on the third ballot some southern delegations began to waver. At this critical point, Senator Huey Long of Louisiana was unleashed to hold Roosevelt's lead in the Mississippi and Arkansas delegations. Long "stormed out on the floor and into the midst of the Mississippi delegation. He shook his fist in the face of Senator Pat Harrison, who was an arrant conservative and cool to Roosevelt, and shouted: 'If you break the unit rule, you sonofabitch, I'll go into Mississippi and break you.' When he went into the Arkansas delegation, he threatened Joe Robinson with the same fate." The delegations stayed with Roosevelt.[27]

Garner certainly had enough support to block Roosevelt's nomination, but he was opposed to "veto" politics. After the third ballot, Garner told Rayburn that, "Roosevelt has a clear majority on every ballot. He is the choice of the convention and ought to be nominated." Releasing his delegates from their commitment to him, Garner underlined his priorities: "Hell, I'll do anything to see the Democrats win one more national election.'" Roosevelt was selected on the next ballot, and Garner was the unanimous choice for the vice-presidency. "All you have got to do is stay alive until election day," Garner advised Roosevelt. "The people are not going to vote for you. They are going to vote against the depression." The Texan made only one public appearance and one radio address on behalf of the 1932 ticket. As he privately told Roosevelt, "Hoover is making speeches, and that's enough for us."[28]

Garner was an individualist, a conservative politician of fiercely independent judgment. Although a conventional segregationist, he opposed the Ku Klux Klan during the height of its popularity in Texas. In an era in which consumption of alcohol and gambling in card games were considered sinful by many southern Protestants, a constituent once confronted Garner with rumors of his fondness for both: "One of his campaign addresses was interrupted by a querulous listener who wanted to know if, in addition to being a wet, it was also true that Mr. Garner played cards. 'Yes,' said the Congressman. 'Game in Room 5, Starr Hotel, directly after this meeting.'"[29]

Garner ran twice as Roosevelt's running mate, but the combination of an increasingly liberal president, oriented toward expanding the northern constituencies of the Democratic party to include organized labor and blacks, with a conservative small-town banker and financier proved unworkable. When Roosevelt broke the news of his plan to expand the number of Supreme Court justices in 1937 to create a liberal majority on the Court, Garner quickly made known what he felt about the proposal. According to Robert A. Caro, "while the presidential message was being read in the Senate Chamber, Garner left the rostrum, stalked into the Senators' private lobby behind the Chamber, and there let a group of Senators know his reaction by holding his nose with one hand and making a thumbs-down gesture with the other." Garner believed that balancing the federal budget was a sacred obligation, and he could not abide the New Deal's deficit financing. More than once, he simply left Washington and returned to Texas to show his disgust.[30]

One fundamentally important change in the rules of the Democratic national convention occurred during the Roosevelt years. In 1936, by a voice vote, the party eliminated the rule requiring a two-thirds vote to nominate a candidate, replacing it with a simple majority vote. Roosevelt forces had long favored the change, which was pushed through quickly and without great public controversy. Most of the southern conservatives had supported the two-thirds rule. Underwood had favored the rule on the grounds that it "would keep the South a great power to prevent in the future the nomination of some individual who might be obnoxious to the South." John Sharp Williams reminded the Mississippi delegation in 1932 that the "two-thirds rule has been for a century the South's defense and it would be idiotic on her part to surrender it." Others, such as South Carolina's James Byrnes, argued that if a candidate "should be nominated by a bare majority of the delegates, it would show such division of sentiment that in the short time before the election it would be difficult for the candidate to heal the breach and lead the party to victory."[31]

One southern conservative conspicuously dissented from the prevailing orthodoxy. Garner thought the cause of the South—and of southern politicians seeking national office—was actually hurt by relying on the two-thirds rule. "The power it gives the South is a negative one," he said. "If the South would stand up for its rights affirmatively, support a Southern man for President when that man is more competent than others instead of merely trying to veto there might be a time when capability rather than place of residence would be the test of availability."[32]

Shifting to majority rule was a fundamental change in the rules of convention politics. In the past, when southerners actually behaved as a "cohesive and determined" minority, the two-thirds requirement allowed them to exert considerable leverage over the policies and candidates of the party. Since 1936, a blocking coalition has required a majority of the delegates. Over the period from 1936 to 1968, the South averaged 23 percent of the delegates to the Democratic national convention. A South mobilized to the hilt could now only provide less than half (47 percent) of the delegates needed to veto an unacceptable candidate. The southerners would have to attract one of every three northerners to make a blocking coalition, compared with only one in eight nonsouthern delegates under the previous rule. A potential presidential candidate without any southern support could now win the Democratic nomination by capturing two-thirds of the nonsouthern delegates, a feasible goal for a popular politician. The shift to majority rule demolished one of the devices by which the South had magnified its political leverage. It left the southerners vulnerable to the superior numbers of the northern wing of the party.

Within the Democratic party the rising forces were located in the large cities of the North. Here labor unions were the backbone of the Democratic party, and blacks, long Republican, had begun to shift toward the Democratic party. "Until 1936," Robert A. Garson argues, "southern Democrats had constituted the mainstay of the Democratic party. They had provided large sums of money for campaigns and had influenced, even determined, the making of the party platform. No Democratic candidate had ever planned election strategies without the full and expected support of the South. But Roosevelt's overwhelming victory suggested that a Democratic candidate could thenceforth make political calculations based on expectations of support from cities, and not necessarily from the courthouses below the Mason-Dixon Line." If this strategy were followed, the party's national candidates and policies would tilt more toward the demands of northern Democratic leaders than toward satisfying the wants of southern Democratic leaders. The result would be "the beginning of the political emancipation of the national Democratic party from the grip of southerners."[33]

The deterioration of the South's position in the national Democratic party was evident at the 1940 convention. At that gathering the Democratic common law marriage of a northern liberal president and a southern conservative vice-president completely disintegrated. Garner was so opposed to Roosevelt's intention to stand for a third term that the vice-president announed his own candidacy. It was a futile gesture. Roosevelt attracted an overwhelming majority on the first ballot, including 76 percent of the southern delegates, while Garner won only the Texas delegation and most of Virginia's votes. The southerners tried to recover by supporting House Speaker John Bankhead of Alabama as the region's replacement in the vice-presidency. President Roosevelt completely ignored their wishes by insisting that the convention nominate Iowan Henry Wallace, a racial liberal, who enthusiastically advocated almost every policy that instinctively appalled conservative white southerners. Unable to form a positive majority for the candidate they preferred, and unable to block the candidate they loathed, the southerners had their first taste of the new realities of convention politics.[34]

Southerners achieved partial gratification on the vice-presidential nomination in 1944. President Roosevelt had by this time acquired legendary status among white southerners. As one conservative southerner acknowledged, Roosevelt was "the Democratic party, the rebel yell, Woodrow Wilson and Robert E. Lee rolled into one," an unbeatable combination of political assets. Vice-President Wallace had managed to alienate both southerners and northern urban leaders, whose combined strength was sufficient to deny him renomination. South Carolina's James F. Byrnes, a consummate insider who had served in the Senate, the Supreme Court, and, during World War II, as the head of the Office of Economic Stabilization, thought he had won the president's endorsement for the vice-presidency. On the Saturday before the convention opened, Byrnes received word from two key Roosevelt supporters, Robert Hannegan, the national chairman of the party, and Edward Kelly, the mayor of Chicago, that, after meeting with the president, "the matter of the Vice Presidency was 'settled.' Kelly told me, 'The President has given us the green light to support you and he wants you in Chicago.'" The next night Byrnes attended a dinner with Hannegan, Kelly, and other political leaders to plan his strategy. There Hannegan told Kelly, "Ed, there is one thing we forgot. The President said, 'Clear it with Sidney.'"[35]

"Sidney" was Sidney Hillman, the head of the Amalgamated Clothing Workers Union, one of the most influential labor leaders in the nation and an intense opponent of Byrnes. Allowing Hillman to pass on Byrnes amounted to a death sentence on the South Carolinian's chances to win the vice-presidency. Byrnes was also strongly opposed by Ed Flynn, the leader of the Democratic party organization in the Bronx. Hillman, Flynn, and President Roosevelt met on the matter, and according to the report received by Byrnes, "Hillman had repeated his argument that organized labor would oppose me because it felt that as a result of the Hold-the-Line order on wages, it had lost many of its gains under the New Deal. Flynn repeatedly asserted to the President that my nomination would cost the President 200,000 Negro votes in New York and that he would lose the State of New York and probably the election. Finally, Mr. Roosevelt had told the labor leaders and Flynn that in view of their statements he would withdraw his approval of my candidacy and would go along with their desire to nominate [Senator Harry S] Truman."[36]

The southern conservatives were furious at their treatment at the hands of the New Yorkers, and nothing better captured the loss of *their* accustomed veto in Democratic presidential politics than Roosevelt's injunction to "Clear it with Sidney." Representatives of the urban North now had the veto. Clearly this was not the same Democratic party that their fathers, grandfathers, and great-grandfathers had known. There was some consolation in the selection of Truman, "who was acceptable to Southern conservatives because of his Confederate antecedents and his Border State background."[37]

The 1940 and 1944 nomination battles revealed the new centers of political gravity in the national Democratic party. Having only recently been readmitted to a place of secondary visibility on the presidential ticket in 1928, 1932, and 1936, the southerners were completely shut out in the 1940s. Southern Democrats had lost battles within the party concerning cultural issues in the 1920s and the influence of labor unions in the 1930s, but both of these controversies were of minor significance compared with the emergence of the issue of southern racial discrimination after World War II.

The End of the Southern Veto on Racial Policy

For generations of Democratic politicians after the Civil War, the combination of the two-thirds rule for nomination, racist attitudes on the part of Democrats, North and South, and the lack of any realistic chance of capturing black votes in northern states deterred any discussion of adopting policies in favor of civil rights at the Democratic national convention. "The South and potential allies from segregated border states (Maryland, West Virginia, Delaware, Kentucky, Missouri, and Oklahoma) could well have ended the presidential aspirations of any candidate posing a threat to the status quo on race," Rubin has emphasized. "In terms of practical political strategy, a candidate who clearly violated the tradition of keeping race a regional rather than a national issue faced the necessity of winning almost all the votes of the non-segregated states, a strategy unlikely to be adopted by serious presidential candidates."[38]

Franklin Roosevelt was the first Democrat whose appeal was so strong in the Northeast, Middle West, and West that he could have been elected four times without any electoral votes from the South and could have been renominated three times without the support of any southern convention delegates. During the Roosevelt years, the South had become a "minority faction in a majority party." The region was vulnerable when its interests directly conflicted with those of the larger faction. If Democratic presidential candidates were no longer "dependent upon the South for the bulk of the party's support," and if winning votes in the North required the adoption of pro–civil rights policies, why should northern Democrats still allow southerners to control the party's racial policies? The answer soon came. The Democratic party's new departure on civil rights policy was rooted in the growing importance of black voters in providing the margin of victory for Democratic candidates in key northern states. In the North, according to James L. Sundquist, "Black voters, who in the 1930s were just entering the Democratic party, were now on the inside, settled, numerically important, and demanding."[39]

President Truman began to respond to the new demands. In 1947, he addressed the annual conference of the National Association for the Advancement of Colored People and promised civil rights legislation. "We cannot, any longer, await the growth of a will to action in the slowest State or the most backward community," the president told the NAACP. In October of 1947, President Truman's Committee on Civil Rights published its report, *To Secure These Rights*, which recommended passage of civil rights laws and an end to segregation. It ignited a political firestorm in the South. According to Garson, white southerners "inundated the White House" with letters of protest: "A North Carolinian wrote: 'Your recent stand and utterances on the Negro question will no doubt cause many thousands of Negroes to vote for you, but this stand of yours will cost you hundreds of thousands of white votes.' And a minister from Florida warned icily: 'If that report is carried out you won't be elected dogcatcher in 1948. The South today is the South of 1861 regarding things that your committee has under consideration.'"[40]

Truman's advisors were divided about his response to the recommendations of the Committee on Civil Rights, but a progressive group led by James H. Rowe, Jr., and Clark Clifford prevailed. Clifford gave the president a 43-page memorandum (authored mainly by Rowe) in November 1947 that provided the political rationale for a strong stand on civil rights. On the basis of the belief that "Negroes, organized labor, farmers and independent progressives would hold the balance of power in the 1948 election," the memorandum urged the president to appeal to these target groups "by making unequivocal demands for a comprehensive housing bill, reestablishment of price controls, total revision of the tax structure, and a rigorous civil rights bill."[41]

Underlying the recommendation to pursue civil rights legislation was the fundamental—and quite startling—assumption that "it is inconceivable that any policies initiated by the Truman administration no matter how 'liberal' could so alienate the South in the next year that it would revolt." To the contrary. In light of the white South's long obsession with the rights of states to determine racial policies, it is inconceivable that southern whites, especially those in the Deep South, would not have rebelled at President Truman's actions.[42]

The revolt was triggered in 1948. Following the new strategy, President Truman gave civil rights issues his highest priority in the 1948 State of the Union Address. "'Our first goal,' Truman announced, 'is to secure fully the essential human rights of our citizens,' which meant 'effective federal action' to curb racial and religious discrimination." The next month he sent to Congress a set of civil rights proposals, including "a fair employment practices law, an antilynching law, protection of voting rights, and a series of other measures that foreshadowed the legislation enacted in the 1950s and 1960s."[43]

Southern segregationists were furious. The Southern Governors' Conference warned that "the President must cease attacks on white supremacy or face full-fledged revolt in the South." A few days later, after an unsatisfactory meeting with the chairman of the Democratic National Committee, a smaller group of southern governors declared that "the Southern states are aroused and the present leadership of the Democratic party will soon realize that the South is no longer 'in the bag.'" Truman began to take notice of the growing southern revolt and tried to diminish the importance of civil rights issues. Now concerned about an open sectional split at the national convention, Truman's representatives tried to compromise the civil rights plank by reverting to the language used at the 1944 party convention.

Because the issue had been explicitly raised, however, the 1944 language was unacceptable to both sides.[44]

The Americans for Democratic Action (ADA) wanted the Democratic convention to go on record with a stronger civil rights position than the Truman administration preferred. Their strategy was "to press vigorously for a full civil rights program, even at the risk of sending the South into full revolt." The ADA liberals encountered great resistance from administration supporters, who did not want to take the civil rights issue so far that it would put the South at risk in the fall election. After much internal debate, as one of the group's leading spokesmen, Hubert Humphrey of Minnesota, recalled, the group decided to "propose a strong plank but we would introduce it with solid praise for President Truman's civil rights program." On the convention floor, Humphrey made the closing argument for the liberals. "There are those who say to you—we are rushing this issue of civil rights," Humphrey said. "I say we are a hundred and seventy-two years late." His concluding lines brought pandemonium to the convention: "There are those who say—this issue of civil rights is an infringement on states' rights. The time has arrived for the Democratic party to get out of the shadow of states' rights and walk forthrightly into the sunshine of human rights." Southerners introduced planks of their own that stressed the "reserved rights of the states" in these matters. "If we are defeated here today," warned Representative Cecil Sims of Tennessee, "you are witnessing the dissolution of the Democratic party in the South."[45]

The result was a decisive victory for the northern wing of the party. The Democratic convention adopted a civil rights position that was far stronger than the proposals desired by the Truman administration. The convention passed a resolution commending President Truman for "his courageous stand on the issue of civil rights." In addition, the party went on record, for the first time in its long history, in support of "(1) the right of full and equal political participation; (2) the right to equal opportunity of employment; (3) the right of security of persons; (4) and the right of equal treatment in the service and defense of our nation." Democrats from other parts of the nation found it politically unsafe, as well as morally repellent, to stand with the southerners. On the roll call in support of the Humphrey position, the vote was much closer but the outcome was the same. The South picked up votes from border and some western Democrats, but it was still defeated by fellow party members from the North, Midwest, and most of the West. Many northern Democrats feared that a weak civil rights position would cause northern blacks to vote for Henry Wallace, thus endangering the presidential and other Democratic candidacies.[46]

In 1948 the southerners lost all of the roll call votes on the party's civil rights position. Virtually complete regional polarization characterized the only southern amendment involving a roll call. The southerners were totally isolated from their fellow Democrats. No longer could white southerners dictate civil rights policies at the Democratic national convention, an institution which had long deferred to them on racial matters. "The South," *Time* concluded, "had been kicked in the pants, turned round and kicked in the stomach."[47]

At this point the convention was bitterly divided. Rayburn, the presiding officer, knew of southern plans for a walkout. Fearing the consequences for Truman of a massive exodus, Rayburn used his discretion as presiding officer to blunt the southerners' initial anger. The Alabama delegation was expected to lead the walkout in response to the roll call vote on adoption of the entire party platform. Rayburn ordered a voice vote rather than a roll call of the states. Once the platform was adopted, Rayburn announced that the chair could entertain no other motions except one to recess. The southerners were outraged. A small portion of the southerners, only 36 of 278 delegates, did walk out the following night, a fraction of those who had previously been ready to bolt. "We bid you goodbye!" shouted Alabama's Handy Ellis. In response, "thirteen members of the Alabama delegation got to their feet and marched up the center aisle to the door, as did the entire twenty-three-man Mississippi delegation. There were a few cheers from the South, but most of the southern delegations sat glumly in their seats while the galleries booed."[48]

The vast majority of southern delegates stayed to express their opposition to President Truman by voting for Senator Richard B. Russell, Jr., of Georgia. A New Deal Democrat, knowledgeable in foreign affairs and national security but a completely unreconstructed segregationist, Russell was the consensus choice of the white South. Russell received the vast majority of the southern delegates' votes, but won almost nothing outside the South. Not since 1860 had the white South been more thoroughly defeated at a Democratic convention. No longer could the conservative whites think of the national Democratic party as their reliable instrument for maintaining racial segregation.

Truman easily swept to victory on the first ballot. No call for unanimity occurred at the end because the southerners, who "sat in sullen wrath through the loud and sweaty demonstrations" celebrating Truman's nomination, were in no mood to be gracious losers. Nor did Truman make any gesture to reconcile the white South. In the fall election, Truman's southern vote fell 25 points below Roosevelt's final share of the vote. The white South has never since given a landslide vote to any Democratic presidential candidate.[49]

The Revival of National Democrats from the South

Although the South was the most resolutely Democratic part of the nation during the first half of the twentieth century, no southern Democrat had the faintest prospect of becoming the party's presidential candidate. Senator Russell expressed the prevailing realities when he observed in 1951 that he was "under no illusions about any southerner being elected President of the United States." At mid-century the principal reason that southerners were limited to second place on the Democratic ticket was their reputation for defending racial segregation and opposing civil rights bills. In his own case Russell was sufficiently realistic to acknowledge that a "southern man of my decided views against the modern trend euphoniously labeled 'civil rights' had no chance for the nomination."[50]

Despite these bleak prospects, two southern senators, Russell himself and Estes Kefauver of Tennessee, did seek the Democratic presidential nomination in 1952. Russell was the acknowledged leader of the southerners in the Senate, one of a small handful of politicians who exercised enormous influence behind the scenes. Kefauver was very different. Elected to the Senate in 1948, he burst on the national scene two years later by chairing televised Senate hearings that investigated organized crime. Many established Democratic politicians, however, viewed Kefauver as a maverick who was hurting big-city Democrats and embarrassing the Truman administration. Southern Democrats in the Senate generally disliked Kefauver.[51]

Kefauver was the first southerner in the twentieth century to seek the Democratic presidential nomination by running a truly national campaign based on personal appearances in northern and western primaries. Kefauver ran as a moderate Democrat who happened to be from Tennessee. As such he faced the dilemma of trying to be progressive enough to win northern votes while conservative enough to retain southern support. Kefauver's campaign is also worth exploring because he pioneered strategies and tactics that were, decades later, used successfully by Jimmy Carter.

In January 1952 Kefauver decided to seek the presidency, regardless of President Truman's intentions. His main issues were a foreign policy of strength, world peace, and clean government. Running against an incumbent president, Kefauver's only chance was to generate popular support in the presidential primaries. In 1952 about one-third of the delegates to the Democratic convention were chosen in the 16 states that held presidential preference primaries. Kefauver planned to enter the important primaries, hoping that a demonstration of popular appeal would impress the convention delegates.[52]

New Hampshire was the first and most important primary. After first dismissing primaries as "eyewash," Truman decided to keep his name on the ballot but to engage in no active campaigning in the state. "The strategy of the Kefauver forces was very simple," Joseph Bruce Gorman argues. "They planned to ride on the senator's national reputation and stress the fact that he was an active candidate who cared enough about New Hampshire's endorsement to come to the state and work for it." Kefauver worked the state's small towns like he was running for a Senate seat in Tennessee. "For the most part of three weeks," Charles L. Fontenay points out, Kefauver "plodded doggedly through the New Hampshire snow, soliciting individual votes like a country constable." He charmed the voters: "Thrusting out a large hand, Kefauver would say: 'My name is Estes Kefauver. I'm running for President of the United States. I'd sure appreciate it if you'll help me.' At his side, redhaired Nancy, chic and charming, would flash a pixie smile and jot down the name and address of the prospective voter for a followup letter as Kefauver chatted with him a minute or two and then moved on."[53]

The results were an upset victory for Kefauver and an embarrassing defeat for President Truman, who formally announced two weeks later that he would not be a candidate for reelection. "The New Hampshire primary," Gorman writes, "turned the 1952 Democratic political situation upside down. The President had been rejected by a majority of his own party in a New England state that preferred a Southern, freshman United States senator to the titular leader of the national party—a man who had almost unanimous backing from higher officials of the state Democratic party and organized labor." Kefauver went on to sweep the other primaries that he entered outside the South.[54]

As a candidate, Kefauver placed little or no emphasis on the maintenance of racial segregation. As a consequence, he was unable to rally support within his presumed southern base. Kefauver's formidable rival in the South was Russell. The Georgia senator had been prevailed upon by southern conservatives to run as a protest candidate against the conservative South's declining influence within the Democratic party. Russell aspired to national leadership, but as an unyielding, militant segregationist he was inescapably limited to a regional following. He had virtually no chance of winning the presidential nomination of the Democratic party.

The two southerners competed in Florida, the only southern state to hold a primary. Russell had previously "soft-pedaled civil rights issues," but "he returned to the attack on this question during his Florida talks. He accused Kefauver of really being unreliable on the civil rights question after the Tennessean had said he would feel 'morally bound' to support a Democratic platform, including an FEPC [Fair Employment Practices Commission] provision, if he were nominated at Chicago. Russell asserted that if he were the candidate and the convention passed such a platform, he would ignore the FEPC plank."[55]

Russell won the Florida primary with 56 percent of the vote, running best in the conservative rural areas and small towns in the north. Kefauver finished second, polling best in Miami and other urban and suburban areas. "Neither candidate had gotten what he needed in Florida," concluded Fontenay. "Russell's poor showing in the urban areas did not support his claim to possess non-regional appeal as a candidate. Kefauver's legend of invincibility at the polls had been broken, and his severe defeat in the rural areas indicated rejection by any genuinely Southern constituency." All in all, the Florida primary "injured both men's chances for the nomination" because neither showed much strength beyond his natural political base. Kefauver continued to win primaries outside the South, while Russell remained nothing more than a regional candidate.[56]

Kefauver arrived at the convention as a weak front-runner. He had more delegates than any other candidate (the other rivals were Illinois Governor Adlai Stevenson, New York Governor Averell Harriman, and Russell), but he was far short of a majority. He was badly organized, and party professionals loyal to President Truman were strongly opposed to him. Kefauver could expect few votes from the southerners, who were again coalescing around Russell. His only option was to work with Harriman and hope eventually to win the New Yorker's delegates.

Because of his strength in the Midwest and West, Kefauver led on the first ballot. As expected, he did poorly in the South, carrying only Tennessee and a handful of Alabama and Florida delegates. Still he remained optimistic. "I think I'm going to win," he remarked after the first ballot. Unknown to Kefauver, though, Harriman and Stevenson had already reached an agreement that the New York governor would throw his support to the Illinois governor if it became clear that Harriman could not win. After the second ballot, both Kefauver and Stevenson gained votes, but Kefauver's lead over Stevenson had dropped to only 38 votes. Harriman had also lost strength. "I don't see any draft movement here. I think the Stevenson strength is about at its peak," Kefauver conjectured. The Tennessee senator completely misread the convention's dynamics after the second ballot; he was living in a fool's paradise. A Tennesse delegate later remembered Kefauver "sitting there with a drink in his hand and a happy, bemused smile on his face, not even realizing that they had already cut his throat." President Truman settled his score with Kefauver by dispatching an aide to ask Harriman to shift to Stevenson. Harriman complied, and the Stevenson bandwagon, augmented by the large bloc of votes from New York, began to roll.[57]

When Kefauver finally realized what had happened, he attempted to address the convention and withdraw as a candidate. The third roll call was already underway, however, and party officials—Rayburn, the presiding officer, and Clarence Cannon, the parliamentarian—refused to let Kefauver address the convention. Instead, Kefauver took a seat at the rear of the platform and sat for three hours while the roll call continued. "To thousands who watched the spectacle on television, it appeared that the party management was deliberately humiliating the man who, with a few words, could have stopped his supporters' last-ditch fight and resolved the nomination in reasonable harmony," Fontenay concluded. When the vote ended, though, Stevenson was still shy of the majority. Finally allowed to speak, Kefauver addressed the convention and called for the party unity that gave Stevenson the nomination.[58]

Among the southern states, only Arkansas gave Stevenson a majority. Most of the southerners supported Russell. Party leaders appeared chagrined by the Dixiecrats' revolt of 1948, as well as by the southerners' lack of enthusiasm for Stevenson, and they again thought it prudent to "balance" the ticket by nominating a southerner for vice-president. Kefauver was considered, but neither the party leaders (Truman vetoed the suggestion) nor the Kefauvers (the candidate, his wife, and his father) were interested. "Kefauver had already said he would not accept the vice-presidential nomination 'under any circumstances,' after talking it over with Nancy," observed Fontenay. "Nancy and Cooke Kefauver were more outspoken. Nancy's reaction was, 'Tell them to go to hell!' and Cooke Kefauver said of Stevenson, 'Let him take the nomination and to hell with it. I don't want Estes's popularity to put this ticket over. . . . Eisenhower will be the next President.'" John Sparkman of Alabama, a national Democrat in all matters other than race, became the candidate. As in 1928, the presence of a southerner on the ticket in 1952 indicated that the Democrats felt insecure about their southern base.[59]

In 1956 Stevenson was the Democratic front-runner in the public opinion polls and among party leaders, but Kefauver again sought the nomination. Kefauver had moved in a more liberal direction on racial issues. In 1955 he announced his approval of the *Brown* decision as "the law of the land" and said that it was "high time people of both races got together and made their plans to comply with it." He refused to sign the Southern Manifesto, a declaration of segregationist principles that was supported by 19 southern Democratic senators and 96 southern House members. Kefauver paid a high price among his fellow southern Democrats for his increasingly liberal positions on civil rights. Southern segregationists favored Stevenson, explained Florida's Senator George Smathers, because "the South is always more apt to go for a northerner who doesn't know any better than for a southerner who should know better, but doesn't." The conservative southerners had disliked and distrusted Kefauver in 1952, but they despised him in 1956.[60]

Kefauver started impressively in 1956. He again won the New Hampshire primary and, one week later, upset Stevenson in Minnesota. Face-to-face campaigning had paid off again for him. Stevenson discarded his aloof style of campaigning and concentrated on the two crucial confrontations with Kefauver in Florida and California. "In both states, Stevenson developed a consuming interest in shaking everyone's hand, with a quick smile and perhaps a joke." Gorman observes that "In California . . . both Stevenson and Kefauver pictured themselves as heirs of the great liberal tradition of the Democratic party; in Florida . . . both stressed the moderation, especially on the civil rights issue, that was thought necessary to win acceptance by Florida Democrats." Stevenson won both primaries, narrowly in Florida, where the race issue was again used against Kefauver, and overwhelmingly in California. Having failed to demonstrate superior popularity among the primary electorate, Kefauver abandoned his campaign.[61]

After winning on the first ballot, Stevenson turned over to the convention the choice of his running mate. A spirited contest developed between Kefauver and Senator John F. Kennedy of Massachusetts. Reversing the outcome of 1928, the South aligned behind the Massachusetts Catholic and rejected the Tennessee Baptist. "The South's dislike for Kefauver was so intense," Gorman concluded, "that Southerners were willing to take anyone who had a chance to beat Kefauver." Some Democratic Catholic politicians, however, were unwilling to take a chance on Kennedy. Although denied the presidential nomination, Kefauver became the first genuinely national Democrat from the South to win a place on the party's presidential ticket. Kefauver's victory, achieved despite the vehement objections of Democrats from his native region, indicated once again that southern conservatives no longer exercised a veto in the Democratic national convention.[62]

The South Returns to the White House through the Back Door

In the 1960 Democratic convention Massachusetts Senator John F. Kennedy demonstrated anew that southern votes were unnecessary to capture the party's presidential nomination. Kennedy won only 3 percent of the southern delegates, most of whom supported Texas Senator Lyndon B. Johnson, but triumphed by winning 68 percent of the votes cast by delegates outside the South. The Massachusetts Senator swept four-fifths of the delegates from the Northeast and Midwest and captured over half of the western delegates.

Kennedy had begun his efforts with a realistic analysis of his strengths and weaknesses among the various state delegations. He announced early and actively pursued the nomination for more than a year. He cultivated Democratic political leaders in major urban areas and hunted delegates across the nation; he entered and won seven party primaries to demonstrate that his Catholic religion was no barrier to winning votes among Protestants. His most important victory occurred in West Virginia, a Protestant state that many observers did not think he could win. Kennedy money and manpower poured into the state, and the Massachusetts Senator upset Senator Hubert Humphrey of Minnesota. Kennedy's apparent strength among Protestants impressed many Democratic professionals, and he arrived at Los Angeles well ahead of the other candidates in the number of delegates.[63]

Kennedy's chief rival was Johnson, the Senate Majority Leader. Johnson had been elected to the Senate in 1948 and had swiftly risen to the top leadership positions in the institution. With the support of Russell, he had been chosen Minority Leader by Senate Democrats after the 1952 elections. When the Democrats recaptured the Senate two years later, Johnson became the leader of the majority party in the Senate after serving only six years in the body. Keenly aware that a southern identity would damage his prospects for national leadership, Johnson presented himself as a Texan, not as a southerner. He established close ties with many Deep South senators, yet kept his distance from the southern caucus. Humphrey observed that Johnson "was a Democrat and a Texan, enjoying the benefits of southern hospitality, southern power, southern support, but who carefully avoided the liabilities of being clearly labeled a Southerner." Yet Texas *was* a southern state, and there were many in the Democratic party who were skeptical about Johnson's national appeal. Johnson had long aspired to the presidency but feared that it might be beyond his reach. Discussing Johnson's yearnings for the White House, James H. Rowe, Jr., a longtime confidante, told a journalist, "I think he wanted it so much his tongue was hanging out; then this other part of him said, 'This is impossible and why get my hopes up? I'm not going to try. If I don't try, I won't fail.'"[64]

Whatever the mixture of motivations, Johnson approached the 1960 Democratic convention in a way very different from Kennedy's strategy. The Texan repeatedly denied in public that he was seeking the nomination and made his formal announcement of candidacy only a few days before the convention. The Johnson forces hoped that Kennedy and Humphrey would fatally wound each other in the primaries, while Johnson would concentrate on running the Senate and simply be available as "everybody's second choice." In such a situation, "Faced with the more liberal alternatives, the South would be his for the asking. All he needed, then, were the border states, a strong showing in a couple of big northern industrial states, and the Far West."[65]

Johnson's search for delegates rested upon a very curious and unpromising strategy. He sought to win support by relying upon members of Congress to deliver blocs of delegates from their states. Johnson's approach could work in the southern states, but there was no magic to the Johnson name outside the South. Rayburn and his colleagues in the Speaker's Board of Education often encountered resistance from House members. On one occasion, Pennsylvania Congressman Bill Green, who was being pursued by the Kennedys, was the target of Rayburn's insistent solicitation. Heading for the door, Green told the gathering he felt like the proverbial "fruit peddler who was constantly being enticed by women customers into trading his fruit for their amorous favors. Finally, with no money to show for the day, he rang one last doorbell. When a voluptuous female appeared, the peddler started to weep. What's the matter, she asked? 'Oh, hell,' the peddler bawled, 'I've already been fucked out of my apples and oranges, and now you're about to get my peaches.' Amid the laughter, Green escaped, completely uncommitted to Rayburn." Johnson arrived at the convention in Los Angeles far shy of enough delegates to be a serious contender. Having entered no primaries, Johnson had forfeited the opportunity to demonstrate popular support outside the South.[66]

Kennedy turned to Johnson as his running mate, a move that upset Kennedy's advisors and many Johnson confidants. Kennedy's motivations for selecting Johnson were complex. In the South Kennedy's position was similar to Al Smith's in 1928. As a Catholic, he could not count on a unified South. Although Kennedy was privately skeptical that Johnson would be able to carry Texas for him, the Kennedy campaign had targeted it as a key state. Johnson's active campaigning promised to make Kennedy competitive in Texas. Kennedy stressed other factors in explaining his decision. "If we win, it will be by a small margin and I won't be able to live with Lyndon Johnson as the leader of a small majority in the Senate," Kennedy reportedly told his close aide Kenneth O'Donnell. The candidate continued: "If Johnson and Rayburn leave here mad at me, they'll ruin me in Congress next month. Then I'll be the laughingstock of the country. Nixon will say I haven't any power in my own party, and I'll lose the election before Labor Day. So I've got to make peace now with Johnson and Rayburn, and offering Lyndon the Vice-Presidency, whether he accepts it or not, is one way of keeping him friendly until Congress adjourns." Thus Kennedy's decision was also influenced by the desire to both flatter and neutralize Johnson.[67]

Why would Lyndon Johnson leave his position as Senate Majority Leader to place himself at the beck and call of John Kennedy? The answers to a question like this are always complex, but the heart of it appears to be Johnson's elemental yearning to become president. Johnson had some obvious liabilities as a presidential candidate—

"southerner, heart attack, lack of charisma, stigma of the oil and gas industry"—according to one list. Though he held the most important leadership position in the U.S. Senate, he had already failed to convert that base of power into a presidential nomination. There was no reason to think it would be any different in the future. With the route from the Senate blocked off, and with Richard Nixon demonstrating that the vice-presidency could be used as a stepping stone to the presidential nomination, Johnson had no alternative: "There was no real reason for Johnson not to take it [the vice-presidency]. He had proved an unsalable product for the Presidency on his own. The only way he was likely ever to reach the White House was the hard way—by first serving as Vice-President."[68]

On one occasion, as Johnson contemplated selecting his own running mate, a member of his staff advised him that a particular senator under consideration would never accept the vice-presidency. "Let me tell you something," the president said. "That's what they said about old Lyndon Johnson in 1960. But when they lead you up on that mountain, and show you those green fields down below and that beautiful White House standing there—you know what you do? You take it. They all take it." Johnson took it, and by the accounts of friends and foes alike, the vice-presidency proved enormously stressful. A natural leader and power seeker, willingly subordinate to no one, Johnson had to hunker down and accept whatever assignments President Kennedy chose to give him. Although his old friend Russell hoped that Johnson could "protect the South" from his new position, Russell also knew the depth of Johnson's ambition to exert national rather than regional leadership.[69]

In 1963 an extraordinary chain of events made possible the Democratic party's first nomination of a southerner for president in 120 years. "We're heading into nut country today," President Kennedy told his wife on the morning of November 22, 1963. "But, Jackie, if somebody wants to shoot me from a window with a rifle," he continued, "nobody can stop it, so why worry about it?" Johnson was, of course, a backdoor president, elevated to the White House that afternoon upon the assassination of President Kennedy.[70]

Johnson quickly consolidated his power by stressing the "continuity" of his administration with that of President Kennedy. The Democratic National Convention occurred only ten months after the assassination. In light of Johnson's early mastery of the office and his passionate efforts to pass the Kennedy program, he was challenged for the nomination only briefly by Alabama Governor George Wallace. Running as a protest candidate, Wallace attracted a sizable vote, but he had no chance of winning the Democratic nomination and he dropped out of the race in July. With nothing to gain and something to lose if he did not do well, President Johnson avoided all of the presidential primaries. Instead, he relied on his influence with Democratic state politicians to assure friendly delegations at the party convention in Atlantic City.[71]

The convention met in late August, less than two months after passage of the Civil Rights Act of 1964. No Democrat from the South sought to mobilize the region at the convention against President Johnson. *Time* reported that "virtually none of the South's senior Democratic politicians were on hand. And for the first time within recent memory, the South played no role of any importance at a Democratic Convention." Instead, the Democratic convention continued to discipline the most conservative of the southern dissidents by requiring Alabama and Mississippi delegates to pledge their support for the Democratic ticket in the fall elections. Most of the Alabama and Mississippi white delegates refused to take such a pledge, and walked out of the convention.[72]

The most explosive controversy concerned whether an all-white delegation, the regular Democrats, or a mostly black delegation, the Mississippi Freedom Democrats, should represent Mississippi at the convention. The most significant part of the eventual settlement of this dispute was an agreement that delegations to future conventions would not be accepted from states that denied blacks the right to vote. It was the first meaningful step toward the racial diversification of southern Democratic delegations to the national convention. All but four of the regular southern delegates in 1964 were white. The handful of black delegates came from Tennessee, North Carolina, and Georgia. In the future, blacks would play larger roles. As Theodore White put it, "The South, reduced over the years from its one-time absolute veto on Democratic nominees, had now been forced to accept the best compromise it could get [on the racial composition of convention delegates]: a four-year delayed sentence." Conservative southern whites were losing control of the process by which they had dominated delegations to the Democratic convention.[73]

Johnson's selection of a running mate was the main uncertainty at the Democratic convention. By the spring of 1964, Robert Kennedy had made clear his desire to be on the ticket. It was a highly unlikely outcome. For years no love had been lost between Johnson and Kennedy, and polls taken in the spring of 1964 showed Johnson running well ahead of Goldwater. In late July, President Johnson informed the attorney general that he would not be on the ticket. Instead, the President turned to Senator Humphrey, the liberal Minnesota Democrat, whose primary assets were his bona fides among liberal Democrats and, even more important, his willingness to be totally subservient to Johnson.[74]

The Johnson presidency was immense in its intentions and mixed in its results. Johnson pushed through more civil rights legislation than any other American president, always against the opposition of southerners in the Congress. As the impact of his civil rights programs expanded to include the entire nation and began to affect areas of life more costly for whites to change, however, Johnson confronted a deteriorating climate for civil rights legislation. On domestic economic issues, Johnson expanded the activities of the federal government. On the consuming question of American involvement in the Vietnam War, he came to be an ineffective hawk, a politician whose leadership so divided the public that he could not command majority support for his war policies. Whether to expand the war, pull out entirely, or maintain the administration's policies, majorities of Americans opposed all of the options on the most important issue facing the nation.[75]

All of these problems eroded public confidence in Johnson's leadership. In 1968 he was challenged in the Democratic presidential primaries by critics of his war policies. Senator Eugene McCarthy of Minnesota announced for President against Johnson. In the New Hampshire primary, Johnson received slightly less than half of the votes, all write-ins, compared with McCarthy's 42 percent. For an incumbent president, this was an embarrassingly weak showing, a sign of massive disapproval of his leadership. To make matters worse for Johnson, Senator Robert Kennedy of New York, the president's most feared and despised rival, whom he called a "grandstanding little runt" in private conversation, also entered the race. The next battleground was Wisconsin, where polls showed him trailing McCarthy. Faced with the prospect of a series of humiliating defeats, Johnson decided to cut his losses. In a dramatic television address to the nation, he announced that he would not seek renomination as the Democratic presidential candidate. So ended in failure the administration of the first southern president in this century.[76]

His defeat was largely due to the pursuit of an unpopular war whose necessity Johnson could never persuasively explain. In later years, however, he attributed his defeat to the anti-southern biases of his enemies. "He was haunted by regional prejudice, and even the attainment of the Presidency did not temper his feelings," David Halberstam argues. "Later, after he had left office, he became convinced that it was his Southern origins, not the war, which had driven him out, that *they* had lain in wait for an issue, any issue, and had used the war, which was their war in the first place, to drive him from office."[77]

The Democratic Debacle of 1968

With Johnson out of the running, Vice-President Humphrey announced his candidacy later that spring. Humphrey was part and parcel of the Johnson administration, tied to its unpopular war policies whether he liked it or not. Privately, Humphrey told his associates, "The President didn't run because he knew he couldn't make it. And he clothed me with nothing. I've been subjected to the worst type of calumny and humiliation. On college campuses they've not only insulted and spit on me but thrown filth at me." It would be no easy campaign. Humphrey did not enter any primaries but concentrated his efforts on the states where delegates where chosen in caucuses and conventions.[78]

Spring 1968 in the United States was one of the most tumultuous and troubled times in this century. Reverend Martin Luther King, Jr., was assassinated in Memphis, Tennessee, in early April. His death was followed by rioting in scores of cities and the "biggest military deployment for a civil emergency in history." Two months later, Robert Kennedy was murdered on the night he won the California primary. Antiwar Democrats had lost their most effective spokesman, and thousands of persons opposed to the Johnson administration's conduct of the war converged on Chicago, the site of the 1968 Democratic convention.[79]

Although President Johnson never appeared at the Chicago convention, forces loyal to him dominated the proceedings, and he set the terms under which Humphrey, his vice-president, could be nominated. "Johnson might be a lame-duck President, but he was not, at least until the Democrats found a successor, a lame-duck party leader," wrote the authors of *An American Melodrama*. "He had invested his massive ego in his conduct of the war, and he was not about to endure the humiliation of seeing the nominee of his party publicly trample on this policy while he served out the last six months of his term." A substantial minority of the delegates to the convention had backed the candidacies of McCarthy and the slain Robert Kennedy, and they were strongly opposed to the nomination of any politician who promised to continue the Vietnam War policies of the Johnson administration.[80]

Into this highly charged convention came Humphrey, once a hero to Democratic liberals but now Johnson's controversial heir. Humphrey entered the convention as a front-runner without much apparent means of political support. His dilemma was the lack of political resources: "The Vice-President had no money, no political base, nothing without Johnson's support." As the convention opened, Humphrey did not possess the votes to be nominated, for the most important delegations, loyal to the president, were withholding support from him.[81]

The key Johnson delegations were Illinois, whose 118 votes were under the tight control of Chicago Mayor Richard J. Daley, and Texas, led by the veteran Johnson associate, Governor John Connally. As its favorite-son candidate, Connally had complete control of the Texas delegation. Through his close ties with the other southern governors, who were in charge of their delegations, Connally could deliver well over 500 convention votes. "The South spoke from strength," James Reston, Jr., observed, "and Connally was its strong man." And the southerners were playing tough. As a concession to the peace groups, Humphrey had called for the elimination of the "unit rule," a provision under which the decision of a state delegation's majority was binding upon all members. It had long been a key technique by which political leaders such as Connally and Daley had wielded the massive strength of their entire delegations, and they were not about to support a nominee who sought to deprive them of their power bases. Connally and Daley withheld their support until they had won concessions on issues of vital concern.[82]

Humphrey understood the necessity of winning the southern votes for his nomination. "With the nomination in balance, Humphrey felt compelled to seek support among the Southern delegations," wrote Carl Solberg. "To such skeptics as [Larry] O'Brien and [Walter] Mondale, who felt that a forward-looking party could only win by concentrating on the big Northern states, he said: 'I've got a lot of friends in the South. They aren't all bad. You can deal with them like I did in the Senate with Eastland and Stennis. They're not so tough.'" Humphrey did not retract his philosophical position in opposition to the "unit rule, but he reassured southern governors that he did not favor abolition of the rule in the 1968 convention."[83]

President Johnson's major concern was to hold Humphrey's feet to the fire of the administration's Vietnam policies. Three times Humphrey had submitted a draft proposal of the party plank on Vietnam to the president, and each time Johnson had rejected it. Finally, the Platform Committee passed an administration-sponsored measure that was labeled the "Johnson-Humphrey" statement on Vietnam. Humphrey had now met the Johnson-Connally-Daley tests, and he was rewarded with the votes necessary to win the nomination. "We've been playing games," Connally told a key Humphrey aide. "Let's forget all this nonsense; we're with you." All of the other southern leaders soon lined up behind Humphrey. The Johnson-Humphrey Vietnam plank was approved by the convention, and Humphrey easily won nomination.[84]

Humphrey's support came primarily from the key ingredients of the disparate Democratic coalition: "the white South, labor, Northern Negroes, and city machine men—between whose elements little love was lost, but which was held together by considerations of shared self-interest." The vice-president, now more strongly identified as Johnson's man and as a supporter of the administration's war policies than as a civil rights crusader, had become much more acceptable to the white southern Democrats than any of the alternatives, especially any antiwar Democrats. Yet Humphrey's victory had come at substantial cost to his candidacy. "To win nomination he presented himself," according to Solberg, "as the candidate offering no change." In a tumultuous year of domestic and foreign upheavals, the American public was not in the market for a status quo politician who had been stamped "approved" by Lyndon Johnson.[85]

The southerners had helped Humphrey obtain the nomination, but he flatly turned them down on the vice-presidency. Connally led a delegation of southern governors to meet with Humphrey to claim the office for the South. Reston has reconstructed the essence of Connally's argument to Humphrey and his advisors:

> The South and the border states had been central to Humphrey's nomination, he opened, and these states would be essential and decisive to his election; indeed, the South represented the margin of victory. They had come to underscore the importance of this and to say that Humphrey's running mate should be someone who would run strongly in their section. . . . To Humphrey and his aides, it was clear that

Connally was going to be their candidate. [Finally, Humphrey took charge of the meeting]:

"Well, fellows, I want you to know I've made my choice. He's not a Southerner, but he's someone you're going to like—*Ed Muskie.*"

Stunned silence fell over the room. Ed Muskie? Of Maine? Maine, with its population of less than a million? With its four electoral votes?[86]

Humphrey went to the Northeast for his running mate, returning to the geographical ticket balancing that midwestern Democrats usually used after the Civil War. It did not work then, and it assuredly did not work in 1968. Even during the long period when the South could be relied upon to supply electoral votes for the Democrats, the combination of midwestern presidential candidate and northeastern vice-presidential candidate had never succeeded. It had even less chance for success with little or no contribution from the South, since it forced the Democratic candidate to capture two-thirds of the electoral vote in the rest of the country.

There was certainly strong political logic in Humphrey's refusal to go south. The region looked virtually hopeless for the Democrats in 1968. Even with a southerner on the ticket, most white southerners would be deciding between Richard Nixon and George Wallace. Yet Humphrey's veto of a southern running mate undercut what little interest still prevailed among southern Democrats to work aggressively on Humphrey's behalf. Although the vice-president emancipated himself from southern conservatives, they had the final say in Humphrey's bid to carry southern states. He captured around a fifth of the southern white vote, and he lost 10 of the 11 southern states. In the fall of 1968, Humphrey ran worse in the South than any Democratic presidential candidate had since 1868.

The 1968 Democratic convention marked the end of an era. It was the final convention in which conservative southern Democrats played major roles. Humphrey needed and received southern assistance both to win the nomination and to pass policy resolutions supporting President Johnson's conduct of the Vietnam War. Yet when the southerners attempted to claim their traditional reward— a place on the national ticket—their weaknesses were all too clear. With the Democrats nominating a ticket headed by a northern liberal, and with Nixon and Wallace fighting for the votes of most southern whites, no persuasive argument could be made that a southern vice-presidential nominee would help Humphrey win many southern electoral votes. Conservative southern Democrats returned home with little to show for their efforts and with a profound reluctance to campaign aggressively for Humphrey.

Moreover, there was good reason to think that the strategic position of the southern conservatives within the Democratic party was bound to deteriorate further. The heavy-handed techniques that established party leaders had used to dominate the 1968 convention produced an intense and widespread negative reaction among Democratic activists. As a result, a commission was created to revise the rules governing Democratic presidential nominations. The subsequent reforms mandated increased representation of women and blacks in the nominating process, shifted political power away from elected Democratic officials, and accelerated the use of primaries to nominate Democratic presidential candidates. All of these factors strengthened the progressive wing of the party at the expense of conservative Democrats.

Gradually relatively progressive Democrats—blacks and liberal to moderate whites—began to dominate southern delegations to the national convention. Effective power in the reformed Democratic party lay mainly with liberals and moderates. As such, the new Democratic party offered little or nothing of value to conservative white southerners. After 1968 truly conservative southern Democrats became an endangered species at Democratic conventions. They essentially abandoned the Democratic convention, the principal institution thorough which their predecessors had tried to guide the selection of presidential nominees.

Declining conservative influence within the Democratic party did not mean that southern conservatives had no impact on presidential politics. Far from it. Beginning with the Goldwater movement of the early 1960s, they emerged as a formidable force—a "southernizing" force—within the Republican party. While southern conservatives in the Democratic party were repelled by much of Johnson's Great Society, southern conservatives in the Republican party helped nominate Barry Goldwater in 1964. While southern conservatives at the Democratic convention supported Humphrey in 1968 as the least obnoxious alternative of a remarkably bad lot, conservative southern Republicans were successfully doing business with Nixon, who was able to satisfy them on matters of mutual interest.

Increasingly during the 1960s, the Republican party became the new party of choice for southern conservatives eager to nominate presidential candidates and to shape the policies of a major political party. Across the South conservative white southerners were re-evaluating their traditional loyalty to the Democratic party. Abandoning the Democratic ship of their forefathers, many climbed aboard the Republican vessel and advanced at a smart clip in the general direction of the captain's quarters. The best way to restore the influence of southern conservatives in presidential politics, they believed, was to establish blocs of acknowledged and respected power within the Republican party.

5

The South and Republican Nominations

During most of its existence, the Republican party had little concern for white southerners. Republican presidential candidates ran so well in the Northeast and Midwest that they needed no votes from the South to occupy the White House. For their part, most southern whites assuredly held intensely negative feelings toward the party of Lincoln, Reconstruction, and the Great Depression.

The few southerners who did take part in national Republican party activities generally backed conservative candidates, but their choices were limited to the men sponsored by northern Republican leaders. Unable to provide any electoral votes for GOP presidential nominees, the delegations of southerners at Republican national conventions were seldom invited into the inner councils of party leadership. Politicians from the Northeast and Midwest set the party's policies and chose its presidential candidates. These northern leaders occasionally needed southern votes at the convention.to nominate a particular northern candidate, but the southerners were essentially subservient to the northerners.

For decades Republican leaders approached presidential campaigns on the assumption that the South was unwinnable. By 1950, however, the Republicans needed to crack the Solid Democratic South. The Great Depression had shattered the Republicans' traditional hold on northern voters, and Republican presidential candidates had lost five consecutive elections between 1932 and 1948. Reduced to the level of a minority party throughout the nation, the Republicans could no longer afford to write off the entire South. At first Republican goals were modest: to carry a few of the region's states and thus block a Democratic sweep. The victories of Dwight

Eisenhower (1952 and 1956) and Richard Nixon (1960) in several southern states vindicated the initial strategy.

These GOP breakthroughs encouraged a new generation of conservative southern Republican leaders to imagine even greater party success, to dream of sweeping the entire South. A Solid Republican South was possible, they believed, *if* the party nominated a strong conservative as its presidential candidate. By presenting voters with a clear choice between a conservative Republican and a liberal Democrat, the southern Republican leaders thought they could attract massive majorities of whites in every southern state to vote for the conservative candidate.

To push the Republican party to the right in its platform and its candidates required wresting power away from northeastern Republicans, who preferred moderate conservatives such as Eisenhower and Nixon, and placing decison-making in the hands of the growing number of southern and western conservatives, whose political hero was Arizona Senator Barry Goldwater. In alliance with conservatives from the rest of the nation, the southern Republicans helped to nominate Goldwater in 1964. Four years later they assisted in the nomination of Nixon, who had made clear his willingness to do business with the southern conservatives. During the 1960s, a profound regional power shift took place within the Republican party. The center of gravity at the Republican convention now rested with the conservative bloc, and the southerners had become key players in the party.

As part of the explanation for the emergence of a Solid Republican South in presidential elections, therefore, it is vital to explore the changing center of political gravity within the Republican national convention. The Republican convention has become the chief institution for conservative southerners to shape party policies and help nominate conservative presidential candidates. If we are to understand the novelty of the South's rising influence in the modern Republican party, it is helpful to examine the regional bases of support for the original Republican party.

The Nineteenth-Century Legacy

The South was originally useful to the Republican party as a target of denunciation. Organized in the 1850s from such disparate elements as "Free-Soilers, Independent Democrats, Conscience Whigs,

Know-Nothings, Barnburners, abolitionists, teetotalers, Germans, and others," the original Republicans felt "an intense antipathy for the South, its customs, its industry, its way of life, and its economic and social philosophy." They were convinced that southern slaveholders controlled the Democratic party, holding hostage the rest of the nation to policies that directly injured the interests of northern and western whites. While most Republicans did not support abolition of slavery in the South, they vehemently objected to the extension of slavery into the territories. They wanted free labor, land grants for homesteads, federal aid in constructing railroads, a protective tariff against imported goods, and an infrastructure to connect an agricultural and industrial society with distant markets. The southerners stood in the way of all of these goals.[1]

Unlike other major nineteenth-century American political parties, whose leaders had appealed to voters in different parts of the nation, the Republicans were the first broadly based American party organized strictly along sectional lines. "With their appeal aimed solely at the North, Republicans planned a strategy for political victory that needed the South not at all, even to win the presidency," William J. Cooper has written. "No major party had ever so completely repudiated the South." The Republican potential for success rested on the sheer size of the North. "By the 1850s," Robert Kelley has noted, "the Northern population—including both whites and blacks—was half again as large as the population of the South. The number of white people in the North was more than double (in a ratio of seven to three) the number in the South. If Southerners had been concerned about Yankees in John Adams' time, now they were faced with a colossus of the North that had enormous strength if it were concentrated and turned in one direction—as now it seemed to be." And when that strength was turned south, white southerners feared, the result would be an attack on slavery.[2]

Unsurprisingly, when the Republican party assembled in Philadelphia in 1856 for its first national convention, no southern delegates were present. David C. Fremont of California, the Republican presidential candidate, received no votes in the South but carried eleven states in the rest of the nation. In the election of 1860, no votes for Abraham Lincoln were recorded in any southern state. With Lincoln's victory, control of the national government passed to new social forces. "Southerners of almost every political persuasion," Cooper has emphasized, "agreed that Lincoln's win provided 'incontrovertible proof of a diseased and dangerous public opinion all over the North, and a certain forerunner of further and more atrocious aggression.'" As a consequence, "practically every white southerner looked upon a future Republican administration with a combined apprehension and anger." The Republican party had no place for the slave South, and the slave South wanted nothing to do with the Republican party.[3]

The Republicans established their northern coalition during the Civil War and consolidated their gains in the decades after the conflict had ended. No one has analyzed the basis of sustained Republican support more succinctly than V. O. Key, Jr.:

> The long period of Republican rule was based on the successful conduct of a domestic war for a high and noble purpose, which iden- tified the Republican party with the Union, with patriotism, and with humanitarianism. Yet the inner strength of Republicanism did not rest on sentiment alone. Sentiment clothed bonds of substance. To the old soldiers—old Union soldiers—went pensions. To the manufacturers of the Northeast went tariffs. To the farmers of the Northwest went free land under the Homestead Act. To railroad promoters went land grants for the construction of railroads that tied together the West and the North—and assured that the flow of commerce would by-pass the South.[4]

The sectional unity of the Republican party was expressed in the regional composition of its presidential ticket. From the combination of Lincoln of Illinois and Hannibal Hamlin of Maine in 1860 to William McKinley of Ohio and Theodore Roosevelt of New York in 1900, the Republican party typically led with a candidate from the Midwest but reached out to the Northeast to balance the ticket.[5]

As for the vanquished and defeated South, the fruits of Republican victory were quite different. Economic development largely bypassed the South. As Richard Franklin Bensel has demonstrated, the Re- publicans used tariff policies, economic subsidies, and military pen- sions to extract revenues from the South (and other peripheral areas of the economy) and redistribute them to key constituencies of the Republican party, all located in the North. These policies "left the southern periphery to shoulder almost the entire cost of industriali- zation; Confederate veterans were not eligible for federal pensions and no indigenous product (save sugar) was protected by the tariff. The periphery was drained while the core [commercial-industrial regions of the nation] prospered."[6]

The Republican party's racial policies were, of course, even more important in arousing the durable hatred of southern whites. Slaves living in areas not controlled by the Union Army were emancipated in 1863, and the Thirteenth Amendment abolished slavery in 1865. The Reconstruction Act of 1867, passed by congressional Republicans over the veto of President Andrew Johnson, imposed military rule on all of the former Confederate states except Tennessee, and it established the terms under which the southern states could be re-admitted to the Union. "The Reconstruction governments in the South were essentially army-of-occupation governments, for the southern region was a conquered country and was treated as such," observed Ralph J. Bunche. "The all-pervading influence was the victorious armed force of the North as symbolized by federal troops." Ratification of the Fourteenth and Fifteenth Amendments further promised to reshape racial practices in the South. Reconstruction and the new constitutional amendments were imposed against the objections of the vast majority of native white southerners.[7]

With the occupying armies overseeing the conduct of southern elections, Republican Presidential candidate Ulysses S. Grant carried five of the seven southern states that had been readmitted to the Union with a biracial electorate in 1868. Four years later, Grant won eight southern states. In the first two elections after the end of the Civil War, the GOP was able to extract electoral votes from the region it had just defeated in combat. As southern whites—many of them former Confederates or Confederate sympathizers—returned to the polls, however, political power began to shift back to the Democrats. In 1876 the Republicans led only in the three southern states where Union armies were still present. So close was the election outside the South that the outcome hinged on disputed election returns from those three states—Florida, Louisiana, and South Carolina. The ultimate result, as judged by an Electoral Commission, gave the election to the Republicans. A grateful President Rutherford B. Hayes then withdrew federal troops from the remaining southern states.[8]

In 1880 the Solid Democratic South appeared for the first time in presidential elections since the cessation of hostilities. The end of Reconstruction destroyed Republican hopes of carrying the region for generations. From 1880 to 1948, the Republicans won only Tennessee in 1920, and Tennessee, North Carolina, Virginia, Texas, and Florida in 1928. Southern Republicans persisted as an embattled minority, winning about one-third or so of the presidential vote in the shrinking southern electorate. Under the winner-take-all rules of the electoral college, however, the preeminent political fact had been established: the Republican party would have to concede the South to the Democrats and could occupy the White House only by winning landslide majorities of the electoral college vote in the rest of the nation.[9]

Nineteenth-century Republicanism permanently alienated most southern whites. "Republicans could not reshape the image they had acquired in the sectional conflict," George Brown Tindall concluded. "They were the northern party which had opposed the right of the South to carry slaves into the territories. They had waged war on the South, freed the slaves, and imposed Radical Reconstruction." Outside the mountains, few southern whites wanted anything to do with the GOP. One former Confederate who had originally been associated with the Republican party expressed the prevailing view: "No white man can live in the South in the future and act with any other than the Democratic party unless he is willing and prepared to live a life of social isolation and remain in political oblivion." In the 1890s the disfranchisement movement eliminated virtually all of the region's remaining black voters, thereby decimating the southern Republican party's largest group of supporters. These trends culminated in the destruction of the GOP as a viable political party in the South. "Racism in the South," Donald J. Lisio concludes, "reduced the Republican party to cliques of officeholders and patronage seekers who exerted their only remaining influence at the Republican national conventions, where they generally cast their ballots for the likely winner in return for control of patronage in their states."[10]

At the Convention: The Politics of "Rotten Boroughs"

By the 1890s, the status of southern delegates at the Republican national convention had become rather peculiar. The southern Republicans could offer GOP presidential candidates no electoral college votes, but their delegates to the party convention could provide an aspiring Republican politician with about half of the votes necessary for nomination. Ever since 1868, when southern Republican parties began to send delegates to the national convention, the South had accounted for about one-quarter of the total delegates. A region which had previously been of no weight whatsoever in the internal politics of the Republican party now sent a delegation only slightly smaller than the groups from the Northeast (32 percent) and the Midwest (26), and considerably larger than the delegations from the Border states (11) and the West (5). The small cliques of Republican leaders in the South were a force to be negotiated with in the internal affairs of the party, a situation which did not please Republican politicians in the Northeast and Midwest.[11]

At first, when Republican presidential candidates Grant and Hayes had been able to carry some southern states, the size of the southern delegation at the national convention provoked no adverse reactions within the party. As the permanence of the new Solid Democratic South began to be widely conceded, however, delegates from other parts of the country began to complain about the excessive weight accorded the southern states—the "rotten boroughs"—in the Republican convention. Republican politicians in the competitive states— New York or Illinois, for example—always worried about the strength of the nominee in *their* states, for an unpopular ticket leader could hurt Republican candidates for lesser offices. The southerners had no such concerns because Republicans did not seriously compete for state and local offices in much of the South. They were far more interested in supporting the likely convention nominee, who controlled party patronage, than they were in evaluating how well the candidate would perform outside the South. Since 1872, they had always supported any Republican incumbent who sought renomination, regardless of his popularity in the more competitive states of the nation. In open seat contests, the southerners went with the candidate who seemed most likely to receive the party nomination, not necessarily the candidate who seemed most likely to win the fall campaign.[12]

The regional tensions within the party exploded in 1912. On that turbulent occasion, "the most prolonged and disorderly Republican Convention in the history of the Party," incumbent President William Howard Taft was challenged by former President Theodore Roosevelt. Taft won a narrow victory, largely because he mobilized enormous support from the "rotten boroughs" of the South, which followed the time-honored principle of supporting the incumbent. Taft won 83 percent of the southern delegates, far higher than his share of the vote in any other region. Yet Taft was very unpopular in some of the nation's most competitive states. Had the vote been limited to delegates from areas of the country where the Republicans had a chance to win in the fall, Roosevelt would have captured the nomination. Unwilling to acquiesce to Taft's victory, Roosevelt abandoned the Republican party and ran as the candidate of the Progressive party. The southern Republicans had helped saddle their party with a candidate so weak that Taft finished third in the popular vote, behind Democrat Woodrow Wilson and Roosevelt.[13]

In the aftermath of this debacle, northern Republicans revised the rules of representation at the convention to reward states where Republicans polled large numbers of votes in competitive elections and to reduce the size of the delegations from states where the party's candidates won few votes. As a consequence of these new rules, southerners fell from 23 percent of the Republican delegates in 1912 to only 18 percent at the 1916 convention. From 1916 through 1952, the southerners averaged 17 percent of the delegates at the national convention.[14]

As the party of Lincoln, at least in principle, the GOP had afforded an opportunity for some blacks to take part in party affairs. In most southern states the small Republican cliques were divided by fierce rivalries between so-called black-and-tan and lily-white factions. The term *black-and-tan* referred to a delegation led by black politicians in combination with a small number of white Republicans who were willing to accept a position of subservience to black leadership and who were labeled by their white opponents, derogatively, as "tans." These groups of party "regulars" were challenged, at various times and in various states, by the *lily-whites*, groups of Republicans under the leadership of whites, who claimed to be the legitimate representatives of southern Republican parties. Some of the lily-white delegations were comprised exclusively of whites, but others included a few blacks who were willing to be subservient to white leaders.[15]

Just as the presence of southern delegations at the national Republican convention was devalued in the early decades of the twentieth century, so too was the presence of blacks in the southern delegations. The turning point in replacing the black-and-tans with the lily-whites had occurred during the administration of President Herbert Hoover. In 1940 Bunche remarked on the changing racial composition of the southern Republican delegations by observing that "the Negro is largely only on the fringes of Republican activity in the South." Key concluded in 1949 that blacks still controlled Republican politics only in Mississippi. As whites moved into the leadership positions of southern Republican parties, there was now little or no place for blacks in the Republican delegations which represented the South at the national convention.[16]

The Emergence of New Leadership

The affinity of southern Republicans for conservative presidential candidates has deep historical roots. In 1952, Alexander Heard contended that "the southern oligarchies have greatly bolstered the conservative wing of the Republican party." Southern Republicans helped to nominate William McKinley in 1896, William Howard Taft in 1908 and 1912, Warren G. Harding in 1920, Calvin Coolidge in 1924, Hoover in 1928, and Alfred Landon in 1936. They backed the losing efforts of Ohio Senator Robert A. Taft in the 1940s. Yet while they worked energetically for these conservative candidates at the party convention, only on rare occasions did southern Republican leaders try to mobilize grassroots voters on behalf of the nominees in the fall campaigns.[17]

"The most signal characteristic of the party's southern 'leadership,'" observed Heard, "has been a lack of interest in winning elections." The traditional southern party leadership did not evaluate prospective candidates in terms of the likelihood of carrying their state or of increasing the number of Republican candidates for state and local offices. The veteran southern Republican leaders, such as R. B. Creager of Texas, B. Carroll Reece of Tennessee, or Perry Howard of Mississippi, had been "big fish in little ponds," with neither incentive nor ability to expand the electoral base of their party. What the Republican party needed in the South was "a militant leadership intent on partisan victory, the necessary objective of a major American political party."[18]

Competitive presidential elections in the South also required a fundamental change in the attitude of national Republican leaders, who ordinarily gave little attention to the southern states. "Presidential campaign managers judge it wasteful to divert resources from hot campaigns in doubtful states to hopeless campaigns in southern states," Heard concluded. "Their candidate can win more easily with electoral votes gathered outside the South than within it—so why bother about building the party in the South?"[19]

Yet at midcentury this complacent attitude was anachronistic. The Republicans had not won a presidential election since 1928. The party leaders had made modest adjustments in the tickets they offered the voters. After the disastrous performance in 1936 of Governor Landon of Kansas, a typical midwestern conservative, the party began to put northeastern candidates at the top of their presidential tickets. In the 1940s it nominated Wendell Willkie and Thomas Dewey, both natives of the Midwest who had become successful lawyers in New York City. Each represented a moderate or progressive Republicanism which did not reject entirely the innovations of the New Deal. In addition, the party had begun to look to the West for vice-presidential candidates to balance the ticket, as indicated by the selections of Senator Charles McNary of Oregon in 1940 and Governor Earl Warren of California in 1948. The Republicans were searching for a new electoral college combination to counter the Democratic gains of the New Deal and Fair Deal. By continuing to concede the entire South, however, they still had to carry two-thirds of the electoral vote in the rest of the nation. At midcentury the Republicans needed to attempt a more radical strategy to recover the White House. They needed to break apart the Solid Democratic South.[20]

At the 1952 Republican convention, the divisions within the GOP over candidates and electoral strategy came to a head. Among the southern delegations, the regular or Old Guard delegates favored Senator Taft, while the Young Turks backed the candidacy of Dwight D. Eisenhower. Taft was a familiar figure to southern Republican leaders, for he was making his third bid for the party nomination. Each time he had sought southern convention delegates, just as his father had done in 1908 and 1912. "Getting the South behind him became a major effort" for Taft in the closing months of 1951, observed James T. Patterson. "He encouraged oil executives in the gulf states who were battling against federal ownership of offshore mineral rights, told audiences that he would campaign throughout the South if nominated, repeatedly denounced a strong Fair Employment Practices Commission, and opposed federal action against racial segregation in primary schools." The doubts about Taft among northerners concerned his limited appeal to independents and Democrats. This was not much of a drawback for the regular southern Republican leaders, however, and they again supported Taft.[21]

Eisenhower was a victorious general whom both parties had sought as a presidential candidate since the end of World War II. Born in Texas, raised in Kansas, with vast experience of the world as a military officer, Eisenhower combined cultural and economic conservatism with an international outlook. He was the candidate of the Dewey wing of the Republican party and represented so-called moderate Republicanism. Eisenhower was exactly the type of candidate that the younger, more aggressive Republican leadership in the South wanted at the top of the ticket, for they believed he could attract votes from independents and conservative Democrats in the South. Indeed, they thought he could actually win some southern states.[22]

Most of the southern delegations were controlled by the regulars. Eight of the southern states split their convention votes in favor of

Taft over Eisenhower, 84 to 38. But in Louisiana, Georgia, and Texas, where upstarts had successfully challenged the Old Guard, Eisenhower defeated Taft, 60 to 9. While Eisenhower won only 51 percent of the vote cast by southern delegates, Taft supporters were not permanently alienated by the outcome. In several delegations, reports stressed the ease by which the losing Taft supporters threw their votes to Eisenhower. The North Carolina "Taftites switched to Eisenhower without much delay," observed one analyst. In Florida, "the Taft delegates readily switched their votes to Eisenhower when the outcome was clear; there were no die-hards." Eisenhower left the convention with much unified and enthusiastic support among the southern Republicans.[23]

Eisenhower had won the nomination by polling a huge vote from the northeastern delegates, taking such important midwestern states as Michigan, Kansas, and Iowa, and winning such western states as Colorado and Oregon. Taft had been unable to hold a solid Midwest, had been denied a cohesive South, and generally had carried only smaller states in the West. The top leadership turned again to the West for the vice-presidential candidate and selected California Senator Richard M. Nixon as Eisenhower's running mate. It was a very powerful ticket. The Republicans were well positioned in the Northeast, Midwest, and West; and, for the first time since 1928, they had a candidate who could win votes in the South, especially in the growing metropolitan areas.[24]

In 1952 something new had happened at the Republican convention. The South had split, with a young, more aggressive, and more competitive leadership taking control of the party in several states. Something new also happened that fall in the South. National Republican strategists abandoned their belief that the South was a lost cause, and Eisenhower won in Florida, Tennessee, Texas, and Virginia.

As a result of Eisenhower's southern victories, the region was entitled to greater representation at the next Republican national convention. In 1956 the southern delegation accounted for 21 percent of the delegates, the largest share it had enjoyed since 1912. Southern Republicans had played an important but essentially peripheral part in Eisenhower's first nomination, and the nominations of Eisenhower in 1956 and of Nixon in 1960 were uncontested. By 1964, though, southern delegates began again to "bulwark the Right wing of the party," their customary role at the Republican national convention. They made their mark on national politics by backing Goldwater, a candidate who expressed the conservatism of the Far West. More than any other individual, Goldwater attracted into the leadership stratum of southern Republicanism a new generation of activists, young white conservatives who were decidely interested in carrying the South for conservative Republican presidential candidates.[25]

The Goldwater Convention

"At some undefined time between 1960 and 1964," observed Theodore H. White, "the Southern Republican party had come of age and sensed its power; it meant never to be ignored again in national politics." At the 1964 convention southern Republican leaders in search of a candidate who could fully express their conservatism came together with a small group of national conservatives in search of delegates for Goldwater, an unannounced and very reluctant candidate. Goldwater's nomination permanently altered the balance of regional power within the Republican party in favor of the South and the West. It was the most divisive struggle for the Republican nomination since the fight between Roosevelt and Taft in 1912. In regional terms, it represented a shift of power from northeastern Republicans—progressives or moderates or liberals, as they chose to refer to themselves—to the Republicans of the South and West—conservatives, as they thought of themselves. The midwestern Republicans were a crucial swing group that eventually sided with the newly emergent forces. The outcome was a fundamental shift in political direction for the Republican party, a major victory for the conservative wing of the party.[26]

Since the nomination of Willkie in 1940, the eastern Republicans had been able to control the outcome of the national convention. Dewey, Eisenhower, and Nixon had all been the candidates of the eastern wing of the party. This wing had long since shrunk to a sizable minority within the party, but it was usually able to prevail by winning defections of support from portions of the Midwest and the West. Even when the northeastern leaders supported Nixon of California in 1960, the ticket was balanced with Henry Cabot Lodge, one of the Boston Brahmins of eastern Republicanism.[27]

Goldwater sharply challenged the easterners' control of the ticket. Four years earlier, Nixon's nomination had been briefly opposed by a group of conservatives favoring Goldwater. The Arizona senator cut off the challenge and moved to make Nixon's nomination unanimous with words that challenged his followers: "Let's grow up, conservatives! If we want to take this Party back, and I think we can some day, let's get to work."[28]

F. Clifton White, a veteran of New York Republican politics, answered Goldwater's challenge by organizing a Draft Goldwater movement. Taking the party to the right, White realized, entailed a new electoral college strategy. While White insisted that he and his fellow strategists never "wrote off" any region or group of potential voters, he acknowledged that "we had to face political realities. I recognized that any conservative candidate—even a dedicated integrationist—would have great difficulty making inroads in the North, although up to this time Senator Goldwater had been amazing us all by the growing popular support in the Northeast." Because a conservative candidate could not count on carrying the Northeast, "the only hope the Republican party had of counterbalancing this tremendous handicap was to win the Southern states."[29]

In order for Goldwater to be nominated, however, White and his fellow conservatives had to develop a strategy to shift the center of political gravity at the Republican national convention. Goldwater's supporters could take advantage of trends in regional representation that had been under way since the early 1950s. Electoral college victories in a small number of southern states had increased the share of delegates from the old Confederacy from 16 percent in 1952 to 21 percent in 1964. If southern Republicans voted as a cohesive bloc, they could provide a conservative candidate with two-fifths of the votes necessary for nomination. "This growth in southern delegate strength," observed Nicol C. Rae, "was a critical factor in moving the center of power in the Republican party away from the liberals of the Northeast and toward the southwestern conservatives." In addition, the potential clout of the West was increasing at the convention. In 1964 western Republicans made up 19 percent of the delegates. All told, a cohesive South and West could offer a candidate four-fifths of the votes needed for victory. With additional delegates from conservatives in the Midwest and Border states, Goldwater would have the votes to win the nomination.[30]

Most of the delegates to the 1964 Republican convention were elected in state conventions, after precinct and district caucuses had chosen delegates. The Goldwater strategy, developed by White and others, was to take advantage of the senator's enormous national popularity among conservatives by concentrating on the selection of delegates to the national convention. By mobilizing conservatives to participate in precinct caucuses, district caucuses, and state conventions, the Goldwater forces hoped to elect their followers to the national convention. Dividing the effort into different regions, White put special emphasis on caucuses in the South, which were being directed by John Grenier, the state chairman of the Alabama Republican party.[31]

This power shift to southern and western conservatives had serious consequences for the party's policies. A meeting of the Republican National Committee in Denver in June of 1963 signaled trouble to the easterners. "There's an insanity in the air around here," confided one easterner, a New York Rockefeller supporter, based on "unmistakable signs that party leaders from outside the industrialized states of the eastern seaboard were seriously contemplating transforming the Republican Party into the White Man's Party." Robert D. Novak reported that "Republican politicians from the low-population states of the West and South in effect were declaring their independence. They were tired of the Easterners' long hegemony. They were determined to seize party control, nominate Barry Goldwater for President, and draft the most conservative party platform since the 1920's. Moreover, these Southern and Western conservatives were determined to break from forceful support of civil rights." To many of the aggressive, deeply conservative southern Republican leaders, Goldwater was a hero, and they "were able to organize their delegations for Goldwater, whose states' rights position on the race issue conformed with southern white sentiments."[32]

Goldwater swept to an easy first-ballot victory. None of the more moderate candidates—Nelson Rockefeller, Henry Cabot Lodge, or William Scranton—was able to build a respectable coalition. In the closing days, hopes of blocking Goldwater centered on Scranton, the governor of Pennsylvania, whose criticisms of Goldwater as an extremist, an irresponsible militarist, and a quasi-racist anticipated labels the Democrats would use in the fall campaign.[33]

The new strategy—building a Republican nomination mainly on the combined strength of the South and West, while isolating the Northeast—worked in 1964. Southern delegations, displaying greater consensus than any other region, ultimately cast 270 of 279 votes (97 percent) for Goldwater. Southerners alone provided 31 percent of Goldwater's total vote, the largest contribution of any region. Although Goldwater was most popular in the South, he also swept the West (84), the Midwest (76), and the Border states (74). Only in the despised East did he falter, winning merely 15 percent of that region's delegates.[34]

Goldwater was especially strong in the Deep South, where many whites were concerned about the federal government's efforts to challenge the customary practices of racial segregation. According to a study of delegates and alternates to the convention from the Deep South states, the Goldwater supporters were "white, high-status Protestants, most of whom had been born and reared in the South—many, in their home state. Approximately half were former Democrats who had been attracted to the GOP because of their displeasure with New Deal, Fair Deal, and New Frontier Democracy or because of their belief in the GOP as the more conservative of the two major political parties."[35]

The response of the Deep South Republican delegations to public policy questions underscored their widespread conservatism. Ninety-five percent of them disagreed with the proposition that "the government in Washington ought to see that everyone who wants to work can find a job," and 93 percent rejected the view that "the government in Washington ought to help people get doctors and hospital care at low cost." On policies involving race relations, 84 percent agreed with the position that "the government in Washington should stay out of the question of integrating the public schools," and 82 percent believed that "the question of voting rights of Negroes should be left to state and local governments" rather than to the federal government.[36]

The Deep South delegations were composed entirely of whites. For the first time in 50 years, for example, Georgia's Republican delegation contained no blacks. The delegation was all white, the state chairman explained, because the delegates were "people who believe in the philosophy expressed by Senator Goldwater, and there have not been many—or any—Negroes in the forefront of this effort."[37]

In the long run, Goldwater's nomination helped the Republican party become more competitive in the South. At the time, though, his campaign was a national disaster. The candidate knew it. As his speech to the Republican convention was being written, the campaign's latest poll was delivered. It showed Johnson beating Goldwater, 80 to 20. Goldwater told his aides, "'Instead of writing an acceptance speech, we should be putting together a rejection speech and tell them all to go to hell.' Everybody laughed, but it wasn't really funny." Neither the candidate nor his speechwriters were in a "conciliatory mood" toward their liberal Republican opponents. Goldwater later explained his acceptance speech this way:

> We went over every word carefully. The most important point we wanted to make was this: The conservative movement aimed to take

the country in a new direction. It seemed politically illogical and personally contradictory for us to offer olive branches to Rocky and the others. If I walked out on that convention dais and embraced Rockefeller, conservatives in the Cow Palace and across the country would have thought it was some political ad paid for by the Democratic National Committee. We'd just been through a bloody war on a host of issues. The libs had called me just about every dirty name in politics. The address had to make clear that this was a historic break. That's exactly what we were doing, breaking with history—taking over the party from the Republican National Committee on down and setting a new course in GOP national politics.[38]

Toward the close of his acceptance speech in San Francisco, Goldwater uttered the famous words that poured salt into the wounds of his opponents:

> Anyone who cares to join us in all sincerity, we welcome. Those who do not care for our cause, we don't expect to enter our ranks in any case. And let our Republicanism, so focused and so dedicated, not be made fuzzy by unthinking and stupid labels.
>
> I would remind you that extremism in the defense of liberty is no vice. And let me remind you that moderation in the pursuit of justice is no virtue.[39]

Goldwater's remarks, which threw down the gauntlet to the Republican opponents he had just beaten, deeply shocked the man who had done more than anyone else to win Goldwater's nomination. Clifton White later recalled that:

> In the trailer I sat stunned as I listened to these words. I had not seen the speech beforehand, nor had any of the men working with me. But none of us had ever expected such a seemingly carefully calculated rebuff to the moderates and liberals within our party and to the millions we had hoped to draw to our cause.
>
> Inside the Cow Palace the crowd cheered insanely, and I wondered if they knew they were hailing disaster and defeat. This was the time for magnanimity, the time for building bridges across the gulfs that separated Republicans from one another and from countless thousands who were not Republicans and probably never would be. But now the magic moment had passed. There would be no recapturing it. Never again would Barry Goldwater have this opportunity.[40]

And so the reluctant and wounded Republican nominee began his campaign against Lyndon Johnson. "We knew exactly where we were going," Goldwater later recollected, "to defeat at the polls and victory in the party."[41]

Nixon and the Southern Conservatives

The South's new importance in Republican presidential politics was confirmed by the outcome of the 1968 nomination battle. Many of the former Goldwater enthusiasts sought to maximize their influence within the Republican party by coalescing around the most electable conservative. Only two candidates, California Governor Ronald Reagan and former Vice-President Richard Nixon, were seriously considered by the southerners. Reagan was their preferred candidate, but his professed lack of interest in the nomination and doubts about his electability undermined his appeal in 1968. Nixon was able to satisfy the southern conservatives on several key issues and appeared to have a much better prospect of winning.

To a large extent, Nixon owed his narrow first-ballot victory at Miami to the size and cohesion of the southern delegations. Seventy-four percent of the southerners voted for Nixon, the highest share of any region, and the South accounted for 33 percent of Nixon's total vote, the greatest of any region. In the internal politics of the Republican party, the South was becoming one of the most significant blocs in determining who would become the GOP's presidential candidate.[42]

In 1966 Richard Nixon was the nation's most prominent and visible Republican politician, but he had no secure geographical base. Normally presidential candidates begin with their home states and adjacent areas, but Nixon could not mobilize any "friends and neighbors" support. He had abandoned his native state of California for New York City in 1962. The California delegation would come to the convention pledged to the candidacy of Reagan, while New York would be under the control of Governor Nelson Rockefeller. Nixon turned to the South to develop a base of delegate strength, for a united and cohesive South could provide almost half of the delegates (46 percent) needed to win the nomination.

As he sought the votes of southern Republicans, Nixon had several assets. He had a vast knowledge of the major players in Republican politics, had worked assiduously in 1966 on behalf of scores of Republican candidates for office, and believed that the Republicans could retake the White House in 1968. Taking immense satisfaction in the large Democratic losses in the 1966 elections, Nixon told an aide, "We've beaten hell out of them, and we're going to kill them in '68." Moreover, Nixon was a master in framing issues for public consumption. "One of Nixon's real skills had long been in stating an issue so as to maximize the number of groups to which it will be acceptable," John H. Kessel has emphasized. In addition, Stephen E. Ambrose is correct in stressing that "Nixon had an instinctive feel for the political responses and prejudices of a broad spectrum of the voting public, heavily but not exclusively the white middle class. Better than anyone else, he knew what those voters feared, and was an authentic spokesman for those fears."[43]

These political talents were in evidence in Nixon's handling of racial questions, always matters of concern to the southern Republicans. "Goldwater had been the southern favorite because he had voted against the Civil Rights Act of 1964," Ambrose pointed out. "Nixon was much too smart, and his well-known commitment to civil rights far too well established, for him to follow Goldwater's lead. He urged southern Republicans to drop the race issue from their campaigns, and whenever he spoke in the South he iterated his support of the Civil Rights Act of 1964 and the Voting Rights Act of 1965." Yet these positions did not undercut Nixon's appeal "partly because southern Republicans could hardly expect a national candidate to endorse segregation after what happened to Goldwater in 1964, partly because Nixon always softened his message by adding that he was for states' rights and opposed to any attempt by Washington to 'dictate' to the South, but mainly because southerners told themselves that Nixon didn't really mean what he said."[44]

Nixon was not a segregationist, and "he privately as well as publicly told GOP candidates that they could never win by trying to outsegregate the Democrats." Nixon became the champion of those whites who were willing to abandon strict segregation but were unwilling to identify with integration, especially integration directed by the federal government. White public opinion in the South had shifted away from a majority favoring strict segregation of the races in 1964 to a majority preferring "something-in-between" segregation and integration by 1968. Nixon's denunciation of segregation and his distaste for more federal intervention captured this "in-between" position, which was essentially conservative on most pending matters of racial controversy.[45]

The southern Republican leaders were cautious, but willing to pay attention to Nixon's overtures. Harry Dent of South Carolina, a key player, recalled that although "Nixon was never unpopular among us southern conservatives, he was never our first love. Nevertheless, he, unlike other eastern Republicans, endeared himself to Republicans across the nation with the constant support for this party's candidates. In 1964, he impressed all the Goldwater devotees and [South Carolina Senator Strom] Thurmond himself with his unrelenting support of the standard-bearer."[46]

Nixon began formal plans to gain the nomination with meetings in January 1967, which included two influential southerners, Fred LaRue of Mississippi and Peter O'Donnell of Texas, both veterans of the Goldwater campaign. Nixon's main liability was the widespread belief that he could not win, and to counter that he needed to demonstrate support in the primaries. Nixon's main rival in New Hampshire was Michigan Governor George Romney. The former vice-president was so strong, and Romney so inept, that the governor dropped out of the race. Nixon subsequently won 80 percent of the vote in the Wisconsin primary, and 70 percent in the Nebraska primary. The remaining hurdle was Oregon, where Reagan and Rockefeller were also entered. Nixon won 65 percent in Oregon, Reagan received 20 percent, and Rockefeller was left with 12 percent. Nixon had demonstrated he could still make a strong showing among Republican primary voters.[47]

With the primaries out of the way, the southern Republicans began to weigh their choices more seriously. Dent's plan for concerting southern influence at the convention, supported by some but not all of the other southern Republican leaders, was "to play hard to get. We vowed to keep the pact to 'hang loose, but hang together' until we could reach the most workable decision on which man to go with—Reagan or Nixon." In May 1968, Reagan met with the southern state chairmen and squandered his opportunity to gain their support. As Dent put it, "a noncandidate can be a noncandidate too long."[48]

Nixon was anything but a noncandidate. "On May 31," Nixon later wrote, "I flew to Atlanta for one of the most important conferences of the pre-convention period. The Southern Republican state chairmen were meeting, and I spent several hours over two days with these officials individually and in various groups. There was no pretense about the purpose of my visit: I was doing serious courting and hard counting." Meeting with several key southern Republicans, including Thurmond and Senator John Tower of Texas, "Nixon assured them he would slow the pace of integration, especially by resisting forced busing as a solution to racial segregation in the schools, and that he would not make the South into a whipping boy for national problems. He promised Thurmond he would use tariffs against textile imports to protect South Carolina's mills, and he promised a strong national defense policy." Nixon had solidified his southern base, especially by winning Thurmond's endorsement.[49]

At the convention Nixon faced two challengers: Rockefeller, who had reentered the race in late April, and Reagan, who announced his candidacy on August 5, two days before the roll-call vote on the nomination. Neither politician had enough strength to beat Nixon, but they hoped to deny him a first-ballot victory. Nixon recalled that "the marriage of convenience between Rockefeller and Reagan was now operating at full force. Rockefeller worked on the Northern and Midwestern states while Reagan tried to breach my Southern flank." Rockefeller's entry was no threat to Nixon's southern support; the New York governor was precisely the type of Republican that the southern conservatives would move heaven and earth to oppose. Reagan was a much more credible threat. As Nixon acknowledges, "it was Ronald Reagan who set the hearts of many Southern Republicans aflutter. He spoke their conservative language articulately and with great passion, and there was always a possibility that Southern delegates could be lured at the last minute by his ideological siren song."[50]

Reagan's belated entry into the race sent shock waves through the Nixon forces, who were completely dependent upon a first-ballot victory. "The chances of a breakaway in the South had suddenly, and nightmarishly, become a very real possibility," wrote the authors of *An American Melodrama*. "Reagan, now an open candidate, was going the rounds of the delegations, and his pitch was brilliantly seductive: they should let it go for a couple of ballots 'just to get an open convention, so that all views get a chance to be expressed.'" The southern delegations were the special targets of last-moment efforts to pry enough votes for Reagan away from Nixon, but Reagan had waited too long to announce his candidacy. F. Clifton White, late of the Goldwater campaign, was Reagan's main delegate hunter. He acknowledged that their "great trouble in 1968 was that the conservative delegates had been preempted for Nixon; preempted, moreover, by the conservative leadership. Besides Barry Goldwater, Strom Thurmond, and John Tower, I could look down lists of names of the delegates from virtually every state in the union and find our 1964 leaders, including members of my original cadre." He complained to Theodore White that, "I've got to drag people across the line, but they've made these half-baked commitments to Nixon, and they wriggle and wriggle and they can't get off."[51]

Thurmond was Nixon's main weapon among southerners against the persuasiveness of Reagan's eleventh-hour entry. The South Carolina senator, attending his first Republican convention, played the kingmaker by holding the wavering southern delegates. Thurmond sent telegrams to southern delegates. "Richard Nixon's position is sound on law and order, Vietnam, the Supreme Court, military superiority, fiscal sanity, and decentralization of power," Thurmond argued. "He is best for unity and victory in 1968." On the telephone his key appeal was that "a vote for Reagan is a vote for Rockefeller." In the end, as Tower put it, the southerners were "the thin gray line which never broke."[52]

Nixon won on the first ballot with only 25 votes to spare. In the South, Nixon carried all of the votes in Missisppi, South Carolina, and Tennessee. He dominated in Florida, Georgia, Louisiana, Texas, and Virginia, and won narrowly in Alabama. He lost in only two southern states, Arkansas to Rockefeller (through the influence of his brother, Governor Winthrop Rockefeller) and North Carolina to Reagan. Outside the South, Nixon captured 73 percent of the Border states, 68 percent in the Northeast, and 64 percent in the Midwest, but only 46 percent of the West.[53]

During the 1960s the southern conservatives became, in Theodore White's astute observation, the "most explosive and purposive bloc in any Republican convention." They were well positioned to exercise profound influence in the internal affairs of the Republican party, for a cohesive southern bloc could deliver nearly half of the delegates needed for a GOP presidential nomination. The southerners helped to move the GOP to the right on a variety of controversial issues, shunting aside most traces of the party's past ties to Lincoln, to Reconstruction, and to the Great Depression. They *southernized* the modern Republican party by helping to nominate Goldwater, an authentic hero to the conservatives, and by assisting in the choice of Nixon, who was willing to play ball with the southerners on matters of common interest.[54]

There was a lag, however, between the success of the southern bloc within the Republican party and the ability of their presidential nominees to sweep the South in the general election. Goldwater carried only the Deep South states in 1964, and Nixon won only Arkansas, Florida, North Carolina, Tennessee, and Virginia in 1968. Despite these initial setbacks, the southern conservatives eventually proved able to dominate both the Republican party *and* the region's presidential voters. In the 1970s and 1980s, to anticipate the rest of the story, the presidential candidates championed by conservative southern Republicans—Nixon, Reagan, and Bush—won landslide majorities from southern white voters. The result was, for the first time in history, the creation of a Solid Republican South in presidential elections.

III

The Dissolution
of the Solid
Democratic South

6

The White Revolt in the Deep South

Of all the ties that bound the South to the Democratic party in the first half of the twentieth century, by far the most compelling and sacrosanct was the shared understanding that the Democratic party was the party of white supremacy. This belief was the essence of the traditional southern political culture. In return for unswerving loyalty to the Democratic party in national elections, southern Democratic leaders expected ample freedom to control race relations within the region.

Signs of strain between southern and northern Democrats were increasingly evident in the 1940s, but solidarity prevailed as long as President Franklin Roosevelt lived. Once President Harry S Truman and key elements of the national Democratic party began seriously to raise the issue of civil rights, however, many of the South's political leaders grew indignant and alarmed. In the presidential elections of 1948, 1964, and 1968, opposition to various civil rights proposals or to actual civil rights victories led to full-fledged protest candidacies aimed primarily at punishing the national Democrats for intervening in southern race relations. These periodic revolts by racial conservatives were an important element of the process by which the Democratic party lost its dominant position in the South.

Strom Thurmond and the Dixiecrats: Truman Would "Destroy Southern Traditions for Harlem Votes"

The first white revolt, the 1948 States' Rights campaign of South Carolina Governor Strom Thurmond, was a reaction to the *possibility* of national civil rights legislation. Truman's public commitment to civil rights legislation was a dramatic break with policies of previous

Democratic presidents. "As always, the South can be considered safely Democratic," Truman had been advised. "And in formulating national policy it can be safely ignored."[1] Following the new strategy of pursuing urban votes, in early 1948 Truman sent specific civil rights bills to the Congress. The controversy continued at the national convention when the Democratic party, for the first time in history, resolved in favor of civil rights rather than states' rights. These developments astonished and outraged racially conservative white southerners and led directly to the creation of the States' Rights Democratic party to protest what they interpreted as the national Democrats' betrayal of the South.

Three days after the Democrats adjourned, some 6,000 white southerners—mostly from Mississippi and Alabama—convened in Birmingham, Alabama, to create an alternative instrument for influencing national politics.[2] Led by two governors from Deep South states, Thurmond and Mississippi's Fielding Wright, the Birmingham gathering had grown out of earlier meetings involving southern governors and other interested participants.

The Dixiecrats, as the States' Rights Democrats were soon known, nominated Thurmond for president and Wright for vice-president, the leaders of the two states with the highest proportions of blacks in their populations. Thurmond and the Dixiecrats did not actually seek to win the presidency. Instead of trying to build a national coalition, they sought to punish Truman and thus signal to other Democratic presidential hopefuls that the presidency could not be won without the Solid Democratic South. Thurmond and Wright were behaving as other southerners had done in the past; they were trying to use the negative power of a "cohesive and determined" minority to block a prize sought by the northern majority.[3]

To deny the presidency to Truman, Thurmond and Wright pursued a straightforward strategy. By sweeping every southern state, they could withhold the South's 127 electoral votes from the Democrats, prevent a Truman victory, throw the presidential election into the House of Representatives, and thus demonstrate the South's utter indispensability to Democratic control of the White House. Although Thurmond generally defined the issue as a question of national interference with the rights of states, control of race relations was undoubtedly the movement's energizing issue. Few black southerners voted in 1948, and racial segregation was both the custom and the law. The Dixiecrats' principal objective was to defend a racial status quo in which black southerners understood and accepted their second-class status.

Thurmond campaigned actively from Texas to Maryland, generally avoiding blatantly racist appeals but nonetheless making plain in speech after speech that racial considerations were at the heart of the Dixiecrats' complaints about the national Democratic party and Truman. "I warn you here and now," Thurmond said in a Labor Day address, "the Civil Rights program is the wedge which can force open the doorway to tyranny." FEPC legislation, Thurmond had been informed, was "'patterned' after a Russian law written by 'Joseph Stalin about 1920.'"[4]

A major address in Augusta, Georgia, gives the flavor of Thurmond's views. "As long as the so-called civil rights program is a part of the Democratic national platform," he predicted, "the people of the South are not going to support the National Democratic nominees for president and vice-president. No one knows that better now than Harry S Truman." As a result of the States' Rights campaign, "Never again will the politicians—Democrat or Republican—ignore the South because 'we are in the bag.'" Truman, Republican nominee Thomas Dewey, and Progressive party candidate Henry Wallace had all "sold their birthrights for minority votes." Moreover, "the three politicians we oppose seem to have forgotten that the South's problem is not a pure question of logic and law," he asserted. "It involves a sense of bitter history and of bitter pride." Attacking anti–poll tax, antilynching, and FEPC legislation as unwarranted and undesirable, Thurmond claimed that "another right these plunderers seek to take from you is the right to pass your own social legislation" by "telling you that you can not pass laws enforcing separation of the races."[5]

Truman's civil rights program was simply "a cheap political trick designed to buy the votes of small but powerful racial minorities in big-city states." Thurmond believed that "the radicals, the subversives, and the Reds" had gained "complete control" of the machinery of the national Democratic party and that the presidency itself was "being perverted to the selfish minority bloc." In need of immediate reform was the national Democratic party. "We are determined the evil forces that seized control of the national party shall be cast out," Thurmond said. "The impurities of that party—Harry Truman and all his followers—will be deposited like sediment on the banks, and the crystal clear waters of pure Americanism will restore our party to its once high place in American history."[6]

None of the Dixiecrats' objectives, according to Thurmond, involved the slightest racial discrimination. "I am not opposed to the Negro. . . . I am not prejudiced," he stated. "But I think in the best interests of law and order, for the integrity of the races, whites and Negroes should be kept separate in schools, theaters, and swimming pools." States' rights did not mean that the South wished to dictate racial practices to the rest of the nation. "We of the South think it is better not to admit persons of other races into churches, restaurants, . . . and other public places," he admitted. "If Massachusetts and other northern states want to encourage such intermingling, let them do it. But we will have none of it here." Any racial tension detected in the South could be blamed entirely on advocates of racial change. "Catering in high places to the favor of professional agitators and mercenary missionaries of ill-will," he argued, "has set the stage for new racial antagonisms which had been almost entirely stamped out over the years by the increasingly enlightened public opinion of our people."[7]

Even before the votes were counted Thurmond proclaimed many accomplishments for the Dixiecrats. As he explained to the nation in an election-eve broadcast, because of his campaign it would henceforth be "unprofitable for any candidate for president to barter away liberty of the American people to win blocs of racial votes." Indeed, the States' Rights showing would restore to the South a measure of prominence "in the political affairs of the nation which it has not fully enjoyed since the War Between the States." Passage of Truman's "so-called civil rights program" was now "improbable."

Thurmond reviewed for the nation the "shameful proceedings of the Democratic national convention" in which southerners were "insulted" by the adoption of a "vicious civil rights plank." As Thurmond elaborated:

> To add insult to injury, President Truman strutted out on the convention hall rostrum and with a great dramatic gesture called an extra session of Congress to enact, among other things, his so-called civil rights program . . .
> My friends, after this kind of treatment, the people of the South had to fight. If we had not, we would have forfeited any claim to the nation's respect.
> When both the Republican and Democratic parties espoused this un-American and Communistic program, the people of the South had no way to express their opposition at the ballot box.
> That is why the States' Rights Democratic ticket entered the field. We

were determined that the people of the South would not be disfranchised in this presidential election.

If we are to back up the effort of Southern members of Congress to block civil rights laws, we must vote the States' Rights ticket. A vote for States' Rights is a vote against the FEPC and against the breaking down of separation of the races in the South.

A vote for Truman, for Dewey, or for Wallace is a vote that says "We want the FEPC and mingling of the races."

. . . [Southerners] will not support a president who will go into the Harlem Negro district as did Truman Friday and promise to destroy Southern traditions for Harlem votes after refusing upon challenge to discuss this issue in the South.[8]

Thurmond's call for a monolithic southern revolt split the region's Democratic leadership. V. O. Key, Jr., showed that in one group of southern states—Tennessee, Virginia, and North Carolina—where the Republicans actually challenged the Democrats in state elections and some congressional contests, Democratic party leaders were opposed to any movement that might split their accustomed vote and possibly hand some victories to the Republicans. These politicians were racial conservatives and generally strongly opposed to President Truman's civil rights policies, but even before the Democratic convention, they had made clear they did not intend to bolt the party. Former Governor Cameron Morrison of North Carolina best expressed their view of how to handle any prospective civil rights legislation. Morrison rejected entirely what he called "this revolting business." Should Truman win the Democratic nomination, "let's step under the Democratic flag and help elect him. Then, we'll let our Congressmen and Senators beat him down when he needs beating."[9] In another three states—Arkansas, Florida, and Texas—the black populations were relatively small, and fewer Democratic politicians wanted to subordinate all other considerations to the single issue of racial policy. The greatest potential for the Dixiecrats had always been in the Deep South (Alabama, Georgia, Louisiana, Mississippi, and South Carolina), among whites who lived in proximity to the heaviest concentrations of blacks. In each of the Deep South states except Georgia, where rival gubernatorial factions did not want to be accused of splitting the Democratic party, the Dixiecrat leaders were able to control the official Democratic parties and thus to run their presidential electors under the label of the Democratic party.

Despite the attempt of the States' Rights party to speak for the entire region, its effective appeal was actually limited to the whites of the Deep South. "The Dixiecrats were not only confined to the South," Alexander Heard concluded, "but largely to a sector within that region."[10] Thurmond won 39 rather than 127 of the South's electoral votes (31 percent), and all but one of those electoral votes came from the Deep South. Because the Democrats secured 69 percent of the southern electoral vote, Truman needed to capture at least 44 percent of the northern electoral vote to win. The president survived the Dixiecrats' challenge by securing 53 percent.

While the Dixiecratic vote came entirely from whites, only about a quarter of white southerners voted for Thurmond. The Thurmond-Wright ticket won overwhelming white majorities in Mississippi, Alabama, and South Carolina as well as a modest white majority in Louisiana (see Table 6.1). In these four states the Dixiecrats captured the state Democratic parties and listed Thurmond, not Truman, as the regular Democratic candidate. Georgia, where Truman appeared on the ballot as the Democratic nominee, deviated from the Deep South norm. By 61 to 20 percent, Truman trounced Thurmond, who ran only two points ahead of Dewey. Most white voters in the Peripheral South ignored the States' Rights ticket. Only slightly more than a tenth of them, compared with 56 percent of the Deep South whites, voted for Thurmond. In all Peripheral South states (Arkansas, Florida, North Carolina, Tennessee, Texas, and Virginia), the South Carolina governor finished third. Thurmond's message of resistance to proposed federal intervention was persuasive mainly to whites who lived in states with substantial black populations.

The profound impact of state boundaries—reflecting differences in racial composition and differences among white political leadership regarding the salience of racial issues—on the grassroots States' Rights vote is evident in Figure 6.1. In Mississippi, Alabama, South Carolina, and (to a lesser extent) Louisiana, States' Rights sentiment resulted in sweeping grassroots majorities. Outside the Deep South Dixiecrat majorities were rare. Thurmond attracted between a quarter and a half of the vote in a few areas (South Georgia, North Florida, West Tennessee), but in hundreds of Peripheral South counties the Dixiecrats secured less than a fourth of the total vote.

In interpreting the Dixiecrat vote, the leading contemporary analysts stressed racist motivations. Both Key in *Southern Politics* and Heard in *A Two-Party South?* demonstrated that white concerns about racial change were at the heart of the Dixiecrats' success. For southern voters, Heard explained, "the Dixiecrats had one principal, effective appeal, the appeal to fear and dislike of people of different color."

Table 6.1 White opposition to federal intervention in southern race relations was most pronounced in the Deep South states: estimated percentage of white vote won by Strom Thurmond, Barry Goldwater, and George Wallace, by state, subregion, and region

Political unit	Thurmond, 1948	Goldwater, 1964	Wallace, 1968
Mississippi	92	91	83
Alabama	84	77	78
South Carolina	76	70	41
Louisiana	52	65	60
Georgia	22	65	51
Arkansas	17	49	46
Tennessee	14	51	39
North Carolina	9	49	37
Florida	16	56	32
Virginia	11	52	28
Texas	10	44	22
Deep South	56	71	63
Peripheral South	12	49	31
South	23	55	40

Note: States are ranked from highest to lowest according to the median white vote cast for the three candidates.

Sources: Estimates calculated by the authors from Alexander Heard and Donald S. Strong, eds., *Southern Primaries and Elections, 1920–1949* (University, Ala.: University of Alabama Press, 1950); appropriate volumes of Richard M. Scammon, ed., *America Votes* (Washington, D.C.: Congressional Quarterly); appropriate volumes of *U.S. Statistical Abstract*; and SRC-CPS presidential-year election studies.

The two political scientists differed, though, over the the future of the protest movement. Key was certainly aware of the potential for a revival of racial conflict in the South, but he was impressed with the Dixiecrats' failure to unify the white South by emphasizing race. "The Dixiecrats beat the drums of racial reaction in 1948 without impressive results; the Dixiecratic movement may turn out to have

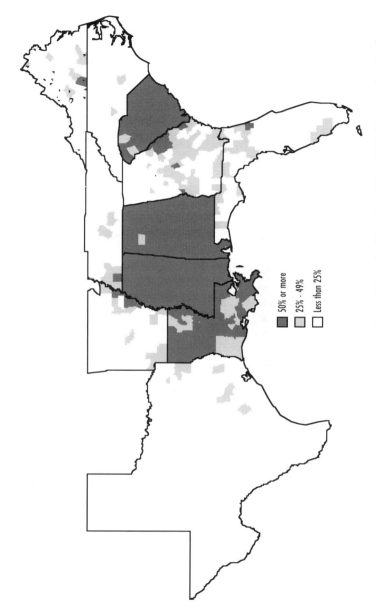

Figure 6.1 The Strom Thurmond vote in 1948. *Source:* Alexander Heard and Donald S. Strong, eds., *Southern Primaries and Elections, 1920–1949* (University, Ala.: University of Alabama Press, 1950).

been the dying gasp of the Old South," he conjectured. Far more realistic, we think, were Heard's conclusions. "Southern concern over the Negro is the most deeply rooted source of political contention in American history," he argued. "In some degree, we pray increasingly small, the concern will persist indefinitely. A movement appealing to those worried about the Negro will be assured of an audience and of at least a measure of support for a long time to come."[11] Heard's words were prophetic, anticipating the pattern of support for Goldwater in the Deep South in 1964 and the main contours of white support for Wallace in 1968.

The Goldwater Campaign: "Forced Integration Is Just as Wrong as Forced Segregation"

The 1964 presidential campaign was contested only months after the passage, signing, and implementation of the 1964 Civil Rights Act. The legislation had divided the nation, and the bill passed only after the longest congressional debate in American history.[12] Overwhelming majorities of northern Democrats and Republicans had voted for the legislation, while over 90 percent of the southern congressmen and senators had voted against the bill. Public opinion polls found a South polarized on civil rights issues between whites and blacks. According to the 1964 National Election Study, more than three-fourths of southern whites believed that the federal government should have stayed out of the question of segregation in public accommodations, compared with more than nine of every ten southern blacks who supported federal action.

President Johnson of Texas had championed the Civil Rights Act, defending it as a just and necessary step forward in providing equality for all Americans. "Whatever your views are, we have a Constitution and we have a Bill of Rights, and we have the law of the land, and two thirds of the Democrats in the Senate voted for it [the Civil Rights Act] and three fourths of the Republicans," the president told an audience of Democrats in New Orleans during the presidential campaign. "I signed it and I'm going to enforce it." By his courageous action, however, Johnson had infuriated many white southerners, who felt betrayed by the first "southern" president in a century. Louisiana Governor John McKeithen, for example, had "informed the president that the 'Negro thing' would cost him the state." Bo Callaway, a Georgia Republican who won a congressional seat in

1964, charged that "Lyndon Johnson had 'turned traitor' to the South."[13]

Arizona Senator Barry Goldwater, the Republican presidential nominee, had been one of the few northern senators who opposed the Civil Rights Act. Goldwater had voted for the Civil Rights Acts of 1957 and 1960, and he told the Senate in the 1964 debate that he was "unalterably opposed to discrimination or segregation on the basis of race, color, or creed." Nonetheless, convinced that the public accommodations and fair employment provisions of the bill were unconstitutional, and persuaded that its effective enforcement would require "the creation of a police state," Goldwater "reluctantly" voted against the Civil Rights Act of 1964. Goldwater was not a segregationist, but by aligning himself with southern congressmen on the Civil Rights Act, he became a highly visible hero to many segregationist white southerners.[14]

The South loomed large in the plans of Goldwater strategists to elect a conservative Republican to the presidency. Republican conservatives, Goldwater's advisors believed, could count on votes in the West and Midwest, but they needed the votes provided by a Solid South to win a majority in the electoral college. "We're not going to get the Negro vote as a bloc in 1964 and 1968," Goldwater said in Atlanta in 1961, "so we ought to go hunting where the ducks are."[15] For Goldwater and like-minded Republicans, the best hunting prospects were among the growing number of southern whites who appeared to be dissatisfied with the Kennedy administration. The Arizona Republican's book, *The Conscience of a Conservative*, as well as his frequent appearances and speeches on behalf of conservative causes, had made him the most visible and popular conservative in American politics. Goldwater held right-wing positions on an enormous number of controversial issues. He was philosophically opposed to most New Deal, Fair Deal, New Frontier, and Great Society legislation. He opposed the expansion of federal activities that began under the Kennedy administration and continued with Johnson's leadership. He differed fundamentally with the Johnson administration on many foreign policy issues, ranging from American relations with the Soviet Union to the conduct of the Vietnam War.

Conservative Republicans could presumably exploit many issues among white southerners, but none seemed so promising as white resentment against federally imposed racial change. There was undoubtedly more to Goldwater's 1964 southern campaign than his opposition to civil rights legislation. The presidential campaign in the Peripheral South, in which Goldwater won about half of the white vote and lost narrowly to Johnson, appears to have been about civil rights *and* other issues. In the next chapter, we shall examine Goldwater's strengths and weaknesses on a broad range of issues within the South. In this chapter, however, we are concerned with Goldwater as a candidate who was attractive to some southern whites primarily because of his visible opposition to federal civil rights legislation.

Just as the Dixiecrats' campaign could not unify the South in 1948, so Goldwater's campaign in 1964 also fell short of sweeping the region. Within the South the Arizona Republican carried Alabama, Georgia, Louisiana, Mississippi, and South Carolina, the five Deep South states that had long been storm centers of white resistance to racial change. Here the Goldwater campaign was primarily a protest against the expansion of federal efforts to enhance and protect the civil rights of blacks.

To Richard H. Rovere, an experienced journalist who watched Goldwater campaign primarily in the Deep South before virtually all-white audiences, the Goldwater movement was "a racist movement and very little else. Goldwater seemed fully aware of this and not visibly distressed by it." The "thousands in the packed stands, the tens of thousands in Memphis and New Orleans and Atlanta and Shreveport and Greenville" who turned out to cheer for Goldwater in a mood of "defiant joy" and to "hoot" at Lyndon Johnson with "thunderous, stadium-filling boos" whenever Goldwater mentioned the president's name, mainly did so, we think, in celebration of the politician who had stood with the majority of white southerners in opposition to the Civil Rights Act of 1964. The Deep South whites who lined the streets and filled the bleachers for Goldwater did not do so because he opposed Medicare or the Tennessee Valley Authority or price supports for agricultural products, or because he wanted to make Social Security voluntary, or because he wanted to get tough with the Russians and tougher with the North Vietnamese. Rovere got it right about Goldwater's passionate support among Deep South whites. "By coming south," he observed, "Barry Goldwater had made it possible for great numbers of unapologetic white supremacists to hold great carnivals of white supremacy. They were not troubled in the least over whether this would hurt the Republican party in the rest of the country; they wanted to make—for their own satisfaction, if for no one else's—a display of the fact that they had found, and were enjoying membership in, one organization that was secure against integration because it had made itself secure against Negro aspirations."[16]

Rovere's assessment of Goldwater's campaign rhetoric in the South is worth emphasizing:

> He did not, to be sure, make any direct racial appeals. He covered the South and never, in any public gatherings, mentioned "race" or "Negroes" or "whites" or "segregation" or "civil rights." But the fact that the words did not cross his lips does not mean that he ignored the realities they describe. He talked about them all the time in an underground, or Aesopian, language—a kind of code that few in his audiences had any trouble deciphering. In the code, "bullies and marauders" means "Negroes." "States' rights" mean "opposition to civil rights." "Women" means "white women." This much of the code is as easily understood by his Northern audiences as by his Southern ones, but there are words that have a more limited and specific meaning for the Southern crowds. Thus, in the Old Confederacy, "Lyndon Baines Johnson" and "my opponent" mean "integrationist." "Hubert Horatio" . . . means "super-integrationist." "Federal judiciary" means "integrationist judges."[17]

On some occasions Goldwater referred specifically to racial questions. The Republican presidential candidate could not bring himself to support the objective of a desegregated society. "Our aim, as I understand it, is neither to establish a segregated society nor to establish an integrated society as such," he declared. "It is to preserve a free society." "Forced integration," Goldwater contended, "is just as wrong as forced segregation." He was emphatically opposed to mandatory busing of school children. "If you ever hear me quoted as promising to make you free by forcibly busing your children from your chosen neighborhood school to some other one just to meet an arbitrary racial quota—look again because somebody is kidding you!" he announced. In one speech, Goldwater asserted "with a sincerely heavy heart, that the more the Federal government has attempted to legislate morality, the more it actually has incited hatreds and violence."[18]

In mid-September South Carolina Senator Strom Thurmond, the former Dixiecrat presidential candidate who had returned to the Democratic party after 1948, dramatically switched his party affiliation to the Republicans and enthusiastically endorsed Goldwater. Now describing himself as a "Goldwater Republican," Thurmond charged that "the Democratic party has abandoned the people. . . . It has repudiated the Constitution of the United States. It is leading the evolution of our nation to a socialistic dictatorship." The following day Thurmond and Goldwater campaigned together in the South. Thurmond vouched for Goldwater at a Greenville, South Carolina, rally, praising Goldwater as a man who "risked the ire of the liberal, left-wing, socialist establishment of this country—even in his own party—in order to stand by his convictions as to the meaning and intent of the founding fathers."[19]

As the election neared Goldwater embraced more tightly his strategy of appealing to the white South. He closed his campaign in Columbia, South Carolina, with a televised speech that was carried on 87 stations across the South. Sharing the platform with an all-star lineup of Deep South segregationists—"James F. Byrnes, Senator Strom Thurmond and Representative Albert W. Watson of South Carolina, former Democratic state chairman James Gray and onetime Representative Iris Blitch of Georgia, and Congressman John Bell Williams of Mississippi"—Goldwater used the occasion to attack the Civil Rights Act of 1964.[20] Surrounded literally by segregationist diehards, Goldwater was pitching his anti–civil rights message so low to the ground that even the least astute of his audience could get the point.

President Johnson did not completely write off the Deep South. Although Johnson vowed that "I am not going to let them build up the hate and try to buy my people by appealing to prejudice," he understood that his advocacy of racial change was angrily resented by many Deep South whites. Johnson's southern campaign consisted mainly of a long train tour headed by Lady Bird Johnson, the president's Alabama-born wife, along with occasional appearances by the president himself. "The Lady Bird Special" was a four-day train trip through nine states, with 47 stops.[21]

Mrs. Johnson was well received in some places, but all was not moonlight and magnolias for the First Lady. She acknowledged that some of her husband's policies were unpopular. "You might not like all I am saying," Mrs. Johnson told an Alabama audience, "but at least you understand the way I'm saying it." As one Johnson official recalled, "We didn't go into any of the easy towns. We went into the toughest, like Savannah. We went through the northern part of Florida; we went where the real 'against' people were." Mrs. Johnson later remembered that she "felt intensely the hostility which certainly did exist, particularly in South Carolina—more in South Carolina than anywhere else by a long shot. There would be banners with unpleasant things like, Go Home, or Fly Home, Lady Bird, something like that. And then if you got up and started to make a speech, some people would begin to make so much noise that you couldn't be heard. It was not frightening. It was not bad, really, but it was enough hostility so that you could feel it, palpably, in the air."[22]

In Charleston she got the silent treatment from upper-class whites. "Part of the day was planned as a sort of sight-seeing trip through the Battery area—lovely old houses along the waterfront where there were magnificent live oaks and stately white houses," Mrs. Johnson said. "As I went down the street in this open carriage with a liveried black driver, I kept noticing that all the houses were shuttered. All the shutters were closed tight. It looked like everybody had left town. Then I began to see signs in windows that said, This House Sold on Goldwater."[23]

President Johnson also made some campaign appearances in the Deep South. "One hundred years is long enough to burden down our future with the divisions of the past," he told an audience in Macon, Georgia. "The time has come—the time is now—to bind up our wounds, to heal our history, and to make our beloved America whole again." At times the going got rough in the Deep South for the president, too. He was booed in Augusta, Georgia, but in due course Johnson silenced the hecklers and won cheers from the crowd:

> I was in an election campaign four years ago . . . and I returned to my home state in the last days of that campaign. We went to the hotel to wash up before we went to a luncheon meeting, but the entrance was blocked and the hecklers were there, and they harassed us and they hounded us and they knocked my wife's hat off, and they spit on us and they called us traitors and they called us treason artists, and they had ugly signs and they dealt not in a single issue that we were debating. They had only to talk about personalities and little petty things because they were little petty people. . . . It took us more than an hour to walk across the block because of the chants and the saliva that was running out of their mouths and, really, some of them were diseased.

There was no more booing from the young Goldwaterites after he finished his story.[24]

Johnson's most memorable visit to the Deep South occurred at New Orleans on October 9, where he greeted the final stop of "The Lady Bird Special." "In the words of Robert E. Lee," President Johnson told the crowd, "let's try to get our people to forget their old animosities and let us all be Americans." Later that night, as the president and his followers approached the Grand Ballroom of the

Jung Hotel to address a large crowd of Louisiana Democrats, he lost his bearings. "'Where're we goin'?' he bellowed. Before he got an answer, he roared, 'I want to know where're we goin'.' Not satisfied with the mumbled answers of those around him, he, in his best Johnsonian earthiness, shouted, 'I don't care if we go to a whorehouse, I just wanta know where we are goin'.'"[25]

Minutes later, Johnson delivered a talk that, "according to many," was "his finest speech of the campaign." It was an aggressive defense and ringing celebration of the Civil Rights Act of 1964, a speech that virtually everyone had advised him not to give in Louisiana. "After completing his prepared remarks, Johnson, encouraged by the friendly and enthusiastic audience, tossed his papers aside and began to speak without notes and from the heart. . . . LBJ talked about the South, its problems, its potential, its future." He praised the Civil Rights Act of 1964 and told "a favorite story of his about a former U.S. senator from Texas who was raised in another Southern state. This man confided to Sam Rayburn that he was tired of racial politics, and that, before he died, he wanted to go back to his old state and speak. 'Poor old state, they haven't heard a Democratic speech in 30 years. All they ever hear at election time is Negro, Negro, Negro.' Was there a Southerner in that room who had never heard such a speech? Would they ever hear it again? Not if LBJ had his way. He pressed on. Race should not be an issue, only 'equal opportunity for all, special privileges for none.'"[26]

A month later, the South spoke in the voting booth in two different voices. We estimate that 55 percent of southern whites repudiated Johnson and voted for Goldwater, while the president received virtually all of the vote cast by southern blacks. Goldwater's strength in 1964, like Thurmond's in 1948, was concentrated among whites in the southern states with the largest black populations. The election returns gave Goldwater victories in all of the Deep South states, while President Johnson narrowly carried all of the Peripheral South states. Goldwater won an estimated 71 percent of the vote cast by Deep South whites, doubling Nixon's estimated share of the vote (35 percent) in 1960. White Mississippians, one of the main targets of the civil rights movement in the early 1960s, went for Goldwater by the same nine-to-one margin that they had given to Thurmond. Elsewhere in the Deep South, Goldwater won an estimated 77 percent of the white vote in Alabama, 70 percent from South Carolina whites, and 65 percent from whites in Georgia and Louisiana. Because the vast majority of blacks were still unable to vote in the Deep South in 1964, the huge white vote for Goldwater translated into a complete GOP electoral sweep of the subregion.

Goldwater's candidacy obviously involved more than a simple protest against national intervention into southern race relations. He tapped into customary Republican sentiment in such areas as East Tennessee, South Florida, and North Carolina's Piedmont. Nonetheless, comparison of the Thurmond and Goldwater grassroots vote (see Figures 6.1 and 6.2) indicates clearly that the strongest support for both candidates emanated from the Deep South states of Mississippi, Alabama, Louisiana, and South Carolina. Goldwater improved on Thurmond's performance in South Georgia, North Florida, West Tennessee, and Southside Virginia. Before 1964 the Republicans had never achieved such widespread grassroots success in the Deep South.

Precinct returns in Deep South cities confirmed the strength of Goldwater among all strata of the white community. In several large cities of the Deep South—Birmingham, Charleston, Columbia, Jackson, Mobile, Montgomery, and Shreveport—Goldwater won at least two-thirds and at times more than nine-tenths of the vote in upper class, upper-middle class, middle class, lower-middle class, and lower class precincts. Eisenhower and Nixon had previously done well among middle-class and more-affluent whites in the Deep South cities. Goldwater retained enormous support among the so-called better sort of whites in these cities, but to this base he added tremendous support from lower-middle-class and blue-collar whites. These lower-status and less-affluent whites in the Deep South had been the traditional backbone of the Democratic party in presidential contests, but they were highly aroused in the 1960s by such practitioners of racial politics as Alabama's George Wallace and Georgia's Lester Maddox. Goldwater won them convincingly and, in so doing, broke the back of the Democratic party among Deep South whites.[27]

We suspect that the Arizona senator was drawing extraordinarily large majorities among the most racially conservative whites in the Deep South. The link cannot be established with the available survey data, for the 1964 NES did not draw representative samples of southern whites in the two subregions. However, the most realistic hypotheses are that the vast majority of Deep South whites were racial conservatives and that most of them voted for Goldwater. Given the opportunity to choose between a symbol of federal intervention and a symbol of states' rights, a heavy majority of Deep South whites

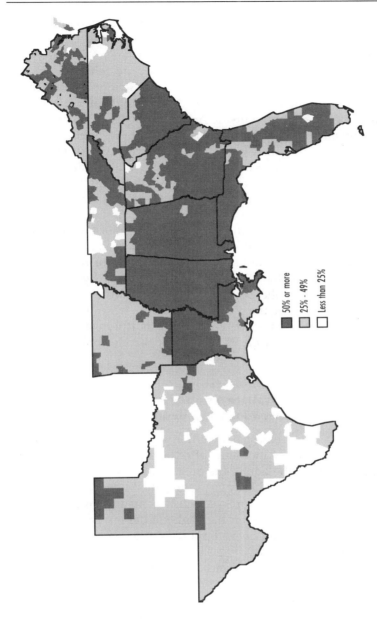

Figure 6.2 The Barry Goldwater vote in 1964. *Source:* Richard M. Scammon, ed., *America Votes,* 6 (Washington, D.C.: Congressional Quarterly, 1966).

50% or more

25% - 49%

Less than 25%

chose the GOP candidate. When Goldwater "directed his 'states rights' appeal at the South, white electorates in the Deep South responded much as their grandfathers would have," Bernard Cosman concluded. "They voted for what they perceived to be the 'candidate of the southern white man.'" And George Brown Tindall summed it up in much the same way: "Barry Goldwater left himself only one center of strength outside Arizona—the Dixiecrat belt where race still prevailed as the central theme of southern politics."[28]

In 1964 the Republicans experienced their worst defeat in a presidential election since the New Deal. As in the States' Rights party's campaign, the Republican's attempt to carry the entire South failed. "In winning the four Dixiecrat states plus Georgia, states which had never gone Republican since Reconstruction," Tindall pointed out, "Goldwater took the core of the old Solid South, but he lost the rest of the region."[29] In the South Goldwaterism succeeded primarily as a movement of racial protest; and as a movement of racial protest, his campaign essentially followed the trail blazed by Thurmond. Goldwater won 52 of the South's 128 electoral votes (37 percent). Because Johnson swept the Peripheral South, his minimum target for national victory was 46 percent of the northern electoral vote. The Democrats actually won 99 percent of the electoral vote in the rest of the nation.

The 1968 Wallace Crusade: "Calling Us Peckerwoods and Rednecks"

"In the name of the greatest people that have ever trod this earth," shouted George Wallace moments after being sworn in as governor of Alabama, "I draw the line in the dust and toss the gauntlet before the feet of tyranny . . . and I say . . . segregation now . . . segregation tomorrow . . . segregation forever." Elected mainly on the strength of his promise to prevent even the slightest desegregation of public education, Wallace seized every opportunity to personify white resistance to black civil rights.

Wallace did not pussyfoot on race. His 1963 inaugural address was saturated with defiance of federal attempts to alter southern racial traditions. Unlike other segregationist governors, who were primarily concerned with holding the line within their own states, the Alabama governor aspired to national leadership. As Wallace informed his audience, he planned to "take the offensive and carry our fight for freedom across this nation, wielding the balance of power we know we possess in the Southland . . . [so] that we, not the insipid bloc voters of some sections . . . will determine" the next president.

Wallace's credentials as a committed segregationist were undeniable. "What I have [previously] said about segregation goes double this day," Wallace asserted. The American Dream, as he saw it, involved development within "separate racial stations. This is the great freedom of our American founding fathers . . . but if we amalgamate into the one unit as advocated by the communist philosophers . . . then the enrichment of our lives . . . the freedom of our development . . . is gone forever. We become, therefore, a mongrel unit of one under a single all powerful government." No listener could doubt that Wallace intended to "Stand Up for Alabama."[30]

Because Alabama was a prime target of the civil rights movement, Wallace had many opportunities as governor to resist racial change. In the spring of 1963, when Birmingham police led by Eugene "Bull" Connor used high-pressure water hoses and police dogs to break up demonstrations protesting segregated public accommodations, Wallace praised Birmingham's "very fine police commissioner" and advised the Alabama legislature that he was prepared to "assist our local governments as they deal with agitators and meddlers trying to destroy our way of life . . . I am beginning to tire of agitators, integrationists and others who seek to destroy law and order in Alabama." President John F. Kennedy's criticism of Birmingham's police brutality left Wallace angry and unimpressed. "The President's lack of candor in refusing to criticize mobs who throw bricks and rocks and bottles and injure authorities and whose clear intent is to incite violence," Wallace remarked, "indicates that the President wants us to surrender this state to Martin Luther King and his group of pro-Communists who have instigated these demonstrations." Wallace refused to participate in "any meeting to compromise on the issue of segregation," and he denounced several white Birmingham leaders who negotiated with civil rights protesters as a "small group of appeasers."[31]

Later that summer, after a federal court ordered the admission of the first black students at the University of Alabama, Wallace used the event to satisfy a campaign pledge to resist school desegregation personally. Claiming that he would fulfill his "covenant" with the people of Alabama "for standing in the schoolhouse door," Wallace appeared on television to inform the state that he would "stand at the University as I promised you I would." Concerned that thousands of furious and well-armed white Alabamians might stampede to Tuscaloosa to help him resist the federal judiciary, Wallace appealed to the general public for calm. "I will be you standing in the door of the University," he explained. "I hope you will stay home and about your work that day." Wallace's nationally televised gesture of defiance—he refused four times to stand aside and let the black students register and solemnly read a proclamation "denounc[ing] and forbid[ding] this illegal and unwarranted action by the central government"—instantly gave him a national presence as a fighting champion of racial segregation.[32]

In January 1964, Wallace began a national campaign against the civil rights legislation pending in Congress. "Under a smokescreen of emotionalism and misrepresentation," Wallace later wrote in *Stand Up for America*, "Congress was preparing a civil rights bill which, if passed, would affect the life of every American." He "knew that someone had to alert Americans to what this pernicious piece of legislation proposed to do to them." Desiring to "give the voters some alternative to the mad rush to federal control over our lives," Wallace entered Democratic presidential primaries in Wisconsin, Indiana, and Maryland. His opponents were Democratic politicians who were standing in, so to speak, for President Johnson. The Alabama governor described his supporters as "concerned parents who wanted to preserve the neighborhood schools, homeowners wanting to protect their investment, union members who wanted to protect their jobs and seniority, small businessmen who wanted to preserve the free-enterprise system, attorneys who believed in the Constitution, police officers who battled organized demonstrators in the streets, and all the little people who feared big government in the hands of phoney intellectuals and social engineers with unworkable theories."[33]

Running against Democratic Governor John W. Reynolds in Wisconsin, Wallace took 34 percent of the vote and returned to a hero's welcome in Alabama. Campaigning next in Indiana, Wallace complained that the civil rights bill "will not help labor, because it does not create one, single job. All it does is take your job and give it to somebody else." He won slightly less than 30 percent of the vote against Democratic Governor Matthew E. Welsh. "We shook the eyeteeth of the liberals in Wisconsin, but we shook their wisdom teeth in Indiana," he told his supporters on election night.[34]

The zenith of his primary campaigning came in Maryland against another Johnson stand-in, Senator Daniel B. Brewster. Wallace was credited with 43 percent of the vote, a figure he later disputed as fraudulent. For the first time, Wallace had won a majority of the white vote in a northern Democratic primary. "They called me a bigot, a liar, a racist, an agitator, a trespasser," he said. "They pictured my supporters with Ku Klux hoods. They called in ten Senators to beat us down, and yet a majority of the white people in Maryland gave me their support. I'm elated. That's more than I ever expected." Wallace had done his best to conform to national standards of behavior in the Maryland campaign. *Newsweek* reported that "he mentioned Negroes rarely and 'niggers' not at all in public until after the polls had closed on election night." But when the returns showed heavy black voting against Wallace, he reverted to his customary idiom. "If it hadn't been for the nigger bloc vote," Wallace told newsmen, "we'd have won it all."[35]

One month later, however, Wallace officially withdrew from the presidential contest. Wallace apparently came under great pressure from Goldwater backers to end his campaign. He had no chance to win the Democratic nomination, and a third-party candidacy would have hurt Goldwater in the Deep South. His Alabama backers were not interested in financing additional activity by Wallace when it seemed certain that Goldwater would be the Republican nominee.[36]

By 1968, however, Wallace was America's foremost opponent of racial change, and he mounted the strongest third-party campaign for the presidency since Theodore Roosevelt in 1912. "Race mixing doesn't work" summarized his basic position on the nation's most momentous social problem.[37] Connoisseurs generally agreed that Wallace exhibited the boldest sneer, the finest snarl, and the most unforced "heh, heh, heh" in American politics.

Above all else, the Wallace movement was a reaction to the racial changes associated with the Great Society. During Johnson's presidency a revolution in civil rights legislation had occurred. Following implementation of the Civil Rights Act, Johnson had encouraged Congress in 1965 to pass the Voting Rights Act (which vastly increased black political participation in the Deep South) and the Elementary and Secondary Education Act (which required school districts to meet increasingly stringent desegregation guidelines established by the Department of Health, Education, and Welfare in order to qualify for federal education dollars). Open housing legislation was enacted in 1967. Riots in many northern central cities and some southern cities further contributed to an atmosphere receptive to Wallace's message of opposition to Washington.

In one form or another, racism permeated Wallace's national campaign. "Let 'em call me a racist," Wallace once told a reporter in a whispered confidence. "It don't make any difference. Whole heap of folks in this country feel the same way I do. Race is what's going to win this thing for me." Wallace became the primary "political entrepreneur" of racial issues, seeking to win nationally by capitalizing on his experience in Alabama.[38]

For public consumption, though, Wallace often put it differently. "The first thing I want to say," Wallace told James Jackson Kilpatrick in a 1967 interview, "is that I'm no racist. Oh, I believe in segregation all right, but I believe in segregation here in Alabama. What New York wants to do, that's New York's business. Same for Ohio. Same for Louisiana. Let them folks decide for themselves." The issues of the 1968 campaign, he thought, would be, "Schools, that'll be one thing. By the fall of 1968, the people in Cleveland and Chicago and Gary and St. Louis will be so God-damned sick and tired of federal interference in their local schools, they'll be ready to vote for Wallace by the thousands. The people don't like this triflin' with their children, tellin' 'em which teachers have to teach in which schools, and bussing little boys and girls half across a city just to achieve 'the proper racial mix.'"

Another set of issues, Wallace predicted, would involve "law and order. Crime in the streets. The people are going to be fed up with the sissy attitudes of Lyndon Johnson and all the intellectual morons and theoreticians he has around him. They're fed up with a Supreme Court that—with a few exceptions—is a sorry, lousy, no-account outfit. . . . I certainly believe in seeing that a defendant gets all the rights he has coming to him. But God dammit, the people have rights too. I'd take one of our fine members of the Supreme Court of Alabama and make him Chief Justice of the United States, and by God you'd see some changes made."[39]

Wallace vigorously attacked both national parties and their presidential nominees (Vice-President Hubert Humphrey for the Democrats, former Vice-President Richard Nixon for the Republicans). "You get a bayonet in yo back with the national Democrats," he claimed, "and you get a bayonet in yo back with the national Republicans." There was no need for Alabamians to defer to the wisdom of national leaders. "These here national politicians like Humphrey and Johnson and Nixon," Wallace explained to one Alabama crowd, "they don't hang their britches on the wall and then do a flyin' jump into 'em every mornin', they put 'em on one britches leg at a time, just like the folks here in Chilton County." Wallace ripped into the former Republican vice-president:

> This Richard Milhouse "Tricky Dick" Nixon, he hadn't got the sense of a Chilton County mule. He comes down here to talk about Alabama politics like it was some kind of his business. Sure, I went over to Mississippi to make a speech a while back, but it was just a philosophy speech over there at the state fair. But I'll tell you, if I had said as much and done as much against the state of Mississippi as "Tricky Dick" Nixon has said and done against the state of Alabama, I wouldn't have the brass to go within a *hunnert* miles of Mississippi, I'd just go around it or over it or something.[40]

As a practical matter, Wallace's strategic goal was the same as Thurmond's—to deny the presidency to the Democrats. The American Independent party became the formal vehicle for Wallace's agenda. As a southern protest candidate in 1948, Thurmond had campaigned primarily in the South, making sporadic ventures into the surrounding Border states. Wallace's "Stand Up for America" campaign took the views of racially conservative white southerners well beyond southern boundaries. Because of his national ambitions, Wallace found it expedient to deemphasize southern and racial themes per se, replacing them with unvarnished attacks on the national news media, federal bureaucrats, and Vietnam war protestors. "And we are going to show them [the national news media] in November," he predicted, "that the average American is sick and tired of all these over-educated ivory-tower folks with pointed heads looking down their noses at us, and the left-wing liberal press writing editorials and guidelines. So we are going to shake them up good in November."[41]

Wallace was firmly anchored in the "hell-of-a-fellow" tradition as practiced by some southern politicians, whose larger-than-life performances on the stump left audiences with unforgettable memories.[42] Speaking in the colloquial style of working-class and rural southern whites, lashing their opponents with sarcasm and ridicule, giving full vent to the frustrations and irritations of their followers, a long line of southern politicians, such as Eugene Talmadge, Huey Long, Theodore G. Bilbo, and Cole Blease, had prevailed by leaving their audiences in a defiant and fighting mood. They bragged about how mean they were, how they punished their opponents. As Talmadge often boasted to his cronies, "I'm just as mean as cat shit."[43] They split voters into unquestioning loyalists and implacable enemies. When Talmadge lay dying in an Atlanta hospital, he was visited by his son Herman:

> "Son," he said, "there was a fellow in here the other day. He told me, 'Gene, you know every man, woman, and child in the state of Georgia is praying for you. Even folks who never prayed before in their lives.'" I said, "I know, Papa." And he just cracked a smile and said, "Half of them are praying I'll recover and half of them that I won't."[44]

More than any other southern politician of his day, Wallace carried on the Talmadge legacies of racism and meanness. Marshall Frady quotes Wallace speaking privately as follows: "Nigguh comes up to a white woman down here like they do up North, tryin' all that stuff, he's gonna get shot. Yessuh. Or get his head busted. That's why we don't have any of that business down here. They know what's gonna happen to 'em." Wallace then got down to the heart of the problem: "Hell, we got too much dignity in government now, what we need is some *meanness.*"[45]

Wallace thrived on controversy and confrontation. His rallies frequently included stormy interludes in which Wallace carefully baited his hecklers ("Sieg Heil!" was their preferred chant) as a means of firing the emotions of his own followers. Fist-fighting, cursing, and taunting were all part of the ambience of a Wallace performance. James Wooten, a southerner who covered Wallace's campaign for the *New York Times*, wrote that "always, there were the hordes of hecklers waiting for him at every stop, sometimes with eggs, sometimes with rocks, sometimes with bags of shit, and he would sneer at them and snarl at them and play them like Heifetz on a Stradivarius, pitting his folks against them, fomenting more tension upon tension until it inevitably and invariably exploded—and he would step back and say with a thin smile, 'Now, now, folks, let's just let the po-lice handle it. They know what they doin'. Just let them handle it, folks.'"[46]

When Wallace spoke at New York's Madison Square Garden, for example, three thousand policemen were required to keep order and protect the candidate. There Wallace toyed with carefully selected representatives of the opposition. "'Hey there, sweetie,' he said, looking toward a long-haired protester to his left in the audience. 'Oh, excuse me,' he added after an appropriate pause. 'I thought you were a girl.'" In Enid, Oklahoma, Wallace informed an appreciative audience of his post-election plans for protesting undergraduates. "'We're going to grab some of these college students by the hair of your head and stick you under the jail,' he said. 'A lot of you evade the draft laws and go to school on taxpayers' money. We're going to put a stop to that too, so some of you'll have to go, along with the working man's son.'"[47]

Wallace often appealed to regional pride when he campaigned in the South. "Both national parties . . . have been calling us pecker-woods and rednecks for a long time," he told a crowd in Albany, Georgia. "And we gonna show them we resent being used for a doormat." "You've asserted your manhood in Texas" when you vote for Wallace, he told Texas admirers. "You've asserted your manhood in our region." Lyndon Johnson might emphasize that "he's a Westerner, and it's all right to be a Westerner," Wallace remarked. "But I tell you, I've never minded saying that I was a Southerner, and I've never apologized for it any place in the country."[48]

As for Nixon and Humphrey, Wallace reminded his Texas audience that they were not southerners at all:

> Referring to Mr. Nixon, he said, "Yes, he looks down his nose at Southerners and Texans, too."
> "I can tell you, they both do," he went on. "They represent the Eastern moneyed interests that have done everything they could to keep the people of our region of the country ground into the dirt for 100 years.
> "And if you can show me one thing the national Republican party has ever done for the average citizen of Texas or Alabama, I'll get out of the race for the Presidency, because you can't show me one thing they've ever done.
> "I ask you from the soul of the South to assert yourselves," he pleaded. "This is the first time in the history of our country that we are solidified in our region all the way from Baltimore to Oklahoma City to St. Louis."[49]

When public opinion polls showed a decline in Wallace's support in the final weeks of the campaign, Wallace accused the "Eastern money power" (including the Rockefeller Foundation) of rigging the polls to support Nixon. "They lie when they poll," he asserted. "They are trying to rig an election. Eastern money runs everything. They are going to be pointed out the liars that they are."[50]

As it turned out, Wallace won 13 percent of the national popular vote. It was more than any third-party candidate had won since 1912, but still too little to throw the election into the House of Representatives. "In most southern states," Seymour Martin Lipset and Earl Raab have pointed out, the Wallace movement "was a major party candidacy. In the rest of the country, however, the Wallace movement was a small radical third party, organized around various extreme right-wing groups."[51] Most northern voters selected either Nixon or Humphrey, and Wallace won only 8 percent of the northern popular vote. Wallace captured 34 percent of the total southern vote, about the same as Nixon received and a few points ahead of Humphrey.

Wallace won an estimated 40 percent of the southern white vote, almost doubling Thurmond's performance 20 years earlier. A large majority of Deep South whites backed Wallace, while less than a third of Peripheral South whites did (see Table 6.1). As they had for Thurmond and Goldwater, Mississippi and Alabama provided the greatest white majorities for the protest candidate. When the geography of the Wallace grassroots vote (see Figure 6.3) is compared with a map of support for Thurmond, the other third-party candidate (Figure 6.1), it is apparent once again that state boundaries powerfully conditioned the two votes. Despite the fact that far more blacks voted in 1968 than in 1948, Wallace won numerous grassroots majorities in every Deep South state except South Carolina, where Thurmond vouched for Nixon. Outside the Deep South Wallace majorities were most prominent in North Florida. While Thurmond rarely won a quarter of the vote in the Peripheral South, Wallace's campaign secured between a fourth and a half of the vote in East Texas and in most of the lowlands sections of the other Peripheral South states. Clearly race was a more salient issue in 1968 than it had been in 1948.

The 1968 NES surveys underscore the centrality of racial segregation in Wallace's appeal among white southern voters and clarify why he failed to carry the entire region. Fifty-six percent of the South's strict segregationists voted for Wallace, but by 1968 this hardcore group represented only 29 percent of white southerners. A slight majority of southern whites (51 percent) now preferred a form of race relations that was neither strict segregation nor desegregation. The preferred candidate for these whites, who constituted the new center of political gravity within the region, was Republican candidate Richard Nixon. Wallace's support dropped to 26 percent among the "intermediate" whites. And among the small but growing band of integrationists in the region—one in five southern whites—Wallace was the worst possible presidential candidate, supported by only 6 percent.

Many of the whites who preferred "something in-between" segregation and desegregation held conservative views on federal responsibility for school integration, the desegregation of public accom-

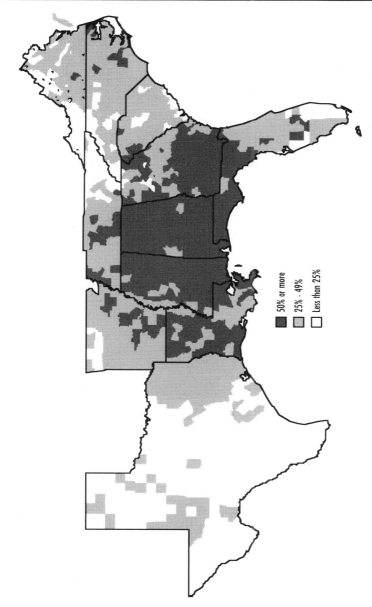

Figure 6.3 The George Wallace vote in 1968. *Source*: Richard M. Scammon, ed., *America Votes*, 8 (Washington, D.C.: Congressional Quarterly, 1970).

modations, and federal supervision of employment practices. Among these voters Wallace faced tough competition from Nixon. Thurmond, the Dixiecrat turned Republican, campaigned across the South in 1968, arguing that a vote for Wallace was a wasted vote and that Nixon would be in a much better position to bring the nation's racial policies more in line with the desires of southern whites.[52] It was an argument that rang true for many southern whites of conservative racial views, especially outside the Deep South.

Most of Wallace's southern white vote—four-fifths according to the NES survey—came from Democrats and independents who leaned toward the Democrats. Relatively little support, mainly in the Deep South, we suspect, came from southern Republicans. Wallace's support ran strongest among whites native to the region, farmers, working-class and lower-middle-class whites, and those whites with the least formal education. Wallace had long presented himself as a champion of the white working man and woman, and in 1968 he "appealed directly to the self-interests of workers and low-income people." Indeed, Wallace compared himself favorably with Goldwater on this point. "In the last election," Wallace said, "Mr. Goldwater was running as a conservative, but he did not have the support and confidence of the working people in our country. For some reason, they feared that he was not in their interest." "I'm no ultra-conservative," Wallace once remarked, "because those ultra-conservatives are conservative about just one thing—money."[53] Wallace's support was strongest among whites without a high school education (40 percent), declined to 34 percent among high school graduates, and plunged to only 17 percent among the region's whites who had attended college. According to the Gallup Poll, Wallace won 53 percent from white southern manual workers, a mere 18 percent among business and professional whites in the region.[54]

Wallace's electoral college vote was quite similar to those won by Thurmond and Nixon. He carried four of the five Deep South states and Arkansas in the Peripheral South, for a total of 46 out of the South's 128 electoral votes (36 percent). Moreover, because Humphrey won only a fifth of the southern electoral vote, Wallace's showing in the Deep South and Nixon's success in the Peripheral South meant that the Democrats needed a substantial majority—three-fifths—of the entire northern electoral vote in order to win the presidency. Humphrey won only two-fifths of the northern electoral vote. With his larger share of the southern electoral vote, Nixon needed only 52 percent of the northern electoral vote, and he actually received 60 percent.

For the first time, the Democrats faced the awesome prospect of reorganizing their presidential election strategy in the North in the face of their candidate's almost total collapse in the South. Since Wallace's candidacy hurt Nixon more than Humphrey, the Republicans emerged from 1968 in good shape, well positioned to attract the "Wallace vote" in future presidential elections.

The Anatomy of White Protest

The presidential campaigns of Thurmond, Goldwater, and Wallace offer considerable insight into the structure of southern politics. Thurmond's and Wallace's regional candidacies were first and foremost expressions of white anger, disgust, and betrayal over potential or actual racial change. Although Goldwater was not a segregationist, his willingness to serve as a symbol of opposition to the Civil Rights Act places him in a similar category with Thurmond and Wallace. But despite the fact that all three protest candidates sought to unify the entire region, none of them came close to carrying all the southern states. What do the votes for Thurmond, Goldwater, and Wallace indicate about political divisions within the South?

Not surprisingly, the protest votes clearly reveal a close relationship between the proportion of blacks in a given location and white racial conservatism. In all three contests the proportion of whites voting for the protest candidate is closely related to the racial composition of the southern states (see Figure 6.4). Generally, the higher the black population, the greater the white vote for Thurmond, Goldwater, and Wallace. Thus in the Deep South, where the percentage of blacks was twice as large as it was in the Peripheral South, substantial majorities of whites favored each of the protest candidates. In the Peripheral South, however, the protest candidates did not win white majorities. Neither of the two southern candidates came close to registering majority sentiment in the Peripheral South, as almost nine-tenths of the whites passed over Thurmond and approximately two-thirds of them rejected Wallace. The southern revolt was preeminently a protest of Deep South whites, most conspicuously the white voters of Mississippi and Alabama.

The relationship between racial composition and white protest can be traced for southern counties as well as for states. For purposes of

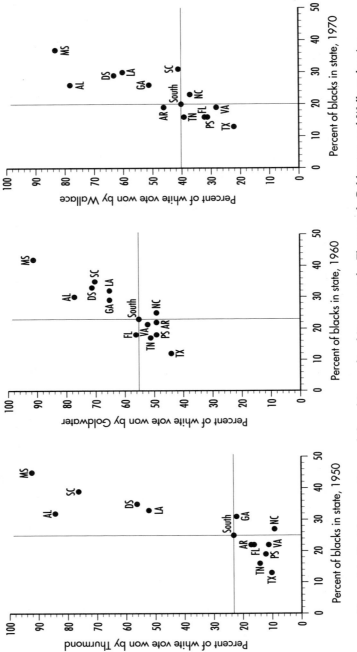

Figure 6.4 Racial composition and the white revolt: white support for Thurmond, Goldwater, and Wallace, by size of black population. *Sources:* Same as Table 6.1.

comparison a "protest county" may be defined as one carried by a protest candidate in at least two out of the three elections of 1948, 1964, and 1968. Figure 6.5 plots the percentage of protest counties among all counties according to the size of the black population. For the entire South the result is a fairly consistent linear relationship between racial composition and protest voting. Counties with small black populations rarely backed protest candidates, whereas large majorities of counties with black populations of 30 percent or greater qualified as protest counties. Figure 6.5 also illustrates the profound difference between the Deep South and Peripheral South in the intensity of racial politics. Segregationist attitudes in the Deep South were so widespread and intense that black populations of 10–19 percent and higher generated exceptionally strong levels of protest voting. In the Peripheral South protest voting was a much weaker political imperative. Few Peripheral South leaders saw politics primarily or exclusively as a matter of race, and whites in areas of high black population exerted less influence in their states' political affairs than did their Deep South counterparts. Thus the shape of protest voting varied remarkably from the Deep South to the Peripheral

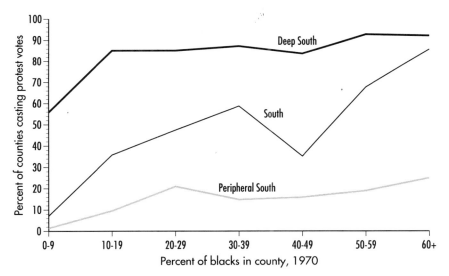

Figure 6.5   The racial structure of the protest vote: percentage of counties classified as protest counties, by percent black of county population, for the South, Deep South, and Peripheral South. *Sources:* Calculated by the authors from sources given in Figures 6.1, 6.2, and 6.3 and the 1970 *U.S. Census.*

South, and the subregional differences help explain the linear relationship for the region as a whole. Most of the many southern
counties with low black populations were located in the Peripheral
South; most of the region's counties with high black populations
were found in the Deep South.

As a final illustration of the sharp subregional differences revealed
by the southern protest votes, consider the geography of the white
revolt mapped in Figure 6.6. Mississippi and Alabama, along with
North Louisiana, stand out as the bedrock of the white revolt, the
areas most supportive of politicians who protested national intervention in regional race relations. In these Deep South jurisdictions
Thurmond, Goldwater, and Wallace each won more votes than any
other candidate.

Protest candidates triumphed in two out of three campaigns in
many other counties. Most of the counties in South Carolina's Low
Country favored Thurmond and Goldwater but not Wallace. In 1968
Thurmond championed Nixon and argued that a Wallace vote was a
wasted vote; the former Dixiecrat was instrumental in splitting the
white vote and denying Wallace victory in South Carolina. In South-
east Louisiana and in scattered counties in North Alabama and South
Carolina's Piedmont, Thurmond and Wallace were victorious but
Johnson defeated Goldwater. South Georgia and North Florida, along
with several counties in Southside Virginia and South Arkansas,
failed to respond to the States' Rights crusade yet supported Goldwater and Wallace.

The geography of protest plainly identifies the Deep South as the
core of the white revolt. North Florida, itself a cultural and political
extension of southern Alabama and Georgia, is the main exception.
Protest candidacies rarely thrived beyond the state lines of the Deep
South. Eighty-four percent of the Deep South's counties, compared
with only 8 percent of the Peripheral South's counties, supported at
least two of the three protest candidates. All told, protest characterized 36 percent of the region's counties.

Figure 6.6 also isolates areas in which a single protest candidate
succeeded. There were only a handful of situations (such as Macon
County, Alabama) in which Thurmond won but Goldwater and Wallace both failed. In 1948 few blacks voted in Macon County, and the
whites who did gave Thurmond a majority of 91 percent. By the
mid-1960s, Macon County contained enough black voters to defeat
Goldwater and Wallace. In a larger number of cases, including South
Florida, East Tennessee, the North Carolina Piedmont, much of

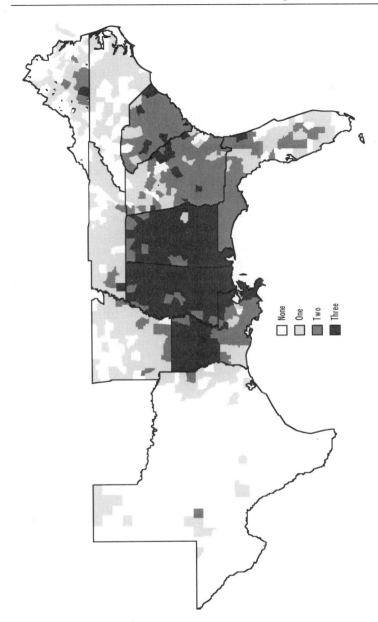

Figure 6.6 The geography of the southern white protest vote: number of times protest candidates (Thurmond, Goldwater, and Wallace) carried southern counties. *Sources:* Calculated by the authors from sources given in Figures 6.1, 6.2, and 6.3.

Virginia, and the Texas Panhandle, Goldwater alone was victorious. Here the Republican party label, rather than racial protest, was the key to Goldwater's success.

The largest number of single protest victories came in 1968 as Wallace's defiant message penetrated areas previously resistant to flamboyant protest. Wallace attracted considerable support in North Georgia and Southwest Louisiana, the only sections of the Deep South that had supported neither Thurmond nor Goldwater. In the Peripheral South Wallace was impressively strong in Eastern North Carolina, Southside Virginia, Middle and West Tennessee, most of nonmountainous Arkansas, and East Texas.

Finally, the map identifies areas of the South where the protest candidates uniformly failed. More than any other southern state, Texas was comparatively hostile to Thurmond, Goldwater, and Wallace. Few prominent Texas politicians paid serious attention to the views and priorities of Deep South firebrands, and Johnson's native-son candidacy in 1964 undermined Goldwater's campaign. Aside from urban areas inhospitable to third-party ventures (such as Miami, Atlanta, Charlotte, and the northern Virginia suburbs), relative indifference to the white revolt was most pronounced in the mountainous sections of Virginia, North Carolina, Tennessee, and Arkansas.

Political Ramifications of the White Revolt

The Thurmond, Goldwater, and Wallace campaigns represent the starkest intrusions of racial politics in presidential elections. Between 1948 and 1968 the broad issue of civil rights moved from the periphery to the center of national politics. In the process many racially conservative white southerners, especially those born and raised in the Deep South, repudiated the political party of their ancestors.

In 1948 the southern social order was rigidly segregated and most black southerners could not exercise the right to vote. For decades white southerners had used their influence within the national Democratic party (in Congress and at the nominating conventions) to maintain the racial status quo. Truman's apostasy in daring to sponsor civil rights legislation stimulated Deep South Democratic leaders to teach their northern counterparts a hard lesson in practical politics. As the Dixiecrats read American political history, southern electoral votes were the cornerstone of Democratic control of the presidency. What better way to demonstrate the folly of trifling with the white

South than to humiliate the impudent Truman? If Thurmond *had* carried all eleven southern states, neither Truman nor Dewey would have won a majority of the electoral college vote. Ultimately the Dixiecrats failed because the Peripheral South states did not share the Deep South's alarm over the faint prospect of federal intervention in southern race relations.

During the next decade and a half, to a degree that must have confused and bewildered southern segregationists of the old school, the worst nightmares of the Dixiecrats were realized as Democratic presidents and northern senators and representatives (both Democratic and Republican) united to support the historic Civil Rights Act of 1964 and the Voting Rights Act of 1965. The States' Righters lost the ideological battle to preserve compulsory racial segregation. Ironically, however, their basic political insight—that the Democratic party would find it difficult to win the presidency without substantial southern support—has been increasingly vindicated by the Republicans' success in presidential elections after the Great Society.

7

The Republican Breakthrough in the Peripheral South

All in all the rebellion of the Dixiecrats in 1948 expressed the dissatisfaction of racially conservative white southerners with Republicans as well as with Democrats. Aside from the Mountain Republicanism found in Tennessee, Virginia, North Carolina, and Arkansas, white southern resistance to the party of Abraham Lincoln was still intense and widespread. Traditional southern hostility to the Republican party was refreshed and reinforced in the twentieth century by the Great Depression, which gave millions of white southerners unforgettable personal experiences of economic disaster under Republican rule. Skepticism about Republican management of the economy reinforced the inherited view of the GOP as a despised northern institution dedicated to the oppression of the white South.

Yet developments without and within the South were converging to create an environment less hostile to presidential Republicanism. At midcentury, V. O. Key, Jr., suggested that the emergence of significant Republican support in the South would "probably depend more on events outside the South than on the exertions of native Republicans. If the balance of power becomes one that clearly requires a Republican fight for southern votes to win the Presidency," the national Republican party might well reassess its traditional indifference to the South. With its 1948 defeat the Republican party had lost five presidential elections in a row, its worst showing in history. No longer could Republicans depend on a cohesive Republican North to offset losses in the South. From the standpoint of electoral college imperatives, the GOP urgently needed to look South. Within the South, moreover, changing socioeconomic and demographic conditions were slowly generating circumstances favorable to genuine competition in presidential elections. An agricultural region was becoming more industrial and commercial. The rise of cities and suburbs increasingly led by a new middle class committed to economic development was creating an electorate more sympathetic to Republican economic views than had previously existed. "If and when Republicans make a real drive to gain strength in the South," Key predicted, "they will find . . . a larger and larger group of prospects susceptible to their appeal."[1]

These trends and developments were much more advanced in the Peripheral South than in the Deep South. When Franklin Roosevelt was first elected president in 1932, the percentage of the total vote cast in Standard Metropolitan Statistical Areas with populations of 250,000 or better was tiny in both subregions. Historically, Atlanta, Birmingham, and New Orleans, all located in the Deep South, were the only large southern cities. By 1950 rapid population growth had created new metropolitan areas in Houston, Dallas, San Antonio, Miami, Nashville, and Memphis, all in the Peripheral South. In 1952 slightly more than a quarter of the Peripheral South's voters lived in large metropolitan areas, compared with 18 percent in the Deep South (see Figure 7.1). Because of its larger urban and smaller black

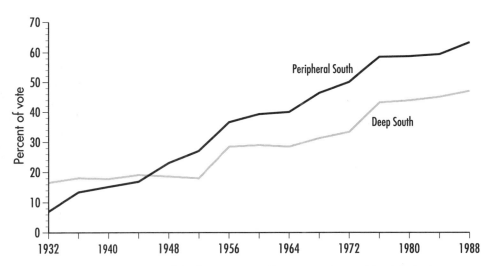

Figure 7.1 Expansion of the large metropolitan sector in presidential elections in the Peripheral South and Deep South, 1932–1988. *Sources:* Richard M. Scammon, ed., *America at the Polls* (Pittsburgh: University of Pittsburgh Press, 1965); and appropriate volumes of Richard M. Scammon, ed., *America Votes* (Washington, D.C.: Congressional Quarterly).

populations and, in some states, a heritage of Mountain Republicanism, the Peripheral South had emerged as a far more attractive target
for GOP presidential efforts than the Deep South.

The 1952 Eisenhower Campaign: "Honored to Come Down"

Provided that the party's historical image could be neutralized, the
steady expansion of the urban middle class represented an opportunity for Republican gains. The Republicans' southern breakthrough
came in 1952, when Dwight D. Eisenhower demonstrated that a
military hero with the popular touch was an inspired solution to the
Republicans' fundamental problem of nominating someone completely unidentified with the failed Republican policies of the past.
"Eisenhower was everybody's hero—the South's as well as the
North's, the Democrats' as well as the Republicans'," observed James
L. Sundquist. "He stood for national unity, national strength, a confident military and foreign policy, above the partisan struggle."[2] Eisenhower was the ideal nominee to make voting for a Republican
presidential candidate acceptable in a region where more than three-
quarters of the white voters still thought of themselves as Democrats.
The central theme of the Republican campaign was to offer the voters
a reasonable alternative to Harry Truman's "mess in Washington,"
an appeal especially attractive to middle-class whites in the region's
large cities and suburbs.

Before 1952 Republican and Democratic presidential nominees customarily did not campaign in the South. Southern loyalty to the
Democratic party made it unnecessary for Democratic candidates to
visit the South, while Republican candidates—recognizing the futility
of their cause in the region—concentrated on winnable northern
states. Eisenhower rejected the conventional political wisdom about
the value of appearing in the South. It had been based, he thought,
on the outdated notions that "the one side owned them and the
other side didn't know how to invade."[3] Eisenhower knew how to
invade. With a general's eye for identifying and attacking potential
enemy weaknesses, Eisenhower shattered this informal rule and
campaigned extensively in the South.

Eisenhower's first official campaign trip, a two-day excursion into
Georgia, Florida, Alabama, and Arkansas, was a deliberate signal
that the Republican party would never again forfeit the South to the
Democrats. As he explained to an audience in Birmingham, a group

of southerners had come to him before he had received the Republican nomination, asking if he would visit the South. "Well, didn't we decide once that we were all going to stay in the same nation?" Eisenhower replied. "Of course, I will be honored to come down." In Little Rock Eisenhower expanded his theme that the South should not be taken for granted. "There is a mounting mass of evidence," he said, "to show that you are in no one's column, that you are not in a captive precinct, and you are going to express your judgment and your decisions as you see fit."[4]

When he later visited Texas, where Democratic Governor Allan Shivers had enthusiastically endorsed him, Eisenhower had further polished his appeal for southern votes:

> The visit to Texas today is a kind of fulfillment for me. When I first considered entering this political race, some of those experienced in politics spoke to me about the South.
>
> I was not a politician then—am not a politician now. So to help my education, this is what they said.
>
> They said Texas had to be counted out—as well as the rest of the South.
>
> When I asked why, they replied, "the [Democratic] Administration has those states in the bag."
>
> I said, "What do you mean, in the bag; they are free people, aren't they?"
>
> "The states of the Solid South," they answered, "no matter how much they are kicked around by the Administration, they are used to it—they are in the bag."
>
> Well, I didn't believe it then and I don't believe it now. . . . No, my friends, Texans are not in anybody's bag.[5]

Eisenhower's appeal for southerners to exercise independent judgments in the presidential contest allowed his supporters to solicit votes from independents and Democrats. Although in every southern state the official Republican party worked hard on his behalf, other organizations emerged to legitimize Eisenhower's candidacy among voters who might "like Ike" but were not Republicans. Sometimes labeling themselves "Democrats for Eisenhower," as in Texas and Florida, or "Virginia Democrats for Eisenhower" in the Old Dominion, or "Eisenhower Democrats" in Alabama, these organizations enabled some southerners to vote for Eisenhower while retaining their traditional party identity. Other groups, such as "Citizens for Eisenhower," "Young Persons for Eisenhower," or "Women for

Eisenhower," made no reference at all to partisanship. Many southern whites apparently viewed Eisenhower either as nonpartisan or as the mildest and least offensive sort of Republican.

The general developed a politician's instinct to exploit regional patriotism. In an appearance at Columbia, South Carolina, "When the band struck up 'Dixie,' Eisenhower leaped up from his chair and shouted to the crowd: 'I always stand up when they play that song.'"[6] Yet Eisenhower was no Dixiecrat. Although the GOP candidate did not emphasize civil rights, in his speeches he made plain to attentive southerners his commitment to equality of opportunity.

In Columbia, for example, where Eisenhower appeared with segregationist Democratic Governor James F. Byrnes, a friendly crowd greeted "with absolute silence" Eisenhower's statement on improving equality of opportunity:

> We will move forward rapidly to make equality of opportunity a living fact for every American. Wherever I have gone in this campaign, I have pledged the people of our country that, if elected, I will support the Constitution of the United States—the whole of it. And that means that I will support and seek to strengthen and extend to every American every right that that Constitution guarantees.
>
> Equality of opportunity was part of the vision of the men who founded our nation. It is a principle deeply imbedded in our religious faith. And neither at home nor in the eyes of the world can America risk the weakness that inevitably results when any group of our people are ranked—politically or economically—as second-class citizens.[7]

Under Eisenhower's leadership the party of Lincoln did not present itself to southern whites as a party of white protest. In both Mississippi and South Carolina Democrats used an Associated Press photograph of Eisenhower eating breakfast with blacks in Harlem to discredit the Republican.[8]

Eisenhower made an early and extensive campaign throughout the South, but the same could not be said of Adlai Stevenson, the Democratic presidential candidate. Democratic leaders were relying on Alabama Senator John Sparkman, their vice-presidential candidate, to hold the South. As late as mid-September, Stevenson's own plans for the southern states remained unclear. Although he did intend to campaign in Texas, the Democratic presidential candidate "wasn't sure" that he planned to make "any major, extensive campaign" in the South. When asked by reporters if he were "worried about 'the apparent defections in the South,'" Stevenson replied, "Not in the least. I expect Texas, Louisiana, and Florida—all of them—to go Democratic, and overwhelmingly."[9]

In reality, however, Stevenson had already endangered Democratic chances of carrying Texas and Louisiana. In these states the major controversy in 1952 concerned whether the federal government or the states controlled certain offshore oil deposits. Stevenson believed that the tidelands belonged to the entire nation, not to the coastal states. He was unwilling to compromise his position when he met with Shivers, an energetic advocate of state control. After an exchange of views in which the Illinois governor "told the Texas governor very frankly that he disagreed with him on the issue," another participant in the discussion "gave the final and (he hoped) telling remonstrance: 'But Governor Stevenson, if you insist on doing that, you can't win.' Coldly and resolutely, Stevenson replied: 'I don't *have* to win.'"[10] By Texas standards of common sense, Stevenson's response was undoubtedly one of the most baffling statements of the purposes of electoral politics ever uttered by a major presidential candidate.

Confronted by a Republican candidate who visited every southern state except Mississippi, Stevenson eventually did campaign in the five southern states most at risk for the Democrats—Virginia, Louisiana, Florida, Tennessee, and Texas. Speaking in New Orleans, he touched on civil rights only in the most general of terms. "As you know," Stevenson said, "I stand on the Democratic Party platform with respect to minority rights. I have only one observation to make on this subject; one that must sadden you as it saddens me. It is that, after two thousand years of Christianity, we need discuss it at all."[11] However, he did not choose to pursue the topic with his Louisiana audience.

John Bartlow Martin, who traveled with Stevenson, best captured the flavor of Stevenson's approach to the South in a speech delivered in Nashville, Tennessee:

> Like all Southern speeches, it was very long and contained a recitation of Stevenson's Southern ancestry; the crowd expected and liked it. He talked at great length about the Democratic Party and the South, calling the people home to the party of their fathers. He recalled their heroes, John C. Calhoun and Cordell Hull and Andrew Jackson. He called the roll of Southern Democrats who presided over powerful House and Senate committees. He recalled how Southern voters had rallied behind Woodrow Wilson, FDR, and Harry Truman. He praised Southern valor under arms. He praised Southern internationalism and resistance to

isolationism. He declared that what the Republicans denounced as Big Government had accomplished much—including TVA; he reminded them that Eisenhower had pledged "there would be no more TVAs" if he was elected. Yet he was careful to say balance must be maintained between economic security and personal liberty and to say that as a Governor he had learned the virtues of states' rights "as a bulwark against Big Government."[12]

Stevenson's efforts were not viewed favorably by all southern Democratic politicians, many of whom carefully distanced themselves from the ticket. Richard Russell, whom many loyalist Democrats had hoped would help "hold the South" for Stevenson, detected disturbing tendencies in the candidate and withheld his endorsement until the waning moments of the campaign. Texan Sam Rayburn, "fighting to the end for every inch of the old ground," was the most prestigious southern Democrat who aggressively worked for Stevenson. William S. White, covering the South for the *New York Times,* observed that "published lists of the seemingly overwhelming numbers of Southern office holders who are stated to be 'back of' Stevenson are far from fully informative. The fact is that most of them have been literally behind the Democratic ticket—far behind. Most of them, in an old phrase, have been simply 'still Democrats—very still.'"[13]

Eisenhower won 50 percent of the vote cast by southern whites in 1952, a spectacular level of support for a Republican presidential candidate. The National Election Study of 1952 showed that Eisenhower captured all of the South's Republicans and four of every five white independents. These groups of voters were very small, however. Only one in eight southern voters were independents, and merely one in nine were Republicans. If Eisenhower's support had been strictly limited to these groups, he would have received only 21 percent of the region's white voters, about the same share of the vote that Willkie and Dewey had polled in the 1940s.

What set Eisenhower apart from the usual lot of Republican presidential candidates in the South was his impressive strength among southern white Democrats. Eisenhower performed well because he won nearly two-fifths of the vote among the region's white Democrats. The general's yield from southern Democrats amounted to an additional 29 percent of the total white vote, considerably more than the votes coming from his meager base of Republicans and independents.

Eisenhower ran much better among white southern women than among white men, the traditional guardians of the region's Democratic political culture. According to the 1952 NES survey, Eisenhower won 59 percent of southern white women and only 41 percent of southern white men. A higher percentage of female voters had been to college than had the males, a characteristic that was also associated with Republican support. Some women may have been troubled by Stevenson's divorce in an era when divorces were uncommon in the South and unheard of for a candidate aspiring to the White House. In the privacy of the voting booth, more than one woman may have answered Eisenhower's call for the exercise of an independent judgment and departed from the straight-ticket orthodoxy of many southern males.

"Building upon the traditional Republicanism of the upper South," Dewey W. Grantham concludes, "Eisenhower ran well in the region's cities and larger towns. His southern victories represented an important breakthrough for presidential Republicanism in the South, and it gave the minority party a new respectability among southerners, particularly middle-class and affluent urbanites and suburban dwellers."[14] George Brown Tindall has observed that "in 1952 middle-class Republicanism began to take on great proportions. To some extent it represented an issue vote against Democratic policies; to some extent in 1952 and increasingly in subsequent elections, a status vote. Republicanism became the style, and a fashion of 'conservative chic' swept through the white suburbs."[15]

Some loyalist Democrats tried to fight back by ridiculing the new interest in Republicanism. Virginia van der Veer Hamilton described Alabama Senator Lister Hill in action:

> Before a Democratic gathering in the ballroom of the Jefferson Davis Hotel in Montgomery, Hill, flailing his arms, pantomimed, mocked, and mimicked his enemies. As his audience roared approval, he jeered: "It is *fashionable* to like Ike. People who have made their financial position—and with government contracts . . . have heard that Mr. and Mrs. So-and-So are for Ike. So they say, 'We'll be for Ike and then perhaps Mr. and Mrs. So-and-So will at long last know that we, too, are nice people.'"[16]

All of this was to little avail. "Checks of urban precincts repeatedly showed a correlation between high income and Republican voting," Tindall concluded. "The most overwhelmingly Republican were the upper-income white residential areas. The areas most heavily for Adlai Stevenson were the black precincts and, to a lesser degree, the low-income white precincts."[17]

The NES surveys clearly show Eisenhower's popularity among the 27 percent of white southern voters who had been exposed to a college education. He won 73 percent from the small group of most highly educated whites, and took 45 percent from another 27 percent who had finished high school but had not proceeded to college. Stevenson was left with a lopsided majority (58 percent) from the 47 percent of southern whites who had not received a high school education in 1952.

Eisenhower did best in 1952 in the southern states where the size of the large metropolitan sector exceeded the urban share of the vote in the region as a whole. In four of the five states with relatively large big-city votes (Virginia, Florida, Texas, and Tennessee), Eisenhower won majority support. Florida best illustrates the phenomenon of urban Republicanism. Republicans benefited in Virginia from Senator Harry Byrd's refusal to back the Democratic ticket; and in Texas and Louisiana the tidelands oil issue hurt Democratic chances (Eisenhower favored letting the states control the matter). Five of the six states with smaller or nonexistent big-city votes gave Eisenhower less support than he received across the region. South Carolina's Republicanism reflected Byrnes's intense opposition to the Democrats' stance on civil rights as well as his confidence in Eisenhower.

The net result of Eisenhower's southern invasion was the disappearance of the Solid Democratic South in the electoral college, a political event of enormous strategic importance in determining which party controls the White House. In 1952 Stevenson won 55 percent of the South's electoral votes, his best showing by far in any region but an unimpressive performance for a Democratic presidential candidate by historical standards. The significance of Eisenhower's breakthrough can be appreciated by comparing the Democrats' northern electoral vote target with the northern electoral vote they won. During the New Deal the Democrats could control the presidency by combining the entire southern electoral vote with no more than 35 percent of the northern electoral vote, an easy task with Franklin Roosevelt on the ballot. Because Stevenson carried little more than half of the southern electoral vote in 1952, he needed almost half—48 percent—of the electoral vote in the rest of the nation to win the presidency. In fact, Stevenson carried no states in the Northeast, Midwest, or West and accumulated only 4 percent of the northern electoral vote. By successfully invading the Democrats' southern base while simultaneously resurrecting its pre–New Deal northern support, the Republicans under Eisenhower invented a new regional approach to winning presidential elections.

In 1952 the regional structure of the Democratic electoral vote was remarkably similar to 1928, when the nomination of a wet Catholic, Al Smith, divided the southern electoral vote and consequently increased the Democrats' target to half of the northern electoral vote (see Table 7.1). Since Smith and Stevenson carried only two northern states apiece, in both 1928 and 1952 the Democrats were swamped in the national electoral vote.

The strategic implications of the Republicans' southern breakthrough in 1952 were profoundly important. If Republican candidates could simply divide the southern electoral vote, the Democrats would necessarily be much more dependent on northern states than ever

Table 7.1   The regional structure of the Democratic party's electoral vote in presidential elections before the Great Society

Region	Democratic percentage of electoral vote					
	1928	1948	1952	1956	1960	1964
South	51	69	55	47	63	63
Border	0	80	35	25	65	100
Northeast	16	14	0	0	91	100
Midwest	0	61	0	0	41	100
West	0	92	0	0	12	95
United States	16	57	17	14	56	90
North	6	53	4	3	54	99
Northern Democratic target	50	44	48	51	46	46
Northern Democratic gap	−44	+9	−44	−48	+8	+53

Note: Each number is the percentage of the electoral vote won by the Democratic nominee within a given area. The northern Democratic target is the minimum percentage of northern electoral votes required for a Democratic victory, given the proportion of electoral votes won by the Democrats in the South. The northern Democratic gap is the percentage point difference between the northern Democratic target and the northern Democratic vote.

Source: Calculated by the authors from Congressional Quarterly, Guide to U.S. Elections (Washington, D.C.: Congressional Quarterly, 1975).

before. Although Harry Truman's northern electoral majority of 53 percent was enough for victory in 1948, Truman's performance was quite weak by New Deal standards. Roosevelt's northern majorities had ranged from 75 percent in 1944 to 98 percent in 1936.

The 1956 Eisenhower Campaign: "I Report to You as Your President"

In 1956, pledging to keep America "going down the straight road of prosperity and peace,"[18] Eisenhower ran for reelection against Stevenson. As a sitting president who had recently recovered from a heart attack, Eisenhower decided that he did not need to barnstorm the country as he had done in 1952. Periodic campaign trips to key states complemented a series of national television appearances that were designed to claim public credit for his administration's achievements in international affairs and domestic policy.

Eisenhower did not enter the South until late October. Planning to visit the four southern states he had carried in 1952, the president made appearances in Virginia and Florida before escalating foreign policy crises forced the cancellation of campaign stops in Texas and Tennessee. Instead, he returned to Washington and "spoke to the people on nationwide all-network radio and television on Eastern Europe and the Middle East. He began, 'Tonight I report to you as your President,' not as a political candidate." Eisenhower's approach to these events abroad, occurring only days before the election, "reinforced the idea that the country could not afford a change in such unstable times and, least of all, lose the service of a President who seemed to be so uniquely fitted to handle what might develop into a military crisis affecting the national security of the United States."[19]

In Miami Eisenhower emphasized peace and prosperity, the two most salient appeals any incumbent president can make. He also took the opportunity to stress his administration's gradual approach to implementing the Supreme Court's *Brown* decision of 1954, which declared racial segregation unconstitutional in public education:

> Four years ago I pledged that, as President of all the people, I would use every proper influence of my office to promote for all citizens that equality before the law and of opportunity visualized by our founding fathers. I promised further to do this with the conviction that progress toward equality had to be achieved finally in the hearts of men rather than in legislative halls. I urged then, as I urge now, the handling of this question, to the greatest possible extent, on a local and state basis.[20]

Eisenhower consistently declined to say whether or not he favored the *Brown* decision.

Stevenson approached his rematch with Eisenhower as a decided underdog. He had been routed in the electoral college four years earlier, and he was now challenging a popular incumbent. In 1952 Stevenson had lost most of the Peripheral South and had been helped in the Deep South by the presence of a vice-presidential candidate from Alabama. In 1956 he again had a southern running mate, but not because of any planned strategy. Stevenson's rival in the 1956 primaries, Estes Kefauver of Tennessee, had emerged as the Democratic vice-presidential candidate after Stevenson had turned the choice over to the convention. Kefauver's moderate to liberal views on civil rights were anathema to Deep South Democrats, and many established Democrats wanted nothing to do with him. Most of Kefauver's campaign appearances were scheduled not in the South but in the Midwest and Far West. Even Kefauver's presence on the ticket was not enough to keep Tennessee from again favoring Eisenhower.

Stevenson tried to straddle the conflicting liberal and conservative wings of the Democratic party by running as a "moderate." In September 1955 the former Illinois governor had met in Texas with Lyndon Johnson and Sam Rayburn, and the two most influential Democrats in the Congress had "urged Stevenson to help put the party on a moderate course. The South, particularly Texas, would be lost, they argued, if the Democratic ticket strayed too far left in 1956. Stevenson promised his cooperation. 'I agree that it is time for catching our breath,' he said. 'I agree that moderation is the spirit of the times.'" To nail down the point, Johnson had a private word with one of Stevenson's key aides as the meeting broke up, "You tell your man that he has to be moderate—be moderate on all these issues—the country's moderate."[21]

Stevenson's effort to compromise sharply conflicting opinions on the *Brown* decision among Democrats, for example, was to agree with the principle of *Brown* but to oppose any use of federal force to implement school desegregation and rely on the gradual processes of education to allow the situation to improve. He repudiated the views of hard-core segregationists, who thought the decision was wrong. Earlier in the year, when asked "if he would 'favor public school desegregation strongly in the South?' Stevenson said 'Oh, yes, it is the law of the land, it has been so enunciated by the Supreme Court.'" "I believe that decision to be right," said Stevenson during the presidential campaign in Little Rock, Arkansas.[22]

Yet he also disappointed some civil rights proponents who wanted to use federal troops to enforce the decision. Speaking before an audience of blacks in Los Angeles early in 1956, he said, "I think that [use of federal troops] would be a great mistake. This is exactly what brought about the difficult Civil War and division of the Union. Now, we will go about these things gradually, because it will be the spirit of man that will make the laws successful and make it possible to enforce them gradually. You do not upset the habits and traditions that are older than the Republic overnight." When questions persisted, Stevenson replied, "'I'm not running for this office for the honor of it, my friend.' Then he said his party represented all the people of the country regardless of race, and he himself would 'do everything I can to bring about [national] unity even if I have to ask some of you to come about it gradually.'"[23]

The civil rights issue "was less important in the general election," Martin contends, "since Eisenhower's own position, in so far as he had one, did not differ greatly from Stevenson's, except that increasingly as the campaign progressed Stevenson urged the President to use his moral authority to solve the problem, while Eisenhower sought to avoid becoming involved and repeatedly said it was a problem for the district courts."[24]

In the Peripheral South, the issue seemed to break in Eisenhower's favor. A voter in East Texas, asked to assess public reaction to the nominees' positions on civil rights, got to the nub of the difference. "The biggest issue in these parts is segregation," he said. "Stevenson has lost ground on that count because people know better now how he stands. They know Ike is also for school integration but think he won't do much about it."[25]

With a popular and trusted incumbent heading the ticket, the Republican party easily prevailed. On election night an "irritated" Eisenhower waited and waited for Stevenson to concede his obvious defeat. "'What in the name of God is the monkey waiting for?' the President demanded. 'Polishing his prose?'" When the Democratic candidate "finally appeared on the television screen to concede, Eisenhower stalked out of the room, saying over his shoulder that the others should stay 'to receive the surrender.'"[26]

In the South the Republican party consolidated its gains of 1952. Virginia, Florida, Texas, and Tennessee, the Peripheral South states that favored Eisenhower in 1952, repeated their performance in 1956. Louisiana, the most urban state in the Deep South, became the first state in that subregion to go Republican. Overall, areas that liked Ike in 1952 stuck by him in 1956. South Carolina and Mississippi, where the Republican vote dropped considerably between 1952 and 1956, were the only exceptions. Mississippi whites were not happy with the president whose appointee as Chief Justice of the Supreme Court had written the school desegregation decision. In South Carolina ex-Governor Byrnes, an enthusiastic supporter of Eisenhower in 1952, repudiated both Stevenson and Eisenhower in favor of Senator Harry Byrd of Virginia. Eisenhower had "said and done enough about integrating the races in the District of Columbia," Byrnes complained, "to cause us to realize that on this subject we need not expect assistance from either major candidate."[27]

In the 1956 election, for the first time since 1872, the Democratic party failed to win a majority of the southern electoral vote (see Table 7.1). As a result, a Stevenson victory in 1956 would have required a stronger electoral college vote in the North than in the South. In any event, by winning only 3 percent of the northern electoral vote, Stevenson fell 48 points shy of his northern target. Increased party competition in the South made Democratic success in the North more essential than ever.

The Kennedy-Nixon Campaign of 1960

"It's time for the Democratic candidates to quit taking the South for granted and it's time for the Republican candidates to quit conceding the South to the Democrats," Vice-President Richard Nixon told an Atlanta audience in 1960. "It's time for Southern voters to start exercising their right to make a choice between the two candidates for the Presidency."[28] By 1960, the South had truly come of age in presidential politics. Nixon became the first Republican presidential nominee to campaign in every southern state. Massachusetts Senator John Kennedy and his running mate, Texas Senator Lyndon Johnson, campaigned aggressively to hold as many southern states as possible for the Democrats.

Democrats still possessed a considerable advantage in the South. Among southern whites, Republicans had increased from 9 to 21 percent during Eisenhower's two terms in office, but three-fifths of the whites still thought of themselves as Democrats.[29] Eisenhower's campaigns had persuaded many white southern Democrats that splitting their tickets between a Republican presidential candidate and Democratic candidates for state and local offices was socially respectable. Carr P. Collins, Sr., a Dallas businessman who headed Texans for Nixon, expressed Republican hopes for the 1960 presidential election. "What we call the old 'brass-collar' Democrat in East Texas that always votes her straight [ticket]," he predicted, "is not going to vote her straight this time . . . I'm telling you one thing: we've just about melted down all the brass collars." Why were fewer southerners voting straight Democratic tickets? As Collins explained the Republicans' approach, "We've made them feel that if they say they are brass-collar Democrats it reflects on their intelligence or their patriotism."[30]

As it turned out, Collins was whistling Dixie about East Texas Democrats. Most of them, as well as other "brass-collar" Democrats across the South, answered Lyndon Johnson's appeal to support the Democratic party. Johnson invoked the old Democratic political religion on a memorable train trip across the South, putting the Republicans on the defensive by asking voters, as he did in one Virginia town, "What has Dick Nixon ever done for Culpeper?"[31]

In reality, both parties encountered great difficulties in the South. Southern Republicans could no longer run Eisenhower, a "nonpartisan" Republican, at the top of the ticket, while the Democrats' selection of a northeastern Catholic to head their ticket revived memories of Al Smith's disastrous 1928 campaign in the South. Civil rights issues were on the front burner of southern politics. In the spring of 1960 black college students began demonstrations to protest segregated public accommodations in cities across the region, and both the Republican and Democratic party platforms contained fairly liberal planks on civil rights. It was no easy matter for either candidate to state positions acceptable to southern whites *and* northern blacks, or to the small but growing number of southern black voters.

Although he never publicly supported the *Brown* decision, President Eisenhower's reputation among segregationists had been damaged by the 1957 Little Rock crisis, when he dispatched troops to enforce school desegregation. Nixon had been an administration spokesman for civil rights, and the vice-president made a point of repudiating segregationist racial practices when speaking in the South. None of these activities helped the Republicans among southern white voters. One northern Alabama newspaper gave the Eisenhower years a scorching review. "We got Earl Warren and the NAACP; we got Little Rock and Federal troops on Southern soil again; we got the rights of the individual states here in the South ground under foot," wrote the Anniston *Star*, "and if Slick Dick Nixon has his way, we will have carpetbag rule all over again."[32]

For his part, Kennedy emphasized to the nation his determination to "establish a moral tone and moral leadership" in the field of civil rights. He criticized Eisenhower because the president "has never indicated what he thought of the 1954 decision." Johnson supported the civil rights platform of the Democratic party, but shrewdly suggested that Democrats use the phrase "constitutional rights" rather than "civil rights" when discussing the issue in the South.[33]

Johnson's acceptance of the vice-presidential nomination and support for the civil rights platform of the Democratic party initially did not go down well with some southern Democrats. As one Texas Democratic official commented, "They nominated an unfriendly candidate [Kennedy], rammed a platform we didn't like down our throats, then said we want your Senator Johnson to help sell the candidate and the platform to the South." "The politicians understand why Johnson pushed through those civil-rights bills," a North Carolina politician said, "but the average voter thinks Johnson sold out the South." Ultraconservative southern whites, individuals unlikely to have supported any Democratic ticket, were enraged. "If Kennedy advisors imagine the South has any deep affection for Lyndon Johnson, they are wholly mistaken," wrote James J. Kilpatrick of the Richmond *News Leader*. "The Texan is widely regarded as a renegade, a turncoat, an opportunist who plays footsie with the liberal Negro bloc."[34] For many southern whites, most of whom were segregationists in 1960, neither ticket was satisfactory.

For southern blacks, who made up less than 10 percent of the actual voters, the choices were also unsatisfactory. Most of the small number of voting blacks in the South had supported Eisenhower in 1956, and many black Protestants, like white Protestants, were troubled by Kennedy's Catholicism.

Nixon announced that he would campaign in each of the fifty states. According to his own account, Nixon "recognized that Kennedy would have a considerable advantage in the big Northeastern industrial states. To balance our anticipated losses there, we needed every Western, Southern, and Midwestern state we could possibly win." About the South, Nixon recalled that "I felt as the Republican candidate I had an obligation to encourage and build on the trend, which President Eisenhower's victories had started in 1952 and 1956, toward a real two-party system in the Southern states."[35]

Theodore White succinctly described the Kennedy strategy: "Nine large states (New York, Pennsylvania, California, Michigan, Texas, Illinois, Ohio, New Jersey and Massachusetts)" held "237 of the 269 electoral votes necessary to elect a President. If these could be swept; and if another 60 or 70 electoral votes could be added by Lyndon B. Johnson in the Old South, and if a few more solid New England or Midwestern states could be counted in—then the election could be won handily."[36] Kennedy campaigned in six southern states, but he knew that he needed help in the region.

The selection of Johnson as his running mate, after the rough campaign that Johnson and Connally had waged against him, signaled Kennedy's geopolitical strategy. It also made clear that John and Robert Kennedy, not Johnson, were in command of the campaign. The power relationships between the Kennedys and Johnson, implicit in Kennedy's victory at the convention, were explicitly spelled out in an episode, chronicled by James Reston, Jr., that occurred prior to Senator Kennedy's September visit to Texas.

With millions of dollars at stake, Texas oilmen were vitally interested in the position of the Kennedys on the depletion allowance for oil and gas producers. In a meeting with Robert Kennedy, the head of the Kennedy-Johnson efforts in Houston, Dub Singleton, asked the campaign manager to approve a statement Singleton had written about the oil depletion allowance. Singleton's hope was that Jack Kennedy would make the statement during his Texas trip.

> Robert Kennedy took the piece of paper and read the draft paragraph: "On the matter of the oil and gas industry, I luckily have the advice and counsel of two men who know more about that than any two men in the world, and that's the Speaker of the House, Mr. Rayburn, and my own running mate for vice president, Lyndon Johnson. On any issue involving the oil and gas industry, of course, I'll counsel with them."
>
> Slowly, Kennedy turned his aquatic eyes on Singleton and tore the paper to bits. "We're not going to say anything like that," he said coldly. "We put that son of a bitch on the ticket to carry Texas. If you can't carry Texas, it [the depletion allowance] is your problem."[37]

In both candidates' strategies, the Solid Democratic South had disappeared. Each sought to win a group of southern states, a part of the whole. Nixon hoped to repeat Eisenhower's gains in Virginia, Florida, Tennessee, and Texas but did not presume he could sweep the region. Kennedy hoped to get 85 or 95 (Texas plus most of the "Old South") rather than the 128 electoral votes cast by the former Confederate states. Both candidates saw the South as a collection of states, rather than as a monolithic and cohesive region. The region had become a competitive battleground in presidential politics, able to go either way depending upon the candidates, issues, and conditions of the moment.

Nixon initially believed that the addition of Johnson to the Democratic ticket would limit his own ability to draw southern votes. His first visit to a southern state, according to one campaign insider, was conceived more to force Kennedy to spend time in the South—and away from the larger industrial states—than to carry states that Eisenhower had been unable to win. Events soon persuaded Nixon to reevaluate his southern prospects, however. Appearing in August at Greensboro, North Carolina, he defended the goals of the Negro sit-in protest: "Any American is entitled to go into a store to buy products, and should have the same right as any other American to use all the facilities of that store without discrimination." Yet Nixon also had a message for whites, for "without saying anything to lose any Negro votes, he got over the idea that the Republican civil rights plank was less drastic than the Democrats." Surprised by the tumultous reception he received, Nixon acknowledged that, "We are going to have to look at these Southern states again."[38]

A week later fifteen thousand people in Birmingham heard Nixon give a "low-key attack on Democratic liberalism that moved his audience of Southern conservatives to rebel yells." *Time* captured Nixon's approach in the Deep South:

> To the conservative Southerners he pictured the Democrats, Northern style, as a party that wants "to progress through spending billions more of the people's money, through increasing the functions, the size and the power of the Federal Government."
>
> Echoing a Southern threat, he predicted that "millions of Democrats will vote for our ticket this year, not because they are deserting their party but because their party deserted their principles." Only once were his remarks met with silence. Bringing up civil rights, Nixon called it a national problem, said simply, "You know my convictions on that issue."

Later in the day, Nixon received an even greater reception in Atlanta, where an estimated 45,000 turned out to see him. It is no wonder that afterwards Nixon told reporters, "The Kennedy-Johnson ticket is in real trouble in the South. They no longer can consider any Southern state safe." Indeed, polls were showing a very large "undecided" vote in the South.[39]

After the first televised presidential debate in the nation's history, however, Nixon's campaign lost momentum. Kennedy established his credentials as a legitimate presidential contender, while Nixon appeared to be a candidate better suited for hospitalization than the White House. A Texas Republican wrote to Nixon's press secretary, "'The first order of the day is to fire the makeup man. Everybody in this part of the country thinks Nixon is sick. Three doctors agreed he looked as if he had just suffered a coronary.' Henry Cabot Lodge, watching from Texas, blurted out at the end of the debate, 'That son-of-a-bitch just lost us the election!'"[40]

Nixon continued to be frustrated by the complex and risky politics of the civil rights issue, vacillating between the incompatible goals of winning large numbers of black votes in northern cities and making inroads among southern whites in the states that Eisenhower had not carried.[41] The contradiction became evident during the second televised debate. On the one hand, Nixon associated himself with the goals of the sit-in movement. "I have talked to Negro mothers," he said. "I've heard them explain—try to explain—how they tell their children how they can go into a store and buy a loaf of bread but then can't go into that store and sit at the counter and get a Coca Cola. This is wrong and we have to do something about it." On the other hand, Nixon stressed that civil rights was a national problem, not merely a problem in the South. "Why do I talk every time I'm in the South on civil rights? Not because I'm preaching to the people of the South because this isn't just a Southern problem. It's a Northern problem and a Western problem. It's a problem for all of us." Later in the debate, he returned to the issue by criticizing Kennedy for putting Johnson on the ticket as his choice for vice-president. "I selected a man [Henry Cabot Lodge of Massachusetts] who stands with me in this field," Nixon remarked, whereas Kennedy "selected a man who had voted against most of these [civil rights] proposals and a man who opposes them at the present time."[42]

Toward the end of October, though, Nixon distanced himself from Lodge precisely on civil rights issues. In a Harlem speech, the Massachusetts Republican promised that "if elected, we will be guided by the following: There should be a Negro in the Cabinet." Nixon, campaigning in California, "instantly backed away from the commitment Lodge had attempted to make for him." Conservative Republicans were shocked. "'Whoever recommended that Harlem speech,' said one Virginia Republican, 'ought to have been thrown out of an airplane from 25,000 feet.'" Nixon biographer Stephen E. Ambrose concluded that "Lodge could hardly have done more to help Kennedy and hurt Nixon. Nixon had hoped to do as well in the South as Eisenhower had in 1956 . . . but immediately after Lodge's pledge the polls showed a sharp decline in Nixon's southern support."[43]

Nixon further lost a chance to win black votes by failing to react when Dr. Martin Luther King, Jr., was sent to a Georgia prison for a technical violation of a previously suspended sentence. Having adopted a more progressive civil rights position in a bid for the votes of northern blacks, he did nothing to follow up on it, while Lodge's unauthorized pledges had cost him many white votes in the South.

Kennedy also faced serious problems in the southern states. Kennedy's Catholicism was a clear political liability in a region where evangelical Protestants constituted the vast majority of the population. The entire structure of authority in Roman Catholicism, with its emphasis on hierarchical decision-making culminating in a single individual, the Pope of Rome, who was believed by Catholics to be infallible in matters of faith and doctrine, made little or no sense at all to most southern Protestants. Southern Baptists, the largest of the Protestant denominations, believed in the absolute separation of church and state. They were concerned about the freedom of Protestants to practice their faith in nations under Catholic control. More than 300,000 requests had been received in the summer of 1960 by the Southern Baptist Convention for a pamphlet entitled "Baptists, Roman Catholics, and Religious Freedom." Specifically, Protestants were skeptical that a Catholic president would give priority to the American national interest if it came into direct conflict with Catholic teachings. By late summer Kennedy was "being openly chastised from many a Protestant pulpit" in the South. In 1960 the skepticism of many Protestants about Catholic politicians would be hard to overcome in the South, where "over half of the Southern presidential vote" was "cast by Protestants who go to church regularly."[44]

When Kennedy came to Texas in September, he met these issues head on before the Houston Ministerial Association. He faced directly the complex issues of church and state and answered questions from the group of Protestants. It was on this occasion that Sam Rayburn got political religion about Jack Kennedy:

> "By God, look at him—and listen to him!" Rayburn shouted while he watched Kennedy tear into the ministers. "He's eating 'em blood raw! This young feller will be a great President!" The next day at Austin and Dallas, Rayburn delivered a hot and fiery speech for Kennedy, hailing him as the greatest Northern Democrat since Franklin D. Roosevelt. "And you people who complain about income taxes," Rayburn yelled

at the Texans, "you should remember that you didn't have any incomes to pay a tax on before Roosevelt came into office."[45]

Kennedy's next boost in the South came at the end of September after the first television debate. The broadcast had an immediate impact upon nine Democratic southern governors, who saw the debate at the annual Southern Governors Conference in Hot Springs, Arkansas, and then congratulated Kennedy by telegram.[46]

In the difficult area of civil rights, Kennedy emphasized to the nation his determination to demonstrate positive leadership. During the second debate, he said that his handling of the Little Rock school desegregation crisis would have been far different from Eisenhower's. Challenged by Nixon to address civil rights when campaigning in the South, Kennedy told a Columbia crowd that Nixon's own statements shifted from region to region. "Up North he talks about legislation. Down here he emphasizes that 'laws alone are not the answer,'" Kennedy charged. "Up there he stresses how quickly he will act in this area. Down here he says, 'I know this is a difficult problem.'" Nixon, Kennedy believed, was "not fooling anyone, North or South." As Kennedy elaborated his own position, he followed Johnson's advice and spoke to the southern audience in terms of "constitutional rights":

> I think it is clear that if we are to have progress in this area—and we must have progress, to be true to our own ideals and responsibilities— then Presidential leadership is necessary so that every American can enjoy his full Constitutional rights and opportunities as an American.
>
> Some of you may disagree with my view, but at least I have not changed my principles in an election year. I have supported this view in all parts of the country, just as I did in Atlanta and Jackson, Mississippi.[47]

Like Nixon, Kennedy pursued the votes of southern whites and northern blacks. His closest political advisors wanted him to avoid any statements that would alienate white Democratic officeholders in the South. Kennedy's phone call to Coretta Scott King expressing sympathy for her husband's imprisonment came at the suggestion of his civil rights advisors and, in due course, became tremendously important in the black community in showing that Kennedy cared about Dr. King. Within the campaign, itself, though, many of the advisors thought it had been a costly mistake. When he learned of it, Robert Kennedy exploded in anger. "With fists tight, his blue eyes cold, he turned on us," wrote Harris Wofford, the main advisor on civil rights matters. "Do you know that three Southern governors told us that if Jack supported Jimmy Hoffa, Nikita Khrushchev, or Martin Luther King, they would throw their states to Nixon? Do you know that this election may be razor close and you have probably lost it for us?"[48]

In October Johnson came alive as a positive force for the Democrats in the South. The Texas senator and his wife Lady Bird boarded the "LBJ Victory Special" in Virginia for a railroad swing through eight southern states (Virginia, North Carolina, Florida, and all of the Deep South). During the trip Johnson "shed all of his preconvention pretence of being a Westerner, not a Southerner" and "campaigned as 'the grandson of a Confederate soldier.'" *Newsweek* reported that "the deeper it went, the thicker Lyndon B. Johnson's drawl seemed to get. 'God bless you, Culpeper, vote Democratic,' he cried in Virginia. 'God bless you, Orange. God bless you, Lexington.' 'Ah wish ah could stay and do a little sippin' and whittlin' with you,' he told the good folks in Rocky Bottom, South Carolina. A thousand times Johnson referred to 'Mah grandpappy' and 'Mah great grandpappy,' to remind Southerners he was one of them."[49]

Johnson was doing more than playing "The Yellow Rose of Texas" at every stop. To "crowds that grew from hundreds in Virginia to thousands down the line," Johnson praised Kennedy, excoriated Nixon, and pleaded for respect for Kennedy's Catholicism. He southernized the civil rights issue for whites, telling them that "Under Jack Kennedy, the Democratic party will guarantee the constitutional rights of every American, no matter what his race, religion, or—what section of the country he comes from." During the trip more than 1,200 southern Democratic politicians came on board to endorse the Kennedy-Johnson ticket, even if many also distanced themselves from the civil rights provisions of the Democratic party platform. "The real business," *Newsweek* reported, "was done by the Senate Majority Leader in eyeball-to-eyeball conversations with the senators and congressmen and governors and other politicos who have it in their power, if anybody does, to sway the South."[50]

The Kennedy-Johnson campaign in Texas was always in doubt. Not only were large numbers of conservatives in revolt, but scars remained among liberal Democrats whom Johnson had treated brutally in winning control of the state Democratic party in 1956. In a "personal and confidential" communication to John Connally, Johnson asked for his "best thoughts" on carrying Texas. "We just must not win the nation and lose Texas," Johnson wrote. "Imagine how the next administration will look upon us."[51]

In the closing days of the campaign, Kennedy pulled ahead among southern whites and blacks. For blacks, the shift away from the Republicans (most of the few blacks who had voted in the South had supported Eisenhower in 1956) to the Democrats was symbolized by Rev. Martin Luther King, Sr., who had earlier announced his intention to vote for Nixon because he could not support a Catholic candidate. After Kennedy's phone call to Mrs. King and his son's subsequent release from a Georgia prison, he switched to Kennedy and used his influence to get other blacks to vote for the Democratic ticket.

Within the South, the NES survey reported that the Kennedy-Johnson ticket won 52 percent of the white vote and a majority of the small black vote. The Democrats did much better among whites native to the region, winning 58 percent, compared with only one-fifth of the much smaller group of whites who had migrated to the South. Kennedy's Catholicism did hurt among southerners. Kennedy ran 17 percentage points behind the "normal Democratic presidential vote" of southern whites. Defections from the Democratic ticket were highest among southern white Protestants who attended church regularly or often.[52]

The Kennedy-Johnson ticket led in seven southern states (Alabama, Georgia, Louisiana, and South Carolina in the Deep South, Arkansas, North Carolina, and Texas in the Peripheral South), the Nixon-Lodge ticket carried three Peripheral South states (Florida, Tennessee, and Virginia), and Mississippi gave a plurality to electors pledged to Harry Byrd of Virginia. In each of the states carried by Kennedy and Johnson, most state and local Democratic politicians and officeholders endorsed the ticket. Grantham concluded that "Kennedy was popular among many southerners; his stand on civil rights appeared moderate, he was dynamic and eloquent, and he seemed to have a genuine interest in the South." All this was not enough, however, and he could not have carried these states without the aid of Johnson. "Not only did Johnson's moderate record and southern background reassure the region's whites," Grantham wrote, "but his strenuous campaign and strong influence among southern Democratic leaders made an indispensable contribution to his party's victory."[53]

In the winner-take-all system, it is easy to lose sight of the closeness of the contests. In 1960, for the third straight time, the Republican ticket was highly competitive in the Peripheral South. Nixon carried Tennessee, Virginia, and Florida, and he ran extremely close races in Texas, North Carolina, and South Carolina. In the two largest states, Kennedy lost Florida by only 45,000 votes and won Texas by merely 46,000 votes. The vice-president was not competitive in Alabama, Arkansas, Georgia, Louisiana, and Mississippi. Only in South Carolina, where former Governor Byrnes championed Nixon, did the Republican vote sharply increase; and only in Louisiana, where Kennedy's Catholicism was helpful in South Louisiana, did the Republican vote dramatically fall. Mississippi repudiated both major parties in favor of a slate of unpledged electors.[54]

"This impressive Republican showing," thought Grantham, "was in part the result of the party's strong campaign throughout the region. But it also reflected the accumulating distrust of the national Democratic party felt by many white southerners, a distrust that was exacerbated by the civil rights movement and by Kennedy's Catholicism."[55] Across the region Nixon ran only three points behind Eisenhower's 1956 vote (46 versus 49 percent), but this modest loss in the popular vote generated a much greater loss in electoral votes. Nixon captured only three of the five southern states Eisenhower had won in 1956, and he failed to carry any state that Eisenhower had lost.

Eisenhower won 52 percent of the southern electoral votes in 1956; Nixon captured only 26 percent in 1960. Nixon's southern failure in the electoral college—only Gerald Ford's 9 percent in 1976 was worse among post-1948 Republicans—meant that he needed 58 percent of the northern electoral vote. Kennedy's strong performance in the South—he secured 63 percent of the electoral vote, only six points behind Truman in 1948—reduced the Democrats' northern electoral vote target to 46 percent. Kennedy actually won 54 percent. Although almost identical to Truman's showing, Kennedy's electoral vote was based far more on the Northeast and far less on the West (see Table 7.1).

The Johnson Landslide of 1964

In 1964 Lyndon Johnson crushed Barry Goldwater in the biggest landslide election since Roosevelt's defeat of Alf Landon in 1936. Johnson's victory came as no surprise to anyone, including the rivals themselves. "If the Republicans nominate Goldwater, and it looks like the damn fools are going to do it," President Johnson told an aide in the spring of 1964, "we'll sweep every part of the country, even New York." Goldwater knew even at the time of his nomination that he could not be elected president.[56] The contest, virtually all observers agree, was not over which candidate would win but how large Johnson's popular vote would be and how many states he would carry.

Part of the explanation for Johnson's victory consisted in the prevailing political conditions. "The prospects were poor for a close race by any Republican candidate in 1964," wrote Stanley Kelley, Jr., "because any Republican candidate was fated to run against a popular incumbent President of the majority party in a time of relative peace and prosperity." Johnson was also helped by Goldwater's conspicuous liabilities. Goldwater was a "minority candidate of a minority party," well to the right of most Americans on many important issues. In addition, Goldwater's habit of giving flip answers to serious questions multiplied doubts about his judgment. A Goldwater activist, Stephen Shadegg, acknowledges that by September, in the eyes of the public, Goldwater "was now the dangerous radical, the advocate of drastic change, the proponent of policies which might take the nation into a nuclear war, alter the domestic economy, destroy Social Security, and bring an abrupt halt to the program of federal farm subsidy."[57]

Lyndon Johnson, of all politicians, knew how to make the most of this promising situation. In August he met with his principal campaign advisors. "'You fellows are the experts,' he said, 'but this is how I see it. I'm the president. That's our greatest asset. And I don't want to piss it away by getting down in the mud with Barry.'" Johnson compared Goldwater's predicament to that of a man trapped in a fire on the third story of a building with a rope tied around his waist: "Now Barry's already got a rope around him, and he's knotted it pretty firm. All you have to do is give a little tug. And while he's fighting to keep standing, I'll just sit right here and run the country." Richard N. Goodwin comments: "And so we had a strategy. Translated into more conventional political terms it meant that we would open the campaign with an assault designed to put Goldwater on the defensive, and then, as he struggled to extricate himself, withdraw to the high ground of constructive statesmanship."[58]

The Johnson campaign's television attacks devastated Goldwater with powerful, emotionally charged imagery. In one riveting advertisement a small girl in a field of daisies dissolved into a nuclear mushroom cloud, while an anonymous voice told viewers, "Vote for President Johnson on November third. The stakes are too high for you to stay home." Another commercial showed a pair of hands—presumably Goldwater's—tearing a Social Security card into pieces. The spots unforgettably associated Goldwater with nuclear devastation and destruction of the Social Security system. They gave millions of voters several things to fear from a Goldwater presidency, and they forced Goldwater repeatedly to explain his positions.[59]

While Goldwater struggled to minimize defections from Republican ranks, Johnson accentuated the positive to the vast majority of the potential electorate—Democrats, independents, and Republicans worried about Goldwater. "And I just want to tell you this," the president announced to a massive crowd of enthusiastic supporters in Rhode Island, "we're in favor of a lot of things and we're against mighty few."[60] The remarks, captured by Theodore H. White, epitomized Johnson's approach to the voters.

In several respects Johnson treated Goldwater as if he were a Texas Republican in the 1950s. He almost never uttered Goldwater's name in public, and he refused to debate the specifics of any issue his opponent raised. Earlier in the spring, Johnson had confided to Goodwin his belief that the American electorate had little interest in political debate. "'What the man on the street wants is not a big debate on the fundamental issues," he said. "He wants a little medical care, a rug on the floor, a picture on the wall, a little music in the house, and a place to take Molly and the grandchildren when he retires.'"[61]

This perspective ruled out a philosophical debate with Goldwater, but it did allow Johnson to portray his opponent as an unstable radical who would threaten to take away what the average citizen now took for granted from the federal government. In a televised address to the nation, President Johnson said that, "We are now told that we, the people, acting through government, should withdraw from education, from public power, from agriculture, [and] from urban renewal." Social Security, TVA, labor unions, and farm programs would all be endangered by a Goldwater presidency. Then the president underscored the essential political point: "This is a radical departure from the historic and basic currents of American thought and action. It would shatter the foundation on which our hopes for the future rest."[62]

With these decided advantages, it was no surprise that, outside the South, Johnson carried every state except Goldwater's Arizona.

In state after state Johnson won huge percentages of the popular vote. He took virtually all of the northern black vote and added large majorities of the northern white vote. According to the 1964 NES survey of white voters outside the South, Johnson received 91 percent of the vote cast by Democrats, 69 percent from independents, and 27 percent from Republicans. In northern and western states the 1964 contest was a runaway Democratic victory.

Matters were very different in the South, however. It *was* surprising that Johnson captured most of the southern electoral college votes despite his prominent leadership in passing the Civil Rights Act of 1964. We estimate that President Johnson won only about 45 percent of the vote cast by white southerners. The vote for Johnson varied markedly in the two subregions of the South. In the Deep South, where he received all of the very small black vote but only 29 percent of the white vote, Johnson was soundly defeated in every state. In the Peripheral South, where the president attracted virtually all of a much larger black vote, as well as an estimated 51 percent of the white vote, he won by comfortable margins in each state. The dynamics of the Goldwater-Johnson contest in the Deep South turned primarily on federal intervention in race relations, while white voters in the Peripheral South went to the polls with more than civil rights on their minds. How Johnson checkmated Goldwater in the Peripheral South in 1964 is an absorbing story, still worth pondering by Democratic presidential candidates who aspire to win southern states.

When conservatives began their efforts in 1961 to nominate Goldwater as the next Republican presidential candidate, President Kennedy was always assumed to be the Arizona Senator's opponent. Goldwater had stumped the South in 1960 on behalf of Richard Nixon. "Don't kid yourself that Jack Kennedy has any love for the South," he told voters. "Don't vote for the Democrats just because your grandfather did. Vote Republican! Just try it once—you've no idea how good you'll feel in the morning."[63] Public opinion polls of the South showed Kennedy faring poorly in 1963. The Goldwater strategists expected to sweep the entire South by offering the region a clear contrast between a northern liberal and a southwestern conservative.

President Kennedy's assassination and the elevation of Johnson to the presidency fundamentally altered the Republicans' chances of carrying all of the southern states. As time passed, the implications for Goldwater's electoral college majority began to trouble F. Clifton

White, who realized that "the whole strategy upon which our campaign to elect Goldwater had been based would now have to be changed. With Lyndon Johnson as President, we could no longer count on capturing the entire South, and particularly the key state of Texas."[64]

Yet Republican strategists were encouraged when Johnson assumed leadership of the fight to pass the Civil Rights Act. The President's reported remark about losing the South (see Chapter 1) was uttered in the immediate aftermath of the passage of the Civil Rights Act of 1964. In August the conventional wisdom was that Goldwater could indeed sweep the South. "The pollsters, the political experts, and the politicians are all saying the same thing about Dixie," wrote *Newsweek*'s columnist Kenneth Crawford. "If the election were held today, they tell us, Barry Goldwater would top Lyndon Johnson in popular vote and walk off with the larger share of the electoral vote of the Old South. At this point not a single state once part of the Confederacy is completely safe for the South's first President since Andrew Johnson." Crawford continued: "There is no great mystery about the reason for this phenomenon. Mr. Johnson has recently pushed through Congress and signed the most comprehensive civil-rights bill ever enacted. Goldwater voted against this bill. . . . So the South appears to have concluded that Mr. Johnson is a turncoat and Goldwater is the man who can save its celebrated 'way of life.'"[65]

As the fall campaign began, the official Republican electoral college strategy still gave great emphasis to the entire South. "On the walls of the various Goldwater headquarters could be seen the maps that plotted this strategy," wrote Theodore White. "Goldwater planners began with the South: they would need to have, and they believed they would have, all eleven states of the Old Confederacy, with a Southern base of 127 electoral votes." There was some realistic basis for initial Republican optimism about the South. Surveys done in mid-September for the Republican National Committee indicated the Johnson administration was most vulnerable in the South. Only 35 percent of the southerners surveyed rated the Johnson administration's performance as excellent or good, and 51 percent evaluated it as only fair or poor. In every other region of the nation, however, large majorities thought the Johnson administration was doing a good or excellent job—an ominous sign for Goldwater.[66]

Goldwater's prospects in the Peripheral South deteriorated during the campaign, in part because of Johnson's skillful presentation of the relevant issues, in part because of Goldwater's awesomely inept campaigning. One example illustrates how Johnson appealed to southerners in the Peripheral South. Before an overflow, enthusiastic audience at the North Carolina State basketball arena in Raleigh, the president gave a southern version of "we're in favor of a lot of things and we're against mighty few." Johnson "made his prepared speech, which was about the Democratic farm program, and then he laid that aside and made another speech, which was about everything," wrote Charles McDowell, Jr. "He could not let the audience go until he had told it all about high corporate profits, high wages, the fight against air pollution, the increased freedom and prosperity of most Americans under a Democratic administration, the military power of the country, his efforts at economy in government, his high opinion of North Carolina statesmen, and his conviction that everyone was going to reason together then get along together and love one another."[67]

By late September public opinion polls revealed a close election within the region, a far different picture from the August surveys. The issues of peace and prosperity were working in Johnson's favor, according to a Louis Harris poll for *Newsweek.* "Goldwater would sweep the South if the election hinged solely on the issue of civil rights; under those conditions, analyst Harris estimates his victory margin would be at least 60 percent. But on virtually all other key campaign issues, Harris reports, Southerners prefer the President to Goldwater. Thus, Southern voters, by margins of 3 to 2, feel Mr. Johnson can best keep the U.S. out of war, work for peace, handle Khrushchev, or respond to a sudden world crisis. If keeping the economy healthy were the determining factor, Southerners would back Mr. Johnson by 57 to 43 percent."[68]

Johnson did not back off from pro–civil rights positions in the South, but he generally emphasized the more popular aspects of his administration's record, while continuously raising questions about his (usually unnamed) rival's positions, judgment, and reliability. He portrayed Goldwater as a reckless and unpredictable candidate who might plunge the nation into nuclear war. "We live no more in the age of the cavalry charge," Johnson said in a Tennessee speech ridiculing his opponent's foreign policy. A nuclear war between the United States and Russia, he argued, would produce 200 million deaths. Campaigning in South Carolina, Johnson said Goldwater had offered "the most radical proposals that have ever been made to the American people."[69]

As a consistent right-wing ideologue, Goldwater faced many practical liabilities in winning votes. Goldwater wanted to campaign as an "honest politician," one who did not trim his views to fit the conventional wisdom of local audiences. He wanted to provide voters with a choice by emphasizing his differences with the Johnson administration on a wide range of policies. However, since many of the policies he criticized were supported by large majorities of the electorate, Goldwater's public statements—as well as the Johnson campaign's versions of Goldwater's positions—sent shock waves through the segments of the population affected by the programs he wanted to modify or abolish. As a method of winning votes, his candor often had the opposite effect. Goldwater's approach amounted to giving citizens quite a few reasons to vote against him.

One prime example of an issue that hurt Goldwater in the Peripheral South was his position on the Tennessee Valley Authority, a New Deal institution that had helped to industrialize Tennessee and sections of adjacent states. Goldwater had long opposed the TVA because of "a clear conservative principle. Washington shouldn't intrude in the private sector and be competing with companies and citizens who already support it through taxation." As Goldwater saw it, TVA "was a big fat sacred New Deal cow" that should be sold off to private power companies. "You would have thought I had just shot Santa Claus," Goldwater later wrote in describing the firestorm of criticism that greeted his suggestion to sell off the institution. "Democrats and Republicans, senior citizens and schoolchildren—all wrote letters defending their empire. The Tennessee Valley was Goldwater Country, but from a conservative viewpoint the statement had to be made. Otherwise, we'd be just an echo of the Democrats—and some fellow Republicans."[70]

The public controversy from this episode, which had begun while Goldwater was seeking the party nomination, had prompted one of his Texas backers, conservative Republican Peter O'Donnell, to criticize Goldwater in a confidential memorandum. According to Clifton White, "The memo took Goldwater to task for 'shooting from the hip' and cited the TVA business. Peter said it was 'an example of kicking a sleeping dog.'" O'Donnell further warned Goldwater that "a series of TVA-type statements could greatly weaken your position. For instance, TVA puts your supporters in an important area on the defensive."[71] Goldwater's loyalists in Tennessee now had the impossible task of explaining to their friends and neighbors why they should vote for a politician who had promised to sell one of the key federal institutions in the state, a source of employment to thousands of Tennesseans. Republican presidential candidates had carried Tennessee in three straight elections, but Goldwater lost to Johnson, 44 to 56, in 1964.

In many respects the Goldwater campaign in the Peripheral South amounted to a series of "TVA-type statements" in which the candidate gave voters in several states specific reasons to vote against him. In Florida, *Time* reported, "Goldwater looked like an easy winner. Then he criticized Social Security in a state full of retired people, [and] derided the moon race despite heavy U.S. space-spending in Florida." Although Florida had twice voted for Eisenhower and once for Nixon, Johnson narrowly won Florida's popular vote, 51 to 49 percent. North Carolina had stayed with the Democrats in the three previous elections, but early in the campaign, Goldwater appeared to be ahead. Goldwater then attacked federal price supports for tobacco in a Raleigh appearance, whereas Johnson had used the occasion of his own Raleigh visit to discuss his administration's agricultural policies. In North Carolina, "Goldwater's farm views helped kill his early lead."[72] Johnson beat Goldwater by 12 points, 56 to 44 percent. In Texas, Eisenhower had twice carried the state, and the Democrats had only narrowly won in 1960. In 1964, with virtually all factions of the Democratic party supporting their native son, Johnson buried Goldwater, 63 to 37 percent, and won by over 704,000 votes.

While Johnson's skillful campaigning induced many whites to vote Democratic, the candidates' contrasting positions on the Civil Rights Act brought virtually all blacks who voted to the Democrats. "We campaigned very heavily not only for President Johnson but against Goldwater," Andrew Young told Merle Miller. "We really weren't looking too hard at President Johnson. We were just scared to death of Goldwater." The Democratic party benefited from the expanding, biracial electorate. Blacks had made much greater progress in penetrating voting booths in the Peripheral South than in the Deep South. In three states of the Peripheral South nearly half of eligible blacks were registered to vote—Arkansas (49 percent), North Carolina (47), and Virginia (46)—while in three other states, more than half of blacks were on the registration books—Tennessee (69), Florida (64), and Texas (58).[73]

The Johnson-Goldwater contest in the southern states sketched a variety of possible outcomes of presidential contests in biracial electorates. Goldwater carried only those southern states in which he managed to attract landslide majorities of the white vote. As discussed in the previous chapter, all of these were Deep South states where more than half of the potential black voters remained unregistered in 1964. Goldwater prevailed in the electorates which most resembled the old southern politics, where the winner was automatically the candidate who received the majority of the white vote. Among the Peripheral South states, a different sort of politics was emerging in which the white majority no longer necessarily determined the winner. In Florida and Virginia, Goldwater clearly won a majority of the white vote yet lost because Johnson captured all of the growing black vote plus a sufficiently large minority of whites. Democratic presidential candidates no longer needed a majority of the white vote to win if they could receive virtually all of the black vote. Indeed, Democratic candidates could win substantial victories—55 percent of the popular vote—by taking all the black vote and splitting the white vote, as occurred in Arkansas, North Carolina, and Tennessee. And a Democratic presidential candidate might win a tremendous landslide, as Johnson did in Texas with 63 percent of the vote, by polling all of the black vote, most of the Hispanic vote, and a clear majority of the white vote.

The NES sample of southern whites in 1964 allows us to take the analysis a step further. There are some drawbacks in the survey, for it understates Goldwater's strength among southern whites. According to our estimates, Goldwater received about 55 percent of the southern white vote, whereas the NES survey shows only 45 percent supporting Goldwater—far too low, given what we know of the actual popular votes. On the other hand, the level of Goldwater support in the NES survey is only four points lower than what we estimate Goldwater received among Peripheral South whites (49 percent), and we think the ten-state sample is a reasonable approximation of public opinion in the Peripheral South in 1964.

Goldwater's fundamental problem in the Peripheral South, the NES data suggest, is that not enough whites were "Goldwater conservatives," much less "Goldwater Republicans." On some racial issues, vast majorities of southern whites favored conservative positions. About seven of every ten southern whites felt that the federal government should stay out of the questions of desegregating places of public accommodations, schools, and jobs. Nearly nine of every ten southern whites thought that the civil rights movement was proceeding too fast and were opposed to the use of busing to achieve racial balance in schools. Majorities of southern whites also agreed with Goldwater's position that state governments, not the federal government, should provide aid to education. Goldwater's emphasis on individual responsibility presumably could resonate with the large majority (62 percent) of southern whites who believed that the individual, not the government in Washington, is primarily responsible for his or her own economic well-being.

In other policy areas, however, Goldwater's positions were *not* supported by majorities of white southerners. The Arizona senator repudiated most of the Johnson administration's conduct of foreign policy, but only 38 percent of white southerners thought the nation's foreign policy was not being well administered, while 47 percent approved of the performance of the administration. Goldwater was strongly opposed to an increased role for the federal government in helping pay for medical care for the elderly, but only 42 percent of southern whites were opposed to Medicare and 50 percent supported it.

Goldwater did best among those white southerners who held conservative positions on the various issues. Philip Converse, Aage Clausen, and Warren Miller correctly argued that "civil rights, while the primary issue in the South, was not the only one. Beyond civil rights, Southerners reacted negatively to the Goldwater positions much as their fellow citizens elsewhere. Many Southern white respondents said in effect: 'Goldwater is right on the black man, and that is very important. But he is wrong on everything else. I can't bring myself to vote for him.'"[74]

Among racially conservative southern whites, support for Goldwater varied according to their positions on other issues of domestic and foreign policy. The indicator of racial feelings that most sharply distinguished Goldwater voters was hostility toward the National Association for the Advancement of Colored People. In 1964, 63 percent of the southern whites surveyed were cold toward the NAACP, and 55 percent of this large group reported a Goldwater vote. Of the southern whites who were neutral or warm toward the NAACP, only one-third voted for Goldwater. Among the southern whites cold toward the NAACP, support for Goldwater varied enormously depending upon the respondents' views on matters of foreign and domestic policy. Goldwater support soared to 86 percent among those cold to the NAACP *and* hostile to the Johnson administration's foreign policy, but dropped to only 15 percent among southern whites opposed to the NAACP but supportive of the Johnson administration's conduct of foreign affairs.

Attitudes about Medicare also were linked to the degree of support Goldwater drew from racially conservative southern whites. The Arizona senator drew only 43 percent among the racially conservative whites who believed that the federal government should subsidize medical care for the elderly, but won 75 percent from those who were hostile toward the NAACP *and* who felt the federal government should not help subsidize medical care for the elderly. Similarly, Goldwater was held to 38 percent of the vote among racial conservatives who also believed that the federal government had primary responsibility for seeing that individuals had a good job and standard of living, but his support increased to 68 among those who were racially conservative *and* who also believed that the individual, not the government, had primary responsibility for his or her own economic well being.

The modern Republicanism championed by Eisenhower and Nixon from 1952 through 1960 had its greatest appeal among the white upper and middle classes in the region's expanding cities and suburbs. Geographically, Republican victories in these elections were concentrated in the Peripheral South, which accounted for 11 out of 12 state victories. Barry Goldwater's 1964 campaign, which we have previously discussed as an example of a racial protest candidacy, clearly marked a new direction for Republican efforts in the South. Goldwater became the Republicans' ideal breakthrough candidate in the Deep South. Unfortunately for the Republicans, Goldwater's policies on other domestic and foreign matters divided whites in the Peripheral South. As a result Goldwater ran strongest in the southern states where Eisenhower and Nixon had run weakest, and vice versa. The 1964 vote split exactly along subregional lines. Goldwater carried every Deep South state and lost every Peripheral South state. Although Goldwater won more southern electoral votes than Nixon (37 versus 26 percent), Johnson captured the same percentage of the regional vote (63) as Kennedy. And since Johnson won even larger shares of the other regions' electoral vote (especially in the West) than did Kennedy, the 1964 election was a Democratic landslide (see Table 7.1).

Although the Goldwater movement was a colossal failure nationally, Goldwater's unvarnished conservatism had considerable success in the South, even in states Goldwater failed to carry. Goldwater was the first Republican presidential nominee to make opposition to racial change—symbolized by Goldwater's criticism of the Civil Rights Act of 1964—a central element in his appeal to conservative white southerners. If the Republicans could position themselves as the more conservative of the major parties on race while keeping their middle- and upper-class base, it might be possible to win sufficiently large white majorities to carry most southern states. In that case they would be far less dependent upon winning a large majority of the northern electoral vote.

For Republican strategists, there was much to ponder in the southern returns. For the first time in American history, the Republican party had won a greater percentage of the popular vote in the South than in any other region. The thousands of conservative activists who had been brought into politics by the Goldwater movement had not abandoned the cause, and the southern Republican party began to appear more promising than the Democratic party as an institution they might influence and perhaps control.

IV

Modern Presidential Politics

8

The New Southern Electorate

The South has experienced more change in the size and composition of its voting population than any other part of the nation. Differences in participation patterns between the South and the North have sometimes been so fundamental that the South seemed to be a separate, and embarrassingly undemocratic, political system. At other times southern participation rates have closely paralleled trends elsewhere. There is perhaps no better way to evaluate political participation in the modern South than by comparing it with previous points in history and with practices in the rest of the nation.

As the size of the presidential electorate has varied, so has the makeup of the region's voters. Originally the southern electorate was composed entirely of white males, who found much to differ about despite their common race and gender. After the Civil War the electorate broadened to include black men. But since most southern whites considered blacks an inferior and illegitimate political force, white Democratic leaders obliterated black voting rights as quickly as conditions permitted. Violence and repression reinforced laws and constitutional provisions in discouraging black participation. In the 1920s white women secured the right to vote, but decades of litigation, civil rights protest, and eventual federal intervention were needed to reopen the electoral system to black men and women. Today the southern electorate is more diversified than ever before.

The Modest Expansion of the Modern Southern Electorate

Contemporary trends in voter participation can best be appreciated by comparing them with voting patterns in previous eras in American history. The election of 1828, the first contest in which a majority of eligible Americans voted for president, provides an appropriate point of departure for comparisons of turnout between the South and the rest of the nation. From 1828 through 1988, the South has *always* lagged behind the rest of the nation in the degree to which its citizens have cast presidential ballots (see Figure 8.1). However, the participation gap between the South and the North has varied enormously over time.[1]

In 1828 more than half of the North's men voted in the presidential election, an achievement not reached in the South until 1840. Over the next two decades, substantial majorities of white men in both regions regularly voted for president. "Before secession in 1860–61," Walter Dean Burnham has observed, "the South's electorate was only somewhat less participant than that outside the region." Although the South never led the nation in turnout, it did not lag much behind the North. The antebellum era presents the picture of a politically engaged and participant white South. Regional political disputes climaxed, of course, in 1860. The stakes in that presidential election

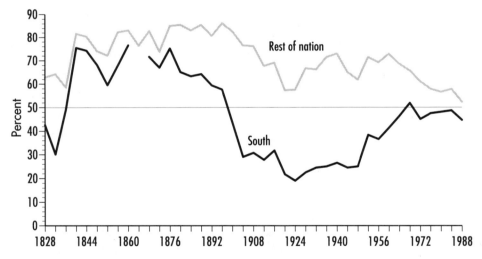

Figure 8.1 Turnout in presidential elections in the South and the rest of the nation, 1828–1988: estimated percentage of voting-age population casting a vote. *Sources:* Walter Dean Burnham, "The Turnout Problem," in A. James Reichley, ed., *Elections American Style* (Washington, D.C.: Brookings Institution, 1987), pp. 113–114; and Harold W. Stanley and Richard G. Niemi, *Vital Statistics on American Politics*, 2d ed. (Washington, D.C.: CQ Press, 1990), p. 79. Harold W. Stanley graciously provided turnout data for 1988.

were so monumental and threatening that record turnouts (an estimated 83 percent of northern white men and 77 percent of southern
white men) occurred in both regions. Almost total regional polarization characterized the election. In the free states Abraham Lincoln
led the Republicans to victory. The slave states divided their votes
between John C. Breckenridge, the candidate of the Southern Democratic party, and John Bell, the nominee of the Constitutional Union
party, while virtually ignoring both Lincoln and Stephen Douglas,
the candidate of the regular Democratic party. Never before had such
high turnout in both regions been associated with such diametrically
opposed results in the South and the North. Secession and war soon
followed.[2]

After the Civil War, over the strenuous protests of many whites,
the southern electorate expanded to include black men. For approximately three decades after the war, both whites and blacks voted in
presidential elections. Whites in some states—especially in the Deep
South—began to reduce black voting after federal troops left the
region, and the southern presidential electorate gradually contracted
between 1876 and 1896. The "shaping" of pure one-party politics in
the South occurred roughly between 1890 and 1910. Southern state
governments either revised their election laws or wrote new state
constitutions giving local white officials fairly complete control over
voter registration. Poll taxes, literacy tests, and subjective tests of
"understanding" were among the formal devices used to sabotage
the letter and spirit of the Fifteenth Amendment of the Constitution.
In some areas intimidation and violence reinforced the new legali-
ties.[3]

Although black men were the main targets of disfranchisement,
the conservative Democrats who led the movement also wanted to
remove many whites with Populist sympathies. When the southern
Democrats' "reactionary revolution" was finished, most blacks and
about half of the whites had been eliminated as voters. In 1896 nearly
three-fifths of southerners voted for president. During the next eight
years participation fell like a rock thrown off a mountain top. By 1904
only three of every ten male southerners of voting age voted in
presidential elections. Nonparticipation became the new southern
electoral tradition. With Democrats controlling every southern state,
with only a token Republican presence, and with Democratic presidential candidates favored so reliably that they did not even need to
set foot in the region, neither the many Democrats nor the few
Republicans had much incentive to vote in presidential elections.[4]

From 1904 through 1948 turnout in the South averaged only about *one-fourth* of the voting-age population. Turnout waxed and waned outside the South, yet normally well over three-fifths of the potential voters participated in presidential elections. Southern participation rates generally trailed those of the North by more than 40 percentage points. Within a supposedly democratic nation, the South stood out as an undemocratic anomaly.[5]

The presidential election of 1952 was a major turning point in the expansion of the modern southern electorate. Some 8.6 million southerners, or 38 percent of the voting-age population, cast ballots in the battle between Adlai Stevenson and Dwight Eisenhower. Eisenhower won more than three times as many votes as previous Republican candidates, and his share of the southern popular vote (48 percent) indicated a genuine competitiveness with the Democrats. During the 1960s the civil rights movement and new federal voting rights legislation motivated many blacks to enter the electorate. Stimulated by a variety of factors, however, an even greater number of whites began to vote. Some 51 percent of the southern voting-age population took part in the 1968 presidential election, the highest participation rate achieved in the South during this century. The three competing presidential candidates offered incentives to a wide spectrum of southern voters. Richard Nixon appealed to middle-class whites, George Wallace excited working-class and lower-middle-class whites, and Hubert Humphrey attracted blacks and a small group of loyal Democratic whites.[6]

Since 1968 southern turnout rates have fluctuated several points shy of a majority. The lowering of the voting age to 18, coupled with the elimination of George Wallace as a candidate and the apparent runaway victory of Richard Nixon, reduced the rate of turnout in 1972. After climbing gradually from 1976 to 1984, southern participation again dropped sharply in 1988. According to estimates made by Harold W. Stanley and Richard G. Niemi, only 45 percent of voting-age southerners voted in 1988, the region's lowest turnout rate since 1964. Although turnout in the modern South is substantially higher than it was during the first half of the century, one abiding characteristic of the region's electorate is that most southerners still pass up the opportunity to vote. The region is now much closer to national standards of turnout, in no small measure because political participation in the rest of the nation has been declining since the early 1960s. Stanley and Niemi estimate that only 52 percent of Americans outside the South voted in the Bush-Dukakis contest.

In recent presidential elections the South has lagged about eight percentage points behind the northern turnout rate. Although the North and the South have not yet converged in their participation rates, the differences between the regions are no longer stark.[7]

The Composition of the New Southern Electorate

The South's traditionally small and almost totally white electorate has given way to a much larger biracial electorate. In 1952 only one-fifth of the South's voting-age blacks were registered to vote. According to the National Election Study, blacks accounted for merely 6 percent of southern voters in that year's presidential election. Blacks did not experience much progress in penetrating the southern electorate during the 1950s. Only 29 percent of eligible blacks were registered in 1960. Because of increased rates of participation by southern whites, blacks still comprised only 6 percent of the region's voters in the 1960 presidential election. Black voter registration was a primary objective of the civil rights movement, and by 1964 an estimated 43 percent of southern blacks were registered to vote. Majorities of blacks were registered in Florida, Tennessee, and Texas; and near majorities of blacks were registered in Arkansas, North Carolina, and Virginia. In every Deep South state, however, majorities of blacks remained *unregistered* prior to enforcement of the 1965 Voting Rights Act. The Voting Rights Act of 1965 was the final triggering event that brought blacks onto the registration rolls in each Deep South state. By 1968 the Voter Education Project estimated that majorities of voting-age blacks were registered in every southern state, a tremendous feat of voter mobilization when set against the region's history of white resistance to black participation.[8]

Impressive as the entry of blacks into the southern electorate has been, it is important to emphasize that whites still constitute most of the South's voters. In 1984 blacks comprised an estimated 17 percent of the South's registered voters. According to the CBS News/ New York Times Exit Poll of the 1988 presidential election, whites made up 83 percent of the southern electorate, while blacks accounted for 14 percent and Hispanics contributed 3 percent. There are about six times as many white voters as black voters in the southern electorate. Because majorities of southern whites and majorities of southern blacks have supported different presidential candidates since 1972, the numerical domination of whites among the region's voters has been of no small consequence in assisting Republican presidential candidates.[9]

In its racial composition, therefore, the modern southern electorate is both different from the past and similar to it. It is different because blacks participate in impressive numbers and whites no longer oppose black voting rights. The abiding continuity between the "old southern politics" and the "new southern politics" is that whites vastly outnumber blacks in the electorate. From 1880 onwards, presidential elections in the southern states have usually turned on which candidate won a majority of the white vote. By heavy majorities whites supported Democratic presidential candidates during the heyday of the Solid Democratic South. After the turbulence of the 1960s had dissipated, large white majorities delivered southern states to Republican presidential candidates in five of the six elections between 1972 and 1988. Only in 1976 was a Democratic presidential candidate able to win by constructing a biracial coalition of virtually all blacks and a sufficiently large minority of whites. The contracted white electorate produced safe Democratic majorities; the expanded biracial electorate has usually yielded Republican presidential victories.[10]

Before 1920 the southern presidential electorate was comprised principally of white males. The modern electorate is very different in term of race and gender. According to the CBS News/New York Times Exit Poll, in 1988 women were a narrow majority—52 percent—of southern voters. White females, who accounted for 43 percent of the southern electorate, were the single largest group of voters. Eight percent of the voters were black women, and another 2 percent were Hispanic females. Each of the three male groups contributed a smaller share of the vote than their female counterparts. White men, once the overwhelming majority of southern voters, made up 40 percent of the total, three points below white females. Black males made up 6 percent of the total electorate, two points lower than black females. Male Hispanics were about a percentage point behind female Hispanics. Thus far individuals have voted more along racial than gender lines, with the Republicans usually winning substantial majorities among both white men *and* white women.[11]

Most southerners, as we have seen, still do not vote in presidential elections. Of the minority who do vote, most are individuals in middle to upper income brackets, as well as individuals who have attended college. Two-thirds of the southern white voters had been exposed to a college education, as had slightly more than half of the southern black voters, according to the 1988 CBS News/New York

Times Exit Poll. Moreover, two-thirds of whites had family incomes of $25,000 or higher, as did 42 percent of black voters. Have-littles and have-nots, white and black, constitute relatively small segments of the region's voters.[12]

Voting Groups in the Southern Electorate

The central features of the presidential electorate in the modern South can be most readily grasped by exploring the political world view of four important groups of voters: blacks, core white Democrats, swing whites, and core white Republicans. As we showed in Chapter 1, each of these groups has provided a distinctive level of support for Republican presidential candidates in recent elections.

These four groups may be considered alternative building blocks for successful presidential campaigns. In each election the major parties strive to construct majority support out of the issues, concerns, and candidates of the day. Republican strategists have tried to expand the Republican base over time, win a majority of the swing voters, and induce substantial defections from the supposedly Democratic core vote. The Democratic presidential strategy has been to unite blacks and the white core Democrats and then attract enough white swing voters to constitute a majority. To understand the four groups' predispositions in presidential elections, we shall assess their feelings toward recent presidential candidates, their likes and dislikes concerning various political symbols, and their preferences on different public policies.

In this analysis we shall rely upon two different sets of surveys. The CBS News/New York Times Exit Polls of southern voters in the 1976–1988 presidential elections will be used to discuss the size and cohesion of the four voting groups, as well as to describe salient demographic features of each group. These exit polls, based upon questionnaires administered to representative samples of southern voters immediately after they had voted for president, are extraordinarily valuable instruments. Their main drawback is the relatively small number of questions asked of the respondents, a limitation inherent in the practical constraints of exit polling by news organizations. To describe more fully the political landscape of the various groups in the electorate, it is necessary to turn to a richer and more detailed set of surveys: the interviews with southern respondents from various National Election Study (NES) presidential-year surveys conducted by the Center for Political Studies of the University of

Michigan. Because of the small size of the regional samples in the NES surveys, our analysis is based upon all respondents, not simply voters.

We have analyzed blacks as a single group, while southern whites have been classified as core Democrats, core Republicans, or swing voters. To place the white respondents of the NES surveys in an appropriate category, we first used the respondents' reports of partisan self-identification to classify them as Democrat, Republican, or independent. We then examined their self-placement on an ideology scale. In the NES surveys respondents were given the following question: "We hear a lot of talk these days about liberals and conservatives. Here is a seven-point scale on which the political views that people might hold are arranged from extremely liberal to extremely conservative. Where would you place yourself on this scale, or haven't you thought much about this?" We classified individuals placing themselves at points 1, 2, or 3 as "liberal," those putting themselves at point 4 as "moderate," and those placing themselves at points 5, 6, or 7 as "conservative." Respondents who had not thought about the question, as well as those who could not place themselves on the continuum, were eliminated from any subsequent analyses. We then classified those white respondents with valid information on both partisanship and ideology into one of three possible categories: core Democrats (liberal and moderate Democrats plus liberal independents), core Republicans (all Republicans plus conservative independents), and the swing groups (conservative Democrats and moderate independents). We shall now show how each of these four major groups in the southern electorate has evaluated a wide variety of presidential candidates, political symbols, and public policy issues.

Core White Republicans

Republican success in the modern South has been based primarily upon the core white Republicans, the region's largest and most cohesive voting bloc. According to the CBS News/New York Times Exit Poll, in 1988 these whites accounted for 44 percent of the entire southern electorate and 53 percent of all southern white voters. Several indicators testify to the political homogeneity of the core white Republicans. Ninety-seven percent of the bedrock Republicans who said they had voted in 1984 recalled casting a ballot for Ronald Reagan, and 94 percent of them approved Reagan's performance as president. More than any other group, the white Republicans plus the conservative independents have collectively set the tone of the South's recent presidential elections.

Such overwhelming unity on behalf of Republican presidential candidates was not limited to Reagan (see Figure 8.2). NES surveys of the electorate have asked respondents to give "thermometer ratings" to various political objects, including presidential candidates. A score of 50 is an expression of indifference or neutrality toward the symbol or person being evaluated. Ratings higher than 50 signify warmth or friendliness toward the particular object, while ratings lower than 50 represent coldness or hostility toward the object. We

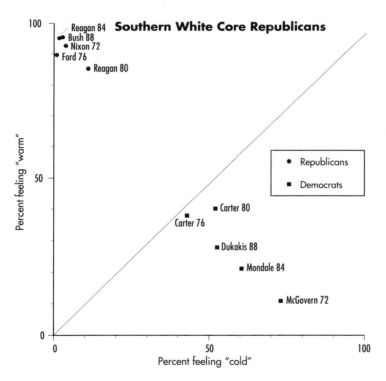

Figure 8.2 The polarized perceptions of southern white core Republicans: percentages of respondents who expressed "warm" and "cold" reactions to Democratic and Republican presidential candidates, 1972–1988. Scores of less than 50 are considered to be unfavorable and are classified as "cold"; scores greater than 50 are considered to be favorable and are classified as "warm." *Source:* NES presidential election year surveys, 1972–1988.

have calculated the percentage of respondents in each group who expressed either "warm" or "cold" evaluations toward the presidential candidates.

Southern core Republicans have consistently appraised presidential candidates along party lines. All five Republican presidential nominees from 1972 to 1988—bunched tightly together in the upper left-hand corner of Figure 8.2—elicited warm ratings from huge majorities of the core white Republicans. All of the Democrats were viewed negatively far more often than positively. With such consensus toward the Republican candidates, white core Republicans have simply repeated their standing decision in favor of the GOP presidential nominee. Spectacular ineptitude and gross policy failures under Republican auspices would probably be needed to induce these bedrock supporters to abandon a Republican presidential nominee in favor of a Democrat.

Underlying the core white Republicans' strong preference for Republican candidates is a broad conservatism in their beliefs and values. Figure 8.3 shows how core white Republicans have evaluated a series of symbolic and cultural objects (including questions about the importance of religion and three examples of the political culture, Edward Kennedy, Jesse Jackson, and Pat Robertson). Whenever possible, we expressed the percentage of respondents expressing favorable or unfavorable views toward these symbols as averages of results from the 1980, 1984, and 1988 surveys. We examined views toward the three politicians for years in which they actively sought their party's presidential nomination (Kennedy in 1980; Jackson in 1984 and 1988; and Robertson in 1988).[13]

The essential druthers of the core white Republicans appear in the positive and negative symbols that generate consensus. They feel exceptionally positive toward southerners, conservatives, the military, the importance of religion, and whites, all symbolic representations of the established order, as well as toward Republicans, the symbol of the emerging party of choice among college-educated, middle- and upper-class southern whites. Core white Republicans feel warmly toward southerners and are proud of the South, even though many may have been raised in other parts of the nation. A landslide majority is favorably disposed toward conservatives, with only a handful of dissenters. Their warmth toward Republicans is almost identical with that toward conservatives, suggesting congruence between the two in the eyes of these GOP supporters.

Several items—radical students, black militants, gays, Edward

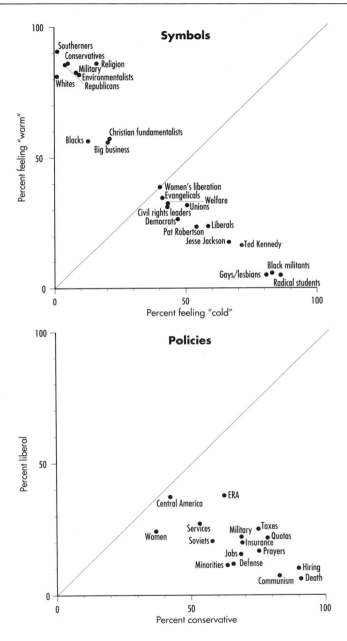

Figure 8.3 Symbols and policy positions of southern white core Republicans. *Source:* Same as Figure 8.2.

Kennedy, Jesse Jackson, Pat Robertson, and liberals—produced high negative consensus. To the core Republican whites, each of these groups or politicians represents extreme or unreasonable views. With the interesting exception of Robertson, all of the negative political symbols represent liberalism or left-wing politics. Core Republicans are especially cold toward racial boldness (Jackson and black militants), unorthodox and disturbing behavior (radical students, gays, liberals), and politicians who epitomize liberalism (Jackson and Kennedy). A Democratic party and Democratic presidential candidates visibly associated with these symbols and politicians become automatically discredited among these voters.

Pat Robertson, the Republican television preacher most identified with charismatic religion, is the one exception to the rule that this group favors conservative symbols. Although core white Republicans prize religion, quite a few of them regard some features of charismatic evangelism—speaking in tongues, praying a hurricane away from the Virginia coast—as embarrassing religious fanaticism. Considered "extreme" even by such fundamentalists (and rivals) as Jerry Falwell, Robertson was not exactly the kind of Republican that the GOP core wanted to see in the White House.[14]

Interestingly enough, core Republicans differed considerably in their reactions to racially charged symbols. Few of them expressed coldness to "blacks" as a group, but more than two-fifths were hostile toward "civil rights leaders," more than half were cold toward Jackson, and more than four of every five disdained "black militants." The more demanding blacks are perceived to be, the less supportive become the core Republicans.

The basic conservatism of the core white Republicans is apparent in their reactions to a number of important public policy issues. In Figure 8.3 the percentage of respondents favoring the liberal position is plotted on the vertical axis and the proportion supporting the conservative position is plotted on the horizontal axis. For questions that were asked more than once during the surveys under review (1980, 1984, and 1988), we averaged the results. As would be expected, the core Republicans are heavily concentrated in the lower right portion—the conservative side—of the scatter diagram. Conservatism predominates on questions involving the primacy of the individual rather than governmental responsibility for economic well-being, racial policies (opposed to quotas and preferential treatment), and the importance of military strength in defending American interests abroad. Over three-fourths of the core Republicans think their federal taxes are excessive.[15]

Although a few issues prompted more moderate or liberal responses, the mindset of the core white Republicans is exactly what is conveyed by the figure: overwhelming consensus in favor of conservative positions on many governmental policies. A few issues, of course, split the bedrock Republicans. In 1984 they were evenly divided over whether the government should become more or less involved in Central America. Most of the core Republicans opposed the Equal Rights Amendment in 1980, but a considerable minority supported it. According to the 1984 and 1988 NES surveys, white core Republicans were also of no single mind about the complex question of abortion rights. The issue is too multi-faceted to be presented visually, but only 16 percent of the core Republicans opposed abortion under any conditions while nearly one-third preferred leaving the decision to the mother. Another third favored abortion if the mother's life were endangered, and less than one-fifth if another need could be established.[16]

The collective portrait of core Republicans is compatible with their consistently solid support for GOP presidential nominees: they are strongly conservative on defense, committed to individual achievement, opposed to racial quotas, convinced they pay too much in taxes, conventionally religious, and cold toward prominent symbols of liberalism such as Jackson and Kennedy. To them the Republican party has become the most promising instrument of economic growth and expansion, while the Democratic party has become the party of taxation, spending, and redistributive politics.

To round out this sketch of the core white Republicans, consider their demographic profile as revealed in the 1988 CBS News/New York Times Exit Poll (see Table 8.1). Alone among the southern voting groups, core white Republicans are disproportionately composed of men (53 percent). Their age distribution is encouraging for future Republican prospects, for they include more younger voters and fewer older voters than do the core white Democrats. Over seventenths of the core Republicans have attended college, and more than four-tenths are college graduates. Economically, core white Republicans are clearly the most affluent southern voting group, with nearly three-quarters receiving a family income of $25,000 or more and with three-tenths (highest among the groups) reporting an income of $50,000 or higher.

Table 8.1 Differences among the voting groups: a demographic profile of the southern core voting groups in 1988 (percent)

	Core white Republicans	Swing whites	Core white Democrats	Blacks	All
Sex					
Male	53	49	42	44	48
Female	47	51	58	56	52
Education					
Some high school	5	10	10	16	9
High school graduate	22	26	31	33	27
Some college	31	27	31	28	30
College graduate	25	18	13	13	19
College plus	16	19	16	9	15
Income ($1,000s)					
Less than 12.5	8	13	15	32	15
12.5–24.9	18	23	27	27	22
25–49.9	44	42	40	28	40
50 or more	30	22	19	14	23
Age					
18–29	21	16	18	28	20
30–44	35	36	35	37	35
45–59	25	22	21	19	23
60 plus	19	26	26	16	22

Source: 1988 CBS News/New York Times Exit Poll.

The White Swing Vote

White swing voters consist of conservative Democrats and moderate independents, who together made up 18 percent of the southern presidential electorate in 1988. Republican candidates have consistently captured a majority of the white swing vote, but a sizable minority has voted Democratic. Higher percentages of white swing voters have evaluated Republican presidential candidates warmly than have done so for the Democratic nominees (see Figure 8.4). However, the Republican advantage among the swing voters has been much smaller than among the white core Republicans. All of the recent Republican presidential candidates were favorably evaluated, as were four of the five Democratic candidates. George Mc-Govern, who drew more hostility than warmth from the white swing group, was the conspicuous exception.

The basis for the Republican advantage as well as the persistence of considerable Democratic strength among these voters appears in their symbolic and policy predispositions (see Figure 8.5). According

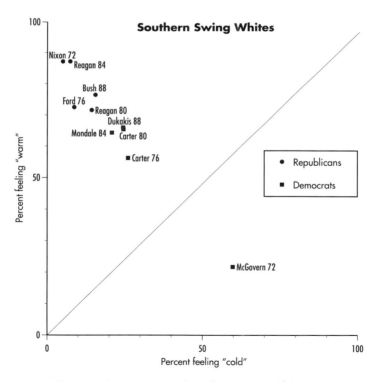

Figure 8.4 The mixed perceptions of southern swing whites: percentages of respondents who expressed "warm" and "cold" reactions to Democratic and Republican presidential candidates, 1972–1988. *Source:* Same as Figure 8.2.

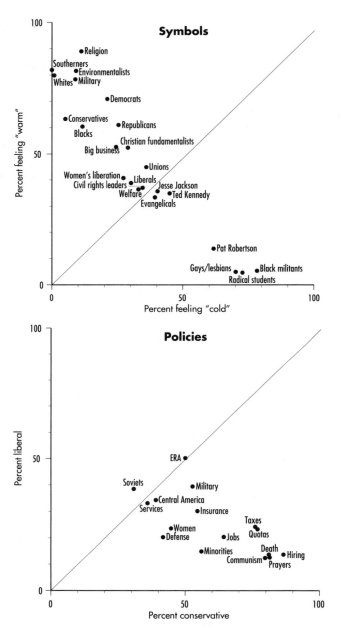

Figure 8.5 Symbols and policy positions of southern swing whites. *Source:* Same as Figure 8.2.

to the NES surveys, they reacted very favorably to southerners, whites, the military, and environmentalists, and most believed that religion was very important in their lives. More swing voters were warm toward Democrats than toward Republicans, and more favorably disposed to conservatives than to liberals. Like the white core Republicans, most were cold toward black militants, radical students, gays, and the chief symbol of charismatic Christianity, Pat Robertson.

Yet on many of the symbols there was no consensus among this group of whites. Included in the gray zone of divisive symbols were unions, civil rights leaders, women's liberation, Christian fundamentalists, and evangelicals. More than two-fifths of the swing whites were cold but over a third were warm toward Jesse Jackson and Edward Kennedy. The groups and politicians drawing mixed reviews sometimes exemplified modern liberalism but also included symbols that represented evangelical Christianity.

The conservative advantage among the white swing voters is more pronounced when the group's policy preferences are displayed. Racial issues generated the most extensive conservative advantage. Most of the swing whites disapproved of preferential racial hiring and racial quotas, wanting blacks and other minorities to advance on the basis of individual achievement rather than through governmental programs. By overwhelming ratios, these whites demonstrated strong cultural conservatism in their support for the death penalty for convicted murderers and their belief that prayers should be permitted in public schools. By more than a three-to-one ratio, they adhered to the individualistic ethic that people should rely on their own initiatives to get ahead rather than holding the federal government responsible for providing jobs and a good standard of living. More than seven of every ten in this group thought in 1980 that they paid too much in federal taxes, while only a minority believed they paid their fair share or too little. With few dissenters, most believed that the United States should prevent the expansion of communism. These findings illustrate the strength of cultural and racial conservatism, the individualistic ethic, and strong opposition to communism among the white swing voters, beliefs that have not escaped the attention of Republican campaign strategists and politicians.

Not all of the policy issues, to be sure, produced lopsided advantages for conservative candidates. On the average, only two out of five swing voters favored expanding the defense budget or encouraging women simply to get ahead on their own. Swing voters disagreed over whether the United States should be involved in Central

America or should attempt to be the world's foremost military power. The group split over whether the government should provide more or fewer services. While most swing voters preferred private medical insurance, more than a third thought the government should provide such insurance. On two important matters the conservative edge disappeared. More preferred conciliation to toughness toward the Soviet Union, and the ERA controversy split the group exactly in half.

Thus a review of the symbolic and policy predispositions of the swing group reveals considerably more support for conservative candidates, symbols, and policies than for the liberal alternatives. Much of the GOP's television advertising is directed at the swing whites. In the most recent presidential elections the Republicans have consistently captured a substantial majority of these voters.

In the 1988 presidential election the demographic profile of the white swing voters closely paralleled that of the entire electorate in terms of gender, education, and income (see Table 8.1). They are split almost evenly between men and women, more than three-fifths have attended college, and a large majority reported family incomes of $25,000 or more. Of the four voting groups, the swing whites had the smallest share of young voters and tied the core white Democrats for the largest share of older voters.

Core White Democrats

Political moderation best describes the collective profile of the South's core white Democrats. These whites are a composite of a sizable group of liberal Democrats, a much bigger group of moderate Democrats, and a very small number of liberal independents. Taken together, they represent the residue of Democratic party strength among southern whites. According to the CBS News/New York Times Exit Poll, they made up 24 percent of the region's voters and 27 percent of the white voters in 1988.

In contrast to the core white Republicans and the swing whites, the NES surveys show that these whites evaluated four of the Democratic presidential nominees (Carter twice, Mondale, and Dukakis) more favorably than any of the Republican candidates (see Figure 8.6). Yet majorities of the white core Democrats also expressed warmth for Nixon, Reagan (in 1984), and Ford. Bush and Reagan (in 1980) received more mixed evaluations, as did McGovern, the Democrats' weakest candidate. While the bedrock Republicans present

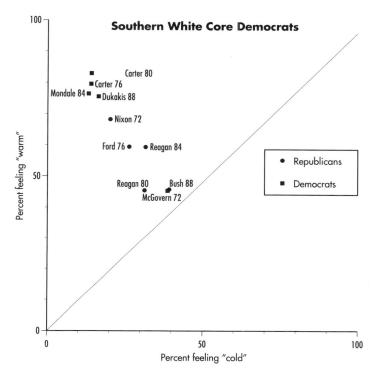

Figure 8.6   The modest Democratic advantage among southern white core Democrats: percentages of respondents who expressed "warm" and "cold" reactions to Democratic and Republican presidential candidates, 1972–1988. *Source:* Same as Figure 8.2.

the image of a *hard* core of loyalists who have polarized views of the rival party candidates, the bedrock Democrats constitute a relatively *soft* core of white loyalists. On the basis of these evaluations, it is easy to see how the GOP has attracted many defectors even among the southern whites most sympathetic to the Democratic party.

The political fragility of the core Democratic whites can be understood by examining their symbolic likes and dislikes and their policy preferences (see Figure 8.7). Unlike their Republican counterparts, who were cohesively attached to conservative symbols and uniformly repelled by the more flamboyant symbols of liberalism, the white core Democrats were simultaneously attracted to some liberal *and* some conservative symbols. They generally rejected the more extreme examples of liberalism (black militants, radical students, gays,

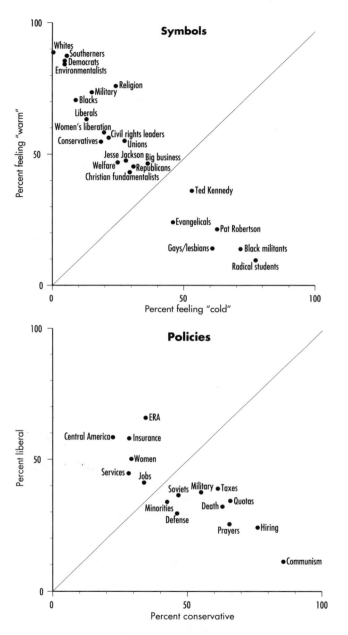

Figure 8.7 Symbols and policy positions of southern white core Democrats.
Source: Same as Figure 8.2.

and Edward Kennedy) and conservative Christianity (evangelicals and Pat Robertson).

Part of what the white core Democrats liked—whites, southerners, the military, the importance of religion, and environmentalists—was similarly appreciated by the other two groups of southern whites. Core Democrats parted company with core Republicans and swing voters in their warmth toward Democrats, blacks, and liberals. The core Democrats disliked many of the same groups and symbols as the other southern whites. Among the symbols and leaders eliciting divided reactions, several liberal symbols (women's liberation, unions, civil rights leaders, Jesse Jackson, and people on welfare) won approval from some core white Democrats but hostility from others. Some conservative symbols (conservatives, Christian fundamentalists, Republicans, and big business) received more favorable than unfavorable reactions from the South's most pro-Democratic group of whites.

The public policies desired by core white Democrats include both liberal and conservative preferences. On the liberal side, most supported bargaining with the Soviet Union as opposed to relying only on military strength, opposed further involvement in Central America, supported government medical insurance, and favored the ERA. By smaller pluralities they wished to maintain rather than curtail public services and thought the government rather than individuals should be responsible for providing jobs. On the conservative side, they strongly rejected preferential hiring and quotas, thus taking positions exactly the opposite of most blacks, the other cornerstone of the Democratic coalition. On defense issues they were emphatically anticommunist and wanted the United States to be the most powerful nation in the world. White core Democrats thought they were overtaxed, and they supported school prayer and the death penalty for murder.

Democratic politicians seeking to attract these voters need to be progressive enough to appeal to liberal whites but conservative enough to interest the larger group of moderate whites. The values and beliefs of core Democrats help explain the group's continued support of Democratic presidential candidates, but they also reveal Republican opportunities. Especially if the Democratic nominee takes liberal positions across the board, the GOP can exploit a wide range of conservative beliefs present among this group. Favorably disposed toward moderate, established Democrats, many of the South's core white Democrats have had more in common and felt more comfortable with Republicans like Ford, Nixon, or Reagan than with Democrats like Kennedy, Jackson, or McGovern.

The most striking demographic characteristic of the core white Democrats is that women constituted 58 percent of the group (see Table 8.1). By contrast, only 47 percent of the core white Republicans were women. In comparison with the entire southern electorate, the core white Democrats were less educated and a disproportionate number were older voters.

Southern Blacks

Blacks, who account for about 14 percent of the South's presidential electorate, have been by far the most reliable and cohesive source of support for Democratic presidential candidates. Michael Dukakis aside, Democratic candidates were favorably viewed by more than four-fifths of southern blacks (see Figure 8.8). While few blacks were cold toward Dukakis, a sizable minority were indifferent, presumably the residue of his prolonged battle with Jackson over the vice-presidential nomination. Every Republican candidate was perceived less favorably than his Democratic opponent by southern blacks. With such favorable evaluations of the Democratic candidates, few blacks have seriously considered Republican candidates.

The overwhelming black support for Democratic presidential candidates is underscored by the group's reactions to symbols and policy alternatives (see Figure 8.9). Southern blacks were warmly disposed toward some symbols they shared with white southerners—southerners, the importance of religion, environmentalists, the military, and whites. Perhaps for different reasons, and with somewhat different understandings, these were some of the most important ties that bound whites and blacks together in the South. Nonetheless, prominent in the symbolic landscape of blacks were also items that were not so favorably evaluated by any group of whites—blacks, Kennedy, Jackson, civil rights leaders, and Democrats. The symbol of black militants illustrates the differences. Black militants were viewed coldly by enormous majorities of core white Republicans, white swing voters, and core white Democrats. Among southern blacks, however, warmth toward black militants exceeded coldness. Such were the symbols that largely united blacks, and separated them not only from the core Republicans and swing whites but also from many core white Democrats.

In their policy preferences blacks were the most liberal of the voting

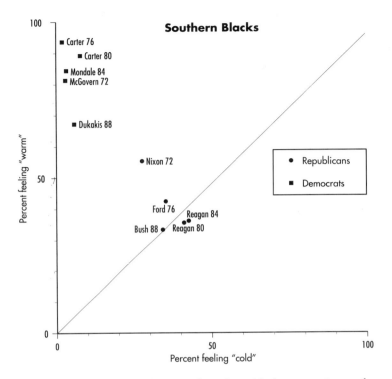

Figure 8.8 The polarized views of southern blacks: percentages of respondents who expressed "warm" and "cold" reactions to Democratic and Republican presidential candidates, 1972–1988. *Source:* Same as Figure 8.2.

groups, though on some issues they were profoundly conservative. Landslide majorities of black southerners favored passage of ERA, the use of quotas in college admissions and preferential treatment in hiring, more government services, and decreased involvement of the United States in Central America. Over three-fifths of southern blacks thought the government, not the individual, should be primarily responsible for a person's economic well-being, a position adopted by only two-fifths of the white core Democrats. By smaller pluralities blacks preferred governmental funding for medical insurance, governmental responsibility for helping blacks and other minorities, and bargaining with the Soviet Union.

Nonetheless, blacks did not take liberal positions on all issues. Blacks were split on the question of whether the United States should try to remain the most important military power in the world, and

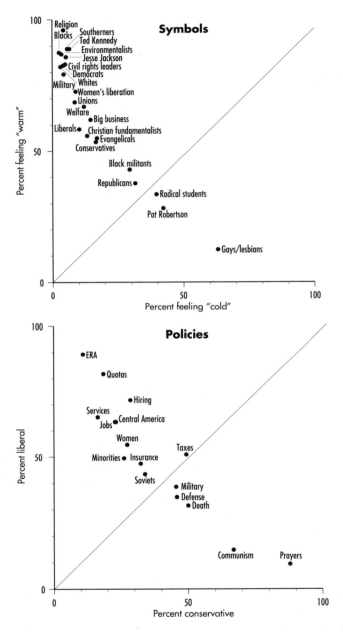

Figure 8.9 Symbols and policy positions of southern blacks. *Source:* Same as Figure 8.2.

over whether the defense budget should be cut or increased. About half of southern blacks supported the death penalty and thought that they paid too much in federal taxes. Blacks were the most conservative of the four groups in their support of prayer in public schools.

The 1988 demographic profile of southern black voters reveals far more women than men, as well as a disproportionate percentage of young voters. The educational and income profiles of black voters differed substantially from each of the white voting groups. While substantial majorities of whites in each voting group had been exposed to a college education, only 51 percent of blacks had gone to college. And while large majorities of each white group of voters reported family incomes of $25,000 or more, only 42 percent of blacks reported such incomes. Nearly one-third of black voters reported an income of less than $12,500.

Each of the four groups surveyed—core white Republicans, swing whites, core white Democrats, and blacks—has its own distinctive profile of likes and dislikes toward presidential candidates, symbols, and policies. In profoundly different ways, white core Republicans and blacks are the most homogeneous groups and display the greatest cohesion, election to election, in their partisan choices.

The General Election

The evolution of the Republicans' advantage in recent presidential elections can be visualized by examining the changing size of the four voter groups—the building blocks of presidential coalitions—for the South and North (see Figure 8.10). Outside the South the core white Republicans constituted the largest voting group, increasing from 36 percent in 1976 to 41 percent in 1988. After leading the core white Democrats by only a few points in 1976 and 1980, they opened a gap of 10 to 12 points in 1984 and 1988. When blacks are added to the core white Democrats, Democratic presidential nominees started off almost equal to the core Republicans: each side's base amounted to around two-fifths of the electorate. Over the four elections the Democrats slipped from a slight lead in 1976 and 1980 in the size of their base vote to a rough parity in 1984 and 1988. However, since the core Republicans have voted more cohesively for their party's nominees than have the two components of the Democratic base, the Republicans have extracted larger yields from their base. White swing voters, who controlled 22 percent of the North's vote in 1988, remain a crucial target of both parties' strategists. Even at their best

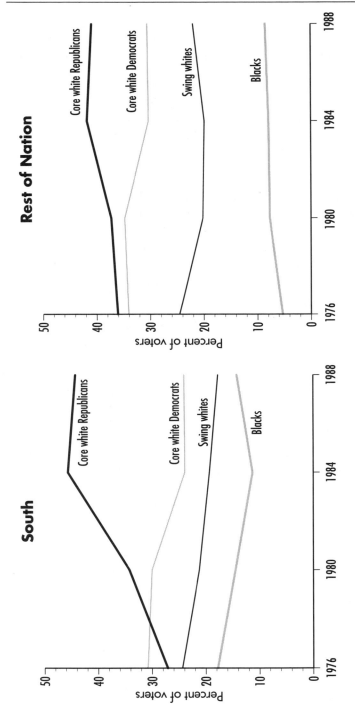

Figure 8.10 The emerging Republican advantage in presidential elections: sizes of the four groups of voters in the South and the rest of the nation, 1976–1988. *Source:* Calculated by the authors from CBS News/New York Times Exit Polls, 1976–1988.

the northern Republicans have remained a minority party still dependent upon the kindness of swing voters and disaffected Democrats to win presidential elections.

In the South core white Republicans have emerged as the biggest and most cohesive voting unit in presidential elections. In 1976 the Republican core amounted to only 27 percent of the region's voters, slightly less than the 31 percent who were core white Democrats and much smaller than the combined total of blacks and core white Democrats (49 percent). Jimmy Carter's southern sweep in 1976 rested upon an electorate in which about half of the participants belonged to groups predisposed to vote Democratic by landslide proportions. By 1980, however, signs of Democratic decay were appearing in the southern electorate. During Carter's presidency core white Republicans displaced core white Democrats as the region's largest group of voters. Although blacks and core white Democrats (45 percent) still outnumbered the reliable Republicans (34 percent), the traditional Democratic advantage was shrinking. The 1980 presidential contest was close, but the cohesive Republicans added enough swing voters and alienated Democrats to carry every southern state except Georgia.

The Reagan years significantly and dramatically increased the size of the Republican base, which rose to 46 percent of the total southern electorate in 1984 and stabilized at 44 percent in 1988. Core white Republicans gave George Bush an extraordinary 93 percent of their vote in 1988, the most cohesive of any voting group in the South. Core white Republicans now cast the most powerful "bloc vote" in the new southern presidential electorate.

Core white Democrats, by contrast, shrank to only 24 percent in 1988. Even when combined with blacks, the Democratic groups constituted only 38 percent of the southern electorate, six points below that of the core Republicans. Neither of the two Democratic groups were as united in support of Dukakis as the bedrock Republicans were for Bush. According to the CBS News/New York Times Exit Poll, 87 percent of southern blacks and 76 percent of southern core white Democrats voted for Dukakis. The Republican core vote yielded 41 percent of the total vote for their candidate, while the comparable Democratic bases provided only 31 percent of the total vote for their nominee.

With neither base providing a majority, white swing voters have become even more crucial targets in the South. The swing vote has always been critical to Republican victories, since Republicans have been and remain a distinct minority of the southern electorate. It was less important historically to Democrats since their biracial base constituted a near majority of the southern electorate as late as 1976. The collapse of the reliable Democratic presidential vote in the South means that the Democrats also need to court this group effectively.

Recent Republican victories in the South must be understood in light of the changing size and cohesion of the four different groups of voters. The emergence of a solid Republican bloc vote in southern presidential politics—a bloc vote that is bigger than any other segment of the electorate—has transformed the setting in which campaigns are waged. In the 1988 election the Republican advantage rested upon its substantial base of core white voters plus a sizable group of swing white voters who have usually favored the Republicans. The Democratic vote came mainly from blacks and core white Democrats, two groups which no longer constitute a majority. These new realities, unprecedented in the history of the region, underlie the establishment of a Solid Republican South in presidential elections.

9

The Progressive Advantage
in Democratic Primaries

Historically, the South followed the counsel of its most successful Democratic politicians and thereby presented a cohesive face at Democratic national conventions. Leaders of the southern Democratic party, exclusively white men, evaluated prospective presidential candidates in light of their views toward the South, their prospects for election, and their possible impact on the fortunes of the South's candidates for state and local offices. In picking delegates to the national party convention, state party leaders generally favored like-minded older white men who enjoyed close ties to important office-holders. With these delegations, the southern Democratic leaders could easily produce a disciplined and cohesive bloc of votes at Democratic conventions on behalf of such candidates as Franklin Roosevelt (1932–1944), Richard Russell (1948 and 1952), Lyndon Johnson (1960 and 1964), and Hubert Humphrey (1968).[1]

Since 1968, however, the route to the Democratic presidential nomination has been transformed. New rules adopted by the national Democratic party diversified each state's delegation to the national convention, shifted power from state party leaders to the candidates themselves, magnified the importance of liberal activist groups in the nomination process, and eventually made the primaries the main arena for determining Democratic presidential nominees. These developments have revolutionized the politics of Democratic presidential nominations in the South. With a primary electorate composed of blacks *and* whites, women *and* men, migrants to the South *and* natives of the region, liberals, moderates, *and* conservatives, it has become more difficult—though certainly not impossible—for a single candidate to sweep the region's primaries.

Over time there has been a striking change in the ideological composition of the Democratic primary electorate. An exodus of many white conservatives has significantly weakened the clout of this group within the Democratic party. Although a substantial minority of participants in southern Democratic presidential primaries still think of themselves as some sort of conservative, the growing importance of blacks, white moderates, and white liberals means that the Democratic primaries in the South now tilt in a moderate to progressive direction. There are far more votes to be won in southern Democratic primaries by candidates who emphasize moderate to progressive themes than by politicians who stress their conservatism.

The appearance of a Solid South at the national convention depends not only on how well rival candidates perform in the ideologically diverse electorate of the primaries, but also on whether the trailing candidates, who now choose and control *their own delegates,* fight to the finish on the convention floor or release their delegates to support the apparent nominee. All in all it is a radical departure from the nomination politics of the past.

The Impact of the New Rules

Traditional methods of choosing delegates did not survive the Democratic party's disastrous 1968 convention. Complaints about inequitable representation were so widespread that the Democratic national convention created a body (the McGovern-Fraser Commission) to recommend changes in the procedures for selecting delegates. True to form, southern Democrats at the 1968 convention "voted overwhelmingly against the proposal for a commission to revise delegate selection rules." However, in 1970 the national party adopted the recommendations of the McGovern-Fraser Commission. Under the new rules state parties were required to open up the process by which delegates were selected and to take "affirmative steps" to ensure that more minorities, women, and young people were included in each state's delegation to the national convention.[2]

In the old days, when delegations were chosen by the top stratum of southern Democratic leaders, women played a minor role in convention politics. Women were only 13 percent of the 1968 southern delegates, but they rose to 36 percent in 1972 under the new McGovern-Fraser requirements. Beginning with the 1980 convention, the national party has required that representation be divided equally between men and women. Women now regularly constitute half of the southern delegations to the Democratic convention.[3]

The new rules also changed the racial composition of southern convention delegations. For many decades after the Civil War, the Democratic party was thought of by whites *and* blacks as a "white man's party" whose racial policies were controlled entirely by racist southern whites. As such, "Before the New Deal, blacks not only stayed away from the Democratic party generally, but were denied the right to participate fully." When blacks first officially appeared at a Democratic convention in Houston, Texas, as alternates in 1928, they were stationed "behind a chicken-wire fence on the convention floor, along with all black spectators." As blacks increasingly entered the northern urban Democratic parties during the New Deal, however, their numbers at the convention gradually increased.[4]

Since 1968 the racial character of southern Democratic delegations has dramatically changed. Through 1960 there were no black delegates from the South at the Democratic convention. Only four southern blacks were regular delegates to the convention that met less than two months after passage of the Civil Rights Act of 1964. In 1968 blacks accounted for 10 percent of the southern delegates, and in 1972 black representation increased to 24 percent. After dropping slightly in 1976, blacks continued to post incremental gains. In 1988 blacks were one-third of the South's delegates to the Democratic convention, a considerably higher figure than their share of the region's population. Increased black representation has been most pronounced in the Deep South, formerly the bastion of conservative white Democrats. Blacks made up 46 percent of the Deep South's delegates to the 1988 Democratic convention. Blacks were one-half of the South Carolina delegation in 1988, only a few points above their representation in Mississippi (47 percent), Alabama (46), Louisiana (45), and Georgia (44).[5]

Liberal activist groups within the Democratic party also benefited from the new requirements for selecting delegates, for the reforms were fundamentally "a shift from a party-based to a candidate-based process of delegate selection." If governors and mayors were no longer kingmakers, the candidates themselves had to attract support from the "interested partisans" and the "organized interests" that had the most at stake in the selection of Democratic presidential nominees. In the Democratic party these interests were often liberal or progressive in their politics, and they included labor unions, civil rights groups, feminists, environmentalists, and many others. These activists sought candidates who would support their policy positions, while the candidates and their campaign managers sought experienced political activists to staff their campaigns. Most convention delegates are now issue activists who have worked for particular candidates.[6]

Ideologically, most Democratic convention delegates are self-identified liberals or moderates. In the Democratic conventions of the 1980s, an average of 44 percent of the delegates were liberals, 45 percent were moderates, and only 5 percent were conservatives. Conservatives are about as welcome at a Democratic national convention as liberals would be at a Republican national convention.[7]

The most important long-term consequence of the new rules has been the expansion of presidential primaries. Through a process of trial and error, it proved far simpler to institute a primary election in which delegates to the Democratic convention would be apportioned in some clear relationship to each candidate's share of the primary vote than to select delegates through caucus or convention systems. In 1988 forty states conducted primaries that influenced the selection of delegates to the Democratic convention. The road to the Democratic presidential nomination inescapably entails competing in many primaries.[8]

Here again practices have changed more in the South than in the rest of the nation. Although southern Democrats customarily used primaries to nominate their candidates for state and local offices, they seldom did so in presidential politics. "I've never thought much of the primaries as a way to decide these matters," Sam Rayburn once observed. Rayburn's disdain for presidential primaries reflected the thinking of most established Democratic politicians. As late as 1968 only Florida held a presidential primary, and its results did not bind the state's convention delegates. Even after the new rules went into effect, the southern states were initially slow to adopt primaries. Three southern states held primaries in 1972, six in 1976, and eight in 1980, before falling back to six in 1984. In 1988, however, stimulated by the effort to show a unified region on Super Tuesday, Democrats in every southern state except South Carolina (a caucus state) held a presidential preference primary. Primaries are now more common in the South than in any other region. In 1988, the vast majority of presidential primaries in the South were open to all registered voters, regardless of party affiliation. In Florida and Louisiana both parties held closed primaries. In North Carolina, only registered Democrats could participate in the Democratic primary, whereas the Republicans permitted voters registered as independents also to take part.[9]

Although more primaries were occurring in the South, relatively fewer southerners were taking advantage of the opportunity to participate. In 1972 Democratic presidential primaries attracted 22 percent of the eligible voters in the southern states holding primaries. Turnout fell to 17 percent in 1976 and dropped again to 14 percent in 1980. The 1988 Democratic primaries drew about 14.5 percent of the eligible voters. During the same period the Republicans did not pick up the slack. In 1972 about 6 percent of eligible voters took part in the three southern Republican presidential primaries. Except for a dip in 1984, when President Reagan was unopposed for renomination, the GOP maintained this modest level of participation. Some 7.4 percent of the South's voting-age population participated in the Republican Super Tuesday primaries.[10]

How have the two parties fared in attracting voters to their southern presidential primaries? In 1972 nearly four times as many southern voters took part in the Democratic primaries as in the Republican primaries. Democrats again won the participation battle in 1988, but their advantage dropped to slightly less than two Democratic voters for every Republican voter. "Republicans have made some headway," Charles D. Hadley and Harold W. Stanley conclude, "but Democrats are still dominant."[11]

Super Tuesday involved a significant fight between Democratic and Republican leaders in attracting white voters. In 1988 the Democrats continued to win, drawing over 60 percent of the whites who voted on Super Tuesday in Arkansas, Louisiana, North Carolina, and Tennessee, about 55 percent in Mississippi, Texas, and Florida, and slightly over half in Alabama, Virginia, and Georgia. Despite the preference of a clear majority of whites for the Democratic primary, the Republicans' ability to secure over two-fifths of the white primary voters in many southern states was a GOP milestone. The Democrats did even better among the region's two minority groups, attracting more than nine of every ten blacks who voted and nearly four of every five Hispanics who went to the polls on Super Tuesday.[12]

Democratic presidential primaries have produced both a Solid South and a Split South. Presidential candidates from the South (George Wallace in 1972 and Jimmy Carter in the next two elections) secured a majority among southern voters in the 1972–1980 primaries, but no politician swept the region in 1984 and 1988. Walter Mondale, Gary Hart, and Jesse Jackson divided the southern vote in 1984, as did Jackson, Al Gore, Jr., and Michael Dukakis in 1988. If several substantial candidates seek the nomination, it would take an espe-

cially skilled and compelling politician to unite the diverse and competing forces that make up the Democratic party in the modern
South. The best way to understand the changes that have revolutionized Democratic presidential nominating politics in the South is
to review the battles over the Democratic nomination, beginning with
the 1972 contest, the first to occur under the liberalized rules.

The Wallace Impact in 1972

In 1972 the crucial southern primary occurred in Florida, where a
large field of Democratic contenders competed for the chance to
oppose President Richard Nixon. Maine Senator Edmund Muskie,
the early front-runner, had been upset by South Dakota Senator
George McGovern in the New Hampshire primary, and both candidates carried their campaigns to Florida. The primary also attracted
former Vice-President Humphrey, Washington Senator Henry Jackson, New York Mayor John Lindsay, New York Congresswoman
Shirley Chisholm, and, most important of all, Governor George Wallace of Alabama.

As a third-party candidate in 1968, Wallace had run well throughout the Deep South and in rural and small-town areas of the Peripheral South. In 1972 Wallace returned to the Democratic party and
seriously attempted to win the party's presidential nomination.
"Send Them a Message" implored Wallace's billboards. Wallace no
longer used explicitly segregationist rhetoric, but his language, ges-
tures, and inflections left no doubt about his ability to communicate
white anger about federal intervention in racial matters. His most
insistent theme was total and unqualified opposition to the busing
of students to achieve racial balance in public schools, a policy Wallace denounced as "the most senseless, asinine, callous, ridiculous
thing this government has ever done."[13]

Taking the hardest possible line on the primary's most explosive
issue, Wallace won Florida with 42 percent of the vote and thereby
emerged as the voice of the white South in the Democratic presidential primaries. Wallace ran best in northern and panhandle Florida,
the most traditional parts of the state, but his appeal went far beyond
these areas. "Wallace, it became obvious that night, was not just a
Southern phenomenon—he was much more than a statewide Florida
phenomenon," observed Theodore H. White. "He was a national
phenomenon and would remain so until shot, two months later, and

removed by a would-be assassin's bullet from national consideration."[14]

Gaining momentum from his Florida victory, Wallace proceeded
to lay waste his rivals in the two other southern primaries. In North
Carolina Wallace contemptuously dispatched his chief rival, former
Governor Terry Sanford. On the same day that Wallace handily
defeated Sanford (50 to 37 percent), he won 68 percent of the vote
in Tennessee. All told, Wallace captured 50 percent of the entire
southern primary vote—and a much larger majority of the white
vote.

As he had done in 1964, Wallace carried his campaign into northern
states. Far and away the best speaker of the Democratic candidates,
he attracted overflow crowds with spellbinding performances. Wallace finished second in Wisconsin, Pennsylvania, Indiana, and West
Virginia. The turning point in the Alabama governor's campaign
came on May 15, when he was shot six times in the stomach and
paralyzed for life after speaking to a crowd in a Maryland shopping
mall. On the next day he won the Maryland (39 percent) and the
Michigan primaries (51 percent), convincingly defeating McGovern
and Humphrey in both states. At this point in the campaign Wallace
had won a larger share of the Democratic primary vote than any
other candidate, and most of his votes had been earned outside the
South. These primaries represented the peak of Wallace's efforts in
1972; his campaign dissipated as Wallace recuperated.[15]

After Wallace was eliminated as a serious candidate, northern and
western Democrats largely divided their votes between McGovern
and Humphrey. McGovern's victory in the California primary finally
decided the struggle, and the Democrats nominated a candidate who,
in his only southern test, had finished far out of the running. At the
convention McGovern drew his greatest support from the West and
Northeast, a very unusual pattern of support for a midwestern Democrat.[16]

In the 1972 Democratic convention the Solid South gave way to a
thoroughly splintered region. On the roll-call vote that awarded
McGovern the nomination, delegates from the South (before
switches) gave Wallace a plurality of 40 percent, followed by 23
percent for McGovern, 11 percent each for Chisholm and Jackson, 8
percent for Sanford, and 5 percent for Arkansas Congressman Wilbur
Mills. Wallace *was* the regional leader, but a majority of southern
delegates supported someone else.[17] The Alabama governor won 75
percent of the vote from the convention delegates of Florida, North

Carolina, and Tennessee, the states with primaries, but these states supplied only one-third of the region's delegates to the national convention. The overwhelming majority of southern convention delegates represented states in which the delegates had been chosen in reformed caucuses or conventions. In these states—Alabama, Georgia, Louisiana, Mississippi, and South Carolina in the Deep South; Texas, Arkansas, and Virginia in the Peripheral South—Wallace had very little support at the Democratic convention. He won only 19 percent of their convention votes and carried only Alabama.[18] Blacks, females, and younger persons were much more prevalent in the caucuses and conventions of these states in 1972 than in 1968, and many of the delegates were moderate to progressive Democrats. Most of the new party activists viewed Wallace as exactly the type of southern politician they wanted to repudiate.

Thus the picture of Wallace as the spokesman for southern white Democrats is far more complex than the results of the primaries alone would indicate. Whites and blacks polarized when "the people" were given a chance to speak, with majorities of southern whites "Send[ing] Them a Message." Yet most of the delegates to the 1972 convention were not chosen in primaries. The Democratic party's insistence on more equitable representation of minorities, females, and young people broke the grip of conservative Democrats on the southern convention delegations. As a result, some southerners stood with Wallace, while others began to support candidates whose main appeal lay in the core Democratic voting groups—blacks, liberal to moderate white Democrats, and liberal independents.

The Carter Achievement in 1976

Early in 1975 the former governor of Georgia, Jimmy Carter, paid a call on Massachusetts Congressman Thomas P. (Tip) O'Neill, Jr., the Democratic Majority Leader of the House of Representatives. Carter informed the startled O'Neill that he would be the Democratic party's presidential nominee in 1976. As O'Neill later reconstructed the conversation, Carter told him that "at the moment . . . I'm only one-half of one percent in the polls. But by the time we get to Madison Square Garden, I'll have this thing wrapped up." After evaluating and dismissing his possible rivals, Carter drove home the point. "Mr. Majority Leader," he said, "I'm telling you right now that I'm going to be nominated on the first ballot, and that in November of next year I'll be elected president of the United States." O'Neill's reaction to Carter's boldness was typical of experienced politicians. "The idea," he said, "that this Georgia peanut farmer, a complete unknown, saw himself as a serious candidate for the highest office in the world struck me as pretty farfetched." O'Neill concluded that the former Georgia governor's scenario was "impossible."[19]

Skepticism was not limited to those who knew little or nothing about Carter. Although Carter enlisted the enthusiastic support of many Georgians ("the peanut brigade"), unfriendly Georgia media ridiculed his campaign. When Carter formally announced his candidacy in December 1974, the *Atlanta Journal* headlined the story, "Jimmy Carter Is Running for What?" Carter himself told the story about a cartoon that had appeared in an Athens, Georgia, newspaper. "They don't like me at all in that newspaper," he said, "so they drew a cartoon with me walking in the road carrying a Carter-for-President sign and the devil walking into hell with a snowball. And this guy is standing there and said, 'I'm betting on the snowball.'"[20]

In 1976, of course, Carter did exactly what he said he would do. His successful fight, against tremendously long odds, remains one of the most genuinely impressive nomination campaigns in the history of the presidency. Carter broke the informal barrier that blocked southern white Democrats from winning their party's most important nomination. The Democratic party had nominated Lyndon Johnson in 1964, but Johnson had the many advantages of incumbency going for him. Carter was the first southern Democrat since 1844 to win the nomination without the benefit of occupying the White House.

Before Carter no southerner in the twentieth century had accomplished both of the two difficult but necessary tasks that faced any serious contender: uniting the region's Democrats while demonstrating significant strength among Democrats in the rest of the nation. Richard Russell and Lyndon Johnson had won cohesive votes from the region's convention delegates in 1948, 1952, and 1960, but they were never able to demonstrate impressive strength outside the South. Wallace had won the 1972 southern primaries but had carried only Maryland and Michigan in the North. Estes Kefauver had been extraordinarily successful, for a southerner, in winning support outside the South in 1952. Nonetheless, Kefauver could attract little support within the South. Carter's unique achievement was simultaneously unifying southern Democrats while running ahead of his rivals, most of the time, outside the South.

Carter had decided to run for president while serving as governor of Georgia in the early 1970s. Taking the measure of prospective Democratic contenders who passed through Atlanta, Carter felt himself their equal or better, a theme expressed in the title of his book,

Why Not the Best? Hamilton Jordan, a trusted aide, devised the imaginative and ingenious Carter strategy. Jordan and Carter assumed the most important factor in determining the outcome of the election, in the post-Watergate era, was the trustworthiness of the presidential candidates, not their positions on the myriad of specific issues that would arise during the campaign. Accordingly, the Carter campaign emphasized the candidate's personal trustworthiness and decency.[21]

Presenting himself as a centrist Democrat, Carter mixed progressive positions on some issues (civil rights, for example) with conservative positions on other issues (fiscal responsibility, for example). Carter applied to a *national* campaign a style of politics that many Democrats in the South had successfully developed after blacks had reentered the southern electorate. Operating in an electorate composed of whites and blacks, liberals, moderates, and conservatives, Democratic politicians had learned how to mix their issue positions to draw support from a broad, biracial spectrum of voters. Carter sought to be progressive enough to attract liberals but conservative enough to hold right-of-center voters. In so doing, he could present himself to the nation as a new and improved type of southern politician, one without a distinctively regional agenda.[22]

Carter's strategy correctly assumed that he needed to demonstrate strength outside the South in order to be taken seriously as a presidential candidate. "We decided early on New Hampshire and Florida; later, we saw that Iowa was a good chance," Carter told a reporter. "We just saw a good chance to build that up [Iowa] with a major media event." In both the Iowa caucuses and the New Hampshire primary Carter hoped to perform unexpectedly well, and then to use the dynamics of favorable media attention to gain visibility as a major candidate. Florida was Carter's make-or-break primary in the South. There he needed to defeat Wallace, still the reigning symbol of the South. Once he bested Wallace in the South, Carter's chances would be further boosted among northern Democrats, who would see him as a "New South" politician capable of winning votes in the principal northern states. Jordan's "run everywhere" strategy emphasized that Carter should enter virtually all of the primaries. Carter's opponents pursued the nomination by selectively entering primaries. Although Carter did not always win, he usually won something in each week of the nominating season, and his total number of delegates began to build toward a majority. Whenever he defeated a rival on territory supposedly favorable to his opponent, so much the better for Carter. His frequent victories offset the inevitable losses.[23]

"Momentum triumphant" best characterizes Carter's 1976 nomination campaign. His style of personal, face-to-face campaigning, reminiscent of Kefauver's techniques, was the centerpiece of Carter's approach. A smiling politician who could "charm the lard off a hog," the former Georgia governor made full use of this talent. "Hi, Bobby, my name's Jimmy Carter and I'm going to be your next President—and I'm going to be a wonderful President," Carter told a small boy in New England, a greeting that epitomized his style of politics. His personal campaigning first paid off in Iowa, where he won that state's caucuses against Democrats who were far better known nationally but who had failed to cultivate local support. Carter then validated his front-runner status by leading a crowded New Hampshire primary with 28 percent of the vote. The remaining candidates, mainly liberals, split the rest of the vote. Carter had become an overnight sensation, the media story of the year, a dark-horse candidate who suddenly seemed a viable contender. His momentum was blunted in Massachusetts, where he ran fourth, but the setback was only temporary.[24]

Florida was Carter's next major challenge. Although Wallace was permanently paralyzed from the waist down, he remained a formidable opponent. In the Florida primary Wallace represented the continuation of "Old South" politics, a combination of opposition to changes in race relations and support for economic populism, a strong national defense, and cultural conservativism. Wallace's entire career amounted to a permanent campaign against the racial and taxation politics of the federal government, a bitter crusade against those presidents, congressmen, judges, and administrators whose policies seemed to be completely out of touch with the values and interests of many whites.[25]

Despite Wallace's strength, Carter too had assets that he could exploit. Carter fully understood the temperament of the Wallacites, for he had won their votes in the 1970 Georgia governor's race. Some of Carter's themes simply expressed in softer and more cheerful language what Wallace had been saying for years. Carter's message was also directed at the anger people felt about Washington politicians, but the former Georgia governor replaced Wallace's sneers and cynicism with hope and optimism about the goodness of the people and the possibilities of positive change. Above all, Carter campaigned in a way that did not permanently alienate Wallace and his supporters, for he needed the Wallace delegates at the party convention and, even more important, the Wallace voters in the fall election.[26]

Although part of Carter's task in Florida was to wedge apart many of Wallace's usual supporters, he also needed to build a "New South" coalition of blacks and whites. Carter had received some black support in his 1966 campaign for the Georgia governorship, when he ran as a populist, nonracist Democrat. Carter finished third that year. In 1970 Carter faced former Governor Carl Sanders, who had emerged as a "New South" governor in the early 1960s and who was expected to put together a biracial coalition. Either unable or unwilling to take black support away from Sanders, Carter sought the nomination by winning a landslide majority among Georgia's white voters. Carter's campaign strategy that year had been to appeal to the largest group of white voters in Georgia, the supporters of Lester Maddox and George Wallace. Pledging in his platform, among other things, "To serve all Georgians, not just a selfish few," "to return control of our schools to local people, within the framework of the law," "to insure that it is never more profitable for able Georgians to stay on welfare than to work," and to "return the control of the Georgia Democratic party to Georgia Democrats," Carter positioned himself as a moderate conservative. He won an overwhelming majority of the white vote.[27]

As a candidate he had not campaigned as a "New South" Democrat. Immediately after he won the election he began to behave as though he wanted the votes of whites *and* blacks. On inauguration day Carter delivered a brief address in which he canceled his conservative campaign rhetoric and surprised many of the whites who had voted for him by calling for a new era of race relations in Georgia. "I say to you quite frankly," Carter told his audience, "that the time for racial discrimination is over." The media response was enormous: "He was on page one of *The New York Times* the next day and on the cover of *Time* magazine a few weeks later as one of the South's 'new voices,'" and "it was Jimmy Carter who became the grinning symbol of the changing region."[28]

When he began to consider running for president, Carter knew that he would need prominent black leaders to vouch for him on civil rights issues in order to receive serious consideration by northern Democrats, as well as to get the votes he needed from southern blacks to help defeat Wallace in the South. Toward this end Carter successfully won endorsements and campaign activity on his behalf from Reverend Martin Luther King, Sr., and Congressman Andrew Young.[29]

Thus Carter entered the Florida primary with the backing of blacks and those whites who wanted to eliminate Wallace, and with the ability to appeal to Wallace's supporters using language and values they could understand. In addition, despite the setback in Massachusetts, he had heightened visibility from his victory in New Hampshire. "One of the major things we had going for us against Governor Wallace in Florida," later explained Jody Powell, a key aide, "was that Jimmy Carter . . . was a Southerner with a real chance to win the nomination. Obviously, there's no better way to do that than to go 'way the hell off yonder to New Hampshire and win a primary."[30]

Relying on blacks, labor unions, and recent migrants to Florida, Carter's "New South" politics finished a few percentage points ahead of Wallace's "Old South" politics, 35 percent to 31 percent. Carter won 449,000 votes, while Wallace took 397,000. Wallace's support declined by over 100,000 votes from his showing in 1972, presumably losing much it to Carter. Carter's narrow victory in Florida was the beginning of the end for Wallace as a significant force within the national Democratic party. Carter's southern popularity surged, while Wallace had to excuse his defeat on the grounds that Florida was not a typical southern state.

In late March North Carolina Democrats gave Carter even greater support. While Wallace continued to exhort voters to "send 'em a message," Carter urged North Carolinians to "send a President" to Washington. Carter won 54 percent of the vote, Wallace 35 percent. North Carolina Democratic leaders were optimistic that Carter could carry the state in the fall. Carter ran well in black precincts, white working-class wards, and upper-middle-class areas. "Were he [Carter] to be nominated," said one county chairman, "he stands a chance to be the first Democratic candidate to carry the state since 1964. It would help the whole ticket." Carter was bringing southern Democrats back to life, as the results in subsequent southern Democratic primaries indicated. He beat Wallace 84–12 in Georgia; 63–17 in Arkansas; and 78–11 in Tennessee. Democratic leaders across the South began to see Carter as precisely the type of Democrat who could carry their states in a presidential contest, an opinion far unlike their evaluations of the Humphrey and McGovern candidacies.[31]

For Wallace the North Carolina primary was a second critical setback. According to Ferrel Guillory, "television cameras picked up the image of a pallid, subdued Wallace, the drooping lines around his mouth and the gaze in his eyes showing the severity of his North Carolina defeat." After this defeat Wallace laid off his country band, a sure sign that the Wallace campaign was coming to an end.[32]

Having won the South, Carter continued to do well elsewhere in the nation. He defeated his chief rivals, edging past Representative Morris Udall of Arizona in Wisconsin, Michigan, and Ohio and beating Washington Senator Henry Jackson in Pennsylvania. Carter's delegates accumulated, the early competitors faded, and not even two fresh entrants, California Governor Jerry Brown and Idaho Senator Frank Church, could deter him, even though they beat him in several primaries. Carter still lacked the delegates necessary for nomination when the primaries ended, but he was so far ahead of any rival that he quickly moved to ensure the support of a majority of the delegates.[33]

On the night of the last primaries Wallace told Carter he was withdrawing from the race and endorsing his fellow southerner. "He said he had been watching on television that night when I said I was proud to be a southerner," Carter recalled. "And he said if I had no objection, he would endorse me the following day." Carter had now unseated Wallace as "the South's political hero." Wallace's withdrawal, combined with the decision of most "undecided" delegates to support Carter, enabled the former Georgia governor to bring a cohesive delegation of southerners to the convention. Carter also spoke with Chicago Mayor Richard Daley, who endorsed him, and with Senator Jackson, who pledged an open expression of support within days. Armed with the delegates pledged to Wallace, Daley, and Jackson, Carter had more than enough delegates. Only Udall and Brown remained in contention, essentially as symbolic candidates.[34]

At the convention Carter captured 89 percent of the southern delegates. He combined this strong southern showing with impressive majorities from the border states (84 percent), the Northeast (79), and the Midwest (77). Only in the West, where Brown carried most of the California delegation, was Carter held to a slim majority (54 percent) of the delegates. As Jordan summed it up on the night of Carter's nomination, "Not bad for a bunch of dumb southerners!"[35]

Carter in 1980: The Renomination of a Weak Front-Runner

As the 1980 presidential campaign approached, President Carter found himself very much on the defensive. His situation in 1979 appeared so bleak that he faced a major challenge for renomination, let alone reelection. Carter's public opinion ratings were "reaching lows . . . unmatched by Richard Nixon in the midst of Watergate,"

Larry M. Bartels noted. "Democratic officeholders nervous about running on a Carter ticket were, literally, lining up to urge Kennedy into the race. And in spite of his own glaring liability—Chappaquiddick and the issue of 'character'—[Massachusetts Senator Edward] Kennedy was beating Carter handily in every national poll."[36]

Just as there was minimal high regard between Lyndon Johnson and Robert Kennedy, so too no love was lost between Carter and Ted Kennedy. "On both ideological and personal grounds," wrote Jack W. Germond and Jules Witcover, "the two men had no use for each other." Carter was confident of beating the Massachusetts senator in a renomination battle, but he had nothing to gain and a great deal to lose from an open fight with the nation's leading liberal Democrat. Every Democratic incumbent since World War II who had faced a serious challenge for renomination had been severely wounded in the process. Once their unpopularity with the voting public was established in the early primaries, both Truman in 1952 and Johnson in 1968 had withdrawn their candidacies.[37]

The Kennedy problem was especially acute for Carter. Open political warfare between himself and the Massachusetts liberal would deepen the already heightened tensions between the southern and northeastern wings of the Democratic party, the two forces that had put Carter in office four years earlier. Carter had won the presidency in 1976 with a fragile and tenuous political base consisting of the South, the Border states, and several northeastern states. A serious challenge from the liberal wing of the party, strongest in the Northeast and California, directly threatened to undermine Carter's electoral college coalition.

Disregarding advice that he could not prevent the renomination of an incumbent president, Kennedy announced against Carter in the fall of 1979. His campaign self-destructed almost immediately, however, when Kennedy could not state a convincing rationale for his candidacy in a television interview seen by millions. Moreover, the Iranian hostage crisis temporarily reversed the President's position. President Carter suspended campaigning to devote full attention to the crisis. Public opinion polls showed a dramatic rise in those who approved Carter's performance, and by the end of 1979 Carter had regained the lead from Kennedy.[38]

Carter then waged "a modern version of the nineteenth-century 'front-porch' campaign," which allowed him to escape public scrutiny during most of the nominating season. Kennedy was not strong enough to beat Carter, but he directed attention to Carter's liabilities.

In the primaries Carter swept all eight southern contests. He also won fifteen of the twenty-four primaries outside the South, including such key states as Illinois, Wisconsin, Indiana, and Ohio. Kennedy won heavily in the Northeast (Massachusetts, Connecticut, New York, Pennsylvania, New Jersey, and Rhode Island) and in California. All in all, Carter won only 51 percent of the total Democratic primary vote in 1980 and Kennedy received 37 percent. Although the incumbent had won enough delegates to be renominated, he had failed to elicit enthusiastic support within his own party. Many liberal activists in the Democratic party had never been comfortable with Carter, and after he had defeated their hero they had even less incentive to work hard for a Carter victory in the fall.[39]

The final confrontation between Kennedy and Carter occurred moments after Carter had finished his acceptance speech at the convention. Senator Kennedy belatedly answered the call of National Democratic Committee Chairman Robert Strauss to join the president on the podium, but "he pointedly avoided giving Carter the satisfaction of the traditional closing-night tableau—the winning candidate and his rival standing together, their hands clasped and raised to demonstrate their shared commitment to a unified campaign against the common Republican enemy, Ronald Reagan." Kennedy shook hands with Carter, waved to the crowd, and then walked around the platform, avoiding any closer contact with President Carter. The nation watched "a president, ostensibly the leading actor in this mock-drama, playing the supplicant, and an unsuccessful one at that." It was a devasting scene. "'It looked like hell,' a reporter suggested later to Strauss. 'It looked worse than hell,' Strauss replied. At the very moment when Jimmy Carter should have been in control of the situation, he seemed instead to fit the picture the country had developed of him over the previous three and a half years—somehow smaller than life." Kennedy had delivered a public insult to President Carter. Carter entered the fall campaign as a very weak and vulnerable incumbent.[40]

The 1984 Primaries: The Triumph of Progressive Democrats

Voters in the 1980 southern primaries had helped President Carter, a centrist Democrat, defeat the challenge of a liberal Democrat, Senator Edward Kennedy. The outcomes of the 1984 primaries were very different, for voters in the southern states kept former Vice-President Walter Mondale, a liberal Minnesota Democrat, in the race. In addition, Mondale was challenged from the left by Rev. Jesse Jackson, a South Carolina–born, Chicago-based civil rights leader who was trying to expand the base of the Democratic party by organizing a "Rainbow Coalition" of blacks, Hispanics, and low-income whites. Together, these liberal candidates attracted 55 percent of the vote cast in the southern Democratic primaries in 1984. The success of Mondale and Jackson rested in part on the changing ideological composition of the southern Democratic electorate. Delighted by the performance and policies of President Reagan, many southern conservatives had abandoned the Democratic party; as a result, the party's remaining electorate was composed largely of moderate to progressive voters.[41]

The Mondale campaign was in desperate trouble when it arrived in Alabama, Georgia, and Florida, the three southern states that were part of the March 1984 "Super Tuesday" primaries. Mondale had long been the front-runner for the Democratic presidential nomination. When he received less than half of the vote in the Iowa caucuses while Colorado Senator Gary Hart finished second with 15 percent, however, the media began to tout Hart as Mondale's most credible challenger. Hart then defeated Mondale, 37 to 28 percent, in the New Hampshire primary. Suddenly the Mondale campaign was vulnerable. Beyond Hart's appeal to young and independent voters, Jackson's support among blacks hurt the Minnesota Democrat.[42]

Appealing to such basic Democratic constituencies as blacks and union members, Mondale aggressively defined the "soul of the Democratic party" by championing the party's traditional liberal values. Mondale lost to Hart in Florida, but his narrow victories in Alabama and Georgia rescued his campaign in early March. In these two Deep South states, a biracial coalition provided him with pluralities of the vote. Indeed, without the support of prominent black politicians in both states, Mondale would not have finished first. In all, Mondale won four of the six primaries held in the South in the spring of 1984 (Alabama, Georgia, North Carolina, and Tennessee), finished second to Jackson in Louisiana, and ran behind Hart in Florida. Mondale won 33 percent of the vote cast in the southern primaries, compared with 31 percent for Hart and 21 percent for Jackson—a decidedly divided South. Even when Mondale "won" in the South, he did not do so decisively. He received over 40 percent of the vote only in Tennessee.[43]

Nor could Mondale take much encouragement from his performance in primaries outside the southern states. He carried Illinois,

New York, Pennsylvania, and New Jersey but lost to Hart in such important states as Massachusetts, Connecticut, Wisconsin, Indiana, Ohio, Oregon, and California, as well as in some smaller states. Mondale beat Hart in many of the caucus and convention states and had more complete slates of delegates than Hart in the primary states, so his number of delegates accumulated. When the primaries ended, Mondale was close enough to a majority of the pledged delegates that he was able to persuade a sufficient number of previously uncommitted delegates to support him.[44]

Much of the drama in the 1984 primaries lay in Jackson's emergence as a serious campaigner. Jackson's candidacy was based mainly on the growing importance of black voters in Democratic primary politics, both in the South and in many of the nation's largest cities. "Hart and Mondale represent advocacy. I represent action," Jackson told black audiences in the South. "At best they represent liberalism. I represent liberation. Both are talking forward and moving backward." Jackson wanted to expand the grassroots constituency of the Democratic party by bringing into it groups of Americans who had not participated fully in the past. "My constituency," he explained to the nation during his address to the Democratic convention in San Francisco, "is the desperate, the damned, the disinherited, the disrespected and the despised." As he further told the convention, "Our flag is red, white and blue, but our Nation is a rainbow—Red, Yellow, Brown, Black and White—we're all precious in God's sight." America, Jackson believed, should be perceived as a political "quilt":

> America is not like a blanket—one piece of unbroken cloth, the same color, the same texture, the same size. America is more like a quilt— many patches, many pieces, many colors, many sizes, all woven and held together by a common thread. The White, the Hispanic, the Black, the Arab, the Jew, the woman, the Native American, the small farmer, the businessperson, the environmentalist, the peace activist, the young, the old, the lesbian, the gay and the disabled make up the American quilt.[45]

In 1984 Jackson's campaign was hindered by Mondale's well-established reputation as a champion of civil rights and by the common belief that Mondale was far more likely than Jackson to win the nomination. Alabama's Joe Reed, an influential black Democratic politician, explained why he had supported Mondale rather than Jackson: "'The question that one always has to answer as a leader,' he said later, 'is, do you tell people the truth or do you tell them what they want to hear? We elected to tell the truth, and that was, we didn't think Jesse could get nominated, and if he got the nomination, he couldn't win.'"[46]

Jackson stimulated black turnout, but he was unable to unite all blacks behind his candidacy. Nor did Jackson draw more than a trace of support from southern whites. CBS News/New York Times Exit Polls suggest that whites accounted for only 2 percent of Jackson's vote in Alabama, 6 percent of his Georgia vote, and 8 percent of his North Carolina vote. Jackson carried Louisiana when many whites followed the advice of Governor Edwin Edwards to skip the primaries, an early example of what could happen in states where blacks turned out in large numbers and whites had little interest in the outcomes.[47]

Both Jackson and Hart carried their campaigns into the Democratic convention. Each candidate addressed the convention, and there were numerous strains, private and public, between Mondale and his two defeated rivals, neither of whom were seriously considered as vice-presidential candidates. At the convention the South remained splintered. Mondale received 54 percent of the southern delegates, with the remaining vote divided between Hart and Jackson. Mondale won larger majorities of the convention delegates from the East, Midwest, and Border states than from the South, but his weakest region by far was the West, where he won only 35 percent of the delegates.[48]

Mondale bypassed both of his principal rivals by selecting New York Congresswoman Geraldine Ferraro as his running mate. Trailing Reagan badly in the polls and facing a deeply divided party, Mondale threw caution to the winds and proudly proclaimed in his acceptance speech that, if elected, he would call for an increase in income taxes to help balance the budget. "I mean business," Mondale informed the nation. "By the end of my first term, I will cut the deficit by two-thirds. Let's tell the truth. Mr. Reagan will raise taxes, and so will I. He won't tell you. I just did."[49]

One person who understood the riskiness of Mondale's message was Lee Atwater, the chief southern strategist for the Reagan campaign, who was "being worked over by a masseur when he heard Mondale's bolt of candor." Atwater later recalled to Germond and Witcover that "I was half-delirious and heard him say that. Coming from my region [the South] and my political background, I knew a tax increase is just outlandish . . . I thought I had literally fallen asleep and was dreaming. I sat up and asked my wife and the masseur, 'Did he really say what I thought he said?'" After a night's sleep Atwater was ready to grade Mondale's promise to raise taxes: "Well, he's getting an A-plus for boldness, but he's going to get an F-minus in the end."[50]

Super Tuesday 1988: The Unsolid South

Reagan's devastating attacks on Mondale in the 1984 campaign were also felt by many southern Democratic officeholders and candidates. Mondale's pledge to raise income taxes to balance the budget powerfully reinforced his image as a "tax and spend liberal," and many southern Democratic politicians avoided any association with the Democratic presidential nominee. Nowhere was the liability of the "Mondale liberal" label used more effectively than in the North Carolina Senate race between incumbent Republican Senator Jesse Helms and Democratic Governor James B. Hunt. "Mr. Hunt doesn't want you to know it," said Senator Helms during a televised debate, "but he's a Mondale liberal and ashamed of it. I'm a Reagan conservative and proud of it." In a previous debate Helms had asked of Hunt, "'What is it about these two figures [Walter Mondale and Ted Kennedy] that you admire so much?' Hunt replied that he had a 'lot of differences' with them and that if he went to the Senate he intended to 'get them to understand why they ought to be more moderate, and maybe more conservative like us Southern Democrats are.'"[51]

Like Hunt, many Democratic candidates across the South viewed Mondale's candidacy as dangerous to their political success. They had generally run with Jimmy Carter in 1976 and 1980, but the 1984 campaign reminded them of the problems they had encountered with Humphrey in 1968 and McGovern in 1972. Many of them believed they could not afford another ticket headed by a politician who could be stigmatized and ridiculed as a "liberal northern Democrat." The Democratic nominating process needed to be changed, they thought, in order to produce a different sort of Democratic nominee, one whom they could genuinely support in the general election.

From these feelings of despair emerged a change designed to enhance the role of the South in the nominating process. A group of influential Democratic state legislators resolved to create a regional primary that would be scheduled early in the nominating season. Six of the southern states held primaries in 1984, and only three of them occurred on the same day early in the nominating process. In 1988 Super Tuesday—as the event came to be known—involved Democratic primaries in ten southern states. (South Carolina Democrats opted for a caucus.) Super Tuesday was scheduled for March 8, only two weeks after the New Hampshire primary. The Iowa caucuses and the New Hampshire primary would still precede the southern regional primary, but much of the original field of candidates would presumably be intact. Because of the large number of convention delegates apportioned that day, it would be virtually impossible for any major candidate to skip the South. Candidates would have to confront the southern electorates if they wished to win the Democratic nomination.[52]

Many leading southern Democrats hoped that Super Tuesday would help nominate a consensus candidate who could bring together the diverse strands of the South's voters. The successful candidate would presumably be a "moderate" or "mainstream" Democrat who could draw from liberal and conservative factions and who would be an asset rather than a liability to southern state and local Democratic candidates in the general election. If the winner of Super Tuesday turned out to be a moderate southern Democrat, so much the better.

From the start many observers viewed Super Tuesday as flawed. After all, Alabama and Georgia had given the liberal Mondale the victories that had kept his candidacy alive in 1984. Ohio Senator John Glenn, the moderate Democrat who had been expected to run well in the South, finished far out of the running after he had made little headway in Iowa and New Hampshire. No unified South had appeared in the six southern primaries held in 1984. In the Deep South, where blacks made up well over a third of the potential primary voters, Super Tuesday raised the distinct possibility that Jesse Jackson might have his biggest day ever in politics. An impressive Jackson performance would increase the number of delegates to the Democratic convention who wished to shift the party more toward the needs and interests of low-income Americans—exactly the positioning that the inventors of Super Tuesday wanted to avoid.[53]

The success of the Super Tuesday strategy also depended upon the emergence of a consensus candidate, a politician of obvious presidential stature who could excite the region's moderate voters while also winning votes from the liberal and conservative wings of the party. Carter had been such a candidate in the 1976 and 1980 southern primaries, but whether a similar type of candidate would emerge in 1988 remained to be seen. In view of the electorate's diversity and the moderate to liberal voting tendencies already evident in 1984, the most likely prospects were that the Super Tuesday primaries would reveal not a single "South" but several different "Souths" and that the more liberal Democrats would again prevail.

With President Reagan ineligible for reelection, many Democrats entered the field. The Iowa caucuses and the New Hampshire primary, however, sharply reduced the number of serious candidates. Representative Richard Gephardt of Missouri and Senator Paul Simon of Illinois finished first and second in Iowa, ahead of Governor Michael Dukakis of Massachusetts. The New Hampshire results put Dukakis in the lead, relegated Gephardt to second place, and virtually eliminated Simon. As Super Tuesday approached, the principal contenders were Dukakis, by far the best funded of the Democrats in the race, and two other candidates who had received no boosts outside the South. Jesse Jackson, already well-known among whites and blacks, was trying for a second time to construct a "Rainbow Coalition" of blacks, Hispanics, and low-income whites; and Tennessee Senator Al Gore, Jr., not widely known outside his home state, sought to become the consensus candidate for southern whites.

In presidential primaries with several candidates, the name of the game is a plurality victory, usually in the range of one-third to two-fifths of the vote. The easiest way for a particular candidate to succeed is to identify groups that are likely to favor the candidate and then to target those states in which the candidate's potential support groups are large enough to generate a plurality. To understand the results of Super Tuesday in the South, it is necessary to grasp the diversity of the region's Democratic primary voters. The candidates faced two rather different subregional electorates, which we have profiled using the CBS News/New York Times Exit Polls of the Super Tuesday voters: voters in the Deep South states (the average of results from Alabama, Georgia, Louisiana, and Mississippi) and those of the six Peripheral South states.

The Democratic primary electorate in the Deep South showed signs of the triumph of the civil rights movement as well as the withdrawal of many conservative southern whites from the Democratic party. In the relatively small arena of Democratic primary electorates, moderate to progressive groups strongly outnumbered white conservatives. Blacks averaged 42 percent of the Deep South Democratic electorate, and core white Democrats, mainly moderates, made up another 29 percent of the voters. Right-of-center whites were still a potent minority force in the Deep South Democratic electorates, but they averaged less than a third of the voters.

Moderate to progressive forces also dominated the Democratic primary electorate in the Peripheral South states, but in a strikingly different way. The effective center of gravity in the Peripheral South lay among core white Democrats rather than blacks. Core white Democrats averaged 40 percent of the Democratic voters, while blacks made up one-quarter of the Peripheral South's Democratic voters. Slightly over one-third of the participants in the Peripheral South were either swing white voters or core white Republicans. In both subregions the ideological diversity of the Super Tuesday electorate enabled different candidates to direct their efforts toward particular segments of the electorate—blacks, core white Democrats, or right-of-center whites.

The diversity of the Democratic primary electorate in the South is even more apparent in Table 9.1, which shows for each southern state the percentage of its Democratic Super Tuesday electorate com-

Table 9.1   The composition of the Democratic primary electorate in the southern states: percentages of blacks, Hispanics, migrant whites, and native southern whites voting in the 1988 Super Tuesday Democratic presidential primaries

	Blacks	Whites raised in South	Whites raised elsewhere	Hispanics
Mississippi	45	43	12	—
Alabama	45	40	15	—
Louisiana	38	46	16	—
Georgia	36	47	17	—
Virginia	35	27	38	—
North Carolina	29	52	19	—
Tennessee	27	56	16	—
Texas	23	43	24	11
Florida	17	26	56	1
Arkansas	13	57	29	—

Note: Rows may not add to 100 because of rounding. States are ranked (highest to lowest) according to the percentage of blacks in the Super Tuesday Democratic primary electorates.

Source: CBS News/New York Times Exit Polls.

posed of blacks, whites raised in the South, white migrants to the region, and Hispanics. The states are ranked according to the size of the vote cast by blacks on Super Tuesday. In five states—all of the Deep South states holding primaries plus Virginia—blacks constituted more than one-third of the voters. In Arkansas, North Carolina, and Tennessee, whites raised in the South supplied a majority of the Democratic primary voters. Florida and Texas, the two remaining states, displayed still different patterns. Florida was the only southern state in which white migrants were the majority. White migrants were only 24 percent of the Texas voters, but Hispanics cast an additional 11 percent of the vote.

These profiles of the subregions and states are relevant in understanding which states and which types of voters were targeted by the different candidates. Jackson clearly planned to capitalize on the growing black presence within southern Democratic parties. Although the breadth of the Rainbow Coalition was questionable, even without much support from whites or Hispanics Jackson would be a strong contestant in any southern state where blacks made up a substantial portion of the voters. Jackson focused on the seven southern states where blacks comprised at least one-quarter of Democratic primary voters.

Because of Jackson's anticipated strength among black voters, none of the white candidates targeted blacks. Dukakis sought the votes of liberal to moderate southern whites and Hispanics, and he was especially active where large numbers of white Democrats raised outside the South had migrated into the metropolitan areas of southern states—Florida, Texas, and Virginia. Gore's appeal was directed toward moderate and conservative whites, especially those born and raised in the region. He sought white votes in his home state, the neighboring Peripheral South states of North Carolina, Arkansas, and Virginia, and the Deep South.

With each candidate focusing on a different set of states and target groups, Super Tuesday illustrated the diverse currents that flow through Democratic primaries in the modern South. Jackson and Gore finished in a dead heat for the region's popular vote, each winning 29 percent. Dukakis took third place with 24 percent of the vote. Jackson won the Deep South states of Alabama, Georgia, Louisiana, and Mississippi. Helped by a large black turnout and a low white turnout, Jackson even carried Virginia. Gore finished first in Tennessee, North Carolina, and Arkansas, a subregional "friends and neighbors" vote in the heartland of the Peripheral South; and

Dukakis won Texas and Florida, the two states least conventionally "southern" in their populations. It was a very unsolid South.

The 1988 Super Tuesday primaries did give Jackson his greatest day in politics and propelled him toward the convention. Jackson was enormously popular among southern blacks and enjoyed the enthusiastic backing of many black grassroots organizations. He won practically all of the black vote, ranging upward from 89 percent in Texas to 96 percent in Alabama and Virginia. Among southern white voters, however, Jackson did not make impressive inroads. His white support varied from 5 percent in Mississippi and Louisiana to 12 percent in Virginia. Jackson thus consolidated his base among black voters, but failed to go significantly beyond it. The pattern of over-whelming black support but minimal white support meant that he did not have the remotest prospect of carrying any southern state in a presidential election, when whites would make up the vast majority of voters.[54]

At the other end of the continuum was Gore, a first-term senator with few obvious "presidential" assets and little name recognition outside Tennessee. He had a solidly liberal voting record in the House and Senate, and he was one of a handful of southern Democrats whose positions on most issues were closer to their northern than to their southern colleagues. Gore campaigned in Iowa and New Hamp-shire but made little headway against a field of better-known and more experienced candidates. Switching tactics, he then denounced the liberal activists who dominated the Iowa Democratic party, down-played the importance of New Hampshire, and began to campaign as a moderate Democrat, strong on defense, who sought to become the consensus candidate of southern white Democrats. Gore fell back on the unlikely scenario of igniting his campaign in the South on Super Tuesday by capturing the votes of moderate to conservative white southerners.[55]

Gore's strategy was seriously flawed. Instead of first establishing himself as a credible candidate outside the South, as Carter had done, he attacked as unrepresentative of the Democratic party the very arenas that Carter had demonstrated a southerner could win. In addition, Gore's effort to distinguish himself from the rest of the field both deemphasized the progressive features of his record and crippled his ability to appeal to the bulk of citizens who vote in Democratic primaries, whether in the South or in the rest of the nation. Even in the South, as we have shown, there are far more moderates and liberals than conservatives in the Democratic primary electorate. Although Gore was able to win pluralities in some states by emphasizing his conservative credentials and southern background, by doing so he was alienating progressive Democrats.

Gore's white support varied markedly. He won majorities of the white vote in Tennessee (87 percent), Mississippi (64), Alabama (64), Georgia (53), and North Carolina (51) and substantial white pluralities in Arkansas (46), Louisiana (44), and Virginia (40). Yet Gore faltered badly among whites in the two largest southern states, winning only 28 percent in Texas and 15 percent in Florida. In each of the southern states a higher percentage of core white Republicans and swing whites voted for Gore than did core white Democrats. Competing against Jackson, he rarely drew more than 3 percent of the black vote.

Having won part of the southern vote by appealing to the most conservative Democrats, Gore was in no position to advance in the North. He became another example of a purely regional candidate, armed with the support of moderate to conservative southerners. Running to the right in a Democratic presidential primary is generally *not* a promising route to the nomination because it cuts against the dominant grain of conviction and opinion among most of the voters. Many northern Democratic voters viewed Gore, if they perceived him at all, as irrelevant. His campaign ended in the lively company of New York Mayor Ed Koch, who upstaged Gore with a blistering anti-Jackson crusade that left Gore in third place with only 10 percent of the New York vote. Eventually Gore withdrew and released his delegates to Dukakis.[56]

To many southerners Dukakis was basically a stranger with an odd name. Like Gore, he rarely won more than 3 percent of the black voters in the southern states. Among white voters he polled well in Florida (53 percent), Texas (38), Virginia (35), and North Carolina (30), but elsewhere he attracted well less than three out of every ten whites. Dukakis was strongest among core white Democrats, but he showed little strength among swing whites or core white Republicans.

Based on his Super Tuesday performance, Dukakis's general election prospects in the South were not good. Dukakis had won two states, Florida with 41 percent and Texas with 33. But these electoral prizes normally vote Republican in presidential elections, and it was most unlikely that Dukakis could carry either the Lone Star State or the Sunshine State with George Bush as the probable Republican nominee. In Arkansas Dukakis finished a distant second. Everywhere else Dukakis ran third. This point is very important. The Massachusetts governor was the type of candidate who—had he been running for a southern governorship in a dual primary state—would not have qualified for the Democratic runoff primary because he failed to finish among the top two candidates.[57]

After Super Tuesday the Democratic nomination was essentially a contest between Dukakis and Jackson. Dukakis defeated Jackson in almost all of the remaining contests, and he entered the convention with a majority of the delegates pledged to his support. The head-to-head confrontation between the white liberal and the black progressive left both men irritated with each other, and their disagreements exposed some of the most important divisions within the modern Democratic party.[58]

The biggest question concerned the vice-presidential nomination. Dukakis's selection of Senator Lloyd Bentsen, a moderate to conservative Texas Democrat, symbolically re-created the "Boston-Austin" axis of the 1960 Kennedy-Johnson campaign, the only type of ticket headed by a liberal northerner that had succeeded since midcentury. Picking Bentsen had the short-term effect of energizing the southern leadership echelon that had sponsored Super Tuesday. However, it simultaneously deepened the conflict between Jackson and Dukakis. Jackson had won more than seven million votes in the primaries, far more than he had obtained in 1984, but on grounds of electability it was inconceivable that Dukakis would choose Jackson as his running mate. It did not help matters that Jackson was not informed personally by Dukakis before he heard the news that the governor had chosen Bentsen.[59]

Personally insulted by this inept manuever, Jackson began to extract his due from Dukakis. At a press conference called on the afternoon of the Bentsen announcement, Jackson left "the door open to letting his name be put forward for the Vice-Presidency at the Convention, and said he'd bring about a dozen platform issues to the Convention floor." In addition, according to Elizabeth Drew, "Jackson turned his grievance, which was a personal one, into one that had been inflicted on all blacks, and at an N.A.A.C.P. convention that night he made a fiery speech. He ended the speech by shouting, to the cheers and applause of the crowd, 'I will never surrender!' and 'I may not be on the ticket but I'm qualified!' and, with the crowd joining in, he repeated, 'Qualified! Qualified! Qualified!'"[60]

The 1988 convention began with Jackson and Dukakis still at odds over the role Jackson would play at the convention and in the fall campaign. After a peacemaking meeting on Monday, the Jackson and Dukakis factions came together, at least temporarily. Dukakis closed the convention with a dramatic acceptance speech. "This election is not about ideology," Dukakis announced, "it's about competence." Whether competence was a sufficiently powerful theme to motivate party unity and attract swing voters remained to be seen.[61]

The Progressive Tilt

Since the late 1960s southern Democratic parties have undergone a virtual revolution. Southerners who vote in Democratic presidential primaries are generally moderate to liberal voters, not conservatives. In turn, the progressive tilt within the small arenas of the Democratic primary electorates in the southern states has influenced the types of candidates who can win presidential primaries and, indirectly, the types of individuals who represent the southern states at Democratic national conventions.

The Super Tuesday vote cast by the core Democratic groups (blacks, white liberal Democrats, white moderate Democrats, and white liberal independents) and the combined vote for Jackson and Dukakis, the two most liberal candidates in the Super Tuesday primaries, are convenient indicators of the relative size of the moderate to progressive forces within the Democratic primary electorate. As Table 9.2 shows, these calculations reveal an ideological center of gravity that greatly favors progressive candidates.

In every southern state the core Democratic voting groups constituted a majority of voters in 1988. If Arkansas is set aside as a case of extraordinarily arrested Republican development, the results are even more revealing. In nine of the ten southern states holding Democratic primaries, the core Democratic voting groups accounted for more than three-fifths of the Democratic primary voters. Furthermore, in all but two southern states (Gore's home state of Tennessee and Arkansas) the combined vote for the two most liberal Democratic presidential candidates amounted to a majority of the total vote. Estimates in each state of the potential Democratic core vote and the actual vote for the two most liberal candidates create a range of liberal strength. If the moderate to progressive forces can unite behind a candidate, they assuredly have enough votes to control Democratic primaries in the South.

This analysis has many implications for strategies in future Democratic presidential primaries. Given the new lay of the land, it is not

Table 9.2 The progressive tilt in the southern Democratic primary electorate: percentages of Democratic core voters and combined votes for Michael Dukakis and Jesse Jackson in the 1988 Super Tuesday Democratic presidential primaries

	Core Democratic voters[a]	Dukakis-Jackson vote[b]
Virginia	73	67
Mississippi	69	53
Alabama	69	51
Florida	68	61
Georgia	68	55
Louisiana	67	51
Texas[c]	64	57
North Carolina	64	53
Tennessee	61	24
Arkansas	51	36

a. The percentage of the Democratic primary electorate accounted for by blacks, liberal white Democrats, moderate white Democrats, and liberal independents. States are ranked from highest to lowest according to the percentage of core Democratic voters in the Super Tuesday Democratic primary electorates.

b. The percentage of the Democratic primary vote won by Dukakis and Jackson.

c. Hispanics are included in the core Democratic groups in Texas.

Sources: CBS News/New York Times Super Tuesday Exit Polls; and Gerald M. Pomper, "The Presidential Nominations," in Gerald M. Pomper and others, *The Election of 1988* (Chatham, N.J.: Chatham House, 1989), p. 40.

surprising that Democratic presidential candidates who emphasized their progressive credentials dominated most of the South's primary elections in 1984 and 1988. The majorities of the vote won by Mondale and Jackson in 1984 and by Dukakis and Jackson in 1988 rest on a durable redistribution of political power favoring the progressive groups within the Democratic primary electorate.[62]

Democrats who are tempted to emphasize conservative themes because of the still sizable fraction of the vote cast by swing whites and core Republicans may indeed be able to win a plurality of the vote, provided the more liberal candidates split the larger moderate to liberal vote. Nonetheless, this is a self-destructive, fruitless way to try to win a Democratic presidential nomination. The Democratic party is simply not going to nominate a candidate who has little or no appeal to at least some of the party's core voting groups.

What the Democrats need are extraordinarily skilled candidates who generate enthusiasm among the party's two essential groups, blacks and core white Democrats, but who are also attractive to the South's swing whites, the conservative white Democrats and moderate independents. Such candidates would give most emphasis to progressive issues and themes, while hedging their liberalism by making some concessions to more conservative voters. Democratic politicians who are already experienced in devising such a broad-based appeal would have an enormous advantage, in a general election campaign, over Democrats who owe their success mainly to particular narrow segments of the party. Above all, the Democratic party should nominate politicians who understand that winning the presidency requires that the candidate develop an appeal that includes—but goes beyond—the Democratic core groups.

Just as the candidates and Democratic primary voters have tilted toward the progressive side, so have southern convention delegates. Women now account for half of the southern delegates to Democratic conventions, and blacks made up a third of the region's delegates in 1988. Southern convention delegates are mainly political moderates or liberals; very few are conservatives. Especially missing are the conservative white southerners who were the dominant regional force in the old days of the hand-picked delegations. If white conservatives traditionally defined the southern presence at Democratic national conventions, they have practically no leverage in the conventions of the reformed party.

The progressive tilt of the Democratic presidential electorate in the South, as well as in the rest of the nation, has contributed mightily to the difficulties encountered by the eventual Democratic nominees in the general election. "With the withdrawal of socially conservative white voters from the nomination process," Thomas Byrne Edsall and Mary D. Edsall have emphasized, "Democratic presidential candidates have negotiated that process in the context of an artificially liberal primary electorate that puts the candidates outside the ideological mainstream and provides them with virtually no training in the kinds of accommodation and bargaining essential to general-election victory."[63]

As political trends within the southern Democratic party have shifted in a liberal direction, the Democratic party has become more isolated and prone to defeat in presidential elections. Presidential campaigns are dramas with three acts—the primaries, the conventions, and the general election. Progressive groups are a working majority within the narrow borders of Democratic primary politics (Act One), and an even larger majority among the South's delegates to the Democratic national convention (Act Two). In Act Three of the presidential play, however, there is no progressive advantage. Instead, the liberal forces constitute a decided minority of the southerners who vote in presidential elections. Because the core Democratic groups make up only about two-fifths of the electorate that chooses the president, Democratic presidential nominees confront a difficult task. By the nature of the situation they are compelled to win considerable support from swing white voters, people who have little influence either in selecting Democratic presidential candidates or in determining the policies of the national Democratic party.

10

The Conservative Triumph
in Republican Primaries

Conservative supremacy within the Republican party has become one of the most significant "givens" of modern American politics. "The Eastern Liberal Establishment so influential in the 1950s and 1960s was now just a memory," observed Jack W. Germond and Jules Witcover in 1989. "The few moderates within the party had been dying off or quitting politics in frustration. The conservative movement was not monolithic, but the Republican party had become monolithically conservative."[1]

No small part of the increased prominence of conservative political forces in the Republican party was due to the party's growing southern wing. Having lost the ability to influence the outcomes of Democratic national conventions, many conservative southerners gravitated to the Republican party as a more attractive and sympathetic institution. Over the years, activists from the South—such as Peter O'Donnell of Texas, John Grenier of Alabama, Clarke Reed of Mississippi, Harry Dent, Strom Thurmond, Lee Atwater, and Carroll Campbell of South Carolina, and Jesse Helms of North Carolina, to list only a few—have been prominent players in Republican presidential politics. In turn, their own regional brand of conservatism helped to shift the GOP's center of gravity further to the right.[2]

During the 1980s, for the first time in history, the South became the largest regional delegation at Republican national conventions. The eleven states of the Old Confederacy accounted for one-fourth of the Republican delegates. If completely united behind a single candidate, southern delegates alone could provide an aspiring candidate with *half* the votes necessary for the Republican presidential nomination.[3]

In the words of Mississippi's Reed, the persistent objective of most southern Republicans has been to back "the conservative who has the best chance of winning the election." More often than not, the South has set the tone of successful campaigns for the Republican presidential nomination. A cohesive South at Republican conventions helped nominate Barry Goldwater in 1964 and Richard Nixon in 1968. Southern support was a key aspect of Ronald Reagan's campaign for the 1980 nomination, and George Bush's massive southern vote in the 1988 Super Tuesday primaries ensured his nomination. In 1976, the one instance in which a majority of southerners preferred the losing candidate, southern Republicans could claim that Reagan's victories in the North Carolina and Texas primaries had kept him in the race and eventually made him the Republican front-runner for 1980.[4]

Southern conservatives customarily exercised their influence at the Republican national convention, but in the past two decades the battlegrounds have expanded to include presidential primaries overwhelmingly dominated by white conservatives. The scheduling of several southern primaries early in the nomination season and the large numbers of delegates at stake have enhanced the South's political leverage within the Republican party.

During the 1970s and 1980s there were three sharply contested fights for the Republican presidential nomination. President Gerald Ford was challenged by Reagan in 1976; Reagan, George Bush, and several others contended for the 1980 nomination; and in 1988 Vice-President Bush faced Robert Dole, Jack Kemp, Pat Robertson, and others. Two other nominations (in 1972 and 1984) involved open-and-shut victories for incumbent Republican presidents. The contested nominations are the subjects of this chapter.

The South and Reagan's Challenge to Ford

"Well, Governor, I'm very disappointed," President Gerald Ford replied to former California Governor Ronald Reagan. "I'm sorry you're getting into this. I believe I've done a good job and that I can be elected. Regardless of your good intentions, your bid is bound to be divisive. It will take a lot of money, a lot of effort, and it will leave a lot of scars. It won't be helpful, no matter which of us wins the nomination." The occasion for the president's irritation was a telephone call from Reagan, announcing his intention to challenge Ford for the Republican presidential nomination in 1976. Ford and his advisors had long hoped—against many signs to the contrary—that Reagan would not be a candidate in 1976.[5]

Ford had good reason to be concerned. As Lee Atwater once explained, "if you're the incumbent . . . and you are being challenged inside your party by the major player in the other wing of the party . . . you are facing two challenges: (a) people saying that this guy is not capable of leading the country, and (b) people saying that not only is he not capable of leading the country, he's not capable of leading this party." Since 1912 no sitting Republican president had ever needed to engage in a protracted fight to win the nomination. In that year President William Howard Taft, with considerable help from the "rotten borough" southern delegations, had been able to defeat former President Theodore Roosevelt at the Republican convention. The Taft-Roosevelt struggle so disrupted the party that Roosevelt's followers could not bring themselves to support Taft. As a direct consequence of the split, Democrat Woodrow Wilson was elected president.[6]

Reagan's challenge of Ford was thus an extraordinary event. It was rooted in Reagan's determination to achieve the presidency, but it also reflected a struggle for ideological control of the Republican party. When President Richard Nixon and Vice-President Spiro Agnew began their second terms in January 1973, conservative southern Republicans were satisfied with their influence and status within the national party. They had helped Nixon and Agnew win the greatest landslide ever recorded for a Republican presidential ticket in the South. Southern Republicans could do business with Nixon, and they had come to venerate Agnew for his ripping attacks on liberal Democrats.

Within months, however, the Nixon-Agnew administration began to disintegrate. In 1973 Vice-President Agnew pled *nolo contendere* to federal charges of using public office for private gain and resigned his position. President Nixon nominated Representative Ford of Michigan, the Minority Leader of the House of Representatives, as his replacement. Ford was a midwestern conservative who had good relations with the various factions of the party, but he was not the kind of dynamic politician who could bring crowds of southern and western conservatives to their feet.

Amidst Agnew's disgrace and the escalating Watergate crisis, Reagan emerged as an unsullied hero for conservative Americans. Nowhere was Reagan more popular than among southern Republicans. In November 1973 the California governor addressed the Mississippi Republican party and received an ecstatic welcome from an overflow audience. "You're one of the key people that we need—we've loved you for a long time," said one of his Mississippi hosts. "Nowhere else in this country are you better understood and respected because these people want you to be the next President of the United States." Reagan "spoke of limited government, welfare reform, and patriotic values," and he "paid homage to the South as the national repository of conservative values." After listening to Reagan's speech, another enthusiastic Mississippian said, "I haven't applauded so much since a Goldwater rally." Reagan was energized by his enthusiastic reception. "If there's a Southern strategy," he told reporters, "I'm a part of it."[7]

As the Watergate crisis expanded to include the possibility of Nixon's impeachment, Reagan continued to consider his options for 1976. In a meeting with close political advisors in May 1974, John P. Sears, a young Washington lawyer who had worked in Nixon's 1968 campaign, "planted the seeds for what became the Reagan challenge to President Ford." According to Lou Cannon, Sears "predicted both that Nixon would not survive and that Ford would not be able to lead the country after he was gone. What Sears was suggesting was the heretical notion that loyalist Reagan could run for President in 1976 no matter what happened. If Nixon lasted, there would be an open run for the nomination. If Ford inherited the presidency, then Reagan could seek the Republican nomination against him in the primaries."[8]

A few months later Nixon's resignation in the face of certain conviction on articles of impeachment elevated Ford to the presidency. One of Ford's most consequential initial decisions was to choose a new vice-president for confirmation by the Congress. In a California press conference Reagan offered the president some unsolicited advice. While emphasizing that he was not personally seeking the office, Reagan urged Ford to look carefully at Republicans with executive experience and to honor "the conservative philosophy" in selecting the new vice-president.[9]

Reagan did not make Ford's short list for the vice-presidency. The final choice lay between George Bush, at that time the chairman of the Republican National Committee, and Nelson Rockefeller, the former governor of New York. Bryce Harlow, a Ford advisor who weighed the alternatives, counseled the president that

> For party harmony, plainly it should be Bush. But this would be construed primarily as a partisan act, foretelling a Presidential hesitancy to move boldly in the face of known controversy. The Rockefeller choice

would be hailed by the media normally most hostile to Republicans. It would encourage estranged groups to return to the party and would signal that the new President will not be the captive of any political faction. As for 1976, a Ford-Rockefeller ticket should be an extremely formidable combination against any opponents the Democrats could offer. Therefore, the best choice is Rockefeller.[10]

Rockefeller's selection was a bold act for President Ford. "Conservatives who might otherwise have been tempted to give Ford a chance were infuriated at the prospect that Rockefeller might inherit the presidency," observed Cannon. "More than any other single act of Ford's, or indeed all of them combined, it was the selection of Rockefeller which fueled national interest among conservatives in a Reagan candidacy." Republican conservatives believed that Rockefeller's brand of moderate, northeastern Republicanism had been decisively rejected at the past three party conventions. At Reagan headquaters, the "selection of their old enemy was an unbelievable insult."[11]

The resolution of the Watergate debacle had transferred the most visible and important leadership positions within the White House from western and border conservatives to a midwestern conservative and a liberal northeastern Republican. It was a kind of regional balance that cut against the dominant ideological tendencies of the modern Republican party. "The essence of the Ford problem," emphasized Harry S. Dent, "was the failure to see the Republican party realistically as the conservative party it is." There was no doubt about the type of Republican candidate the conservatives desired. "Give a Republican a choice of Goldwater or Reagan versus almost any other Republican," Dent insisted, "and the purist yearning in his heart is difficult to suppress." In this curious turn of events southern and western conservatives had been relegated to a secondary position in the Republican party by two politicians who had neither been nominated by the party nor elected by the voters. Nixon and Agnew's downfall and their replacement by Ford and Rockefeller motivated conservative Republicans to risk losing the White House temporarily in order to regain control of "their" party.[12]

Eventually the conservatives extracted their revenge on Rockefeller. After a private meeting with President Ford in which the two leaders discussed "the growing strength of the GOP's right wing," Rockefeller removed himself from the 1976 ticket. Ford accepted Rockefeller's decision. "I was grateful for his expression of unselfishness, his willingness to do what was in the best interests of the party and the country—and me," he later wrote. "At the same time, I was angry with myself for showing cowardice in not saying to the ultra-conservatives, 'It's going to be Ford and Rockefeller, whatever the consequences.'"[13]

Reagan formally announced his candidacy in November 1975. By all accounts, the Ford organization greatly underestimated the seriousness of the Reagan challenge. Surrounded largely by associates from his days in the House of Representatives, and with his nomination campaign headed by Howard "Bo" Callaway, a former Georgia congressman who proved to be an inept manager, Ford was poorly prepared to fight. In the campaign's early stages Ford benefited largely from Reagan's mistakes. Reagan had given a new speech, the "$90 Billion Speech," in which he proposed massive shifts of programs from the federal government to state and local governments. As usual, Reagan was unprepared to answer detailed and specific questions about his proposals, and Ford strategists exploited these weaknesses to put Reagan on the defensive in the early primaries.[14]

President Ford barely won New Hampshire, 51 to 49 percent. It was a very weak showing for an incumbent president, but a severe disappointment to Reagan, who had expected to win. Ford's narrow win in New Hampshire did wonders for him in Florida, the first southern primary. The Ford campaign "hammered away at the $90 billion and Social Security issues and painted Reagan to the elderly Florida voter as someone who would upset the *status quo*." Ford again won a narrow victory, 53–47. By allying himself with key Republican organizations, Ford then won by a more decisive margin in Illinois, Reagan's native state. Despite these losses, Reagan was not about to quit. "You have to recognize he made some pretty bad movies," explained Sears, his campaign manager. "It must have been pretty embarrassing. But he knows that if you make a bad movie, you don't stop making movies."[15]

North Carolina's Republican primary, however, completely reversed the early momentum of the campaign. The Ford-Reagan contest became entangled in a test of strength between two rival Republican organizations. Ford was supported by Republican Governor James B. Holshouser, a moderate conservative, while Reagan was backed by the Congressional Club, the political organization created by Senator Jesse Helms and his chief strategist, Tom Ellis. These right-wing conservatives began counseling Reagan to sharpen his attacks on Ford's conduct of foreign policy. Jules Witcover reported that Reagan "hit at Ford with every issue he could think of, from the

Panama Canal and detente to the bloated Washington bureaucracy and the excessive political use of his incumbency." Greatly aided by Helms's organization in getting conservatives to the polls, Reagan beat Ford for the first time. There was no question about the importance of this victory. "North Carolina was the turning point of Reagan's political career," Cannon pointed out. "It kept him in the race to Kansas City, and it made him the presumptive presidential nominee in 1980."[16]

Reagan returned to national attention on May 1 with a tremendous victory in Texas. More than 400,000 voters, a record turnout, took part in the Republican primary. Reagan won two-thirds of the vote and all of the delegates. In Texas Reagan was able to attract the followers of George Wallace, whose career was being eclipsed by the rise of Jimmy Carter. Reagan then used his success among independents and conservative Democrats in Texas to make the case that he would be a far stronger general election campaigner in the South than President Ford would be. "If the Democratic nominee is to be Jimmy Carter," Reagan told an audience in Shreveport, Louisiana, "I will tell you now that I offer the best opportunity for victory for what we believe in." Three days later he won in Alabama and Georgia. Reagan faltered only in Tennessee, when he revived memories of Goldwater by suggesting that the status of the Tennessee Valley Authority should be reexamined. Outside the South the western states provided most of Reagan's support.[17]

Yet Reagan's surge did not last. The Ford organization improved as the campaign persisted. When the primaries drew to a close, Ford led Reagan in delegates but still lacked a majority. As the sitting president, Ford was in a far better position to bargain for the votes of wavering delegates. From then on the battle was waged delegate by delegate, among the caucuses and the uncommitted. The outcome was in doubt until the convention itself. Following the advice of Sears, Reagan tried to attract delegates by announcing that Senator Richard Schweiker of Pennsylvania, a moderate Republican, would be his vice-presidential candidate. This tactic did not work. It weakened Reagan among his conservative base and attracted few moderate Republicans. Ford even picked up some votes from southern conservatives, who felt betrayed by Reagan's selection of a moderate to balance the ticket.[18]

At the convention the result was a sharply regionalized division within the Republican party. Ford's support came from the Midwest, the Northeast, and most of the Border states, while Reagan captured landslide majorities of Republican delegates from the West and South. By and large the southern delegations led the fight for Reagan. They provided about a third of his vote, more than any other region. A few southerners supported Ford because they disagreed with Reagan's selection of Schweiker. Most of the southerners, though, vastly preferred Reagan to Ford. The balloting produced a very narrow victory for the incumbent president, after a campaign in which Reagan had sharply and effectively attacked Ford's leadership on foreign policy.[19]

Like Taft, Ford survived the nomination fight only to lose the general election. Ford's nomination substantially weakened the appeal of the Republican ticket in the party's newly developing southern base. It left southern Republicans divided and unhappy, lukewarm in their commitment to elect Ford—and created an ideal situation for a comeback by a Democratic candidate from the South. In addition, it positioned southern Republicans to argue that success in the South depended upon the nomination of a more conservative candidate.

The Reagan Victory in 1980

Reagan emerged from the battle with Ford as the front-runner for 1980. Many doubts persisted about the suitability of the sixty-nine-year-old politician, however, and Reagan's expected candidacy did not deter a large group of Republicans from seeking the 1980 presidential nomination. Conservatives Robert Dole, Philip Crane, and John Connally, moderate conservatives George Bush and Howard Baker, and liberal John Anderson also entered the contest.

Inside the Reagan campaign there were many conflicts among his advisors. Operational control of the Reagan candidacy rested with Sears, who had managed the 1976 effort. Employing a "front-running strategy," Sears sought to present Reagan as the "presumed nominee" of the party, almost as though Reagan were an incumbent seeking renomination rather than a candidate who had to prove his worth against a competitive field. The strategy of damage prevention dictated that Reagan avoid debates and press conferences; the strategy's drawback was that it prevented Reagan from using his exceptional speaking skills to best advantage.[20]

Sears was also concerned that Reagan would be perceived as another Goldwater, as a Republican whose appeal was limited to conservatives. As a consequence, "Sears had tried to persuade Reagan to appeal more to moderate Republicans—a tactic that angered Reagan's more conservative backers." An effort to broaden Reagan's base appeared to be more properly suited for the general election than for the Republican primary, where conservatives made up most of the voters. In addition, Sears targeted the campaign more toward building support for Reagan in parts of the country where he had been relatively weak in 1976—the Northeast and Midwest—than toward capitalizing on areas of previously demonstrated strength—the South and West.[21]

Many of the aides who had served Reagan as governor of California—Ed Meese, Michael Deaver, and Lyn Nofziger—as well as the national campaign chairman, Senator Paul Laxalt of Nevada, disagreed with at least some parts of Sears' strategy for winning the nomination. In fall 1979 Nofziger and Deaver departed the campaign, leaving Sears in complete control of Reagan's fortunes.[22]

Sears' strategy was tested first in the Iowa caucuses. Reagan had enjoyed a large lead in Iowa during the previous fall, but he dropped sharply in the Iowa polls when he passed up the state's major televised debate. The former California governor did little serious campaigning in the state. After making a televised speech in Iowa on the Saturday before the vote, Reagan returned to California. Confident of victory, Reagan was watching a private showing of a new movie with friends in Hollywood when he received the unexpected news that he had been beaten by Bush. Reagan was stunned. "There are going to be some changes made," he told Meese.[23]

"Rather than wrecking Reagan," Cannon argues, "Iowa freed him from the shrouds in which his managers had wrapped him, permitting him to campaign as a natural candidate drawing on the resources of his own personality." No longer the assured front-runner, Reagan ran as though all his hopes for the presidency depended upon the outcome of the New Hampshire primary. "In a transformation as swift as any ever made at Central Casting, the high-flying and disengaged frontrunner became the bus-bound accessible underdog. Weekends were out. During one stretch Reagan campaigned for twenty-one consecutive days, mostly by bus in New Hampshire, with a couple of side trips to the early primary states of South Carolina and Florida." He participated skillfully in the scheduled debates, and, on the day of the New Hampshire primary, he even changed campaign managers, dismissing Sears and two other aides. William Casey was installed as the new campaign manager, and before long other members of Reagan's California group returned. Reagan began playing to his strength as a politician. He emphasized conservative themes that had worked for him in the past and for which there were natural majorities among Republican primary voters.[24]

As a result of "massive voter shifts in the closing days of the campaign," Reagan won a tremendous victory in New Hampshire. He polled nearly half of the vote and beat Bush by more than two-to-one. Reagan monopolized the vote from New Hampshire conservatives (63 percent), and he won almost a third of the vote cast by moderates and liberals. Although the New Hampshire win revived Reagan's front-runner status, the next two primaries in New England gave mixed results. Reagan finished first in Vermont with 30 percent of the vote, but he dropped to third in Massachusetts with 29 percent.[25]

Reagan put the 1980 Republican nomination out of his competitors' reach with four decisive southern victories in early March, a vindication of the Sun Belt strategy of relying on previously established strength among Republican voters. The first of the southern primaries occurred on March 8 in South Carolina. The main contenders were Reagan, Bush, and Connally, a former conservative Democrat turned Republican. Reagan's operation in South Carolina was directed by Lee Atwater and Representative Carroll Campbell. They used direct mail, telephone banks, and get-out-the-vote tactics to provide Reagan with 55 percent of the vote. Despite endorsements by Senator Strom Thurmond and former Republican Governor James B. Edwards, Connally finished a distant second and quit the race. Bush plummeted to 14 percent of the vote, and Atwater later recalled that the Reagan forces had "pounded him into the dirt" in the South.[26]

South Carolina was a prelude to Reagan's success in the remaining southern primaries. Three days later Reagan won 73 percent in Georgia, 70 percent in Alabama, and 56 percent in Florida. After decisive wins in these four southern primaries, Reagan was unstoppable. Later in the primary season Reagan won 75 percent of the Republican primary vote in Louisiana, 67 percent in North Carolina, 74 percent in Tennessee, and 89 percent in Mississippi. Only in Bush's adopted Texas was the contest close, and even there Reagan prevailed with 51 percent. In states where the Republican primary was open to crossovers, Reagan apparently attracted many conservative Democrats and independents. In Alabama, for example, more voters turned out for the Republican primary than for the Democratic contest between Carter and Kennedy.[27]

The regional patterns in the Republican primaries are worth emphasizing. Geographically, Reagan's candidacy was based on the Sun Belt; southern and western states accounted for 42 percent of the vote cast at the Republican convention, and Reagan won every primary held in these regions. Reagan also did well in the Midwest, winning every state except Michigan. It was in the Northeast, as usual, that Reagan encountered his greatest difficulties, but even here he ran much stronger than in the past. At the convention the Republican party united around Reagan. Northeastern Republicans had refused to work for Goldwater, but Reagan won their support. Impressed by Bush's tenacity, the Reagan strategists rewarded him with the vice-presidential nomination. Some conservatives were outraged, but Bush helped to moderate the ticket for the general election. For the first time in history, the Republicans combined the West and the South on the same ticket.[28]

In the South the Republicans had a presidential candidate who could run competitively against Jimmy Carter in most states. Indeed, if Reagan could draw slightly more of the white vote than Ford had won in 1976, Carter could be beaten in the South. The nomination of a more consistently conservative politician motivated southern Republicans to support the national ticket aggressively, which they had declined to do for President Ford four years earlier.

The 1988 Bush Nomination: Running as "Ronald Reagan, Jr."

Two weeks after the 1984 elections, George Bush chose Atwater to direct his effort to win the Republican presidential nomination in 1988. Atwater was a skillful and tenacious strategist who was adept at positioning candidates for success in primaries and in general elections. He had also earned a reputation, over the years, as a master of negative politics. His early experience had been in running Republicans against Democrats in the South, where he helped Republicans win by assaults on the policies, reputation, and character of the Democratic opponents. Informed by close attention to his three favorite books, Plato's *Republic*, Machiavelli's *The Prince*, and Sun Tzu's *The Art of War*, he brought a scorched-earth, take-no-prisoners, total-warfare style to political campaigning. If he were given enough money, Atwater once explained, "I guarantee you I can get the negatives up on anybody."[29]

Atwater and Bush decided to reap the benefits of Bush's loyalty to Reagan by taking advantage of the president's extraordinary popularity among Republican primary voters. "George Bush in many respects was Ronald Reagan, Jr.," Atwater later stated. "It was his own personal strategy of sticking with Reagan right on through. I think it paid off. It would definitely pay off big in the primary. Even in the midst of the Iranian thing, I knew that Ronald Reagan was a deity in our party."[30]

Doing well in the southern primaries was integral to Bush's success. When Democratic legislators created the regional primary that became known as Super Tuesday, Atwater turned the event into a tremendous asset for Bush. Atwater believed that "if we were able to position South Carolina appropriately," Bush would be the main beneficiary of the 1988 Super Tuesday primaries. Just as a Reagan victory in the 1980 South Carolina Republican primary had set the stage for Reagan's sweep of three southern Republican primaries the following week, so in 1988 the winner of an early South Carolina primary might possess a great advantage in the *ten* southern states that would hold their primaries three days later on Super Tuesday.[31]

A convincing Bush victory in South Carolina, Atwater hoped, would ignite a complete sweep of the southern states for Bush. If Bush failed to win the previous primaries, Super Tuesday could become a "firewall" that would extinguish the momentum of any rival candidate. If Bush were able to win New Hampshire, victory in all of the southern primaries could provide the vice-president with an unbeatable advantage. Bush would be so far ahead of the other candidates in the number of delegates that, for all practical purposes, the nomination fight would be over after Super Tuesday. Rival campaign managers understood—and feared—what Atwater was doing. Long after the election, at a conference where all of the 1988 campaign managers gathered to analyze the campaign, Edward Rollins of the Kemp campaign paid homage to Atwater's vision: "Lee obviously understood the South better than anybody in this room and, by moving the South Carolina primary forward, he set a strategy that was almost impossible to beat."[32]

The South Carolinian quietly began to solicit support for Bush from the Republican establishment across the South. By the summer of 1987, Atwater was able to gather "some three hundred prominent southern supporters [of Bush] at the Buckhead Ritz-Carlton in

Atlanta. . . . The political muscle on display there was impressive. The delegations from each state seemed to include most of the leading Republican Party leaders and almost all of the region's most talented campaign operatives."[33]

As for South Carolina, it was not difficult for Atwater and Governor Campbell to line up strong support for Bush, just as they had done for Reagan eight years earlier. The vice-president was willing to do his part to attract the state's Republicans. "Jesus Christ is my personal savior," Bush told a group of evangelical ministers in Greenville, South Carolina. "That declaration may have sounded a little strange coming from an Episcopalian from Connecticut," commented Germond and Witcover, "but it was important here in a state in which half the voters claimed to be 'born again' Christians."[34]

The South was all the more important for Bush because his campaign manager expected to lose Iowa. Just as Reagan's appearance had not deterred other opponents in 1980, so too was Bush challenged by a large group of rivals, including Kansas Senator Robert Dole, Representative Jack Kemp, and Pat Robertson. In March 1987, Atwater had taken his own soundings in the state where the first caucuses would be held. As he later recalled the experience, "I made the assessment that I didn't see how we could win Iowa. We decided that we should never say that publicly and that we should fight hard in Iowa but we had to be prepared to lose Iowa."[35]

A Bush loss in Iowa was not necessarily fatal, however, for the outcome of the Iowa caucuses had never been a determining factor in winning the Republican presidential nomination. In 1980 Reagan had been upset by Bush in Iowa but had recovered with a decisive victory in New Hampshire. Atwater proceeded to strengthen Bush's chances in New Hampshire by cultivating Republican Governor John Sununu. "After we made the Iowa decision," Atwater recalled, "I made a personal decision that I never announced to anyone: I was going to New Hampshire to meet with John Sununu. . . . I went to dinner at his house at 6 o'clock and I said to myself, 'I ain't leaving here 'till this guy commits.' About 11 o'clock, when he hadn't committed, I said, 'John, I ain't leaving until we get this thing worked out. Here it is 11 o'clock, so let's get it done or I'll be here till the 15th.'" Sununu agreed to head the Bush effort in New Hampshire.[36]

Bush's defeat in Iowa was worse than expected, far worse than Reagan's narrow loss in 1980. The vice-president of the United States finished sixth among all candidates. He ran behind Dole and Robertson in the Republican caucus, but he also received fewer votes than the top three candidates in the Democratic caucus. Bush desperately needed a victory in New Hampshire.[37]

Bush and his advisors responded with a blend of positive and negative campaigning. Like Reagan in 1980 after his Iowa defeat, Bush became an accessible, hands-on candidate in New Hampshire. He drove a forklift truck, an eighteen-wheeler, and a snow plow. He drank restaurant coffee with locals, always accompanied by Governor Sununu. His campaign advisors wanted to attack Dole, his main rival, with a television commercial that accused the senator of straddling the possibility of a tax increase. Bush resisted running the ad for several days, but finally agreed on the Saturday before the primary. The campaign's pollster told Bush that "he was now running about two points behind Dole." The vice-president was surprised: "'What the hell is going on?' Bush asked. 'I thought we were five points up.' Then he added: 'Well, if we're two points down, that's a different ball game.'" After listening to arguments by Atwater and others, he allowed them to run the attack on Dole, which saturated the state in the closing days of the campaign. Winning the New Hampshire primary with 38 percent of the vote, Bush was well positioned to put the nomination away as the primaries moved south, into authentic Reagan country.[38]

Instead of simply conceding South Carolina to Bush—and thereby devaluing the results—Dole, Robertson, and Kemp attempted to beat him in the stronghold of Atwater and Republican Governor Carroll Campbell. Atwater put Bush in the back seat of the vice-presidential limousine (no more truck driving was needed) and sent him on the same tour of South Carolina towns that Reagan had taken in 1980, and Campbell mobilized his organization on behalf of Bush. The outcome was an easy victory for Bush. Attracting a record Republican primary turnout of 195,000 voters, Bush won 49 percent of the popular vote and all of the convention delegates. Dole, Robertson, and Kemp split the remaining vote. In the warmup for Super Tuesday Bush had routed his opponents.[39]

On March 8, Bush won an even larger share of the popular vote (57 percent) in the ten southern Republican primaries. Bush's fortunes were powerfully aided by the popularity of President Reagan among Republican primary voters. According to the CBS News/New York Times Exit Polls in ten southern states, an average of 88 percent of Republican Super Tuesday voters approved of Reagan's conduct of the presidency. Bush won the votes of 61 percent of these Reagan supporters. Among the small proportion (12 percent) of Republican primary voters who disapproved of Reagan, Bush averaged only 31 percent of their votes. Running as "Ronald Reagan, Jr." was the main asset the vice-president enjoyed in the southern primaries.[40]

In addition to winning the Republican primaries decisively, Bush appeared to be well positioned to carry the southern states in the presidential election. He had very high approval ratings across a wide variety of demographic categories in the southern Republican primaries, according to the CBS News/New York Times Exit Polls. Very popular among the core white Republicans, he was also favorably evaluated by swing whites and the small number of core white Democrats who voted in the Republican primaries. His profile of support in the primaries indicated that he would be a formidable Republican candidate in the southern states.

While Bush was showing broad strength, Robertson, his chief southern rival, collapsed as a serious candidate. A longtime television minister from Virginia Beach, Virginia, Robertson's specific brand of Biblical literalism was charismatic Christianity. Part of Robertson's problem had "to do with the divisions within the evangelical movement between the charismatics—who speak in tongues and believe in faith healing, and of whom Robertson is one—and the fundamentalists," Elizabeth Drew pointed out. "In state after state, Robertson got the vote of charismatics but didn't do particularly well among fundamentalists." Indeed, Bush, the "born-again" Episcopalian, performed well among the fundamentalists. The limits of Robertson's appeal among Republican voters were vividly sketched in his approval ratings. Among those voters with opinions, in every state about two-thirds of the Republican Super Tuesday voters disapproved of Robertson, while merely one-third, on the average, approved of him. Only a "miracle" could give him the nomination, Robertson concluded after the Super Tuesday results.[41]

Bush's Super Tuesday victories gave him an enormous lead in convention delegates. "Prior to Super Tuesday, Bush and Dole had secured the support of equal shares of national convention delegates," observed Charles D. Hadley and Harold W. Stanley. "After Super Tuesday, Bush had the backing of 74 percent of the delegates selected, Dole only 17 percent." Dole vowed to continue the fight, but it was a hollow threat. The next primary was Illinois, where Bush, who was supported by Republican Governor James Thompson, easily defeated Dole.[42]

The 1988 Republican nomination came to an early closure in the southern states. Voting virtually as a cohesive bloc, the South provided such a mass of delegates that no competitor had any realistic chance of winning. Never before had such a huge regional primary occurred, and never before had it been so cohesive. Once again, the South had demonstrated that—if united—it could powerfully aid a Republican candidate in winning the party nomination. The South's contribution to Super Tuesday was perhaps the most striking evidence in recent years of the influence of the united conservatives on behalf of the most electable conservative candidate. In sweeping the southern Republican primaries so convincingly, Bush had become the favorite to win the general election in the South against any of the three Democratic candidates—Dukakis, Jackson, or Gore—each of whom had won only parts of the Democratic South on Super Tuesday.[43]

The Republican Primary Electorate

Following the innovations of the Democrats, Republicans have begun to use primaries to allocate delegates to their presidential nominating convention. In 1980 eight southern states held Republican presidential primaries that attracted a total of 2,187,000 voters. Eight years later, when all eleven southern states held GOP primaries, the number of voters increased to 3,860,000. Record turnouts occurred in all but one of the southern states in 1988. Participation in the Texas Republican primary, for example, jumped from 527,000 to 1,015,000, while the Florida GOP primary electorate increased from 614,000 to 901,000. In the Deep South, Georgia led the way, as turnout doubled from 200,000 to 401,000. Only in Tennessee, where Al Gore's presence in the Democratic primary may have attracted some Republican support, did the number of voters in the Republican primary fall short of previously established records.

Although turnout has been increasing, the southern Republican primaries are still rather small in size. In 1980 an estimated 6 percent of the eligible voters participated in the Republican primaries. Eight years later only 7 percent voted in the highly publicized Super Tuesday Republican primaries. The 1988 GOP contests attracted only 4–9 percent of eligible voters in the southern states, hardly a sign of great interest on the part of most southerners (see Table 10.1). As an institution, the Republican presidential primary has no historical roots in the South. Moreover, in every southern state in which the Democrats held a competing primary in 1988, the Republicans attracted far fewer voters. The GOP was most successful in Florida,

Table 10.1   The small southern Republican primary electorates in 1988

	Share of all primary voters	Estimated share of white voters	Share of eligible adults	Turnout (in 1,000s)
Florida	41	45	9	901
Georgia	39	49	9	401
Virginia	39	49	5	234
Texas	36	45	8	1015
Alabama	35	48	7	214
Mississippi	31	44	9	159
Tennessee	31	37	7	254
North Carolina	29	36	6	274
Louisiana	19	27	5	145
Arkansas	12	13	4	68

Sources: Congressional Quarterly voter returns; estimates from CBS News/New York Times Super Tuesday Exit Polls. South Carolina is excluded because the Democratic party held a caucus rather than a primary.

Georgia, and Virginia, where they accounted for about two of every five voters in the Super Tuesday primaries. In Arkansas and Louisiana, by contrast, the Republicans drew very few voters.

Because Republican primaries have interested few blacks and Hispanics, GOP turnout rates depend mostly on the number of white voters the Republicans can attract. According to the CBS News/New York Times Exit Polls, GOP primaries in Georgia, Virginia, and Alabama attracted nearly half of the whites who voted in those states on Super Tuesday. About 45 percent of whites voted in Republican primaries in Florida, Texas, and Mississippi; and more than one-third of the whites chose the Republican primary in North Carolina and Tennessee. Only in Louisiana and Arkansas did relatively few whites take part in the Republican Super Tuesday primary. These figures are important, for they signify growing white interest in Republican rather than Democratic presidential nominations.

The Republican primary electorate is almost completely white. In a region in which blacks constituted 14 percent of the voters in the 1988 presidential election and 31 percent of all Democratic primary voters, blacks were conspicuous by their absence from the Republican primaries. Although blacks were not excluded from the Republican primaries, few chose to participate. Blacks averaged 2 percent and whites 97 percent of all voters in the Republican Super Tuesday primaries.

Republican primary voters are more affluent and better educated, on the average, than their Democratic counterparts. According to the CBS News/New York Times Exit Polls, 69 percent of the Republican primary voters had gone to college, compared with 56 percent of Democratic primary voters. Differences in reported family income were also striking. More than a quarter (26 percent) of the Republicans reported incomes in excess of $50,000, compared with 15 percent of the Democratic voters; at the other extreme, 45 percent of the Democrats (versus 28 percent of the Republicans) had family incomes of less than $25,000.

Republican and Democratic primary voters differ enormously in their political behavior. Three different indicators tell essentially the same story of strongly united Republicans but deeply divided Democrats (see Table 10.2). Of the 1988 Republican primary voters who had voted in 1984, 96 percent had chosen Reagan. By contrast, only 57 percent of the Super Tuesday Democrats had voted for Democratic candidate Walter Mondale four years earlier. Among the Republicans favorable evaluations of Reagan persisted in 1988, with nearly nine of every ten approving Reagan's performance as president. One-third of the Super Tuesday Democrats, on the average, also approved of Reagan's performance as president, thus indicating a substantial group of potential Republican votes in 1988. Finally, participants were asked about their voting intentions in the presidential election. Four-fifths of the Republicans, but only about two-thirds of the Democrats, thought they were certain or highly likely to vote for the eventual nominee of their party. In each comparison voters in the Republican primaries were far more unified and supportive of their party's presidential prospects than were the Democratic primary voters.

The Republican advantage in party unity can best be understood in terms of the relative sizes of the four voting groups we have analyzed: blacks, core white Democrats, swing whites, and core white Republicans. Figure 10.1 compares the percent distribution of the two parties' primary voters in 1988. The Republican primary electorate is far more homogeneous than the Democratic primary electorate. Core white Republicans, accounting for 80 percent of the voters, completely dominate the small arena of GOP primary politics. These white voters are resolutely conservative in their views on most

Table 10.2 United Republicans and divided Democrats: mean political characteristics of participants in southern Super Tuesday primaries, 1988

	Voters in Republican primaries	Voters in Democratic primaries
1984 presidential vote		
Reagan	96	43
Mondale	4	57
1988 approval of Reagan		
Approve	87	34
Disapprove	13	66
Fall vote intention		
Certain/probable same party	80	65
Can't say	16	21
Rival party	4	14

Sources: Calculated from CBS News/New York Times Exit Polls in 10 southern states, March 1988. Each percentage is the average response of the participants in the ten surveys.

policies, in their symbolic likes and dislikes, and in their high approval ratings of Republican presidents. Core white Republicans were the backbone of Bush's support in 1988. Most of the remaining GOP primary vote is cast by swing whites, leaving only tiny contributions by core white Democrats and blacks.

The dominant position of the core white Republicans in Republican primaries does not harm the party in presidential politics because core white Republicans constitute a majority of southern white voters (53 percent) and a plurality of all voters (44 percent) in the general election. Swing whites, the second biggest group in the Republican primary, make up an additional 18 percent of the presidential electorate. A majority from the swing voters, combined with a cohesive vote from the core white Republicans, is large enough to carry the South for a Republican presidential candidate.

A quite different situation confronts the Democrats. Neither core white Democrats nor blacks are numerous enough to dominate the

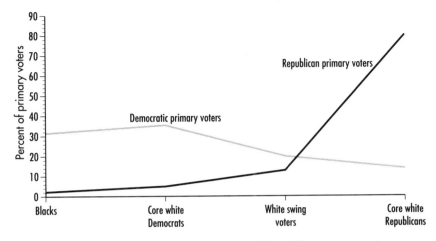

Figure 10.1 The vastly different Democratic and Republican primary electorates in the South: mean percentages of blacks, core white Democrats, white swing voters, and core white Republicans in the 1988 Democratic and Republican Super Tuesday electorates. *Source:* Calculated from the 1988 CBS News/ New York Times Exit Polls of voters in Democratic and Republican presidential primaries in ten southern states.

primary electorate. Indeed, in 1984 and 1988 there were acute divisions in the southern Democratic primaries between candidates supported by core white Democrats and those preferred by blacks. Even if the two groups eventually agree to back the same candidate in the fall campaign, the dominant groups in the Democratic primary collectively make up less than two-fifths of the general election voters. Moreover, because the core white Democrats do not support their party's nominee at the high rates characteristic of blacks and core white Republicans, the white "base" of the Democratic party yields fewer votes for the party nominee. Consequently, even a Democratic candidate who can unite the party's two bases remains a long way from victory in the general election. One of the ironies of modern southern politics is that, even with a much smaller number of voters, the Republican primary electorate more closely resembles the actual composition of voting groups in the general election than does the larger group of Democratic primary voters.

With such conservative dominance in the southern Republican primary electorate, leaders of southern delegations to the national conventions have been able to exert formidable influence over the policies and candidates of the Republican party. The result has been a distinct "southernizing" of the national Republican party. Having played a central role since 1968 in the nomination of every Republican presidential nominee except one, and having become the largest source of convention delegates, the South will assuredly loom large in the strategies of future conservative candidates who seek to lead the Republican party.

As the southern Republicans moved the national party to the right, its candidates in the presidential elections of the 1980s ran exceedingly well in the South. Reagan and Bush captured landslide majorities of the white vote in all three elections. The result has been the continuation of a Solid Republican South, in which the eleven states of the old Confederacy, for the first time in history, have become the most Republican part of the nation in presidential elections.

11

Republican Dominance
after the Great Society

During Lyndon Johnson's presidency the dynamics of southern politics changed drastically. The Civil Rights Act of 1964 was soon followed by the Voting Rights Act of 1965, and these laws reshaped political participation and restructured party loyalties. Black voter registration increased sharply (especially in the Deep South), with most new black voters entering the electorate as Democrats. Intervention by a Democratic administration on behalf of the rights of black southerners did not escape the attention of racially conservative whites, many of whom began to reexamine *their* options in presidential elections.

The creation of a biracial electorate in the South fundamentally altered the customary rule of thumb for determining the winner in a two-candidate contest. In the old southern politics, before blacks voted in large numbers, the winner was automatically the candidate who received a majority of the votes cast by whites. This rule no longer held. A candidate who received few votes from blacks now had to poll a landslide majority of the southern white vote (the specific percentage depending on the size and cohesion of the black vote) to obtain a bare majority of the region's total vote.

This chapter focuses on Republican strategies for building winning coalitions based almost exclusively on white votes, strategies that have been increasingly successful in the South since the Great Society. To understand the outcomes of presidential elections in the modern South, we will need to grasp the size of the white majorities Republican presidential candidates need for victory if they receive virtually no support from blacks. Figure 11.1 contrasts the southern Republicans' white necessities (the percentage of the white vote Republicans have needed to carry the South in presidential elections)

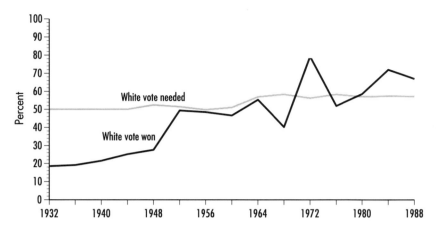

Figure 11.1 The southern white Republican vote in presidential elections: percent of white vote needed for a majority compared with percent of white vote won, 1932–1988. *Sources:* Calculated by the authors from Richard M. Scammon, ed., *America at the Polls* (Pittsburgh: University of Pittsburgh Press, 1965); appropriate volumes of Richard M. Scammon, ed., *America Votes* (Washington, D.C.: Congressional Quarterly); appropriate volumes of *U.S. Statistical Abstract;* and NES presidential-year election studies.

with their white realities (the percentage of the white vote actually won by the Republicans).[1]

During the New Deal, in the days of the Solid Democratic South, Republican candidates never attracted as many as three out of every ten white votes. Eisenhower's 1952 campaign, however, initiated a period of close competition for white support. Since 1964 the Republicans' failure to attract substantial black support has meant that majorities on the order of 57–58 percent of the white vote have been the Republicans' target for winning a majority of the entire southern vote (see Figure 11.1). Aside from 1968 and 1976, when the campaigns of George Wallace and Jimmy Carter temporarily undermined Republican success among whites, the Republicans have exceeded this target in post–Great Society elections, usually by wide margins.

The greater the size and the stronger the cohesiveness of the black vote conceded by Republicans to the Democrats, the larger the white vote needed by the Republicans to win a given election. Because there are proportionately more black voters in the Deep South than in the Peripheral South, Republicans need a bigger white vote there to offset the preferences of black Democrats. In the Deep South

Republican presidential candidates have generally required about 61 percent of the white vote in order to win, while roughly 55 percent of the white vote in the Peripheral South has been sufficient to produce a subregional majority. Winning substantial white majorities has been—and still remains—the central political imperative of modern Republican presidential campaigns.

The conversion of the South's traditional white Democratic majorities into Republican majorities is a crucial development in presidential politics. In the presidential elections of 1972–1988, the median Republican vote cast by whites in the southern states was 67 percent (see Table 11.1). In the Deep South, Republican presidential candidates have attracted a median white vote of 72 percent, 11 percentage points higher than they have needed. In the Peripheral South, the

Table 11.1 White Republicanism in the South: estimated white vote for Republican presidential candidates after the Great Society (percent)

Political unit	1968	1972	1976	1980	1984	1988
South Carolina	48	85	55	64	82	79
Mississippi	17	100	60	62	79	76
Georgia	36	90	42	47	73	72
Alabama	16	83	50	59	73	71
Virginia	51	76	56	59	72	69
North Carolina	46	78	51	57	73	68
Louisiana	28	77	57	63	76	68
Florida	45	78	51	62	71	67
Tennessee	43	75	48	55	65	65
Arkansas	36	80	42	53	68	63
Texas	45	73	53	59	70	61
Deep South	29	86	52	58	76	72
Peripheral South	45	76	52	59	70	65
South	40	79	52	59	72	67

Source: Estimates calculated by the authors. States are ranked from highest to lowest according to the median percentage white Republican vote for the 1972–1988 presidential elections.

median white vote of 65 percent for Republican presidential nominees has been 10 percentage points higher than their minimal target among whites. With white majorities of this magnitude, GOP presidential candidates have been able to carry southern states without significant black support.

The repositioning of the Republican and Democratic parties on racial issues has played no small part in enabling the Republicans to attract the landslide white vote needed for victory in the biracial electorate. In *The Making of the President 1960*, Theodore H. White speculated on the electoral advantages that might accrue to the Republican party by modifying its image as the party of Lincoln, the party of civil rights. "If they adopt a civil rights program only moderately more restrained than the Democrats'," White argued, "the South can be theirs for the asking; and with the South, if it comes permanently to Republican loyalties, could come such solid addition of electoral strength as would make Republicans again, as they were for half a century, the majority party of the nation and the semipermanent stewards of the national executive party."[2]

No Republican presidential candidate, of course, has campaigned in the openly segregationist style so common in the old southern politics. Nonetheless, from Goldwater's vote against the Civil Rights Act of 1964 and Nixon's vocal opposition to "forced busing" in 1968 to Ronald Reagan's coolness toward civil rights laws in the 1980s and George Bush's veto of the Civil Rights Act of 1990, Republican presidential nominees and Republican presidents have consistently taken significant positions in opposition to the wishes of most blacks. And as the national Democratic party came to be widely perceived as the party more beholden to blacks, the Republicans have been positioned to win the votes of those whites who did not think of themselves as Republicans but did not like the candidates and policies of the national Democratic party. It was no accident that the collapse of the Democratic party among white voters in the South came after passage of civil rights legislation.

As V. O. Key, Jr., made abundantly clear in *Southern Politics*, the greater the proportion black in a given area, the more distinctively "southern" the political behavior of the whites. The racial structure of southern white presidential Republicanism after the Great Society provides a stunning modern example of the profound impact of black concentrations on white political behavior. In the southern states the size of the median white vote for Republican presidential candidates increases as the proportion of blacks in the population rises (see Figure 11.2). All six states whose black populations exceeded the black percentage for the entire South (the Deep South states and North Carolina) had median white Republican votes above the GOP regional percentage. The highest median Republican presidential votes during the 1972–1988 elections occurred among whites in the Deep South states of South Carolina (79 percent) and Mississippi (76). Four of the five Peripheral South states with relatively smaller black populations fell below the southern median for white Republicanism. Virginia alone had a slightly higher rate of white support

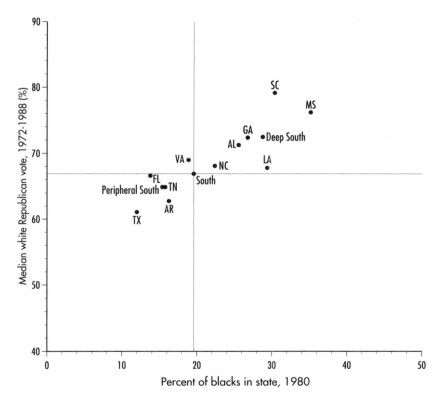

Figure 11.2 The racial structure of the white Republican vote in the southern states: median white Republican vote in the 1972–1988 presidential elections, by percent of blacks in population in 1980. *Sources:* Same as Figure 11.1 and 1980 *U.S. Census.*

for Republican presidential candidates than its racial composition would indicate.

Important as racial questions have been, we do not believe Republican presidential candidates have attracted massive white majorities solely on the basis of racial appeals. In election after election, other issues—the conduct of the nation's foreign policy, the management of the economy, the imposition of federal taxes, and the defense of traditional cultural values—have intertwined with racial considerations in erecting and maintaining the clear Republican advantage among white southerners. The Republicans have generally been able to aim a wide and varied arsenal of weapons at the Democrats in the region's presidential campaigns since the Great Society. Their success, no less than the transformation of the Republican party from an institution generally despised by southern whites into a party which has recently enjoyed remarkable victories in the South, has been a most significant development in American politics.

The 1968 Nixon Campaign: "On the Other Hand"

"In 1968," wrote Richard Nixon in his *Memoirs*, "the South was to be one of the most important regions in terms of winning both the nomination and the election." The former vice-president clearly understood that Alabama Governor George Wallace, not Democratic nominee Hubert Humphrey, was his chief competition for the votes of southern whites. "The Deep South had to be virtually conceded to George Wallace," Nixon later wrote. "I could not match him there without compromising on the civil rights issue, which I would not do. But I would not concede the Carolinas, Florida, Virginia, or any of the states on the rim of the South."[3]

How did Nixon intend to compete against Wallace for these white votes? He expressed a tough stand on law and order, urged a stronger national defense, offered to use tariff policy to protect textiles, and supported conservative justices on the Supreme Court. Most of all, Nixon offered a more sympathetic understanding than he had in the past for the views of most southern whites on civil rights policies. When he ran for president in 1960 the GOP candidate had declined to stake out a civil rights position clearly distinguishable from the Democrats. Eight years later, however, Nixon positioned himself as a "centrist" alternative to the more racially liberal Humphrey and the more racially reactionary Wallace.

Nixon contended, for example, that his firm advocacy of law and order had been misunderstood. "When an individual talks about the necessity for order, or law and order, people think it is a code word for racism." It was a view Nixon rejected, but not all observers were convinced. Nixon's "emphasis on the crime rate, civil disobedience and restlessness among minority groups had, obviously, two purposes: to tap the general discontent among whites and to counter George Wallace with a velvet-glove version of the mailed fist with which Wallace saluted the white backlash," observed Jules Witcover. In so doing, Nixon "could give his allies in the South and blue-collar North raw material with which to lure Wallacites into the GOP ranks."[4]

On the most controversial racial issue of the day—the use of federal funds as a lever to stimulate school desegregation—Nixon positioned himself as a "middle-of-the-road" politician. In a television interview prepared for the Carolinas, Nixon summarized his views as follows:

> I believe . . . that the Supreme Court decision was a correct decision, Brown versus the Board of Education.
>
> But, on the other hand, while that decision dealt with segregation and said that we would not have segregation, when you go beyond that and say that it is the responsibility of the Federal Government and the Federal courts to, in effect, act as local school districts in determining how we carry that out, and then to use the power of the Federal Treasury to withhold funds or give funds in order to carry it out, then I think we are going too far.
>
> In my view, that kind of activity should be very scrupulously examined and in many cases I think should be rescinded.[5]

Nixon's "centrist" approach to civil rights issues had many political advantages. As Witcover argued, the former vice-president

> could say all the things Wallace was saying about law and order, street violence, the Supreme Court's babying of "the criminal forces," excessive concentration of power in Washington and all the rest of the red-neck litany, but with greater restraint. Next to the ranting Wallace, that was easy. Why throw your vote away on Wallace, who couldn't win, when you could get the essentials of what you wanted in the more reasonable, infinitely more respectable Nixon? It was a question that did not have to be belabored in the border states and Dixie.[6]

To carry the targeted southern states Nixon relied heavily on the advice and support of two South Carolinians, Senator Strom Thurmond and Thurmond's principal aide, Harry S. Dent, who directed the Nixon effort in the South. Dent concentrated on "south side Virginia, North Carolina, Tennessee, South Carolina, Georgia, and Florida." "In the early days of the campaign," Dent later wrote, "I tried to get the Nixon staff to go along with a statement from Nixon indicating some favor for 'freedom of choice' in public school desegregation and against forced busing of school children." Later in the campaign, Nixon took the positions Dent had advocated. In October, when vice-president Humphrey "claimed full credit for all civil rights legislation and endorsed the Supreme Court's recent decision outlawing the Court's earlier 'freedom of choice' ruling," Dent ran an advertisement comparing the different positions of Nixon and Humphrey on the implementation of school desegregation.[7]

Senator Thurmond, a pragmatic conservative who had led the Dixiecrat revolt in 1948, campaigned across the region in favor of Nixon. Speaking before an audience of whites at a country club in Lake Charles, Louisiana, in October, Thurmond "acknowledged that Mr. Nixon, while he would make 'a good President,' was not an ideal candidate for the South. . . . 'He's not going to do everything you're going to like or everything I'm going to like.'" He added however, that Nixon could achieve the goal of "stopping the liberals." Wallace could not win the presidency, he emphasized. "What we've got to do," Thurmond told the audience, "is go out here and show people that a vote other than for Mr. Nixon could end up a vote for Humphrey." Thurmond's "overwhelming distaste" for Humphrey, his old civil rights adversary, was evident. "I warn you now," he said, "if the race goes to the House [of Representatives], Mr. Humphrey might walk off with it . . . God forbid! We can't let it happen!"[8]

A fighting northern liberal if there ever was one, Humphrey forthrightly defined the 1968 election as a "referendum on human rights" and accused both Nixon and Wallace of exploiting "the fears and hates aroused by this issue." As Humphrey elaborated his criticism of Nixon:

> My Republican opponent is no racist. He is a fair and just man. But he and the Republican party have chosen this year to join forces with the most reactionary elements in American society.
>
> They have adopted a Southern strategy very similar to Mr. Goldwater's in 1964. And, I mean the old South—not the new South I mean to win.
>
> They are openly competing with Mr. Wallace for the votes of people

who at very best want to put the brakes on our progress toward full opportunity.[9]

Wallace, finding less than a dime's worth of difference between the two major parties, denounced both Nixon and Humphrey for supporting the early civil rights movement and civil disobedience:

> Mr. Humphrey and Mr. Nixon, back in '60 when it started, you ought to read the statements they made.
>
> Mr. Nixon said, "It's a great movement. It's constitutional," yessiree . . . Mr. Humphrey said, "I'd lead a revolt," and now they all stand saying, "We've got to have law and order in this country."[10]

His opponents "ought to help bring about law and order," Wallace argued, because "they helped to destroy it by kowtowing to a group of anarchists that folks like you and me said we ought to do something about." Wallace attacked Nixon as a supporter of civil rights legislation and as a member of the Eisenhower administration that appointed Earl Warren Chief Justice and dispatched troops to Little Rock in 1957 to uphold the Supreme Court's school desegregation decision.[11]

Nixon's strategy concerning Wallace was basically to deny him legitimacy by refusing to debate him or even mention his name. He did not wish to attack Wallace directly for fear of undermining his own effort to win the support of Wallacites who might yet be persuaded that their first choice could not possibly be elected president. Early in October, by coming to the South and explicitly attacking Wallace and Nixon as contributing to racial division, Humphrey forced Nixon to alter slightly his original strategy. Speaking in Nashville and Knoxville, Humphrey charged that Wallace was seeking "to deliberately inflame the fears, frustrations and prejudices of our people—to bring this nation to the brink of broadscale civil disorder." The same objectives, Humphrey said, "are also found in the perfumed, deodorized, detergentized campaign of my Republican opponent—a man who has deliberately courted the most radical extremist elements in his own party—who continues this appeal in his speeches—and who will be fully in their debt should he win the Presidency."[12]

Several days later, in Atlanta, Nixon found an opportunity to sympathize with the frustrations of Wallace supporters while simultaneously attacking Wallace as unqualified to be president. Wallace, Nixon remarked:

is against a lot of things that the American people are frustrated about—the rise in crime, the conduct of our foreign policy, what's happened to American respect around the world.

I am against a lot of those things . . . The difference is I'm for a lot of things, and that's what we need now.

We need policies at home that will go beyond simply saying that, well, if somebody lies down in front of my Presidential limousine, it will be the last time he lies down in front of it.

Now look here. No President of the United States is going to do that, and anybody who says that shouldn't be President of the United States.[13]

Having attacked Wallace as not "fit to be President," Nixon reverted to his standard practice of ignoring Wallace. In campaign appearances the following day in Greenville and Spartanburg, South Carolina (with Senator Thurmond at his side), Nixon received a tumultuous welcome. Republican leaflets stressed Nixon's attacks on school busing, and the bumper sticker of the day was "Help Strom Elect Nixon."[14]

Outside South Carolina, in 1968 Nixon could not compete effectively with Wallace among Deep South whites for the role of chief opponent of civil rights. Nor did Nixon wish to play that role. Wallace won twice as many Deep South white votes (63 percent) as Nixon (29) and eight times as many as Humphrey (8). In the Peripheral South, however, Nixon received a plurality (45 percent), while Wallace won 31 percent and Humphrey got 24 percent. Humphrey's best showing among whites was a second-place finish with 34 percent in Texas. In every other southern state the Democratic nominee ran third among whites.

Nixon's "centrist" strategy on civil rights issues paid off. According to the NES surveys, he received 56 percent of the vote cast by the majority of southern whites who wanted some form of race relations "in-between" segregation and desegregation. In addition, he won 44 percent among those who preferred desegregation. He did worst among the hard-core segegationists (23 percent), the vast majority of whom supported Wallace.

While racial issues were central in the contest between Nixon and Wallace in the South, widespread dissatisfaction with the conduct of foreign policy also worked to Nixon's advantage. The Johnson administration's Vietnam War policies, as well as its handling of other foreign affairs, gave the Republicans an opening. Sixty-two percent of southern whites were dissatisfied with the conduct of American foreign policy in 1968 while only 24 percent were satisfied. Nixon won 54 percent among the large majority of southern whites who believed that American foreign policy was not being well conducted.

According to the NES surveys, Nixon won 86 percent of the vote cast by Republicans and independents who leaned toward the GOP, as well as 65 percent among the pure independents. He also captured one in five votes among whites who were favorably disposed toward the Democratic party. Nixon's vote came mainly from middle-class and college-educated whites in the South. After analyzing precinct returns in a number of southern cities in 1968, Numan V. Bartley and Hugh D. Graham concluded that "Nixon ran best in higher-prestige neighborhoods, where his economic conservatism and law-and-order defense of social stability appealed to affluent urban and suburban whites throughout the region." Nixon did better in the region's metropolitan counties than in the smaller cities and rural areas.[15]

Wallace's candidacy meant that the Republicans—like Eisenhower in 1952 and 1956 and Nixon in 1960—had to settle for part of the Peripheral South's electoral votes. In 1968 Nixon won 45 percent of the southern electoral vote, so the Republicans needed at least 52 percent of the northern electoral vote. With strong support from the West, Midwest, and Border, he carried 60 percent of the northern electoral vote. Strategically, Nixon succeeded in positioning the Republican party to the right of the Democrats on civil rights and to the left of Wallace (and Goldwater). If the Republicans could keep their Peripheral South white support and add to it the Deep South whites who had voted for Goldwater and Wallace, the Republican party would be in excellent shape to dominate future presidential elections in the South.

1972: The Nixon Landslide

As Kevin P. Phillips argued in *The Emerging Republican Majority*, the political significance of Nixon's 1968 victory lay in the electorate's sweeping rejection of "Democratic liberalism." The "repudiation visited upon the Democratic party for its ambitious social programming, and inability to handle the urban and Negro revolutions," he suggested, "was comparable in scope to that given conservative Republicanism in 1932 for its failure to cope with the economic crisis of the Depression." In "the emerging Republican majority" that Phillips discerned, the South was expected to be an electoral cornerstone of presidential Republicanism. Peripheral South whites were already tending toward Republicanism in presidential politics, and Phillips argued that Deep South whites would eventually follow suit. "For national political reasons, the Republican party cannot go to the Deep South," whereas "the Deep South must soon go to the national GOP." In this process Phillips emphasized that "maintenance of Negro voting rights is essential to the GOP. Unless Negroes continue to displace white Democratic organizations, the latter may remain viable as spokesmen for Deep Southern conservatism."[16]

In 1972 Nixon found himself in a position similar to that of Lyndon Johnson in 1964: a popular incumbent president facing a weak and controversial opponent. According to the 1972 NES survey, 80 percent of southern whites and 55 percent of southern blacks were warmly disposed toward Nixon. As a South Dakota Democrat who took liberal positions on a wide variety of economic, civil rights, foreign policy, and cultural issues, Senator George McGovern was—beyond doubt—the weakest candidate the modern Democratic party has ever run in the South. While 81 percent of southern blacks were also favorable toward McGovern, merely 29 percent of southern whites gave him warm ratings. Like Johnson, Nixon had the experience to make the most of this opportunity for a landslide victory. These conditions produced—for the first time in American history—a Solid Republican South.

There was never any mystery about the outcome of the 1972 campaign. In early September Nixon led McGovern by 34 points in the Gallup Poll. Much as Johnson had done with Goldwater, Nixon played the role of "President" to the hilt while portraying McGovern as a naive and dangerous radical. As Nixon saw it, McGovern's defense policies involved a "move toward war," his domestic policies implied the "confiscation of wealth," and his strange ideas on welfare would "make it more profitable for a person to go on welfare than to go to work." Indeed, Nixon framed the election as a choice between the "work ethic" and the "welfare ethic."[17]

Although racial issues were not central in 1972, Nixon did align himself with majorities of whites on the conservative side of two controversies. He attacked politicians (like McGovern, though names were not mentioned) who favored "the involuntary busing of schoolchildren away from their neighborhoods for the purpose of achieving racial balance." Such "zeal" only undermined "the cause of good race relations, of orderly desegregation and of quality education." And he strongly denounced employment "quotas." "The reasons [for quotas] are often well-intentioned," he explained. "Quotas are intended to be a short cut to equal opportunity, but in reality they are a dangerous detour away from the traditional value of measuring a person on the basis of ability."[18]

Like Eisenhower, Nixon traveled far less extensively in his reelection campaign. His main southern trips included Texas and Georgia. He campaigned against "permissive" judges in South Texas and attended a gathering of "Democrats for Nixon" at John Connally's ranch. When he later visited Atlanta, he was "engulfed by throngs of applauding whites."[19]

McGovern too spent very little time in the South. In early September he made a rare appearance at the Southern Governors' Conference, where he announced that he had "every intention of waging a hard campaign to carry the South." McGovern was opposed in principle to having a southern strategy. "'I don't think a person ought to have a Southern strategy,' he said. 'I think it's an insult to the people of the South to think that they somehow have to be coddled.'"[20] So much for McGovern's southern campaign.

In 1972 Nixon achieved the most overwhelming southern white vote—79 percent—ever won by a Republican presidential candidate. About three-quarters of Peripheral South whites voted Republican, as did 86 percent of whites in the Deep South. The landslide, a product of Nixon's popularity and McGovern's unattractiveness, occurred in every southern state (see Table 11.1). Nixon achieved this result by adding much of the Wallace following to his original base of support. "In the South," observed White, "the Wallace vote moved en masse to Richard Nixon. A CBS analysis . . . showed that the 1968 Wallace voters in the South had gone for Richard Nixon by three to one."[21] In every southern state Nixon's 1972 vote was within a percentage point of the combined vote for Nixon and Wallace in 1968.

Nixon's breadth of support among southern whites was astonishing. He carried 95 percent of the white Republicans, 79 percent of the pure independents, and over 80 percent of the weak Democrats and independents who leaned toward the Democrats. In addition, he took nearly half (49 percent) of the strong Democrats. His support among southern blacks increased from 4 percent in 1968 to 16 percent in 1972.

Nixon ran best, as would be expected, among white southerners with conservative views on specific issues and symbols. McGovern was such a weak candidate, however, that Nixon often won majorities from those groups taking the most liberal position on various issues. Two examples from the NES surveys will suffice to illustrate. Nixon captured 92 percent of those white southerners who wanted to achieve total military victory in Vietnam, but he also won a majority among the southern whites who believed that the United States should pull out entirely from Vietnam. With the help of the Wallacites, Nixon won 94 percent of the vote cast by the region's white segregationists, but he also captured 79 percent from those who preferred some form of race relations that was neither strict segregation nor complete desegregation and 73 percent among those southern whites who favored desegregation.

The 1972 presidential election was a milestone for the Republican party, the first campaign in which the Republican nominee won the *entire* southern electoral vote. The strategic implications of the victory cannot be overemphasized. By sweeping the entire South, the Republican party no longer needed to win a majority of the electoral vote in the North, the historical base of Republicanism. In fact, the Republicans could have prevailed with all of the South and merely 34 percent of the northern electoral vote. Nixon's showing was the culmination of Republican efforts since 1952 to invade the Democratic South.

Having won the greatest electoral victory of any Republican president, Nixon and the Republicans promptly threw it away with the Watergate scandal. Four years later, after the humiliating (and unprecedented) resignations of both Vice-President Spiro Agnew and President Nixon, former Governor Jimmy Carter of Georgia used the South as his principal electoral base to win back the presidency for the Democrats.

The story of Carter's 1976 presidential campaign will be told in the next chapter. Here we shall simply observe that President Gerald Ford, Nixon's successor, was ill-equipped by experience and inclination to repeat Nixon's performance in the South. In the severest test of the Republican strategy of emphasizing white majorities, Ford won clear majorities of the white vote in Mississippi, Louisiana, Virginia, South Carolina, and Texas (see Table 11.1). Yet even with this white advantage, the size and cohesiveness of the black vote cast against Ford was sufficient to deny him a statewide victory save in Virginia. Ford's poor showing in the South cost the Republicans the presidency. Because Ford won only 9 percent of the southern electoral vote, the Republicans' northern target increased from 34 percent in 1972 to 63 percent in 1976. Ford received 56 percent, a

substantial majority of the North's electoral vote but still seven points shy of the share he needed for victory.

1980: Reagan Revives the Republicans

The setting of the 1980 presidential election offered little realistic chance that Jimmy Carter could be reelected. As William Schneider has observed, "Carter entered the 1980 campaign with the lowest job approval ratings of any incumbent president since Gallup began taking these measurements in the 1940s." In July 1980, only 21 percent of Americans approved of Carter's performance as president. "These ratings, which went widely unnoticed during the fall campaign," Schneider stresses, "were ultimately to be the determining factor in the election outcome."[22]

Carter's approval rating was low mainly because of the nation's economic and foreign policy problems. A major recession coincided with double-digit inflation in 1980, a situation hardly conducive to an incumbent president's reelection. In addition, the Iranian hostage crisis epitomized the administration's weaknesses in foreign affairs. Carter was in the position of an unpopular incumbent running for reelection but unable to point to a record of "peace and prosperity." His only chance for victory was to press with vigor and imagination the working assumption of his campaign manager, Hamilton Jordan, that "the American people are not going to elect a seventy-year-old, right-wing, ex–movie actor to be president." As Jack W. Germond and Jules Witcover put it: "Because Carter could hardly run on his record, the focus would be on the dangers of turning to Ronald Reagan in the next four years."[23]

The contest between Carter and Reagan offered a clearer ideological contrast than the 1976 race. Reagan was far more popular among southern conservatives than Ford. His southern advisors made the most of his appeal. As the campaign progressed it became increasingly evident that Reagan was attracting some of the whites who had supported Carter out of regional pride in 1976. Reagan also especially courted evangelical Christians, as illustrated by his early October visit to the Reverend Jerry Falwell's Liberty Baptist College in Lynchburg, Virginia.[24]

Symbolically, the opening round in the 1980 presidential campaign in the South was Reagan's appearance in early August at the Neshoba County Fair in Philadelphia, Mississippi. For decades the fair had attracted Mississippi politicians who championed "states' rights," by which they meant racial segregation. Before an audience of some 10,000 whites, Reagan offered philosophical reassurances. "I believe in states' rights; I believe in people doing as much as they can at the private level," Reagan told the fairgoers. If elected, he would "restore to states and local governments the power that properly belongs to them."[25]

In 1964 three civil rights workers had been savagely murdered in Neshoba County. Although Reagan may have been ignorant of this fact and of the connotations of "states' rights," his southern handlers assuredly were not. Reagan's implicit message to racially conservative southern whites was, "I'm on your side, folks." To black leaders who had risked their lives in the civil rights movement, the implication of the remarks was quite different. As Andrew Young later translated Reagan's affirmation of "states' rights," the term "looks like a code word to me that it's going to be all right to kill niggers when he's President." The Carter White House immediately repudiated Young's characterization.[26]

Throughout September the Carter and Reagan campaigns attacked and counterattacked with racially oriented charges. Carter began his official campaign at a northern Alabama rally with Wallace in attendance in which Carter denounced the Klan: "As the first man from the Deep South in 140 years to be President of this nation, I say that these people in white sheets do not understand our region, and what it's been through." On the same day in Detroit, Reagan ridiculed Carter for "opening his campaign down in the city that gave birth to and is the parent body of the Ku Klux Klan." Reagan's facts were wrong, as Carter quickly pointed out. "I resent very deeply what Ronald Reagan said about the South and about Alabama and about Tuscaloosa when he pointed out erroneously that I opened my campaign in the home of the Ku Klux Klan." As Carter continued, "I think it was uncalled for. I think it was inaccurate, and I think it was something that all Southerners will resent." In a statement of clarification the Reagan campaign contended that Reagan did not mean to imply "that Mr. Carter was in any way sympathetic to the Klan," nor did Reagan "believe there is any place for the Klan in the hearts of the people of the South."[27]

In mid-September Carter used the pulpit of the Ebenezer Baptist Church in Atlanta to accuse Reagan of appealing to racial fears. "You've seen in this campaign the stirrings of hate and the rebirth of code words like 'states' rights' in a speech in Mississippi, in a campaign reference to the Ku Klux Klan relating to the South," Carter said. "This is a message that creates a cloud on the political horizon. Hatred has no place in this country." Two days later, at a press conference, Carter explained that he was not calling Reagan a racist. "I did not raise the issue of the Klan, nor did I raise the issue of states' rights," Carter explained. "And I believe that it's better to leave these words—which are code words to many people in our country who have suffered discrimination in the past—out of the election this year. I do not think that my opponent is a racist in any degree."[28]

The Reagan campaign denied any racism on Reagan's part and attacked a Carter advertisement placed in black publications as a resort to racism by the Democrats. According to the ad, the Carter administration had appointed a record number of black judges, "Cracked down on job bias. And created 1 million jobs." The text concluded: "That's why the Republicans are out to beat him." The Carter campaign withdrew the ad.[29]

While charges and denials of racism were commonplace, both candidates used nonracial issues to solicit votes. Above all, Reagan attacked Carter on economic issues. "Mr. Carter has not answered for the economic misery he's caused," Reagan said in Florida. Speaking later in the month at Texarkana, Texas, Reagan broadened his attack. "In place of confidence, he has given us ineptitude," Reagan charged. "Instead of steadiness, we have gotten vacillation. While Americans look for confidence, he gives us fear." As Reagan saw it, Carter's performance in office amounted to "a tragicomedy of errors."[30]

The Reagan campaign also criticized Carter as a betrayer of southern values. Former Mississippi Governor John Bell Williams, for example, denounced the president before a responsive crowd in Columbus, Mississippi. As Germond and Witcover described the scene:

"Jimmy Carter took us down the boulevard of broken promises," the arch-conservative Williams told thousands at an old-fashioned, flag-waving barbeque. Other Democrats, he reminded them, say they have to vote for Carter because "he's a Southerner born and raised in the South." And he asked: "Do you see any indication of it in the last four years?"

The crowd roared: "No!" To which he answered: "You won't see any of it in the next four either."[31]

For his part, Carter frequently attacked Reagan as a threat to world peace and generally not "a good man to trust with the affairs of this nation in the future." His strongest ridicule of the Reagan campaign occurred in Texas. Given a pair of cowboy boots, Carter displayed them to a Waco crowd and explained their functions. "'I grew up on a farm and I know you need hightop boots for things besides stomping Republicans,' Mr. Carter said. 'As you well know, Republicans have a habit of spreading a lot of horse manure around right before an election. And lately, as you also know, it's getting pretty deep all over this country.'"[32]

Mutually bitter feelings characterized the two presidential candidates. In a Dallas television interview, Reagan sharply attacked Carter:

> Criticizing each other belongs in a campaign—to criticize policies you disagree with—but I think Carter has lowered himself to a personal type of attack against me. And it's an attack based on falsehoods and distortions.
>
> He doesn't know me enough to charge me with being a racist. He doesn't know me enough to suggest that I am trigger-happy and would cause a war and so forth, such things as saying if I were President I would separate Christians from Jews, blacks from whites and so forth. This is a personal type of campaign that's unworthy of the office he holds.
>
> I can hardly have a warm feeling in my heart for someone who's been attacking me on a personal basis for many months now in the campaign.[33]

The South was a critical battleground in the 1980 presidential election. Because Carter's 1976 victory had rested fundamentally on his southern strength, it was essential that Carter again sweep the South. By the same token, Reagan's southern campaign officials believed that Carter was quite vulnerable in the South. Ford had won 53 percent of the white vote in 1976, but Reagan looked to be a more formidable competitor for white votes. If Reagan could run only five percentage points stronger than Ford had among southern whites, the Republicans could take back the southern states from Jimmy Carter.

Representative Carroll Campbell and Lee Atwater of South Carolina developed a strategy of forcing Carter to campaign in the South, his natural base, which diverted him from seeking votes elsewhere in the nation. As Campbell later recalled, the South was Carter's "home base, his centerpiece, and without it he would be lost." The aim of the Republican strategists was to "make Carter come home and do battle on his own turf. If he has to defend the soil of the

South, he will leave his flanks to the north and west wide open and vulnerable."[34] Campbell explained how he and Atwater put the plan into execution:

> After the convention we organized loosely around our strategy. We got our little task force together and went around the South and hammered away here and there. We took 'em on on the issues, held press conferences in little towns, did all the grass-roots pushing, and they began to feel the rumblings up in Washington. They knew that things were coming apart on them down South.
>
> We scheduled Reagan into the South early, made a quick blitz, had a couple big hoorah visits, and then we sent him along the way to the areas outside the South that he had to go to win early. It gave us a fast reacquaintance with the people down here, it shook Carter's strength, and in that respect we forced Carter back into the South early in the game. And when he diverted his previous plans to go elsewhere, he looked especially vulnerable in his home.[35]

The success of the Campbell-Atwater strategy of eroding Carter's strength within his natural base was evident in the closing days of the race. "In these final days of the campaign both candidates were spending most of their time in states that should have been part of Carter's base as a Southerner and Democrat—Reagan because the opportunity was there for breakthroughs, Carter because he could not feel confident they would not slip away," wrote Germond and Witcover. "Indeed, the fact that the President felt obliged to go into South Carolina, Tennessee, and Mississippi was a certain sign of his vulnerability; none of these states should have been a question for him at that point in the campaign."[36]

In 1980 Reagan did well enough among whites to reclaim the South for the Republican party. Carter dropped from 47 percent of the southern white vote in 1976 to only 36 percent in 1980. Reagan won white majorities in every state except Georgia (see Table 11.1), and his share of the regional white vote narrowly exceeded the Republicans' white target in the South (see Figure 11.1). Reagan won majorities of white voters in every educational and income category.

During Carter's presidency core Republicans displaced core Democrats as the largest group of white voters in the South. According to the CBS News/New York Times Exit Polls of white southern voters, core Democrats barely outnumbered core Republicans, 36 percent to 34 percent, in 1976. By 1980, however, 40 percent of southern white voters were core Republicans, while some 35 percent remained core Democrats.

The 1980 exit polls revealed that Reagan lost two voting groups in the South, blacks (9 percent) and white core Democrats (32 percent). The former California governor won 60 percent among the region's white swing voters and 89 percent among white core Republicans. Reagan benefited enormously from the troubled economy. He won 78 percent among the nearly two-fifths of southern whites who felt their family finances had worsened over the past year. Reagan captured 56 percent of a larger group of whites whose finances had remained the same. He dropped to 41 percent among the small group of southern whites (18 percent) who reported improvements in their family finances during the last year of the Carter administration. The hostage crisis in Iran also worked to Reagan's advantage. According to the 1980 NES survey, Reagan won 78 percent from the large majority of southern whites (63 percent) who disapproved of President Carter's handling of the crisis, but he won only 31 percent from the much smaller group who approved of Carter's actions.

Reagan's white support in the South was always highest among the most conservative voters. According to the NES surveys, Reagan polled huge majorities, for example, among whites who believed they paid too much in federal taxes, who wanted to increase defense expenditures, who wanted to reduce government services rather than expand federal programs, who wanted blacks and other minorities to rely on their own efforts rather than those of government in getting ahead, who were cold or indifferent toward blacks and civil rights leaders, who opposed ratification of the Equal Rights Amendment, and who were warm toward big business.

By successfully executing the Republican southern strategy based on uniting whites of different economic and social status while writing off most blacks, the Republicans demonstrated even more convincingly than in 1972 how important the South could be to winning the White House. The 1980 election was the second occasion after the Great Society in which Republican success in the South—winning 91 percent of the southern electoral vote—sharply reduced the Republicans' northern target. The GOP needed only 37 percent of the northern electoral vote, a target that was easily surpassed. Reagan's southern victory was all the more impressive because it was achieved against an incumbent Democratic president from the Deep South.

The 1984 Reagan Landslide

In many ways the 1984 general election was a replay of 1972. In both campaigns popular conservative Republican incumbents had the good fortune to be matched against liberal Democratic challengers from the Midwest. Reagan's success in reducing income tax rates contrasted vividly with Walter Mondale's statement when he accepted the nomination that he would raise income tax rates, with the political advantage clearly going to Reagan.

Mondale, like Humphrey and McGovern, was an ideal opponent from the standpoint of Republican strategists. As a proud champion of economic, social, and racial liberalism, Mondale could easily be attacked an an "ultraliberal" northern Democrat whose values ran counter to dominant white opinion in the South. "My opponent has made an enormous tax increase his first option, the centerpiece of his campaign," Reagan said in a Corpus Christi speech. "Well, I think he's a little confused. Doesn't he know you don't want greater taxes, you want a greater Texas?" Before an audience of appreciative college students, again in Texas, Reagan argued that the Democrats "just don't understand that the American people are tired of the tax-and-tax, take-and-take mentality."[37]

The political liabilities of Mondale's pledge that, if elected, he would increase taxes to reduce the budget deficit were apparent in the CBS News/New York Times Exit Poll on election day. Mondale's position solidified the core white Republicans and both groups of white swing voters against him, while it split core white Democrats (54 percent supported Mondale's position, 46 percent opposed a tax increase). Mondale received 88 percent of the vote from the southern core white Democrats who supported the need for a tax increase, but only 50 percent among members of this group who opposed a tax increase.

In fashioning their easy reelection, Reagan's strategists viewed the South as an essential part of the Republican base. "The Sun Belt has the lion's share of electoral votes, and the three megastate anchor of the Sun Belt is Texas, California and Florida," Atwater explained in late October. "It became clear to us very early in this contest that if we nailed down the West and the South with those three states as an anchor that we could spend the rest of the campaign challenging him on his turf."[38] Money and personal appearances not needed in the safe southern and western states could be directed to more competitive states in the Midwest and the Northeast.

Part of the reason for growing Republican optimism about the South had to do with shifts in the underlying political predispositions of the white electorate. The revival of Reagan's popularity as the economy came out of recession stimulated a sizable expansion in the core white Republicans at the expense of the core white Democrats.

From 1980 to 1984, the core white Republicans increased from 40 to 52 percent of southern white voters, according to the exit polls. At the same time core white Democrats dropped sharply, from 35 to 25 percent. After four years of Reagan Republicanism, the cohesive group of pro-Republican white voters was twice as large as the less cohesive but most pro-Democratic group of southern white voters.

Although Mondale's southern campaign commenced with bold talk, matched against Reagan there was never any realistic chance for Mondale to win the minority of white votes he needed to combine with most black votes to carry southern states. Early in September the southern Democratic party chairs met with Jesse Jackson to plan an agenda for Mondale's campaign in the South. "We are declaring," Jackson announced, "a new era of Southern political involvement in the national political scene." As Jackson continued, "It is time to shift from racial battlegrounds to economic common ground. Never before have we come together as we have today to coalesce leadership." Southern Democratic chairs, aware that enthusiastic black participation was crucial to Democratic competitiveness, welcomed Jackson's offer to campaign in their states. In a wildly optimistic appraisal, the Virginia Democratic chair, Alan A. Diamonstein, said "Nobody at this meeting is willing to concede that we'll lose the white vote in the South." Since the Democrats had not carried the southern white vote for decades, Diamonstein's statement was simply wishful thinking.[39]

Mondale wisely spent little time in the South. He made one puzzling appearance in Mississippi, a state where whites were to reject him by a margin of four to one. Almost an entire day was spent in Tupelo, where his only public appearance was at a high school rally. There the former vice-president was heckled, cat-called, and grilled concerning his views on religion, abortion, and homosexual rights.[40]

There was never any doubt that Reagan would win the landslide white majorities necessary to compensate for token black support (see Figure 11.1). Seventy-two percent of whites favored the conservative Reagan over the liberal Mondale, an avalanche of white support exceeded among Republicans only by Nixon's 79 percent against McGovern. Reagan's white vote ranged from a low of 65 percent in Tennessee to a high of 82 percent in South Carolina.

Among the major voting groups in the South, the CBS News/New York Times Exit Poll shows that Reagan won an extraordinary 96 percent among the white core Republicans and 65 percent from the white swing voters. He also took 29 percent of the vote cast by white core Democrats, and managed to extract 10 percent from southern blacks.

Reagan's fortunes were enhanced by the nation's recovery from the recession of 1981–1982. According to the 1984 CBS News/New York Times Exit Poll of southern white voters, 70 percent believed the economy had improved during the previous four years, and 91 percent of these voters voted to reward Reagan with a second term. The Republican president even drew a majority from those southern whites who contended that the economy had remained unchanged, and he lost only among the small group (18 percent) who thought the economy had worsened during the previous four years.

By winning the South's entire electoral vote, the Republicans needed only one-third of the electoral vote in the rest of the nation to reelect Reagan. In fact they swept all of the North except Minnesota and the District of Columbia and thus achieved an electoral triumph comparable to Nixon's in 1972.

Relentless Sledgehammering: The 1988 Bush Campaign

In the 1988 presidential election Vice-President George Bush faced a potentially strong challenge from Massachusetts Governor Michael Dukakis. Bush temporarily faded from public attention after he cinched the Republican nomination in the primaries, while Dukakis rose in the polls as he defeated Jesse Jackson. Gallup Polls in March and April showed Bush holding leads of only four and three points over Dukakis in the South. An early June poll, in the wake of Dukakis's victory over Jackson in the California primary, showed the Massachusetts governor with an 11-point lead over Bush. Two weeks later, Bush again had gone ahead of Dukakis by seven points in the South, but he continued to trail elsewhere.[41]

In this setting of uncertainty and concern about Bush's success in the fall election, Republican campaign strategists began in early summer to execute a strategy designed to elevate Bush by discrediting Dukakis as a potential president. The sledgehammer campaign Bush waged against Dukakis was thoroughly familiar to observers of partisan politics in the South. As Thomas B. Edsall observed, the 1988 Bush campaign amounted to a "classic southern Republican challenge to a 'national' Democrat," a type of campaign that Republicans have often conducted in the region.[42] Directly assailing Dukakis's character, judgment, and values, Bush aggressively nailed his opponent to the wrong side of a host of conservative issues and sacred symbols.

Campaign manager Lee Atwater summarized the Bush campaign's strategy in a postelection interview. "The strategic concept was developed way before we knew who the Democratic nominee was," Atwater said. "Whoever it was, we had to paint him as a frostbelt liberal who is out of the mainstream, and is not in tune with the values of the mainstream voters. What we did was find the actual issues that allowed us to paint the picture."[43]

Careful examination of Dukakis's public record generated a bumper crop of words and deeds that could be exploited with devastating effect among white southerners. "There are only four words we need to mention," claimed the director of Bush's Tennessee campaign. "ACLU. Gun Control. Furlough. Taxes. Down here, one of those four is bound to hit home." Bush's Texas campaign manager discerned an abundance of "hot button" issues to exploit. "It's almost like going down the list, shutting your eyes, and saying, 'Where should we hit him this week?'" Simply on the issue of being "soft on crime," which many Republicans considered Dukakis's most vulnerable area, numerous stones could be hurled. "Whether it is the furlough program, Dukakis' opposition to the death penalty, vetoing mandatory sentencing for drug dealers or gun control—the mix of these four issues is overwhelming," said Lanny Griffin, the Bush campaign's chief southern strategist.[44]

Once the voters were fully alerted to Dukakis's past positions, Republicans were confident that the governor's efforts to present himself as a nonideological, pragmatic moderate would collapse and that he would be isolated as a liberal. If the Bush campaign could convincingly "paint" Dukakis as an unadulterated northern liberal— a Teddy Dukakis—then all the advantages conservatives hold over liberals in the South would come into play. Very few southerners identify themselves as political liberals, and they are easily outvoted by conservatives. Moreover, many "moderates" take conservative positions on a variety of social, racial, defense, and some economic questions. Aware of the ideological tilt against liberalism among the region's white voters, the Republicans sought to make the election a referendum on Massachusetts-style liberalism.

Throughout his southern campaign Bush fiercely denounced Dukakis's judgment and values. One example illustrates the tone of the Bush assault. On August 27, in the East Texas town of Longview, Bush assumed the role of a "bare-knuckled, street-brawler" as he "launched one of his harshest, most sharply worded attacks on . . . Dukakis, portraying his opponent as a 'liberal Massachusetts governor' who opposes gun ownership, the Pledge of Allegiance, prayer in public schools, and is weak on crime." According to the *Washington Post*, "The crowd loved the rhetoric, cheering each new attack." As one retired white man put it, "'Texans are basically conservative. They believe in God and the right of the individual,' he said. 'They still pray a lot in public schools down here. I guess it's against the law, but they're still doing it. Bush is really talking about where we live.'"[45]

Especially devastating to Dukakis's campaign was the story of Willie Horton. A black man convicted of first-degree murder, Horton took advantage of Massachusetts' policy of prison furloughs to escape from prison. While at large Horton raped and terrorized a white woman. As a symbol of misplaced sympathy for murderers at the expense of innocent citizens, the Horton episode was political dynamite against Dukakis in the South, as well as in other parts of the nation. Using a black convict to depict Dukakis as soft on criminals illustrated the persisting importance of racial appeals. As Edsall has emphasized, the Horton case implicitly focused "on one of the traditionally most divisive and frightening examples of race relations: the black rapist and the white woman, an image exploited in the past by southern segregationists."[46]

On other matters of concern to southerners the Republican campaign accentuated the positive, especially the peace and prosperity they identified with the Reagan presidency. The Bush campaign stressed huge differences between Bush's experience and Dukakis's inexperience in international affairs and national security policy; claimed that the arms reduction treaty signed by President Reagan with the Soviet Union proved the wisdom of strengthening the military before bargaining with the Russians; accused the Massachusetts governor of wanting to raise taxes in contrast to Bush's convention pledge ("read my lips") of no new taxes; and favorably contrasted economic recovery under the Reagan-Bush administration to high rates of inflation and interest under the last Democratic administration.

Bush's aggressive mixture of negative and positive campaigning gave southern whites several reasons to stick with the Republican candidate. As the fall campaign proceeded, Republican ranks closed around Bush, and the vice-president developed growing support among white independents and Reagan Democrats. Bush's slashing attacks on Dukakis resolved whatever doubts some southern Republicans might have held about his ability to take the fight to the

Democrats. For example, North Carolina Senator Jesse Helms, who had not endorsed any candidate in the primaries, was fully on board for the fall campaign. "My supporters back the Bush-Quayle ticket 102 percent," he announced. "Dukakis is the best thing Bush has going for him," Helms emphasized. "People look at Dukakis and they get frightened. They're scared to death."[47]

The Bush organization and the state Republican parties used paid and free media, direct mail, and phone banks to identify, inform, and bring to the polls registered Republicans and white swing voters—moderate independents and "Reagan Democrats." After all, the sledgehammer strategy had been originally designed to unite and mobilize Republicans and to appeal to the values, beliefs, interests, and fears of independents and conservative Democrats. Most of the white swing voters, Bush strategists believed, would reject a candidate associated with the positions Republicans attributed to Dukakis. "After they have had a chance to be better acquainted with the two candidates," Griffin said, "they are siding overwhelmingly with us. Among ticket splitters and Reagan Democrats, we are getting enough to win."[48]

Southern Democrats approached the 1988 campaign as regional underdogs but with considerably more optimism than in 1984. President Reagan's retirement meant that the Democrats would compete against a weaker opponent. Yet the Democrats faced significant problems in carrying the region. There were far fewer southern Democrats in 1988 than in 1980; and liberals continued to be a beleaguered and unpopular minority, vastly outnumbered by conservatives and moderates. Geographically, the Democrats' traditional base of support had collapsed, while the Republicans' consistent support had rapidly expanded in many cities and suburbs.[49] A Democratic victory in the South required the right candidate and the right campaign. Southern Democrats got neither from Dukakis, and again they suffered a lopsided defeat.

Dukakis initially refused to write off the South. "If anyone tells you that we can't win the South, or that we can't win in the West, or that we can't win in the great state of Texas," Dukakis told the Texas state Democratic convention, "don't you believe it." Interviews with chairmen and executive directors of state parties led David S. Broder to conclude that, "after hiding from their national ticket four years ago, southern Democratic officials are telling aides of the Massachusetts governor that Vice President Bush does not have their region's electoral votes locked up—unless Dukakis decides to default."[50]

Dukakis's apparent southern strategy had three parts. He first sought to position himself as a moderate, pragmatic Democrat skilled in the art of governing rather than as a liberal Democrat. Second, Dukakis tried to capitalize on the feeling of many southern Democrats—widespread in the spring and summer of 1988—that Bush was weak and beatable. Finally, he attempted to regain the support of conservative Democrats and independents by selecting Texas Senator Lloyd Bentsen as his running mate. None of these efforts worked.

In his acceptance speech to the Democratic national convention, Dukakis asserted that the 1988 election was about "competence" rather than "ideology." "It's not about meaningless labels," Dukakis said. "It's about American values. Old-fashioned values like accountability and responsibility and respect for the truth."[51] Dukakis blended progressive and conservative themes in his effort to appeal to southerners.

As part of his progressive appeal he urged "good jobs at good wages for every citizen in the land, no matter who they are or where they come from or what the color of their skin." In August, campaigning in Birmingham, Dukakis eulogized the four black girls killed by a church bombing in 1963, and pledged that "we will not rest until every form of bigotry and racism and religious intolerance will be banished from this land."[52]

Yet the Massachusetts governor also stressed conservative themes when campaigning in the South. Robin Toner captured the spirit of a June campaign swing: "In three days of traveling the South, the New Englander had tried hard to immerse himself in this region's political culture, and to dispel the notion that another liberal northern Democrat had captured the nomination and was about to lead the ticket on another doomed crusade across the South." The Democratic nominee "was doing his best to avoid the labels that can mean political catastrophe in the deep South—such as 'ultraliberal.' He was talking about fighting crime and illicit drugs. He was talking about strengthening families." According to T. R. Reid, the purpose of Dukakis's southern trip was "to create a positive image for this largely unknown Democratic Yankee" by showing "a picture of a tough crime-fighter, a worthy commander in chief for the war on drugs."[53]

Although Dukakis's attempt to present himself as a moderate who had something to offer both progressive and conservative southerners made political sense, the real question was whether his self-definition would prevail against the expected Republican efforts to define him as a Teddy Kennedy liberal. Susan Estrich, his campaign manager, foresaw the attacks but professed little concern. "I expect the Republicans will be very negative about Dukakis. They've run out of positive things to say about Bush. We're ready for it."[54]

Some of the southern Democrats, though, much more experienced in the type of campaigning Republicans had practiced against moderate to liberal Democrats, were quite worried about the coming onslaught. "In one way or another," reported Broder, "most of the southerners express fears that Republicans will move to label Dukakis a typical northeastern liberal, whose values are alien to the 'God, flag, and country' psychology of the South." As one veteran southern campaign manager argued, "Symbolism is important in the South. People will tolerate a good deal of difference on policy, but if they don't think you share their values, they write you off."[55]

As the campaign proceeded Dukakis's self-definition collapsed. "Initial reaction to the governor here in the South was positive," concluded John Dillin. "But in August and September, the governor's political standing was devastated among white Southerners on gun control, the death penalty, the Pledge of Allegiance and prison furloughs—visceral issues that grabbed the public's attention." For weeks Dukakis mounted no effective counterattack against the Republican charges, much to the disgust of southern Democratic leaders. Al LaPierre of the Alabama Democratic party complained that "we know how to run and do what the Republicans are doing—a down and dirty campaign. We're used to it."[56]

The net impact of the Republicans' multiple attacks on Dukakis's beliefs, values, and past behavior was to make him unacceptable not only to Republicans but to many southern white swing voters. Analyzing interviews with Reagan Democrats and independents, Kenneth R. Weiss discovered that "all but a handful of these Southern swing voters consider themselves either conservative or moderate in their political beliefs. From this political orientation, two out of three of these voters believe Dukakis is 'too liberal.'" In addition, the candidate's name "sounded strange" to some southerners. "President Dukakis just doesn't sound like an American president," said one Tennessee voter. "It sounds like somebody in Indonesia or Greece or someplace overseas."[57]

The second initial basis for Democratic optimism involved a gross underestimation of Bush's strength as a campaigner. Broder's interviews with southern Democratic leaders underscored the point that "much of the increased optimism about Democratic inroads in the South rests less on an estimate of Dukakis' strengths than on Bush's perceived weaknesses." A few weeks later Toner reported that "many of these Southern Democrats smell the possibility of victory" and that "some party leaders seemed delighted at the prospect of a race against Vice President Bush." Jim Hightower, the populist Texas Commissioner of Agriculture, predicted Bush's defeat. "We're not just going to drive little Georgie Bush out of office," Hightower claimed. "We're going to drive him plumb crazy." Frank Holleman, the South Carolina state chair, believed "Bush is a fundamentally weak personality and a weak candidate. That's why we have a chance."[58] Scorn for Bush peaked at the Democratic national convention, where numerous speakers mercilessly ridiculed the vice-president.

There was certainly some justification for the Democrats' eagerness to take on Bush, since his performance in the Republican primaries was inconsistent. At times Bush looked like an authentic leader; at other times he seemed a parody of leadership. Bush operated in Reagan's shadow and did not emerge as an independent figure until the Republican national convention. Nonetheless, the Democrats' contempt for Bush blinded them both to his potential strengths in the general election and to the likelihood that his managers, Atwater, James Baker, Roger Ailes, and Robert Teeter, all highly experienced in the crosscurrents of national campaigns, would know how to make the most of the material at hand. In the end southern Democrats underestimated Bush and overestimated Dukakis.

During the Super Tuesday campaign Dukakis had already revealed a tin ear for the subtleties of southern political culture. He essentially advised southerners that they were the same as Americans everywhere. This conclusion may or may not be true, but it contradicted the belief of many southerners that they possessed a special culture in which they took enormous pride.[59] It was not surprising that Dukakis (and his Massachusetts advisors) would fail to take seriously the potential political damage arising from Bush's shrewd attacks on the governor's beliefs and values.

When Dukakis campaigned in the South before the convention, he was everywhere advised to balance his ticket with a southerner. Apparently convinced that he could not make inroads into the region solely on his own strength and Bush's weaknesses, Dukakis chose the most popular Democrat in Texas to broaden the ticket's appeal

to white southerners. Senator Lloyd Bentsen had repeatedly demonstrated his ability to unite all wings of the fractious Texas Democratic party. His selection as the vice-presidential nominee immediately brought support from many moderate and conservative
Democratic elected officials and state party leadership in the region.

Apart from activating officeholders and politicians who had a personal stake in a Democratic presidential victory, the real question
was whether rank-and-file southern Democrats and many independents would support the Dukakis-Bentsen ticket. In "his role as a
Southerner working the Southern territory for a Yankee," Bentsen
pleaded with Democrats to return to the party: "'This year Michael
Dukakis reached out to the South,' he said. 'He chose one of you.
He took the extra step to bring us home again. He came here and
listened to us. He campaigned among us. He asked a Southerner to
join him on the ticket, and one reason I accepted was because I want
to help bring Texas and Tennessee and Arkansas and Mississippi
back into the Democratic party.'"[60]

The strategy was only partially successful. It did not win back all
of the conservative Democrats, nor did a majority of white independents vote Democratic. Party leaders acknowledged that "having Mr.
Bentsen on the ticket means little to the average voter. 'You don't
have guys out there driving Trans Ams with Bentsen stickers,' said
one Democratic activist. 'It's at a higher level.'" The nub of the
problem was that Democratic politicians were no longer opinion
leaders for many voters. "Most voters today," observed Hastings
Wyman, Jr., in *Southern Political Report*, "make up their minds independent of state and local leadership."[61]

By September the Dukakis campaign was in trouble, and its prospects worsened after the first presidential debate. "Nowhere in the
South are the Democrats running any better than even," reported
Douglas Jehl in early October. "'We're really sucking wind down
here,' said one state director who spoke on condition he not be
identified." On Saturday, October 1, a secret meeting of Dukakis
campaign officials from the "Big Five" states (North Carolina, Tennessee, Arkansas, and Georgia, plus the border state of Kentucky)
took place in Atlanta to "fashion a fallback strategy that will focus
on the five southern states where a Democratic victory still seems
possible." Dukakis officials from other southern states were not invited to attend, a sign that the Dukakis campaign was writing off
most of the region a month before the election. After the second
debate polls showed Dukakis virtually out of the race in all the

region's states, and the governor's organization largely abandoned the South to concentrate on 18 states outside the region.[62]

The 1988 presidential election added a fresh verse to the new song of a Solid Republican South. Just as Nixon had done in 1972 and Reagan in 1980 and 1984, the Bush campaign unified its base, won most of the independents, and took a respectable share of the region's Democrats. Even though Dukakis ran a stronger race than Walter Mondale had among southern Democrats, he secured little support from the large majority of southern voters who were not Democrats.

Republican strategists were light-years ahead of their Democratic counterparts in assessing the vulnerabilities of the opposition and in selecting the specific "hot button" issues and symbols that could motivate anti-Dukakis feelings. In a slashing rhetorical style that owed something to the political warfare that George Wallace had conducted against his enemies, Bush personally savaged Dukakis's record. Yet the Bush victory was not based entirely on the exploitation of negative feelings toward Dukakis. The vice-president stressed his close ties with President Reagan, his superior experience in national decision-making, and the Republicans' accomplishments in maintaining peace and promoting prosperity.

An *Atlanta Journal-Constitution* poll conducted in the first week of October, for example, showed that the ingredients of Republican success were settling into place. According to Tom Baxter, "Mr. Bush's eight years as vice president have made him better known than Mr. Dukakis among Southern voters and given them greater confidence in his experience and abilities." A month before the election, Bush had managed "to shape the focus of the campaign around the same issues the Republicans have used to win the region in four of the past five presidential elections: defense, crime, and patriotism." Moreover, the issue of relative economic prosperity had begun to work in Bush's favor. Baxter noted that "most people think they are financially better off than they were when Mr. Reagan first was elected. Therefore they seem more likely to listen to Mr. Bush when he discusses the progress made since the 'bad old days' of high inflation and double-digit interest rates under President Jimmy Carter and less likely to agree with Mr. Dukakis's claim that in real terms most middle-class voters have lost ground." As William Graham, Bush's North Carolina coordinator, put it, "If we can't sell peace and prosperity, we don't deserve to win."[63]

Bush essentially reconstructed the coalition of voting groups in the

South that had given strong support to Reagan. According to the CBS News/New York Times Exit Poll, Bush won 93 percent of the vote cast by core white Republicans and 58 percent among white swing voters in the South. In addition, he captured 24 percent of the core white Democrats and 13 percent among black southerners. By combining his strength among independents and Reagan Democrats with his powerful mobilization of the Republican base vote, Bush was able to win 67 percent of the region's white voters. He thus easily exceeded his southern target among the 83 percent of the southern electorate who were white. The Bush campaign was a resounding success.

The vice-president greatly benefited from the popularity of President Reagan. According to the CBS News/New York Times Exit Poll, 72 percent of southern white voters approved of Reagan's performance in the White House, and Bush captured 89 percent of these voters. By contrast, Bush won only 15 percent of the much smaller group of southern white voters who disapproved of President Reagan's performance. Favorable economic conditions among southern white voters also aided Bush's candidacy. Bush won 88 percent of the majority of southern white voters (56 percent) who believed the economy was better in 1988 than it had been in 1980. In addition, he won a majority (57 percent) among the one-fifth of southern white voters who thought the economy was unchanged over the Reagan years. Bush lost overwhelmingly only among the small group of southern whites who contended that the economy had worsened during the past eight years.

Just as Nixon and Reagan had done before him, Bush drew upon a variety of conservative appeals to attract his massive white vote in the South. According to the 1988 NES survey, Bush ran best among those southern whites who thought having a strong military was "very important," who believed the United States should remain the most powerful nation in the world, who were staunchly anticommunist, and who favored increased spending on national defense. On domestic economic issues, Bush was supported by southern whites who believed in reducing governmental services and programs rather than in expanding them, who supported private health insurance rather than a program of public health insurance, and who believed that individuals themselves, not the government, should be primarily responsible for getting a good job. On racial issues, Bush received disproportionate support from southern whites who believed that the pace of racial change was proceeding too fast, who opposed quotas and preferential hiring, who believed that blacks and other minorities should help themselves rather than rely on the government to get ahead in society, and who were cold toward civil rights leaders. On cultural issues, Bush drew heavily from southern whites who favored the death penalty for persons convicted of murder and from those who were cold toward homosexuals.

By winning the entire southern electoral vote, the Republicans once again could capture the presidency by securing only a third of the electoral vote outside the South. Bush finished with 72 percent of the northern electoral vote.

National Consequences of Change in the South

The emergence of a Solid Republican South has been a pivotal event in modern presidential politics. From 1880 through 1948 the Republican party essentially wrote off the South. Eisenhower's 1952 and 1956 campaigns were highly successful when measured against the Republicans' previous inability to penetrate the South, but neither Nixon in 1960 nor Goldwater in 1964 had Eisenhower's popular appeal. In terms of electoral votes, Nixon was as competitive in the three-way race of 1968 as Eisenhower had been in 1952. With the collapse of the Wallace movement in 1972, the Republicans were finally positioned to win the substantial white majorities they required to sweep the South's electoral votes. In every subsequent election save 1976 a new Solid South appeared, this time under Republican auspices.

Once the South contributed no electoral votes at all to Republican presidential campaigns. Commencing with Eisenhower's races, however, the South began to provide a small portion of the electoral college votes needed for a Republican majority. In 1952, for example, Eisenhower's southern breakthrough gave the Republicans 21 percent of the electoral votes necessary for victory. Since 1968 the South's contribution to Republican control of the White House has increased enormously. Southern states alone gave Nixon 48 percent of the electoral votes he needed to win reelection in 1972. The South's contribution to Republican presidential candidates slipped to 4 percent in Ford's 1976 loss to Carter, rose to 44 percent in Reagan's victory in 1980, and amounted to a slight majority—51 percent—of the electoral votes needed to elect Reagan in 1984 and Bush in 1988. A completely solid Republican South in the presidential elections of the 1990s would provide 54 percent of the electoral votes needed to win the presidency. Its unmatched size and potential unity make the South the grand regional prize of presidential elections.

The creation of a Solid Republican South in most recent presidential elections has revolutionized the regional dynamics of presidential campaigns. Because of its southern gains, the Republican party has not needed northern electoral majorities to control the presidency. Increasing Republican competitiveness in the South from 1952 through 1968 reduced the Republicans' northern electoral vote target to much smaller majorities (50 to 55 percent). The decisive change occurred in the aftermath of the Great Society. Beginning in 1972 the Republicans usually could win the presidency with only a small minority—33 percent in 1984 and 1988—of the northern electoral vote. If the Republicans again secure the entire southern electoral vote in the presidential elections of the 1990s, they will need only 31 percent of the electoral vote outside the South in order to win. A Solid Republican South, if it can be retained, gives the Republicans the luxury of targeting key northern states (California being the most obvious) while compelling the Democrats to win 69 percent of the northern electoral vote, an extremely difficult task in "normal" political times.

Between the New Deal and the present the Republicans' northern target has been cut roughly in half. Aside from the GOP's close defeat in 1976, the Republicans have exceeded their northern goals by substantial margins. Winning the South thus makes it much easier for the Republicans to succeed in the North. By understanding and fully exploiting the dynamics of southern politics, the Republicans have thus far succeeded in building and rebuilding the large white majorities necessary to carry the South. Southern victories have in turn given Republican presidential candidates a vital hedge against possible northern defeats.

A final point needs to be made about the role of the South in presidential politics. The best political base is the one that can be repeatedly secured with the least expenditure of time and money. Just as the South had traditionally functioned as a cheap and safe Democratic base in presidential politics, so the South today usually serves as an inexpensive and promising Republican stronghold. It is no small advantage to Republican campaigns to be able to pour extra resources into key northern states on the reasonable assumption that the southern states are relatively safe.

12

The Democratic Interlude

Since the administration of Lyndon Johnson, prospects for Democratic presidential candidates in the South have been bleak. Each of the northern liberals nominated by the party—Hubert Humphrey, George McGovern, Walter Mondale, and Michael Dukakis—was easily defeated by his Republican opponent. Only when a southerner, Jimmy Carter of Georgia, headed the national ticket have the Democrats been competitive in the South in recent presidential elections, and only once, in 1976, was even Carter successful in carrying most of the southern states. The political events and developments that have increased the attractiveness of Republican presidential candidates to most white southerners have made the Democrats the party of choice among most black southerners and a minority of whites.

The Democratic strategy for winning in the South has been quite straightforward. Democrats have attempted to construct biracial majorities based on most of the black vote and a sizable minority of the white vote. Beginning with Lyndon Johnson's 1964 campaign, Democratic presidential nominees have usually won around nine-tenths of the southern black vote. Assuming that Democratic candidates continue to mobilize and to sweep the southern black vote, the main uncertainty for the southern Democrats will be attracting enough white support to be competitive.

Figure 12.1 compares the white vote needed for a Democratic presidential majority in the South with the white vote the Democrats actually won. Through 1944 the Democrats achieved the landslide white majorities traditionally associated with the South's "white man's party." In 1932 and 1936 Democratic loyalty and the impact of the Great Depression resulted in more than four-fifths of southern whites supporting Franklin Roosevelt, but his final campaign, in

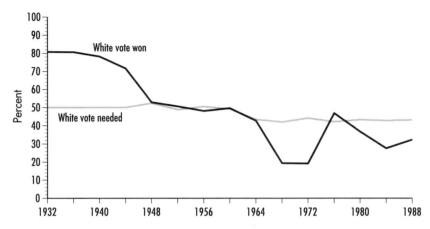

Figure 12.1 The southern white Democratic vote in presidential elections: percent of white vote needed for a majority compared with percent of white vote won, 1932–1988. *Sources:* Calculated by the authors from Richard M. Scammon, ed., *America at the Polls* (Pittsburgh: University of Pittsburgh Press, 1965); appropriate volumes of Richard M. Scammon, ed., *America Votes* (Washington, D.C.: Congressional Quarterly); appropriate volumes of *U.S. Statistical Abstract;* and NES presidential-year election studies.

1944, was the last time the vast majority of whites voted Democratic. White support declined sharply in 1948 after President Harry Truman made civil rights a national Democratic priority. Between 1948 and 1964 the Democrats' southern white vote gradually shifted downward, and then it plummeted below 20 percent in 1968 and 1972. Since 1968 the Democratic white vote has never risen above one-third except when a native southerner, Jimmy Carter, headed the Democratic ticket. Not even Carter won majorities of the southern white vote.

Figure 12.1 documents the profound racial change in the Democratic presidential vote from the New Deal through the 1980s. In the old days when very few blacks could vote, the Democrats needed only small majorities of the white vote in order to win the region. In modern elections the certainty of black support for the Democrats has meant that Democrats need well less than half the white vote in order to win the South. Roughly 42–43 percent of the white vote, when added to about 90 percent of the black vote, generally constitutes a narrow majority of the entire southern vote. Winning enough white support has been the basic Democratic problem. Only in 1976, when Carter won 47 percent of the white vote, have the Democrats exceeded their targets of slightly more than two-fifths of the southern white vote.

Because there are proportionately more blacks in the Deep South electorate than in the Peripheral South electorate, the Democrats need a smaller percentage of the white vote in Alabama, Georgia, Louisiana, Mississippi, and South Carolina. Slightly less than two-fifths of the white vote would be sufficient for a Democratic victory in the Deep South. Partly because racial considerations are more salient in the Deep South, however, when northern liberals have run for president the Democrats have attracted a lower percentage of white votes in the Deep South than in the Peripheral South. In the Peripheral South the Democrats need to win about 45 percent of the white vote, a greater percentage than in the Deep South. In neither subregion (1976 excepted) have they secured enough white support to win.

As a consequence of losing majority white support, the Democrats' modern imperatives are twofold. Democratic candidates must attract a large and unified vote from southern blacks while winning a sufficiently large minority of the vote cast by southern whites. Unless both objectives are achieved, the Democratic party cannot carry southern states in presidential contests. Although black southerners have consistently voted Democratic by overwhelming margins in presidential elections, acquiring substantial white support has been another matter entirely. As a result, the Democrats' biracial southern strategy has been very difficult to execute except when the party's presidential nominee has been a white southerner. Having examined the Republicans' modern southern victories in the last chapter, here we shall concentrate on the 1976 Carter campaign, the one example of a successful southern strategy for the Democrats.

The 1976 Carter Campaign: The South "Cannot Be Taken for Granted or Jeopardized"

The 1976 presidential election, in which former Georgia Governor Jimmy Carter challenged incumbent (but unelected) President Gerald Ford of Michigan, gave the Democrats their best opportunity to capture the presidency since 1964. Ford had gained the White House after the resignations in disgrace of both Vice-President Spiro Agnew and President Richard Nixon. Shortly after taking office Ford pardoned Nixon for any possible criminal acts. Ford's standing in the polls immediately fell, and never again did a majority of Americans approve of his conduct of the presidency. Ronald Reagan's attempt to win the 1976 Republican presidential nomination further weakened Ford within his own party. A "pause" in the nation's recovery from recession occurred in the fall of 1976, allowing Democrats to claim they would better manage the economy.[1]

Moreover, Ford was such a clumsy and awkward candidate that his own advisors were brutally skeptical about his ability to make a convincing case for reelection to the voters. Stuart Spencer, Ford's main campaign strategist, concluded that Ford's weaknesses as a candidate were so formidable that he should stay in the White House and be "presidential" as much as possible. "Mr. President," Spencer bluntly told Ford in a White House meeting, "as a campaigner, you're no fucking good!" Public opinion polls in early September gave Carter a two-to-one lead over the incumbent president. Capitalizing on voter distrust of Washington, Carter presented himself as a Georgia "farm boy" who would restore the honor of the presidency.[2]

Carter's electoral strategy assumed that a Solid South or something very close to it was essential to a Democratic victory. "The Southern states provide us with a base of support that cannot be taken for granted or jeopardized," wrote Carter campaign manager Hamilton Jordan in an important memo on general election strategy. "The Republicans cannot win if they write off the South. Consequently, we have to assume that they will challenge us in the South. I believe that they will challenge us in those larger Southern and border states that they view as contestable—Texas, Florida, Maryland, and Missouri. I believe we can win each of those four states."[3]

Although Carter's strategists fully understood the importance of the South as an electoral base, Jordan cautioned against emphasizing the role of the South in public discussion:

> Although the Southern states provide us with a rich base of support, it would be a mistake to appear to be overly dependent on the South for victory in November. It would be harmful nationally if we were perceived as having a "Southern strategy." The strength of the South in the electoral college is quite obvious to the media. But to the extent that regional bias exists in this country—and it does—there would be a negative reaction to a candidacy that was perceived as being a captive of the Southern states and/or people. Sad but true. Southern regional pride can be used to great advantage without unnecessarily alienating potential anti-Southern voters.[4]

Carter campaigned extensively in southern black churches, where his Baptist faith was a formidable asset. "His appeal was unique for a white politician. One had only to watch the reception Carter received in black churches," observed Kandy Stroud. Not all southern blacks, of course, rallied to the Carter cause. In the final weekend of the campaign, a highly publicized controversy erupted when a black resident of a nearby town was rebuffed in his attempt to join the Plains Baptist church of which the Carters had long been members. The episode may have cost Carter some black votes.[5]

As a native Deep Southerner who had defeated but not alienated George Wallace in the Democratic primaries, Carter was positioned to win some white support on the basis of regional pride alone. "Isn't it time we had a President without an accent?" Carter would ask of audiences in the South.[6] With a brilliant smile and an effective speaking style, Carter knew how to campaign among southerners. Drawing on many years of teaching Sunday School in Plains, Georgia, Carter brought "some of the mannerisms and methods of a Sunday School teacher" to the presidential campaign trail. As Charles Mohr described Carter in action:

> In his opening speech Monday morning at Warm Springs, Ga., Mr. Carter told the crowd that President Truman had a slogan on his desk and asked, "Does anyone here remember what it was?"
>
> As a chorus of voices shouted, "The buck stops here," the Democratic Presidential candidate, smiling happily, said, "That's right," and went on to accuse President Ford of evading the responsibilities of his high office.
>
> Since then, Mr. Carter has several times asked questions for which there are simple, expected answers, and Mr. Carter has led his audiences in the answers. Sometimes he asked his listeners to raise their hands if a relative is jobless, or even if they know that stock car automobile races occur on Labor Day in Darlington, S.C.
>
> "Southern Baptist dialectic," an onlooker called it the other day.[7]

Carter began the campaign by linking himself to President Roosevelt, the most popular Democrat in the twentieth-century South. He then associated himself with one of the South's most popular spectator sports by flying to South Carolina for the Darlington 500. Carter circled the track, "grinning and waving," to a tumultuous roar of approval from a crowd of 70,000. "Every single stock-car racer in the country is a supporter of mine," Carter later told a crowd of 25,000 at the Norfolk Botanical Gardens.[8] The former Georgia governor's nonthreatening and familiar style helped him win the confidence of many southern whites who were disenchanted with the national Democratic party.

In the final month of the race the Carter campaign used several television advertisements to generate regional pride on behalf of the southern candidate. Martin Schram reported the reaction of Pat Cadell, the Carter campaign pollster, to the ads: "They were blatant—waving the bloody rebel flag. . . . And they were very effective." The script for one of these commercials read as follows:

ANNOUNCER: On November 2, the South is being readmitted to the Union. If that sounds strange, maybe a southerner can understand. Only a southerner can understand years of coarse, anti-southern jokes and unfair comparison. Only a southerner can understand what it means to be a political whipping-boy. But, then only a southerner can understand what Jimmy Carter as President can mean. It's like this: November 2 is the most important day in our region's history. Are you going to let it pass without having your say? Are you going to let the Washington politicians keep one of our own out of the White House? Not if this man can help it.

CARTER: We love our country. We love our government. We don't want anything selfish out of government, we just want to be treated fairly. And we want a right to make our own decisions.

ANNOUNCER: The South has always been the conscience of America—maybe they'll start listening to us now. Vote for Jimmy Carter on November 2.[9]

Unlike Humphrey and McGovern in the two previous campaigns, Carter carefully balanced conservative and liberal themes. Asked by a reporter "if he thought his acceptance speech [at the Democratic national convention] was liberal or conservative," Carter replied, "I think the speech not inadvertently shifted back and forth between the liberal and the conservative."[10] While this revealing answer generated laughter from the national press corps, Carter was simply expressing the basic formula by which most successful Democratic politicians in the South have maintained their biracial coalitions against Republican competitors.

Well aware that the Republicans would attempt to discredit Carter with many white voters by labeling him an "ultraliberal," the Carter campaign used a Birmingham, Alabama, rally to stress several conservative views. To the delight of Governor Wallace, Carter told an enthusiastic crowd that "we Southerners believe in work, not welfare." As James T. Wooten reported, Carter "was clearly more emphatic [than usual] in his commitment to balanced Federal budgets, fiscal moderation, a strong national defense, a more efficient bureaucracy, and 'an end to the welfare mess.'" Wallace frequently "smiled and nodded his approval from his nearby wheelchair as Mr. Carter stirred his audience with refined echoes of familiar Wallace themes." In return Carter reaped the benefit of Wallace's praise: "Oh, how I've longed to see a Deep Southerner, like you and me and Jimmy Carter, in the White House."[11]

But if Carter successfully courted Wallace, he also campaigned as an undisguised advocate of civil rights who believed that the civil rights legislation of the 1960s was "the greatest thing that ever happened to the South." In a Mississippi appearance where he was joined by the state's veteran segregationist senators, James O. Eastland and John C. Stennis, Carter praised the South's transition from a segregationist to a biracial society. "The changes were made not solely by the Supreme Court, or solely by the Congress," Carter declared. "The changes were made by literally hundreds, even thousands of school board members, city councilmen, county officials and others who did accept complete and total integration in the South."[12]

To Carter's mixture of conservative and progressive themes was added a populist promise of tax reform calculated to please most Democrats. "I would never increase taxes for the working people of our country and the lower and middle-income groups," Carter promised in St. Louis. "But we will shift the burden of taxes to where the Republicans have always protected—on the rich, the big corporations and the special interest groups—and you can depend on that if I am elected."[13]

Fortunately for the Democrats, the Ford organization had far less understanding of southern politics and the South's importance to Republican success than had previous Republican strategists. "For us the South was a long shot," President Ford later acknowledged. "Florida was touch and go; the only Southern state we felt sure we would win was Virginia."[14] Ford was less popular than Reagan among southern Republicans, and the Ford campaign initially faced the difficult task of rallying the southerners following Reagan's defeat at the Republican national convention.

In early September, with Ford trailing badly in the polls, Senator Robert Dole of Kansas, the Republican candidate for vice-president, expressed the Ford campaign's basic attitude toward the South. "We don't have any Southern strategy; we think it's a matter of philosophy," Dole said. "As soon as Governor Carter is revealed as the liberal he is, we think there will be a big shift in the South." Earlier in the summer Dole had even tried to label Carter as "Southern-fried McGovern."[15] But it proved far more difficult to pin the "liberal" label on Carter, who had a record that blended progressive and conservative themes, than on McGovern or Humphrey.

After appearing to concede much of the South to Carter, the Ford campaign's internal polling indicated that the president had a chance to win in Louisiana, Mississippi, Virginia, North Carolina, Florida, and Texas. Encouraged by the polls and hoping to force Carter to spend more time in the South, Ford made a three-day southern trip in late September. Campaigning on Mississippi's Gulf Coast, Ford attacked Carter as a big spender. "There are people running for this office of president that want to add more spending, bigger and bigger deficits, more and more inflation," Ford said. "We're against that." Ford's entire southern trip stressed "aggressively conservative themes."[16]

Although Carter's huge lead in the polls evaporated as the campaign progressed, ultimately Carter carried ten of the eleven southern states. Carter attracted sufficiently large white minorities that, when added to landslide black support, enabled the Democrats to implement their biracial southern strategy. He drew white majorities in only three southern states: substantial white majorities in Georgia, his home state, and Arkansas, one of the South's least urbanized states, and a slight white majority in Tennessee. Elsewhere southern whites preferred Ford to Carter, but the minority of whites who voted Democratic was great enough, taking black voting into account, to enable Carter to win every remaining state except Virginia (see Table 12.1).

Carter won 47 percent of the southern white vote, a gain of 28 percentage points over McGovern's support in 1972. According to the NES survey, Carter ran much stronger among whites native to the South (winning 50 percent of this group) than among white migrants to the region (40 percent). Native whites were more likely to be Democrats than were the migrants, of course, but they were also more susceptible to Carter's appeals to regional pride. According to the CBS News/New York Times Exit Poll, Carter captured 82 percent from southern blacks and 71 percent among the core white Democrats. Carter won 46 percent among white swing voters in the region, and only 10 percent of the core white Republicans backed Carter.

Carter's achievement among white voters is best understood by

Table 12.1   White Democracy in the South: estimated white vote won by Democratic presidential candidates after the Great Society (percent)

Political unit	1968	1972	1976	1980	1984	1988
Texas	34	26	46	37	30	38
Arkansas	19	19	58	42	31	36
Tennessee	19	22	51	42	34	34
North Carolina	18	20	48	39	27	32
Florida	23	22	47	31	29	33
Louisiana	12	15	40	33	23	30
Virginia	21	22	40	33	27	30
Alabama	4	14	48	36	25	28
Georgia	13	10	58	50	27	27
Mississippi	0	0	36	35	20	23
South Carolina	12	13	44	32	17	20
Deep South	8	11	47	38	23	26
Peripheral South	24	23	47	36	30	34
South	19	19	47	37	28	32

Source: Estimates calculated by the authors. States are ranked from highest to lowest according to the median percentage white Democratic vote for the 1972–1988 presidential elections.

comparing his breadth of support on questions of race relations with that of Hubert Humphrey in 1968. According to the 1968 NES survey, Humphrey carried 50 percent of the small group of southern whites who preferred desegregation, but attracted only one-fifth of the vote cast by the much larger group who wanted either strict segregation or "something in-between" desegregation and segregation. A question dealing with the pace of racial change showed the same pattern. Humphrey won 47 percent of the white southerners who thought the speed of racial change was "about right," but only 20 percent from the much larger group of southern whites who believed that changes in race relations were moving "too fast."

Carter won 46 percent of the vote from the most racially liberal southern whites in 1976, but he also captured 47 percent from the strong segregationists and 46 percent among the intermediate group of whites. He carried 48 percent of the southern whites who thought the pace of racial change was about right, but also received 48 percent from those who believed that race relations were changing too fast. Endorsed by leading black politicians *and* by George Wallace, Carter positioned himself as a racial moderate. By neutralizing the racial issue as a liability among southern white voters, Carter brought back to the Democratic party many southern white voters who had voted Republican or who had supported Wallace's American Independent party in 1968. He was thus able to get the plurality of the white vote needed to carry southern states.

The former Georgia governor brought together most of the white southerners who were still sympathetic, rather than indifferent or hostile, to the Democratic party. In 1976, according to the NES survey, 62 percent of southern whites were warm toward the Democratic party, and Carter won 65 percent of this group's vote. Among the 38 percent of southern whites who were not favorably disposed toward the Democrats, Carter received only 23 percent of the vote. The hard core of Carter's white support in the South came from the one-third of voters who believed that the Democrats did a better job of handling unemployment than did the Republicans.

The NES survey showed Carter winning 55 percent of the vote among southern whites who had not received a high school education, 48 percent among the region's white high school graduates, and 41 percent among the growing group of whites who had attended college. He ran 32 percentage points higher among the least educated whites than Humphrey had done, 20 points better among high school graduates, but only 12 points better among whites who had attended college.

Carter won 91 percent of the southern electoral vote, the best showing by a Democratic candidate since Franklin Roosevelt's total sweep of the South in 1944. Having carried the South decisively, Carter needed only 37 percent of the electoral vote outside the region to win the presidency. Carter received 44 percent of the northern electoral vote, enough to defeat Ford by a margin of 55 to 45 percent in the electoral college.

Four years later a besieged President Carter could no longer retain enough white support against Reagan to carry any southern state except Georgia. Even in his native state Carter won no more than a bare majority of the white vote. With a southern base that was reduced to 9 percent of the regional electoral vote, Carter's northern target soared to 63 percent. In fact Carter won no more than 9 percent of the northern electoral vote. Carter's loss of the South to a California conservative illustrates the Democrats' difficulty in implementing their southern strategy.

The Problem of Northern Democratic Liberals

For decades few prominent southern Democrats have run for statewide office under the banner of liberalism. Campaigning as a proud liberal ordinarily invites a beating, and a bad one at that. In *The Transformation of Southern Politics*, Jack Bass and Walter DeVries observed that the southern Democratic governors in the 1970s "by and large were moderates, but not liberals—'liberal' remained a suspect political label in the South." Most successful southern Democrats have continued to position themselves as moderates, as some variation of conservative progressive or progressive conservative.[17] Liberalism still has such negative connotations with so many white voters that few experienced Democrats would seriously consider so describing themselves.

None of the northern liberal Democrats who have run for president since 1968 mounted serious campaigns across the entire South. Snickers, horselaughs, and pungent expressions of disbelief greeted the nominations of Humphrey in 1968, McGovern in 1972, Mondale in 1984, and Dukakis in 1988.[18] All of these northern liberals proved to be easy targets for Republican attacks as "liberals" or "ultraliberals."

The Democrats' dilemma in presidential politics is that words and deeds that may be disastrously impolitic in the South may be acceptable and even expected in some areas outside the region. Championing vanguard positions on a variety of racial, economic, social, or cultural issues—taking stances that most experienced southern Democratic politicians would instinctively regard as foolhardy and outlandish—may simply be smart politics in northern states like Minnesota, Massachusetts, New York, or California. Because of the increased power of the liberal Democratic activists and related interest groups in presidential nominations after 1968, many of the Democratic presidential nominees have entered the general election campaign with political records that are baffling and unacceptable to most of the white southerners who vote.

Republican candidates and strategists, armed with a better feel for white southern political culture, have been quick to seize the advantage. Nixon, Reagan, and Bush all shared with the southern electorate their inability to understand why their Democratic opponents would want to bus schoolchildren away from neighborhood schools, or raise federal income taxes, or not allow children to recite the Pledge of Allegiance, or give first-degree murderers vacations from life sentences. "I just can't understand why Democrat X wants to do Activity Y" has been almost a generic Republican formula for undermining the reputation of Democratic presidential candidates. And there can be no doubt that Republican presidential nominees have generally known which side of a sacred symbol or explosive issue to be on.

McGovern, a bold critic of America's participation in the Vietnam War as well as an articulate champion of economic, racial, and social liberalism, was undoubtedly the weakest Democratic nominee in modern times. Southern Democrats ran over themselves trying to repudiate McGovern. The aggressive and unapologetic liberalism of Humphrey and Mondale placed them in the forefront of the Minnesota Democratic party, but many of their sincere convictions and goals appeared to be—or could be made to appear to be—radical departures from common sense to most southern white voters. Dukakis spent much of his campaign attempting to disguise his Massachusetts liberalism, to no avail.

Unsurprisingly, none of the northern liberal Democrats have appealed to more than a small fraction of southern whites. Figure 12.1 provides estimates of the share of the southern white vote won by Democratic candidates from 1968 through 1988. Humphrey and McGovern, running in the most tumultuous of times, received the smallest white votes of the northern liberals. Deep South whites especially rejected the Democrats in 1968 and 1972, with no more than a tenth of them backing Humphrey or McGovern. Slightly fewer than a quarter of Peripheral South whites voted Democratic. After the Carter interlude the northern liberals performed slightly better than in 1968 and 1972. Mondale and Dukakis attracted respectively 28 and 32 percent of the region's white vote. Subregional differences narrowed slightly, but Deep South whites remained less attracted to the northern Democratic nominees. Of the 44 presidential campaigns in the 11 southern states between 1968 and 1988 involving Democratic nominees who were northern liberals, not a single one attracted a white vote that reached 40 percent. The median white vote was 23 percent.

We can further demonstrate the Democrats' problem in the region by examining the net Republican yields from the southern counties that are usually Democratic or usually Republican or that move back and forth between the parties in presidential elections (see Table 12.2). If we compare the results when northern liberals are on the ballot with Carter's two campaigns, the Republicans' underlying advantage is readily apparent. The greatest Republican victories—in 1972 and 1984—have involved choices between liberal northern Democratic challengers and conservative incumbent Republican presidents.

In Nixon's landslide reelection the South's Republican counties gave him a surplus of 4.5 million votes, to which he added a plurality of 1.6 million votes from swing counties and a plurality of 0.2 million votes from counties that were usually Democratic in the 1972–1988 elections. The result was a Republican plurality of 6.3 million votes in the South.

Carter's grassroots appeal in 1976 was unique. With the Republicans temporarily on the defensive because of the Watergate scandal, Carter carried his Democratic base with a surplus of 0.5 million votes, defeated Ford by 1.3 million votes in the southern swing counties, and neutralized the Republicans in their large base. But Carter could not repeat his initial success. Four years later his plurality dropped slightly in the Democratic counties and more substantially in the swing counties. Carter lost because Reagan achieved a plurality of 2.4 million votes in the Republican counties.

In 1984 Mondale narrowly carried the Democratic counties, while losing the Republican counties by over five million votes and the swing counties by almost a million. Dukakis repeated the process in

Table 12.2 The Republican grassroots advantage in the South: net Republican gains or losses in Usually Democratic, Swing, and Usually Republican counties in the 1972–1988 presidential elections (in millions of votes)

Type of southern county	1972	1976	1980	1984	1988
Usually Republican counties	+4.5	0.0	+2.4	+5.2	+3.9
Swing counties	+1.6	–1.3	–0.5	+0.9	+0.5
Usually Democratic counties	+0.2	–0.5	–0.4	–0.2	–0.3
Entire South	+6.3	–1.7	+1.4	+5.9	+4.1

Source: Calculated by the authors from appropriate volumes of Richard M. Scammon, ed., *America Votes* (Washington, D.C.: Congressional Quarterly). All figures are rounded to the nearest tenth of a million votes.

1988, winning a plurality only in the usually Democratic counties. Bush's plurality of 3.9 million votes in the Republican counties and 0.5 million votes in the competitive counties gave him a comfortable regional lead of 4.1 million votes.

The southern failure of the northern liberals is obvious. Dukakis and Mondale achieved modest pluralities only in the Democratic counties, and McGovern ran so poorly that he even lost the party's base. The Republicans' grassroots advantage—their ability to generate surpluses to offset surpluses in the Democratic base—flows from the sheer size of the usually Republican counties. In 1988 *two-thirds* of the entire southern vote was concentrated in counties that normally vote Republican. Reliably Democratic counties, by comparison, controlled only *8 percent* of the regional vote. With eight times as many voters living in Republican as in Democratic counties, the Republicans can be defeated in the South only if—like Ford in 1976—they fail to generate substantial surpluses from their base counties.

Southern Democrats and the Electoral College

After the Civil War and Reconstruction the Democratic party was primarily a party of the South, with some northern support of uncertain dimensions. Conversely, the Republican party was a thoroughly nonsouthern enterprise, preeminently a party of the rest of the nation. Under the terms of American two-party politics that prevailed through 1944, total Democratic control of the South meant that the Democrats could capture the presidency by winning only slightly better than one-third of the electoral vote found outside the South. The New Deal period was the only era in post–Civil War American history in which the Democrats won four consecutive massive electoral victories in the North as well as carrying the Solid South. Control of the South gave the Democrats plenty of room to maneuver outside the South but compelled the Republicans to win almost two-thirds of the entire northern electoral vote.

Presidential elections since the Great Society have been the mirror image of the New Deal period. The inescapable political consequence of the Democrats' recent southern failures has been an increase of major proportions in the Democrats' target for northern electoral votes (see Table 12.3). With the exception of 1976, the minimal share of the northern electoral vote required for a Democratic victory has ranged from 60 percent in 1968 to 67 percent in 1984 and 1988. In no

Table 12.3 The regional structure of the Democratic party's electoral vote in presidential elections after the Great Society

Region	Democratic percentage of electoral vote					
	1968	1972	1976	1980	1984	1988
South	20	0	91	9	0	0
Border	38	6	84	37	6	18
Northeast	81	11	70	3	0	47
Midwest	23	0	35	8	8	23
West	14	0	4	4	0	19
United States	35	3	55	9	2	21
North	40	4	44	9	3	28
Northern Democratic target	60	66	37	63	67	67
Northern Democratic gap	−20	−62	+7	−54	−64	−39

Note: Each number is the percentage of the electoral vote won by the Democratic nominee within a given area. The Northern Democratic target is the minimum percentage of northern electoral votes required for a Democratic victory, given the proportion of electoral votes won by the Democrats in the South. The Northern Democratic gap is the percentage point difference between the Northern Democratic target and the Northern Democratic vote.

Sources: Calculated by the authors from Congressional Quarterly, *Guide to U.S. Elections* (Washington, D.C.: Congressional Quarterly, 1975); and appropriate volumes of Richard M. Scammon, ed., *America Votes* (Washington, D.C.: Congressional Quarterly).

election did the Democrats approach this level of support. Should the Democrats continue to lose the entire South in the 1992, 1996, or 2000 presidential elections, they would have to win 69 percent of the electoral vote outside the South in order to elect a president.

Thus far there have been only eight presidential elections—won by Andrew Jackson in 1832, James Buchanan in 1852, Woodrow Wilson in 1912, Franklin Roosevelt in 1932, 1936, 1940, and 1944, and Lyndon Johnson in 1964—in which the Democrats won 69 percent or more of the northern electoral vote. In all of these campaigns the South and the North were both overwhelmingly Democratic. Even Johnson captured 63 percent of the southern electoral vote in 1964.

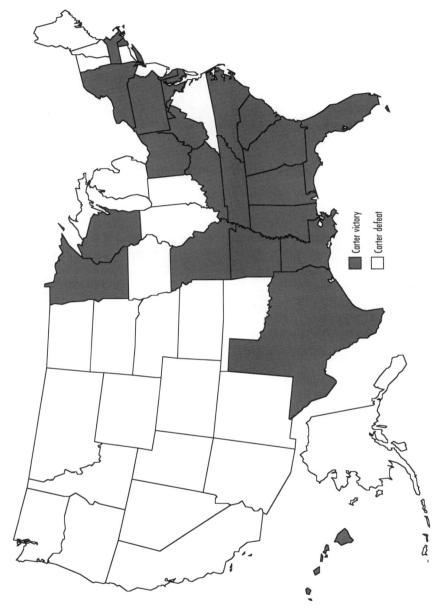

Figure 12.2 The geography of Jimmy Carter's victory in 1976. *Source:* Richard M. Scammon and Alice V. McGillivray, eds., *America Votes,* 12 (Washington, D.C.: Congressional Quarterly, 1977).

There is no example in American history of the Democrats losing the entire South but winning the presidency by securing almost seven-tenths of the northern electoral vote.

The emergence of a fairly Solid Republican South in presidential elections has thus radically altered the regional structure of presidential politics. Carter's 1976 campaign (see Figure 12.2 as well as Table 12.3) helps to show the advantage of *not* losing the South. Because Carter almost swept the South, he could realistically look to the Border, the Northeast, and (to a lesser extent) the Midwest for the 37 percent of the northern electoral vote he needed to win. Assuming hypothetically that the other Democratic presidential nominees—the northern liberals and Carter in 1980—had been as successful in the South as Carter was in 1976, only Humphrey would have won enough northern electoral votes to capture the presidency.

So long as the Republicans continue to win the entire South, the Democratic party will be in the strategic position of the Republican party before 1952. Only by winning seven out of every ten northern electoral votes can the Democrats prevail. Although it is conceivable that the Republicans could so misgovern the nation as to leave the South the only bastion of presidential Republicanism, the practical difficulty of executing a purely northern Democratic strategy should not be underestimated.

13

As the South Goes

As the united South goes, so goes the nation. The modern South is the largest, the most cohesive, and, arguably, the most important region in the United States in terms of establishing the partisan direction of presidential politics. In every one of the nine presidential elections between 1932 and 1988 in which a single party captured all or nearly all of the South's electoral votes, the South has been on the winning side. During the New Deal the Solid Democratic South gave the Democratic party around half of the electoral votes needed to elect Franklin D. Rooosevelt to four straight terms. Between 1948 and 1968, as racial issues emerged and as Republican competition intensified in the region, the South was divided in presidential politics. Since 1972 the white South has returned to its tradition of casting a monolithic electoral vote. With the sole exception of Jimmy Carter's victory in 1976, the Republicans have benefited from the restoration of southern unity.

Throughout history presidential elections in the South have usually been decided by the preferences of a majority of white voters. New partisan and racial dynamics in southern presidential politics have emerged from the tremendous upheavals of the 1960s. The Republican party, for decades viewed by many whites as an antisouthern organization, has attracted white support for its presidential candidates beyond the imagination of most Republican leaders. Once completely excluded from the affairs of the Democratic party, southern blacks have become the most loyal supporters of Democratic presidential candidates. Since whites far outnumber blacks among southern voters, Republican presidential candidates have been the net beneficiaries of these cross-cutting trends. The ability of white majorities to control the outcome of presidential elections, despite the establishment of a biracial electorate, remains one of the most significant continuities in southern politics.

Yet the emergence of Republican domination in presidential elections is only part of a more complex story. As the South goes, so also goes control of the Senate and the House of Representatives. In congressional elections the partisan outcomes have been remarkably different. Democrats have continued to win impressive majorities of southern seats in the House of Representatives and, apart from the early 1980s, in the Senate. In its congressional representation the South has remained more *Democratic* than the rest of the nation. Since areas outside the South have also been sending Democratic majorities or near-majorities to Congress, the South has been running with the grain of national tendencies. Just as capturing the South has given the Republicans an immense advantage in presidential politics, so the preservation of Democratic majorities in southern congressional delegations has been critically important in assuring Democratic leadership of Congress.[1]

A comparison of the Democrats' proportion of southern electoral votes with their shares of southern House and Senate seats clearly distinguishes their sustained congressional successes from their presidential failures (see Figure 13.1). These different outcomes express the complexity of political conflict in the modern South. Presidential and congressional elections in the South reflect two fundamentally different strategies for victory. Presidential contests display an enormous racial polarization: about two-thirds of southern whites customarily support the winning Republican candidate, while around nine-tenths of southern blacks vote for the losing Democratic nominee. In Senate and House elections, however, the typical outcome in the South is a Democratic victory based on a coalition of most blacks and a substantial minority of whites. Whether these divergent patterns persist or a single pattern comes to predominate in the South will help to determine which political party controls the elective branches of the national government.

The Great White Switch

The magnitude of the transformation in the presidential voting habits of southern whites—which we shall call the Great White Switch—can be portrayed by comparing the size of the white majorities won by Democratic presidential nominees during the New Deal period (the height of white support for the national Democratic party) with

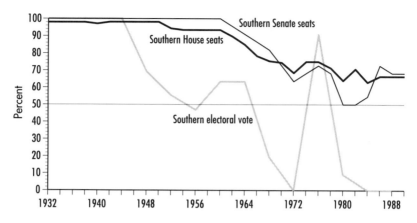

Figure 13.1   Presidential versus congressional Democracy in the South: percentage of southern electoral votes won by Democrats compared with percentage of southern Senate and House seats controlled by Democrats, 1932–1990. *Sources:* Calculated by the authors from Congressional Quarterly, *Guide to U.S. Elections* (Washington, D.C.: Congressional Quarterly, 1975); appropriate volumes of Richard M. Scammon, ed., *America Votes* (Washington, D.C.: Congressional Quarterly); and appropriate issues of *Congressional Quarterly Weekly Report*.

the size of the white majorities that Republican presidential candidates attracted during the 1972–1988 campaigns (see Figure 13.2). In both periods the median white vote was characterized by overwhelming majorities in the entire region, both subregions, and all eleven states.

During the New Deal President Roosevelt symbolized hope for an impoverished region. At the same time, fully understanding the obstructive power of southern segregationists in Congress, Roosevelt took great pains not to challenge white control of southern race relations. Under these dual conditions of economic promise *and* racial status quo, the vast majority of southern white voters remained loyal Democrats. Among southern whites the median Democratic vote in the 1932–1948 presidential elections was 78 percent. The average white Democratic vote varied from a low of about two-thirds in Tennessee to an astonishing 95 percent in South Carolina and Mississippi.

By the early 1970s the Republican party was positioned to replace the Democratic party as the choice of most southern white voters in presidential elections. In the aftermath of the civil rights movement,

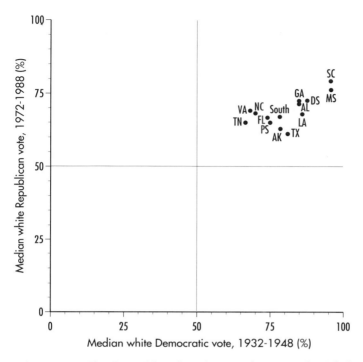

Figure 13.2 The Great White Switch in southern presidential elections: over-whelming white Democracy in the New Deal period followed by overwhelming white Republicanism after the Great Society. *Sources:* Calculated by the authors from Richard M. Scammon, ed., *America at the Polls* (Pittsburgh: University of Pittsburgh Press, 1965); appropriate volumes of Richard M. Scammon, ed., *America Votes* (Washington, D.C.: Congressional Quarterly); appropriate volumes of *U.S. Statistical Abstract*; and NES presidential-year election studies.

federal intervention to enforce the civil rights laws of the mid-1960s, and the waning of the Wallace movement, as well as for all of the nonracial reasons (economic, foreign policy, cultural) why whites might prefer Republican presidential candidates, the Republican party emerged with the votes of substantial majorities of white south-erners. According to our estimates, the median white Republican vote in the 1972–1988 presidential elections was 67 percent. In both periods the southern states with the largest black populations regis-tered the heaviest white majorities.

The three presidential elections of the 1980s illustrate the breadth of Republican support among southern whites. According to the CBS

News/New York Times Exit Polls, Republican presidential candidates in the South averaged 93 percent among core white Republicans, 61 percent among swing white voters, and 28 percent among core white Democrats.

Bush and Reagan ran well among the most affluent and most educated southern whites, just as Dwight Eisenhower had done in the 1950s, but these groups alone are insufficient to provide the landslide white majorities needed by the Republicans. As Republican presidential candidates began to emphasize a conservative agenda that included racial, defense, tax, and cultural issues, they penetrated formerly Democratic strongholds of southern lower-middle-class and blue-collar whites. In each of the presidential elections during the 1980s, according to the CBS News/New York Times Exit Polls, Republican presidential candidates won majorities from *every* educational and income category of southern white voters, including even those whites with the *lowest* family incomes and the *least* formal education.

So pronounced was the Great White Switch that Republican presidential candidates in the 1980s elections drew greater support among white voters in the South than they did among whites in the rest of the nation (see Table 13.1). For example, Bush's southern white vote of 67 percent was 10 points higher than his support among whites outside the South. These regional differences are considerably diluted, of course, when the predominantly Democratic votes of the South's larger group of black voters are taken into account. Even so Bush ran seven points stronger within the South than he did outside it. The South expressed, in a heightened form, the presidential voting patterns characteristic of the entire nation.

The South and Republican Strategy

What must the Republican party do to keep the South reliably Republican? Because the Republicans have gained the upper hand in southern presidential politics, their imperatives for continued success have ironically become those succinctly stated by Hamilton Jordan in formulating Jimmy Carter's 1976 campaign strategy. For the Republicans now as for Carter then, the South must not "be taken for granted or jeopardized."[2] Both points are important.

The Republicans' southern success in the 1980s creates the possibility that an essential political base might be assumed so safe that its interests and values could be ignored or given lip service. There

Table 13.1   Consequences of the Great White Switch: greater support for Republican presidential candidates in the South, by region and race

| | Percent voting Republican | | | |
	1976	1980	1984	1988
White voters only				
South	53	61	72	67
Rest of nation	52	55	63	57
Difference (S − N)	+1	+6	+9	+10
All voters				
South	46	53	64	59
Rest of nation	50	51	58	52
Difference (S − N)	−4	+2	+6	+7

Sources: Calculated by the authors from CBS News/New York Times Exit Polls of presidential elections, 1976–1988. All figures are rounded to the nearest percent.

appears small likelihood, however, that the Republicans will neglect their southern white base. With the single exception of the 1976 Ford campaign, all of the Republican presidential campaigns since Nixon's in 1968 have recognized and skillfully exploited the tremendous opportunities in the South. Indeed, for two reasons the South stands to become even more important to the GOP in the future. Winning southern primaries is critical to securing the Republican presidential nomination, and the region will control an even larger number of electoral votes in the 1990s.

Substantively, the GOP will probably continue to nominate presidential candidates who take conservative positions over a wide range of issues. The party's sole modern defeat came with the nomination of a moderately conservative midwestern Republican who had little appreciation of the strategic importance of carrying southern states. Prevailing political conditions will dictate the specific issues to be raised, but Republican presidential candidates will probably continue to emphasize the foreign policy and military successes of the Reagan and Bush administrations, support large defense and military expenditures, stress the necessity of a well-equipped and high-tech military in defending American interests in the world, and champion various expressions of cultural conservatism. They will presumably continue to oppose increases in federal income tax rates, the expansion of most domestic government programs, and any civil rights legislation that could be interpreted as involving racial or sexual quotas or preferences. These are the clusters of issues that Nixon, Reagan, and Bush have emphasized with marked success among southern white voters.

Although the Republicans have a considerable advantage over the Democrats, they are not invulnerable, given how quickly events can change the outcomes of presidential elections. In the 1920s the Republicans easily won three presidential elections before the Great Depression devastated them in 1932. The Republican landslide of 1972 was followed by the Watergate scandal and their defeat in 1976. Republican victories after the Great Society do not mean that the GOP will always prevail in the future. Because the Republican party has mortgaged itself to the necessity of winning substantial majorities of the large and diverse white population, it will be open to challenge if and when the Democratic alternative seems preferable to most black voters and to a large minority of whites.

Political majorities, as V. O. Key, Jr., cogently argued, must always be reconstructed, election by election:

> Such evidence as can be mustered suggests that the popular majority does not hold together like a ball of sticky popcorn. Rather, no sooner has a popular majority been constructed than it begins to crumble. The maintenance of a supportive majority requires governmental actions, policies, and gestures that reinforce the confidence of those who have placed their faith in the Administration. Yet to govern is to antagonize not only opponents but also at least some supporters; as the loyalty of one group is nourished, another group may be repelled. A series of maintaining elections occurs only in consequence of a complex process of interaction between government and populace in which old friends are sustained, old enemies are converted into new friends, old friends become even bitter opponents, and new voters are attracted to the cause—all in proper proportions to produce repeatedly for the dominant party its apparently stable and continuing majority.[3]

Provided that Republican presidential campaigns do not take the South for granted, the greater threat to continued Republican success lies in the possibility that some combination of Republican policy failures, disappointing economic performance, and the nomination of a conspicuously flawed GOP candidate could jeopardize the party's landslide white majorities. Foreign policy ventures which end in failure, economic recession which reaches deeply into the southern white middle class and working class, an inability to communicate a sense of national purpose, serious disunity within the ruling party itself—these and other possibilities might contribute (as they did in 1952, 1960, 1968, 1976, and 1980, for example) to a widespread feeling that new leadership is needed in the White House. The basic Republican challenge is to sustain its control of the presidency despite the international and domestic problems and conflicts that inevitably generate disagreement and opposition.

During the period after the Great Society, as we have already shown, the Republican party developed its broadest base of support in history. In terms of practical politics, the states that usually vote Republican in presidential elections will cast almost *three-fourths* of the nation's electoral vote in the 1990s, a figure exceeded in American history only by the size of the reliably Democratic electoral vote during the New Deal.

If the Republicans can continue to carry the South, what are the party's prospects in presidential elections? Beginning with the presidential election of 1992 and continuing through the election of 2000, the South will control 27 percent of the nation's electoral votes. If the Republicans can sweep the South's 147 electoral votes, they can win the presidency by capturing only 31 percent of the 391 electoral votes located outside the South. Let us further assume that the Republicans also carry the 12 Northern Republican Bedrock states, those states in which the 1968–1988 Republican presidential vote averaged 55 percent or better. Oklahoma, New Hampshire, Indiana, Kansas, Nebraska, North Dakota, Alaska, Arizona, Idaho, Nevada, Utah, and Wyoming would give the Republicans 65 more electoral votes, for a total of 212. Under these conditions the Republicans would need just 18 percent (58 electoral votes) of the remaining 326 electoral votes. Finally, let us assume that the Republicans win California's 54 votes, the grand prize of the electoral college. Although California's presidential elections are usually close, since midcentury the Golden State has gone Republican in every election except 1964. If the Republicans win the entire South, the Northern Bedrock Republican states, and California, they would be only four votes short of victory. Under these circumstances they would need no more than 1.5 percent of the 272 electoral votes left in the rest of the nation.

Because the South is much bigger than either the Northern Bedrock Republican states or California, keeping the South totally Republican should be the single most important Republican priority. If the Republicans can reconstruct the Solid Republican South, they will be exceedingly hard to defeat in a presidential election.

The South and Democratic Strategy

It is difficult to exaggerate the strategic implications of the Democrats' uncompensated loss of the Solid South in presidential elections. When the Democrats lost their traditional southern base and failed to counter that development by winning fresh support outside the South, the regional foundations of presidential politics were revolutionized. For generations after the period of Civil War and Reconstruction, the South was the nation's principal bastion of presidential Democracy. In no other part of the country was there a compelling tradition of voting Democratic election after election. Only during the exceptional circumstances of the New Deal did the Democratic party develop substantial state-level support outside the South.

The collapse of the Democrats' southern base has meant that the Democrats commence presidential campaigns without a sizable bloc of assured electoral votes. In a reverse of New Deal electoral patterns, the Republicans begin from strength while the Democrats start from scratch. Democratic electoral majorities must be constructed ad hoc and de novo. Because the Democrats have no large base of dependably Democratic states, majorities must be built in many states out of the raw materials of current events, issues, and personalities. The Democrats are fundamentally dependent upon widespread distress among voters focused upon a Republican White House to give them the opportunity to argue persuasively that "it's time for a change."

In presidential elections the national Democratic party occupies an "if and when" status, the hallmark of a weak competitor dependent upon the mistakes of its opponent. The Democrats' modern presidential prospects are reminiscent of the Republicans' chances during the New Deal. In both eras the party out of power had no southern base and hence was forced to wage presidential campaigns on northern electoral votes alone. "If and when" situations typically stimulate a great deal of wishful thinking and angry second-guessing on the part of the frustrated politicians and activists of the "out" party. Much of this behavior recalls the old East Texas adage:

> If "ifs" and "buts"
> Were candy and nuts,
> We'd all have a Merry Christmas.

Just as the Republicans made little headway in presidential politics during the New Deal era, so the Democrats fundamentally await more promising conditions, conditions generating fewer "ifs" and "buts," to contest the presidency.

Because the Republicans' rhetoric generally meshes with the beliefs, values, and aspirations of many middle-class and working-class whites as well as affluent whites, Democratic presidential candidates have been forced to state their case in terms of the possibility of disastrous future outcomes. Democratic arguments and warnings about hard times ahead have been less persuasive than Republican appeals to current feelings of "peace and prosperity" and national pride. If and when the nation's fortunes do turn out to be as bleak as some Democrats warn, and if and when Republican presidents and their policies can plausibly be blamed for bad times, Democratic presidential candidates will find a more receptive audience in the white South.

And yet it will not be easy for the Democrats to regain presidential standing in the South. The national Democratic party has lost so much stature among so many southern white voters that significant changes in white perceptions of the consequences of Republican rule will probably be required before many of the disaffected whites again pay serious attention to Democratic presidential candidates. Republican rule needs to be convincingly discredited by events, as it was during the administrations of Herbert Hoover and Richard Nixon.

If that time should come, Democrats would still need a message and a messenger to be considered a realistic alternative. In international affairs the Democrats have suffered politically because of their inability to use American military power successfully. Neither Johnson's escalation of the Vietnam War nor Carter's inability to rescue American hostages from Iran generated images of Democratic presidents as effective commanders-in-chief. The Republican record has not been a string of unbroken successes, but President Reagan's actions against Libya and Grenada and Bush's intervention in Panama resulted in the effective use of military force to achieve specific objectives. Far more important were Bush's actions in 1990–91 to force Iraq to abandon Kuwait. The Gulf war compellingly underscored the different approaches of Republican and Democratic leaders to the identification and the protection of American interests abroad.

Republican presidents have obviously been far more willing to use military force in international crises. When they have succeeded (as in the war with Iraq), they have reaped the political benefits of a resurgent pride in American military power. The opposition of large majorities of Democrats in the House and Senate to President Bush's decision to use military force in January 1991 against Iraq is the most dramatic expression of these long-standing differences. The Democrats need a foreign policy message that does not appear to concede protection of America's international interests to the Republicans.

In addition, the Democrats need a domestic agenda that identifies both unresolved problems and their solutions and that suggests how corrective measures can be financed without alienating potential Democratic voters. The key to political acceptability is persuading voters that various expenditures make sense as long-term investments: providing education that equips the next generation of Americans to be truly knowledgeable and competitive in a global economic environment; building (or rebuilding) the nation's infrastructure of highways, water supply systems, and airports; extending health care provisions for millions of Americans who do not have medical insurance; ensuring the solvency of the nation's financial system; reducing the budget deficits of the federal government; and protecting the environment. On these matters the Republican record has been far less impressive and much more open to effective political attack.

The most difficult issue for the Democratic party to confront is civil rights, for it is impossible to satisfy fully the conflicting preferences of most whites and most blacks. As Thomas Byrne Edsall and Mary D. Edsall have forcefully observed, "Race is no longer a straightforward, morally unambiguous force in American politics; instead, considerations of race are now deeply imbedded in the strategy and tactics of politics, in competing concepts of the function and responsibility of government, and in each voter's conceptual structure of moral and partisan identity." If the national Democratic party aggressively champions policies that Republicans can plausibly attack as involving "preferential treatment" for minorities, it runs the risk of further alienating whites. Alternatively, if the Democratic party pursues only those civil rights policies consistent with the principle of securing "an equal opportunity to participate and to compete and to gain a measure of justice" for all citizens, it runs the risk of alienating many blacks who believe that such policies provide too little assistance to minorities.[4]

Intensely held differences of opinion about civil rights issues constitute an intractable political dilemma for the Democratic party, one with considerable potential for further splitting the fragile Democratic coalition. Compounding the problem and deepening the frustration of many Democratic activists is the fundamental reality that most blacks, unlike most whites, have no practical alternative to the Democratic party. Because most blacks—like most southern whites in the old days—have written off the Republican party, their basic alternatives in presidential elections are to vote Democratic or not vote at all. Southern whites unhappy with Democratic civil rights policies, however, do not have to forgo voting, for the Republican party offers a more conservative alternative.

Can Democrats Win in the South?

While their recent record in presidential politics is decidedly disappointing, it is only in the contest for the White House that Democratic candidates in the South have been at such a lopsided disadvantage. The Democratic party has continued to win impressive majorities of southern seats in the House of Representatives and (the early 1980s excepted) in the Senate. Most of the region's governors, state legislators, and other elected officials are Democrats. Examining the electoral coalitions that support successful Democratic candidacies in the South may suggest how Democratic presidential candidates might position themselves to attract a larger white vote, while maintaining support among blacks.

Exit polls conducted by CBS News and the New York Times reveal the essential differences between the South's *winning* and *losing* Democratic campaigners in the 1980s. Table 13.2 profiles selected Democratic winners in several campaigns for the Senate (Lloyd Bentsen of Texas, Terry Sanford of North Carolina, John Breaux of Louisiana, Robert Graham of Florida, Howell Heflin of Alabama, and James Sasser of Tennessee). The victorious Democrats in senatorial races usually won large majorities from blacks and core white Democrats—thus unifying the party's bases—as well as capturing a majority from white swing voters.

It is also instructive to examine the southern Democratic losers (see Table 13.3). Carter, Mondale, and Dukakis all drew strong support from the two Democratic groups of voters, but they lost decisively among white swing voters and won very few votes from core white Republicans. Similar problems plagued the Senate campaigns of Wayne Dowdy in Mississippi in 1988 and of James Hunt in North Carolina, Lloyd Doggett in Texas, and William Winter in Mississippi in 1984.

The main difference between success and failure for southern Dem-

Table 13.2 Profiles of winning Democratic candidates in the South: percentage of the vote won by various Democratic candidates for the Senate among blacks, core white Democrats, white swing voters, and core white Republicans

	Blacks	Whites		
		Core Dems	Swing voters	Core Reps
Bentsen 88	93	91	62	27
Sanford 86	90	84	57	8
Breaux 86	89	66	53	13
Graham 86	83	81	64	29
Heflin 84	94	82	60	34
Sasser 82	92	84	72	20

Sources: CBS News/New York Times Exit Polls.

Table 13.3 Profiles of losing Democratic candidates in the South: percentage of the vote won by various Democratic candidates among blacks, core white Democrats, swing white voters, and core white Republicans

	Blacks	Whites		
		Core Dems	Swing voters	Core Reps
President				
Carter 80	89	64	36	5
Mondale 84	90	71	34	4
Dukakis 88	89	75	42	7
Senate				
Dowdy 88	87	66	41	7
Hunt 84	89	75	36	14
Doggett 84	89	77	40	6
Winter 84	74	47	24	6

Sources: CBS News/New York Times Exit Polls.

ocratic politicians is the breadth of their appeal among white voters. The extent of white support the various Democratic candidates can draw depends in part on how the candidates position themselves on issues. Most successful southern Democrats try to offer something of value to the most liberal groups in their coalition, but they generally make some overtures toward the values and interests of moderate to conservative whites.

Democrats *can* win in the South, but victory normally requires a candidate who balances liberal positions on some issues with conservative positions on other issues so that he or she both unites the party faithful—blacks and the core white Democrats—and appeals to a sufficiently large group of white swing voters. The Democrats need a presidential candidate who can craft a message that will unite Democrats and attract those southerners who do not consider themselves members of the party. Without a balanced message and a persuasive messenger, the Democrats will not be well positioned to seize any opportunities presented by Republican disarray.

The Democratic Dilemma: Retaining the White Moderates

The southern party system is still in transition (see Figure 13.3). Blacks have remained overwhelmingly Democratic, according to the exit polls of presidential elections. Indeed, blacks are even more Democratic—and less Republican—than were southern whites in the 1950s. Among white southerners, however, only liberals have retained an overwhelmingly Democratic orientation. Their partisan profile is similar to that of black southerners. About three-fifths of white liberals think of themselves as Democrats, with the remainder split between independents and Republicans.

Since 1976 the South's white conservatives have registered astonishing shifts away from Democracy and toward Republicanism. In 1976 there was no partisan majority among southern white conservative voters. A small plurality still considered themselves Democrats, the second largest group was made up of independents, but only 30 percent of the white conservatives labeled themselves Republicans. In each subsequent election dramatic increases have occurred in the percentage of southern white conservatives who identify themselves as Republicans. By 1980, 40 percent were Republican; four years later, 52 percent identified with the GOP; and in 1988, 60 percent of southern white conservatives did so. Among southern white conservatives the Republican party has emerged as the party

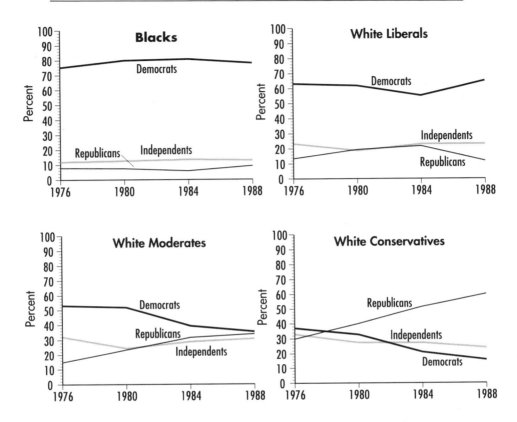

Figure 13.3 The changing party balance among voters in the South: partisan tendencies of blacks, white liberals, white moderates, and white conservatives, 1976–1988. *Source:* Calculated by the authors from CBS News/New York Times presidential exit polls, 1976–1988.

of choice in presidential elections. Support for the Democratic party among these voters has steadily declined, and in 1988 only 16 percent of white conservative voters still described themselves as Democrats.

The most interesting and important group of voters, from the standpoint of the South's future partisan balance, are southern whites who think of themselves as moderates.[5] With white conservatives anchoring the Republicans, and with blacks and white liberals disproportionately Democratic, the prospects for continued Republican growth or for persisting Democratic strength in the South may well depend upon the political tendencies of the white moderates.

Although no dominant tendency has yet emerged, the Republicans have been the main beneficiaries of recent trends among the moderates.

In 1976 a majority of the white moderate voters (53 percent) were Democrats, while only 15 percent called themselves Republicans. Democrats outnumbered Republicans by more than three-to-one among this group of voters, and they constituted much of Jimmy Carter's strength. Since 1976, however, the percentage of Democratic moderates has declined and the percentage of Republican moderates has increased. By 1988 the moderates were split three ways. Merely 35 percent of the moderate voters were still Democrats, while 34 percent identified with the GOP and 31 percent thought of themselves as independents. Indeed, the moderates in 1988 closely resembled the conservatives in 1976 (see Figure 13.3). The Democrats' historical advantage among this critical group of voters has almost vanished.

It is difficult to overstate the importance of these trends among the South's white moderates. Without the votes of white moderates, the Democratic party would simply not be competitive against the Republicans in statewide elections. If the Democrats should ever lose the moderate vote decisively, support for their candidates would be limited to blacks and liberal white Democrats. The party would then be free to be as liberal as it wished to be on a wide range of issues, but it would be hopelessly outvoted in elections. If the Democrats lose the white moderates, they will become a permanent minority party in the South.

White moderates are crucial to Democratic success, for their votes usually provide the margin of victory. In Carter's successful 1976 contest, he won 51 percent of the vote cast by white moderates. In the next three presidential elections Democratic candidates suffered landslide rejection by the white moderates. Carter won only 41 percent in 1980, Mondale dropped to 37 percent in 1984, and Dukakis attracted only 41 percent in 1988. As fewer white moderates identify with the Democratic party, it has become even more difficult for Democratic presidential candidates to capture them.

In the successful Senate races previously discussed in this chapter, most of the winning Democratic candidates carried landslide majorities (60 percent or higher) of the vote cast by white moderates: Bentsen of Texas (62 percent), Sanford of North Carolina (60), Graham of Florida (61), Heflin of Alabama (63), and Sasser of Tennessee (68). The exception was Breaux of Louisiana, who carried only 48 percent of the white moderate vote. On the other hand, not even winning 54 percent of the white moderates was enough to enable Governor Hunt of North Carolina to defeat incumbent Senator Helms in 1984. The other three Democratic losers attracted well less than half of the white moderate voters. Dowdy of Mississippi received only 42 percent, Doggett of Texas won 41 percent, and Winter of Mississippi carried only 26 percent among white moderates. Democratic candidates in the South who cannot carry substantial majorities of the white moderate vote either lose or narrowly prevail.

With so much riding on the candidates' ability to win the white moderate vote, the future of competitive politics in the South, may well turn on whether Democratic politicians can revive their previous levels of support among moderates or whether the Republicans can improve their performance. Although the moderates have voted Republican decisively in presidential elections, they have split their tickets on a candidate-by-candidate basis in major statewide contests. Accordingly, most southern Democratic leaders stress the importance of nominating a moderate for the presidency. As Alan A. Diamonstein of Virginia, the chairman of the Southern Caucus of the National Democratic Committee, has observed, "If [national leaders] don't come out with a moderate candidate, we're going to be defeated in the South."[6]

The South and National Democratic Strategy

The national Democratic party and its presidential nominees have three options for the South in presidential politics. They can completely write off the South, campaign hard in every southern state, or run in several carefully selected states.

National Democratic leaders publicly disavow any suggestion of conceding the South. Addressing leaders of Democratic parties in the southern states in Raleigh, North Carolina, in June of 1991, Democratic Party Chairman Ronald H. Brown assured the audience that "there is no strategy [for the general election] that excludes . . . the South. No such strategy would make any sense."[7] The historical record indicates that conceding the entire region to the Republicans indeed makes little sense as a winning strategy. Doing so would forfeit 147 electoral votes, 54 percent of the total needed for victory. No Democrat in American history has ever been elected president on the strength of northern electoral votes alone.

Because of the Democratic party's poor record in the South since the Great Society, however, it might be necessary for the Democrats to pioneer a new route to the presidency. The outlines of a winning presidential strategy can be faintly detected in Dukakis's performance outside the South. If a future Democratic nominee could carry *all* the states won by Dukakis plus *all* the states in which he polled at least 45 percent of the popular vote, the Democrats could win a narrow victory without a single electoral vote from the South. The campaign would have to concentrate on a carefully selected group of states located in the Northeast (Connecticut, Massachusetts, New York, Pennsylvania, Rhode Island, and Vermont), the Border (District of Columbia, Maryland, Missouri, and West Virginia), the Midwest (Illinois, Iowa, Michigan, Minnesota, South Dakota, and Wisconsin), and the West (California, Colorado, Hawaii, Montana, New Mexico, Oregon, and Washington). Victories in all of these states would generate 275 electoral votes, five votes to spare.

The riskiness of this northern strategy is obvious. A Democratic nominee would have virtually no margin for defeat in any of the northern target states. A full-fledged northern strategy—a Democratic version of Abraham Lincoln's Republican strategy in 1860—would allow the Republicans to assemble over half of their required electoral majority more or less unchallenged in the South. As a result the Republicans could concentrate their campaign resources on the most promising combination of northern states (starting with California!) needed to checkmate the Democrats. Republican money and campaign appearances not needed to secure the South could be channeled to a host of encouraging northern states.[8]

Southern Democrats have hardly been enthusiastic about an exclusively northern strategy to win the White House. In 1991 A. L. May of the *Atlanta Constitution* captured reactions typical of many leading southern Democrats to talk of abandoning the region in the presidential contest. "You got to carry the South or you're dead," emphasized Virginia's Diamonstein. And according to Georgia Democratic Chairman Ed Sims, "The lesson of the past presidential races is not that you write off the South. The lesson is that you get a candidate who can run in the South."[9]

On the other hand, a Democratic strategy that assumed the entire South could go Democratic would waste scarce political resources unless a Republican administration experienced major setbacks and the Democrats nominated a candidate who could elicit genuine enthusiasm in the region. A candidate from the South would probably have more chance of carrying some southern states than would a nominee from outside the region, but not even a southerner at the top of the Democratic ticket would guarantee a Solid Democratic South.

In the absence of a total Republican collapse, the most reasonable strategy for the Democrats would be to concentrate on northern states but to allocate some campaign resources to a small number of southern states—Arkansas and Tennessee, for example, plus any others that might be experiencing severe economic difficulties in the election year—where majority biracial coalitions might be constructed. Denying the Republicans a complete sweep of the South is probably the most realistic outcome that the Democrats can hope for in the near future.[10]

In trying to find more southern white votes to combine with black support, gender might be the demographic key to improved Democratic fortunes. The Republicans have clearly demonstrated that it is possible to write off most black support and still win, but they cannot afford to write off most blacks *and* half of the region's white women. If the Democrats can promote issues that have more appeal to white females, the Republicans would have greater difficulty securing the large white majorities they need for victory. Thus far this has not happened, for Republican presidential candidates averaged 69 percent from white men and 64 percent from white women in the South during the three elections of the 1980s.

The South and the Nation

To provide a final geopolitical perspective on presidential elections, we shall group the 50 states according to their partisan voting patterns before and after the Great Society. From the standpoint of each major party, a state can be considered a continuing success, a gain, a loss, or a continuing failure. For example, a continuing Republican success is a state that was usually Republican in both periods, while a continuing Republican failure identifies a state that was not dependably Republican in either period. A Republican gain is a state that was usually Republican after the Great Society but not before it; and a Republican loss indicates a state that was Republican before the Great Society but not subsequently. (See Chapter 3 for an application of these terms to the nation's counties.)

Figure 13.4 maps the gigantic turnaround in the Republicans' fortunes in presidential elections before and after the Great Society. The 22 states with a record of continuing Republican success include three

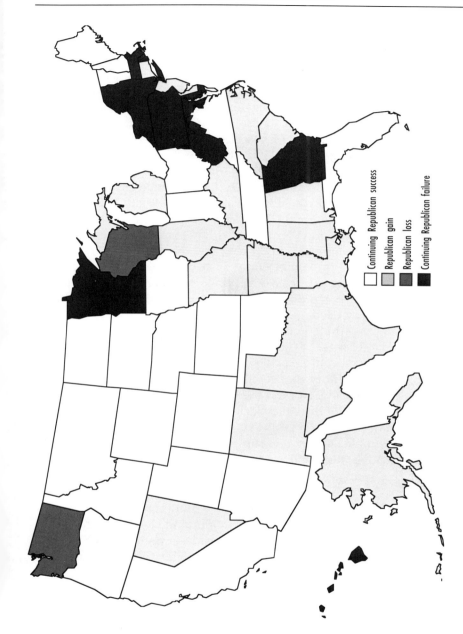

Figure 13.4 Presidential Republicanism before and after the Great Society: 1952–1964 state classifications compared with 1968–1988 state classifications. Southern states classified according to 1972–1988 elections. *Source:* Calculated by the authors from appropriate volumes of Richard M. Scammon, ed., *America Votes* (Washington, D.C.: Congressional Quarterly).

in the South (Florida, Virginia, and Tennessee), but most of them are located in the West and Midwest. In the presidential elections of 1992, 1996, and 2000, the continuing Republican successes will together cast 40 percent of the electoral vote. Another 34 percent of the electoral vote is concentrated in the 17 states which recently experienced Republican presidential gains. Included in this category are all of the remaining southern states except Georgia. The addition of these states to the Republican base that was developed in the 1950s and early 1960s gives the GOP its huge head start toward winning the presidency.

Republican gains after the Great Society far outnumbered Republican losses (Wisconsin and Washington). The continuing Republican failures (New York, Pennsylvania, Massachusetts, and Rhode Island in the Northeast, Maryland, West Virginia, and the District of Columbia in the Border, Minnesota in the Midwest, Hawaii in the West, and Georgia in the South) contain only 22 percent of the electoral vote. If the Republicans can simply continue to carry most of the states where they have a proven record of success, they have the electoral majority they need.

For the Democrats the comparable map is literally devoid of a significant political base (see Figure 13.5). Not one state qualified as a continuing Democratic success. The District of Columbia was the nation's only political entity that regularly voted Democratic before and after the Great Society. Nor did the Democrats create impressive new state-level bases after the Great Society. Minnesota, with a native son on four Democratic national tickets during the 1968–1988 campaigns, was the single Democratic gain.

Unlike the Republicans, the Democrats lost more states than they gained. The five southern states which qualified as Usually Democratic states in the 1952–1964 elections were all Democratic losses after the Great Society. Finally, 41 of the 50 states, possessing 85 percent of the electoral vote, represented continuing Democratic failures. Careful pondering of the two maps provides a visual education in the enormity of the Democrats' task in finding the right candidate and the right set of issues with which to hammer the Republicans.

The South in American Politics

In the past, observers of the South found a different, exceedingly distinctive part of the country. Traditionally the region was fascinating and consequential precisely because it seemed to be so radically

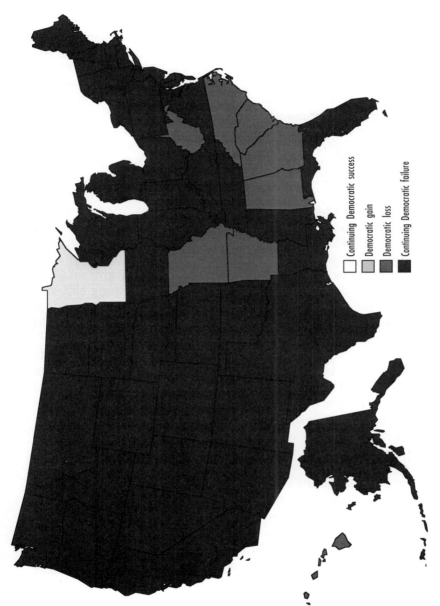

Figure 13.5 Presidential Democracy before and after the Great Society: 1952–1964 state classifications compared with 1968–1988 state classifications. Southern states classified according to 1972–1988 elections. *Source:* Same as Figure 13.4.

unlike the rest of the nation. While most eligible Americans voted in presidential elections outside the South, only small minorities of eligible southerners bothered to vote. Racist institutions pervaded the country, but the southern states had the most intricate, highly developed, and legally required systems of institutional racism. Whereas other parts of the nation experienced more active competition between the major political parties, effective political competition in the South occurred (if at all) within the confines of a single political party. For many decades after the Civil War, the South supported Democratic presidential candidates and resolutely sent Democrats to Congress. The standard qualifying phrase was "except, of course, for the South," and it was applied to a stupendous range of institutions, attitudes, and behavior.

The contemporary South reveals—sometimes in exaggerated form—political outcomes characteristic of the entire country. Regional differences in presidential and congressional politics have typically become matters of subtlety and nuance, matters of degree and emphasis. Political developments in the region are fascinating and consequential precisely because they appear to be so similar to tendencies in the rest of the nation. The modern qualifying phrase should run, "*especially* so in the South."

As the largest and usually most cohesive region in the nation, the South often controls the votes that influence which parties dominate the executive and legislative branches of the national government. Whether the region will continue to produce Republican landslide white majorities in presidential elections while it produces Democratic biracial majorities in many congressional and senatorial contests is among the most compelling and critical questions confronting the nation.

Today, one looks at the South and sees America. There is abundant reason to pay close attention to future political developments in the South, for it now shapes the trends and sets the pace of national political outcomes and processes. Above all, this is the portrait of a *vital* South, a region once again at the center of struggles to define winners and losers in American politics.

Notes
Index

Notes

1. The Republican Edge

1. Confidential source.
2. *Wall Street Journal*, September 6, 1988.
3. Peter Applebome, "The Battle for Texas," *New York Times Magazine,* October 30, 1988, p. 66.
4. Earl Black and Merle Black, *Politics and Society in the South* (Cambridge, Mass.: Harvard University Press, 1987), pp. 259–264.
5. See, for example, Kevin P. Phillips, *The Emerging Republican Majority* (Garden City, N.Y.: Anchor Books, 1970), pp. 187–289; Numan V. Bartley and Hugh D. Graham, *Southern Politics and the Second Reconstruction* (Baltimore: Johns Hopkins University Press, 1975), pp. 81–135; James L. Sundquist, *Dynamics of the Party System,* rev. ed. (Washington, D.C.: Brookings Institution, 1983), pp. 269–297; Dewey W. Grantham, *The Life and Death of the Solid South* (Lexington: University Press of Kentucky, 1988), pp. 149–203; and Kirkpatrick Sale, *Power Shift* (New York: Random House, 1975), pp. 89–152.
6. Joseph A. Califano, "Tough Talk for Democrats," *New York Times Magazine,* January 8, 1989, p. 28.
7. Goldwater voted against the Civil Rights Act of 1964. For his recollections about the Civil Rights Act, see Barry M. Goldwater with Jack Casserly, *Goldwater* (New York: Doubleday, 1988), pp. 3, 171–173, 193–194.
8. *Washington Post Weekly National Edition,* August 8–14, 1988.
9. Alexander P. Lamis, *The Two-Party South* (New York: Oxford University Press, 1984), p. 26.
10. Harold W. Stanley emphasizes multiple reasons for Republican success in the South, although he places considerably less emphasis on race-related factors than we do. See "The 1984 Presidential Election in the South: Race and Realignment," in Robert P. Steed, Laurence W. More-land, and Tod A. Baker, eds., *The 1984 Presidential Election in the South* (New York: Praeger, 1985), pp. 315–322. On the role of race in American

politics generally, see Thomas Byrne Edsall with Mary D. Edsall, *Chain Reaction: The Impact of Race, Rights, and Taxes on American Politics* (New York: W. W. Norton, 1991); and Edward G. Carmines and James A. Stimson, *Issue Evolution* (Princeton, N.J.: Princeton University Press, 1989).

11. For a similar cross-classification of the entire electorate, see Gerald M. Pomper, "The Presidential Election," in Marlene Michels Pomper, ed., *The Election of 1980* (Chatham, N.J.: Chatham House, 1981), p. 86.

2. The South and the Electoral College

1. V. O. Key, Jr., *Southern Politics in State and Nation* (New York: Knopf, 1949); Jasper Berry Shannon, *Toward a New Politics in the South* (Knoxville: University of Tennessee Press, 1949); Charles S. Sydnor, *The Development of Southern Sectionalism, 1819–1848* (Baton Rouge: Louisiana State University Press, 1948); C. Vann Woodward, *The Origins of the New South, 1877–1913* (Baton Rouge: Louisiana State University Press, 1951); C. Vann Woodward, *The Burden of Southern History*, rev. ed. (Baton Rouge: Louisiana State University Press, 1968); Avery O. Craven, *The Growth of Southern Nationalism, 1848–1861* (Baton Rouge: Louisiana State University Press, 1953); George B. Tindall, *The Emergence of the New South, 1913–1945* (Baton Rouge: Louisiana State University Press, 1967); David M. Potter, *The South and the Concurrent Majority* (Baton Rouge: Louisiana State University Press, 1972); and Charles S. Bullock III, "Regional Realignment from an Officeholding Perspective," *Journal of Politics*, 50 (August 1988), 553–574.

2. John Shelton Reed, "Southerners," in Stephan Thernstrom, ed., *Harvard Encyclopedia of American Ethnic Groups* (Cambridge, Mass.: Harvard University Press, 1980), p. 944.

3. Potter, *South and the Concurrent Majority*, pp. 29, 3.

4. Donald L. Robinson, *Slavery in the Structure of American Politics, 1765–1820* (New York: Harcourt Brace Jovanovich, 1971), pp. 168–206.

5. Potter, *South and the Concurrent Majority*, p. 3.

6. William J. Cooper, Jr., *The South and the Politics of Slavery, 1828–1856* (Baton Rouge: Louisiana State University Press, 1978), pp. 105–106.

7. Ibid., pp. 105–106.

8. Ibid.; James L. Sundquist, *Dynamics of the Party System*, rev. ed. (Washington, D.C.: Brookings Institution, 1983), pp. 74–105.

9. Robert Kelley, *The Cultural Pattern in American Politics* (New York: Knopf, 1979), p. 227.

10. Potter, *South and the Concurrent Majority*, p. 61.

11. Woodward, *Origins of the New South*, p. 460.

12. Ibid., pp. 1–74.

13. E. E. Schattschneider, "United States: The Functional Approach to Party Government," in Sigmund Neumann, ed., *Modern Political Parties* (Chicago: University of Chicago Press, 1956), pp. 194–215; E. E. Schatt-

schneider, *The Semi-Sovereign People* (New York: Holt, Rinehart, and Winston, 1960), pp. 78–85; Sundquist, *Dynamics of the Party System*, pp. 134–169; and Walter Dean Burnham, "The System of 1896: An Analysis," in Paul Kleppner et al., *The Evolution of American Electoral Systems* (Westport, Conn.: Greenwood Press, 1981), pp. 147–202.

3. The Changing Geography of Presidential Elections

1. All of the results reported in this chapter were calculated by the authors from Edgar E. Robinson, *The Presidential Vote: 1896–1932* (Stanford, Calif.: Stanford University Press, 1935); Richard M. Scammon, ed., *America at the Polls* (Pittsburgh: University of Pittsburgh Press, 1965); and appropriate volumes of Richard M. Scammon, ed., *America Votes* (Washington, D.C.: Congressional Quarterly).

4. The South and Democratic Nominations

1. V. O. Key, Jr., *Southern Politics in State and Nation* (New York: Knopf, 1949), p. 317.
2. *Newsweek*, August 15, 1960.
3. See William J. Cooper, Jr., *Liberty and Slavery* (New York: Knopf, 1983), pp. 70–191; Nobel E. Cunningham, Jr., *The Jeffersonian Republicans* (Chapel Hill: University of North Carolina Press, 1957); Thomas P. Abernethy, *The South in the New Nation, 1789–1819* (Baton Rouge: Louisiana State University Press, 1961); and Charles S. Sydnor, *The Development of Southern Sectionalism, 1819–1848* (Baton Rouge: Louisiana State University Press, 1948).
4. William J. Cooper, Jr., *The South and the Politics of Slavery, 1828–1856* (Baton Rouge: Louisiana State University Press, 1978); and Donald B. Cole, *Martin Van Buren and the American Political System* (Princeton, N.J.: Princeton University Press, 1984), pp. 142–378.
5. David M. Potter, *The South and the Concurrent Majority* (Baton Rouge: Louisiana State University Press, 1972), p. 14; and James S. Chase, *Emergence of the Presidential Nominating Convention, 1789–1832* (Urbana: University of Illinois Press, 1973), p. 265.
6. Cole, *Martin Van Buren*, pp. 381–405.
7. Eric Foner, *Free Soil, Free Labor, Free Men: The Ideology of the Republican Party before the Civil War*, (New York: Oxford University Press, 1970).
8. Cooper, *Liberty and Slavery*, pp. 258–267; and James M. McPherson, *Battle Cry of Freedom* (New York: Oxford University Press, 1988), pp. 214–216.
9. Potter, *South and the Concurrent Majority*, p. 26.
10. Wilfred E. Binkley, *American Political Parties*, 2d ed. (New York: Knopf, 1954), p. 260.
11. Congressional Quarterly, *Guide to U.S. Elections* (Washington, D.C.: Congressional Quarterly, 1976), p. 132.
12. Potter, *South and the Concurrent Majority*, p. 52.

13. The growth of one-party, Democratic control of the southern electorate in the decades after the end of Reconstruction is thoroughly analyzed in J. Morgan Kousser, *The Shaping of Southern Politics* (New Haven: Yale University Press, 1974).

14. Binkley, *American Political Parties*, pp. 260–277, 301–320.

15. C. Vann Woodward, *The Origins of the New South, 1877–1913* (Baton Rouge: Louisiana State University Press, 1951), pp. 23–50, 235–290, 456–481.

16. Ibid., pp. 477–478; and Evans C. Johnson, *Oscar W. Underwood* (Chapel Hill: University of North Carolina Press, 1980), pp. 18–105, 170–192.

17. Woodward, *Origins of the New South*, p. 478–481; Potter, *South and the Concurrent Majority*, pp. 62–63.

18. Robert K. Murray, *The 103rd Ballot* (New York: Harper & Row, 1976), p. 24.

19. Ibid.

20. Matthew and Hannah Josephson, *Al Smith: Hero of the Cities* (Boston: Houghton Mifflin, 1969), p. 367.

21. Richard L. Rubin, *Party Dynamics* (New York: Oxford University Press, 1976), p. 117.

22. Richard O'Connor, *The First Hurrah* (New York: G. P. Putnam's Sons, 1970), p. 198.

23. George B. Tindall, *The Emergence of the New South* (Baton Rouge: Louisiana State University Press, 1967), pp. 246–247.

24. Ibid., p. 250; Martha H. Swain, *Pat Harrison: The New Deal Years* (Jackson, Miss.: University Press of Mississippi, 1978), p. 23; and Key, *Southern Politics*, p. 318.

25. Frank Freidel, *F.D.R. and the South* (Baton Rouge: Louisiana State University Press, 1965); Tindall, *Emergence of the New South*, pp. 385–387; and Arthur M. Schlesinger, Jr., *The Crisis of the Old Order* (Boston: Houghton Mifflin, 1957), pp. 295–314.

26. D. B. Hardeman and Donald C. Bacon, *Rayburn* (Austin: Texas Monthly Press, 1987), pp. 137–140.

27. T. Harry Williams, *Huey Long* (New York: Knopf, 1969), p. 581.

28. Hardeman and Bacon, *Rayburn*, pp. 137, 141; Tindall, *Emergence of the New South*, p. 387; Bascom N. Timmons, *Garner of Texas* (New York: Harper & Brothers, 1948), p. 168; and Marquis James, *Mr. Garner of Texas* (Indianapolis: Bobbs-Merrill, 1939), p. 130.

29. James, *Mr. Garner*, p. 83.

30. Robert A. Caro, *The Path to Power* (New York: Knopf, 1982), pp. 561, 557–566.

31. Johnson, *Underwood*, p. 401; Rubin, *Party Dynamics*, p. 114; and James F. Byrnes, *All in One Lifetime* (New York: Harper & Brothers, 1958), p. 94.

32. Timmons, *Garner*, p. 161.

33. Robert A. Garson, *The Democratic Party and the Politics of Sectionalism* (Baton Rouge: Lousiana State University Press, 1974), p. 8.

34. Tindall, *Emergence of the New South*, p. 693.

35. Garson, *Democratic Party,* p. 12; and Byrnes, *All in One Lifetime,* pp. 226–227.
36. Byrnes, *All in One Lifetime,* p. 228.
37. Tindall, *Emergence of the New South,* p. 728.
38. Rubin, *Party Dynamics,* p. 111.
39. Potter, *South and the Concurrent Majority,* pp. 60, 62; and James L. Sundquist, *Dynamics of the Party System,* rev. ed. (Washington, D.C.: Brookings Institution, 1983), pp. 273.
40. Garson, *Democratic Party,* pp. 221, 224–225.
41. Ibid., pp. 230–231.
42. Ibid., p. 231.
43. Irwin Ross, *The Loneliest Campaign* (New York: New American Library, 1968), p. 56; and Sundquist, *Dynamics of the Party System,* p. 274.
44. Sundquist, *Dynamics of the Party System,* p. 275; and Ross, *Loneliest Campaign,* pp. 64, 62–65, 111–139.
45. Ross, *Loneliest Campaign,* pp. 123, 125; and Hubert H. Humphrey, *The Education of a Public Man* (Garden City, N.Y.: Doubleday, 1976), p. 113.
46. Congressional Quarterly, *Guide to U.S. Elections,* p. 91; and Ross, *Loneliest Campaign,* p. 124.
47. *Time,* July 26, 1948.
48. Hardeman and Bacon, *Rayburn,* pp. 336–337; and Ross, *Loneliest Campaign,* p. 127.
49. *Time,* July 26, 1948.
50. Gilbert C. Fite, *Richard B. Russell, Jr., Senator from Georgia* (Chapel Hill: University of North Carolina Press, 1991), pp. 272–273.
51. See Charles L. Fontenay, *Estes Kefauver* (Knoxville: University of Tennessee Press, 1980), pp. 99–229; Joseph Bruce Gorman, *Kefauver* (New York: Oxford University Press, 1971), pp. 20–159; and Paul T. David, Malcolm Moos, and Ralph W. Goldman, eds., *Presidential Nominating Politics in 1952,* Vol. I: *The National Story* and Vol. III: *The South* (Baltimore: Johns Hopkins University Press, 1954).
52. Gorman, *Kefauver,* pp. 110–111.
53. Ibid., pp. 119, 123; and Fontenay, *Estes Kefauver,* pp. 194–195.
54. Gorman, *Kefauver,* p. 129.
55. Fite, *Russell,* pp. 285–286.
56. Fontenay, *Estes Kefauver,* p. 204.
57. Ibid., pp. 224–225.
58. Ibid., pp. 225–229.
59. Ibid., p. 231.
60. Gorman, *Kefauver,* pp. 235, 237.
61. Ibid., pp. 234, 224–248; and Fontenay, *Estes Kefauver,* pp. 244–265.
62. Gorman, *Kefauver,* pp. 260, 249–265; and Fontenay, *Estes Kefauver,* pp. 266–284.
63. See Theodore H. White, *The Making of the President 1960* (New York: Atheneum, 1961), pp. 26–58, 78–179.
64. Humphrey, *Education of a Public Man,* p. 163; and Merle Miller, *Lyndon*

(New York: G. P. Putnam's Sons, 1980), p. 236. For background on Johnson's career, see Robert A. Caro, *The Path to Power* (1982) and *Means of Ascent* (New York: Knopf, 1990); Ronnie Dugger, *The Politician* (New York: Norton, 1982); and Alfred Steinberg, *Sam Johnson's Boy* (New York: McMillan, 1968).

65. Hardeman and Bacon, *Rayburn*, p. 435.
66. Ibid., p. 436; White, *Making of the President 1960*, pp. 43–46; and James Reston, Jr., *The Lone Star* (New York: Harper & Row, 1989), pp. 183–196.
67. Kenneth P. O'Donnell and David F. Powers with Joe McCarthy, *"Johnny, We Hardly Knew Ye"* (Boston: Little, Brown, 1970), p. 193.
68. Hardeman and Bacon, *Rayburn*, pp. 433, 442; see also Caro, *The Path to Power*, pp. xiii–xxiii.
69. O'Donnell and Powers, *"Johnny,"* p. 399; and Fite, *Russell*, p. 379.
70. O'Donnell and Powers, *"Johnny,"* p. 25.
71. Theodore H. White, *The Making of the President 1964* (New York: Atheneum, 1965), pp. 32–63.
72. *Time*, September 4, 1964.
73. White, *Making of the President 1964*, pp. 294–295.
74. David Halberstam, *The Best and the Brightest* (New York: Random House, 1972), pp. 401–536; and White, *Making of the President 1964*, pp. 271–304.
75. Analyzed by the authors from the 1968 National Election Study Survey of the Electorate, Center for Political Studies, University of Michigan.
76. Carl Solberg, *Hubert Humphrey* (New York: Norton, 1984), p. 325; Theodore H. White, *The Making of the President 1968* (New York: Atheneum, 1969), pp. 62–125; and Lewis Chester, Godfrey Hodgson, and Bruce Page, *An American Melodrama* (New York: Viking, 1969), pp. 51–141.
77. Halberstam, *Best and Brightest*, p. 435.
78. Solberg, *Humphrey*, pp. 342, 301–354.
79. Ibid., pp. 327; White, *Making of the President 1968*, pp. 150–223; and Chester, Hodgson, and Page, *American Melodrama*, pp. 142–179, 297–372.
80. Chester, Hodgson, and Page, *American Melodrama*, p. 524.
81. Ibid., p. 542; and Reston, *Lone Star*, pp. 349–368.
82. Reston, *Lone Star*, p. 351; Chester, Hodgson, and Page, *American Melodrama*, p. 538–563; and Solberg, *Humphrey*, p. 359.
83. Solberg, *Humphrey*, pp. 358, 355–371.
84. Reston, *Lone Star*, p. 360; and Solberg, *Humphrey*, pp. 359–60.
85. Chester, Hodgson, and Page, *American Melodrama*, p. 542; and Solberg, *Humphrey*, p. 360.
86. Reston, *Lone Star*, p. 369.

5. The South and Republican Nominations

1. Wilfred E. Binkley, *American Political Parties*, 2d ed. (New York: Knopf, 1954), pp. 206, 216; Eric Foner, *Free Soil, Free Labor, Free Men: The Ideology of the Republican Party before the Civil War* (New York: Oxford University

Press, 1970); and William E. Gienapp, *The Origins of the Republican Party* (New York: Oxford University Press, 1987).

2. William J. Cooper, Jr., *Liberty and Slavery* (New York: Knopf, 1983), p. 256; and Robert Kelley, *The Cultural Pattern in American Politics* (New York: Knopf, 1979), pp. 221–222.

3. Cooper, *Liberty and Slavery*, p. 271; convention results and election returns are from Congressional Quarterly, *Guide to U.S. Elections* (Washington, D.C.: Congressional Quarterly, 1975), pp. 128, 270–271.

4. V. O. Key, Jr., *Politics, Parties, and Pressure Groups*, 4th ed. (New York: Crowell, 1958), pp. 185–186.

5. Binkley, *American Political Parties*, pp. 206–259, 278–300; generalizations about the regional composition of the Republican presidential tickets are based upon information in Congressional Quarterly, *Guide to U.S. Elections*, pp. 190–191.

6. Richard Franklin Bensel, *Sectionalism and American Political Development, 1880–1980* (Madison: University of Wisconsin Press, 1984), pp. 62–63.

7. Ralph J. Bunche, *The Political Status of the Negro in the Age of FDR* (Chicago: University of Chicago Press, 1973), p. 16.

8. C. Vann Woodward, *Reunion and Reaction: The Compromise of 1877 and the End of Reconstruction*, rev. ed. (Garden City, N.Y.: Doubleday, 1956); and Eric Foner, *Reconstruction* (New York: Harper & Row, 1988), pp. 564–587.

9. J. Morgan Kousser, *The Shaping of Southern Politics* (New Haven: Yale University Press, 1974); and Dewey W. Grantham, *The Life and Death of the Solid South* (Lexington: University Press of Kentucky, 1988), pp. 1–25.

10. George Brown Tindall, *The Disruption of the Solid South* (Athens: University of Georgia Press, 1972), p. 15; Kousser, *Shaping of Southern Politics*, pp. 1–44; Hanes Walton, Jr., *Black Republicans* (Metuchen, N.J.: Scarecrow Press, 1975), pp. 36–37; and Donald J. Lisio, *Hoover, Blacks, & Lily-Whites* (Chapel Hill: University of North Carolina Press, 1985), p. 36.

11. Congressional Quarterly, *Guide to U.S. Elections*, pp. 132–144.

12. On southern Republicanism in the nineteenth century, see Richard B. Sherman, *The Republican Party and Black America* (Charlottesville: University Press of Virginia, 1973); Vincent P. DeSantis, *Republicans Face the Southern Question* (Baltimore: Johns Hopkins University Press, 1959); Walton, *Black Republicans*; and Alexander Heard, *A Two-Party South?* (Chapel Hill: University of North Carolina Press, 1952), pp. 115–129, 220–226.

13. J. Hampton Moore, *Roosevelt and the Old Guard* (Philadelphia: Macrae Smith Co., 1925), p. 266; and Congressional Quarterly, *Guide to U.S. Elections*, pp. 149, 284.

14. Sherman, *Republican Party*, pp. 102–120; and Congressional Quarterly, *Guide to U.S. Elections*, pp. 151–166.

15. Liscio, *Hoover, Blacks, & Lily-Whites*, p. 37; and Walton, *Black Republicans*.

16. Walton, *Black Republicans*, p. 163; and V. O. Key, Jr., *Southern Politics in State and Nation* (New York: Knopf, 1949), p. 289.

17. Heard, *Two-Party South?*, p. 122.

18. Ibid., pp. 97, 105.
19. Ibid., pp. 115–116.
20. Steve Neal, *Dark Horse* (Garden City, N.Y.: Doubleday, 1984); and Richard N. Smith, *Thomas E. Dewey and His Times* (New York: Simon and Schuster, 1982).
21. James T. Patterson, *Mr. Republican* (Boston: Houghton Mifflin, 1972), pp. 509–510.
22. Smith, *Dewey and His Times*, pp. 575–608; and Stephen E. Ambrose, *Eisenhower: Soldier, General of the Army, President-Elect, 1890–1952*, (New York: Simon and Schuster, 1983), pp. 500–549.
23. Paul T. David, Malcolm Moos, and Ralph M. Goldman, eds., *Presidential Nominating Politics in 1952*, Vol. III: *The South* (Baltimore: Johns Hopkins University Press, 1954), pp. 39, 129; and Congressional Quarterly, *Guide to U.S. Elections*, p. 166.
24. Ambrose, *Eisenhower: Soldier*, pp. 550–572; and Roger Morris, *Richard Milhous Nixon* (New York: Holt, 1990), pp. 625–866.
25. Heard, *Two-Party South?*, p. 122.
26. Theodore H. White, *The Making of the President 1968* (New York: Atheneum, 1969), p. 239; Theodore H. White, *The Making of the President 1964* (New York: Atheneum, 1965), pp. 64–169, 200–231; and John H. Kessel, *The Goldwater Coalition* (Indianapolis: Bobbs-Merrill, 1968), pp. 25–119.
27. White, *Making of the President 1964*, pp. 71–72.
28. Ibid., p. 93.
29. F. Clifton White with William J. Gill, *Suite 3505* (New Rochelle, N.Y.: Arlington House, 1967), pp. 174–175.
30. Nicol C. Rae, *The Decline and Fall of the Liberal Republicans* (New York: Oxford University Press, 1989), p. 56; calculations of regional size based upon data in Congressional Quarterly, *Guide to U.S. Elections*, pp. 166–169.
31. White, *Suite 3505*, p. 261.
32. Robert D. Novak, *The Agony of the G.O.P. 1964* (New York: Macmillan, 1965), pp. 176–178; and Rae, *Decline and Fall*, p. 55.
33. White, *Making of the President 1964*, pp. 205–231; Kessel, *Goldwater Coalition*, pp. 91–119; and Novak, *Agony of the G.O.P.*, pp. 416–469.
34. Calculated from data in Congressional Quarterly, *Guide to U.S. Elections*, p. 169.
35. Bernard Cosman, "Deep South Republicans: Profiles and Positions," in Bernard Cosman and Robert J. Huckshorn, eds., *Republican Politics* (New York: Praeger, 1968), p. 105.
36. Ibid., p. 94.
37. Ibid., p. 109.
38. Barry M. Goldwater with Jack Casserly, *Goldwater* (New York: Doubleday, 1988), p. 185–186.
39. Kessel, *Goldwater Coalition*, p. 118.
40. White, *Suite 3505*, pp. 14–15.
41. Goldwater, *Goldwater*, p. 166.

42. Calculated from data in Congressional Quarterly, *Guide to U.S. Elections*, p. 171.

43. Stephen E. Ambrose, *Nixon: The Triumph of a Politician, 1962–1972* (New York: Simon and Schuster, 1989), pp. 100, 122, 80–156; Kessel, *Goldwater Coalition*, p. 185; and Jules Witcover, *The Resurrection of Richard Nixon* (New York: G. P. Putnam's Sons, 1970), pp. 104–323.

44. Ambrose, *Nixon: Triumph*, p. 89.

45. Ibid.; and Earl Black and Merle Black, *Politics and Society in the South* (Cambridge, Mass.: Harvard University Press), pp. 196–210.

46. Harry S. Dent, *The Prodigal South Returns to Power* (New York: Wiley, 1978), p. 76.

47. White, *Making of the President 1968*, pp. 52, 134–136.

48. Dent, *Prodigal South*, pp. 80, 73–104.

49. Richard M. Nixon, *The Memoirs of Richard Nixon* (New York: Grosset & Dunlap, 1978), p. 304; and Ambrose, *Nixon: Triumph*, p. 155.

50. Nixon, *Memoirs*, pp. 304, 309.

51. Lewis Chester, Godfrey Hodgson, and Bruce Page, *An American Melodrama* (New York: Viking, 1969), p. 457; F. Clifton White, *Why Reagan Won* (Chicago: Regnery Gateway, 1981), p. 111; and White, *Making of the President 1968*, p. 240.

52. Dent, *Prodigal South*, p. 87; and Nixon, *Memoirs*, p. 309.

53. Calculated from results in Congressional Quarterly, *Guide to U.S. Elections*, p. 171.

54. White, *Making of the President 1968*, p. 239.

6. The White Revolt in the Deep South

1. Robert A. Garson, *The Democratic Party and the Politics of Sectionalism, 1941–1948* (Baton Rouge: Louisiana State University Press, 1974), p. 231.

2. Ibid., p. 281.

3. V. O. Key, Jr., *Southern Politics in State and Nation* (New York: Knopf, 1949), p. 317.

4. *Columbia State*, September 7, 1948.

5. Ibid., September 24, 1948.

6. Ibid., September 26; October 2, 1948.

7. Ibid., October 2–3, 1948; and *New Orleans Times-Picayune*, October 27, 1948.

8. *Columbia State*, November 2, 1948.

9. Key, *Southern Politics*, p. 336.

10. Alexander Heard, *A Two-Party South?* (Chapel Hill: University of North Carolina Press, 1952), p. 25.

11. Ibid., p. 27; and Key, *Southern Politics*, p. 671.

12. Charles and Barbara Whalen, *The Longest Debate* (New York: New American Library, 1986).

13. Theodore H. White, *The Making of the President 1964* (New York: Atheneum, 1965), p. 382; Roman Heleniak, "Lyndon Johnson in New Or-

leans," *Louisiana History*, 21 (Summer 1980), 265; and Stephen Hess and David S. Broder, *The Republican Establishment* (New York: Harper & Row, 1967), p. 339.

14. *Congressional Record*, June 18, 1964, pp. 14,318–14,319. See also Barry M. Goldwater with Jack Casserly, *Goldwater* (New York: Doubleday, 1988), pp. 172–173.

15. Hess and Broder, *Republican Establishment*, p. 340.

16. Richard H. Rovere, *The Goldwater Caper* (New York: Harcourt, Brace & World, 1965), pp. 135, 140–143.

17. Ibid., pp. 143–144.

18. *New York Times*, September 11; October 17, 24, 1964.

19. Ibid., September 17, 18, 1964.

20. Ibid., November 1, 1964; and John H. Kessel, *The Goldwater Coalition* (Indianapolis: Bobbs-Merrill, 1968), p. 216.

21. White, *Making of the President 1964*, p. 382; and Merle Miller, *Lyndon* (New York: G. P. Putnam's Sons, 1980), p. 396.

22. Kessel, *Goldwater Coalition*, p. 232; and Miller, *Lyndon*, pp. 396–397.

23. Miller, *Lyndon*, p. 397.

24. Charles McDowell, Jr., *Campaign Fever* (New York: Morrow, 1965), pp. 220, 222–223.

25. Heleniak, "Johnson in New Orleans," pp. 263, 265.

26. Ibid., p. 274.

27. Bernard Cosman, *Five States for Goldwater* (University, Ala.: University of Alabama Press, 1966), pp. 59–91.

28. Ibid., p. 62; and George Brown Tindall, *The Disruption of the Solid South* (Athens, Ga.: University of Georgia Press, 1972), p. 64.

29. Tindall, *Disruption*, p. 64.

30. *Birmingham News*, January 14, 1963.

31. *Montgomery Advertiser*, May 4, 8, 9, 13, 1963.

32. *Birmingham News*, June 5, 6, 11, 1963.

33. George C. Wallace, *Stand Up for America* (Garden City, N.Y.: Doubleday, 1976), pp. 84–87.

34. Ibid., p. 90; *Newsweek*, May 18, 1964.

35. *Time*, May 29, 1964; *Newsweek*, June 1, 1964.

36. Jody Carlson, *George C. Wallace and the Politics of Powerlessness* (New Brunswick, N.J.: Transaction Books, 1981), pp. 38–41.

37. *New York Times*, September 22, 1968. Four years earlier Wallace had expressed his views on the desirability of integration more crudely. "All these countries with niggers in 'em have stayed the same for a thousand years," he told a reporter. "Tell me any place where white people and niggers mix." *Newsweek*, June 1, 1964.

38. Marshall Frady, *Wallace* (New York: New American Library, 1968), p. 7; and Walter Dean Burnham, *Critical Elections and the Mainsprings of American Politics* (New York: Norton, 1970), p. 142.

39. James Jackson Kilpatrick, "What Makes Wallace Run?" *National Review*, April 18, 1967, pp. 402–403.

40. Frady, *Wallace*, pp. 20, 26.
41. *New York Times*, September 3, 1968.
42. See W. J. Cash, *The Mind of the South* (New York: Knopf, 1941).
43. William Anderson, *The Wild Man from Sugar Creek* (Baton Rouge: Louisiana State University Press, 1975), p. 103.
44. Herman E. Talmadge with Mark Royden Winchell, *Talmadge* (Atlanta: Peachtree Publishers, 1987), p. 57.
45. Frady, *Wallace*, pp. 8–9. See also Robert Sherrill, *Gothic Politics in the Deep South* (New York: Grossman, 1968), pp. 255–301.
46. James Wooten, "Wallace and Me: The End of the Road," *Esquire*, November 1978, p. 96.
47. *New York Times*, October 25, 31, 1968.
48. Ibid., September 15; October 18, 1968.
49. Ibid., October 18, 1968.
50. Ibid., October 10, 27, 1968.
51. Seymore Martin Lipset and Earl Raab, *The Politics of Unreason* (New York: Harper & Row, 1970), p. 383. For an ingenious analysis of the Wallace vote in the South, see Gerald C. Wright, Jr., "Contextual Models of Electoral Behavior: The Southern Wallace Voter," *American Political Science Review*, 71 (June 1977), 497–508.
52. For an insider account, see Harry S. Dent, *The Prodigal South Returns to Power* (New York: Wiley, 1978), pp. 73–117.
53. Lipset and Raab, *Politics of Unreason*, pp. 345–346; and Sherrill, *Gothic Politics*, p. 292.
54. Lipset and Raab, *Politics of Unreason*, pp. 388–389.

7. The Republican Breakthrough in the Peripheral South

1. V. O. Key, Jr., *Southern Politics in State and Nation* (New York: Knopf, 1949), p. 674. See Earl Black and Merle Black, *Politics and Society in the South* (Cambridge, Mass.: Harvard University Press, 1987), pp. 3–72; and Lewis M. Seagull, *Southern Republicanism* (Cambridge, Mass.: Schenkman, 1975).
2. James L. Sundquist, *Dynamics of the Party System*, rev. ed. (Washington, D.C.: Brookings Institution, 1983), p. 284.
3. *New York Times*, September 4, 1952.
4. Ibid.
5. Ibid., October 15, 1952.
6. George Brown Tindall, *The Disruption of the Solid South* (Athens, Ga.: University of Georgia Press, 1972), p. 51.
7. *New York Times*, October 1, 1952.
8. Ibid., November 3, 1952.
9. John Bartlow Martin, *Adlai Stevenson of Illinois* (Garden City, N.Y.: Doubleday, 1976), p. 680.
10. Wilson W. Wyatt, Sr., *Whistle Stops* (Lexington, Ky.: University Press of Kentucky, 1985), pp. 104–105.

11. Martin, *Stevenson of Illinois,* p. 722.
12. Ibid., pp. 723–724.
13. Gilbert C. Fite, *Richard B. Russell, Jr., Senator From Georgia* (Chapel Hill: University of North Carolina Press, 1991), pp. 296–298; and *New York Times,* November 2, 1952.
14. Dewey W. Grantham, *The Life and Death of the Solid South* (Lexington, Ky.: University Press of Kentucky, 1988), p. 127.
15. Tindall, *Disruption,* p. 52.
16. Virginia Van der Veer Hamilton, *Lister Hill* (Chapel Hill: University of North Carolina Press, 1987), p. 190.
17. Tindall, *Disruption,* pp. 52–53.
18. *New York Times,* September 13, 1956.
19. John Bartlow Martin, *Adlai Stevenson and the World* (Garden City, N.Y.: Doubleday, 1977), p. 384; and Joseph Bruce Gorman, *Kefauver* (New York: Oxford University Press, 1971), pp. 273–274.
20. *New York Times,* October 30, 1956.
21. D. B. Hardeman and Donald C. Bacon, *Rayburn* (Austin: Texas Monthly Press, 1987), p. 402; and Martin, *Stevenson and the World,* pp. 210–211.
22. Martin, *Stevenson and the World,* p. 258; and *New York Times,* September 16, 1956.
23. Martin, *Stevenson and the World,* pp. 258–259.
24. Ibid., p. 266.
25. *New York Times,* October 16, 1956.
26. Stephen E. Ambrose, *Eisenhower: The President* (New York: Simon and Schuster, 1984), p. 370.
27. *New York Times,* October 30, 1956.
28. *Newsweek,* September 5, 1960.
29. Black and Black, *Politics and.Society,* p. 237.
30. *New York Times,* September 7, 1960.
31. *Time,* October 24, 1960.
32. Grantham, *Life and Death,* p. 150.
33. Harris Wofford, *Of Kennedys and Kings* (New York: Farrar, Straus, Giroux, 1980), p. 63.
34. *Newsweek,* August 15, 1960; and *Time,* August 29, 1960.
35. Richard Nixon, *Six Crises* (Garden City, N.Y.: Doubleday, 1962), pp. 320–321.
36. Theodore H. White, *The Making of the President 1960* (New York: Atheneum, 1962), p. 247.
37. James Reston, Jr., *The Lone Star* (New York: Harper & Row, 1989), pp. 196–197.
38. *Time,* August 29, 1960.
39. Ibid., September 5, 1960.
40. Stephen E. Ambrose, *Nixon: The Education of a Politician, 1913–1962* (New York: Simon and Schuster, 1987), p. 575.
41. White, *Making of the President 1960,* pp. 203–205, 272.

42. *New York Times*, October 8, 1960.

43. *Newsweek*, October 24, 1960; and Ambrose, *Nixon: Education*, p. 580.

44. *Time*, September 5, 1960; and Angus Campbell, Philip E. Converse, Warren E. Miller, and Donald T. Stokes, *Elections and the Political Order* (New York: Wiley, 1966), p. 91.

45. Kenneth P. O'Donnell and David F. Powers with Joe McCarthy, *"Johnny, We Hardly Knew Ye"* (Boston: Little, Brown, 1970), p. 210.

46. Ibid., p. 214.

47. *New York Times*, October 11, 1960.

48. Apart from these political reactions, Robert Kennedy was outraged by the judge's action and later telephoned him to urge the immediate release of Dr. King. Wofford, *Kennedys and Kings*, pp. 19, 21.

49. *Time*, October 24, 1960; and *Newsweek*, October 24, 1960.

50. *Time*, October 24, 1960; and *Newsweek*, October 24, 1960.

51. Reston, *Lone Star*, pp. 197–198.

52. Campbell, Converse, Miller, and Stokes, *Elections and the Political Order*, pp. 86, 89.

53. Grantham, *Life and Death*, p. 152.

54. Although Johnson was endorsed by Mississippi Senator James O. Eastland, the reasons Eastland mustered for supporting Johnson speak volumes about the alienation of Mississippi whites from the national Democratic party. "I don't always agree with Lyndon Johnson," Eastland told white Mississippians, "but you have to give him credit. He took everything relating to integration out of those civil rights bills [that did pass]. . . . He has always opposed Congress' implementing the segregation decisions of the Supreme Court." *Time*, October 17, 1960. Not even that sort of endorsement was sufficient for Mississippi whites, who narrowly preferred Senator Harry Byrd over the Kennedy-Johnson ticket.

55. Grantham, *Life and Death*, p. 151.

56. Richard N. Goodwin, *Remembering America* (Boston: Little, Brown, 1988), p. 283; and Barry M. Goldwater with Jack Casserly, *Goldwater* (New York: Doubleday, 1988), p. 184.

57. Stanley Kelley, Jr., "The Presidential Campaign," in Milton C. Cummings, Jr., ed., *The National Election of 1964* (Washington, D.C.: Brookings Institution, 1966), p. 78; Philip E. Converse, Aage R. Clausen, and Warren E. Miller, "Electoral Myth and Reality: The 1964 Election," *American Political Science Review*, 59 (June 1965), 323; and Stephen C. Shadegg, *What Happened to Goldwater?* (New York: Holt, Rinehart and Winston, 1965), pp. 198–199.

58. Goodwin, *Remembering America*, pp. 303–304.

59. Ibid., p. 305; and Theodore H. White, *The Making of the President 1964* (New York: Atheneum, 1965), p. 339.

60. White, *Making of the President 1964*, p. 365.

61. Goodwin, *Remembering America*, p. 257.

62. White, *Making of the President 1964*, p. 375.

63. *Time,* October 17, 1960.
64. F. Clifton White with William J. Gill, *Suite 3505* (New Rochelle, N.Y.: Arlington House, 1967), pp. 248, 252.
65. *Newsweek,* August 17, 1964.
66. White, *Making of the President 1964,* p. 332; and Shadegg, *What Happened to Goldwater?* p. 222.
67. Charles McDowell, Jr., *Campaign Fever* (New York: Morrow, 1965), p. 205.
68. *Newsweek,* September 28, 1964.
69. *New York Times,* October 25, 27, 1964.
70. Goldwater, *Goldwater,* pp. 195–196.
71. White, *Suite 3505,* p. 226.
72. *Time,* October 30, 1964.
73. Merle Miller, *Lyndon* (New York: G. P. Putnam's Sons, 1980), p. 398; and David J. Garrow, *Protest at Selma* (New Haven: Yale University Press, 1978), p. 19.
74. Converse, Clausen, and Miller, "Electoral Myth and Reality," p. 330.

8. The New Southern Electorate

1. Walter Dean Burnham, "The Turnout Problem," in A. James Reichley, ed., *Elections American Style* (Washington, D.C.: Brookings Institution, 1987), pp. 113–114; and Harold W. Stanley and Richard G. Niemi, *Vital Statistics on American Politics,* 2d ed. (Washington, D.C.: CQ Press, 1990), p. 79.
2. Burnham, "Turnout Problem," p. 115.
3. J. Morgan Kousser, *The Shaping of Southern Politics* (New Haven: Yale University Press, 1974).
4. Ibid., pp. 11–44, 261–265.
5. V. O. Key, Jr., *Southern Politics in State and Nation* (New York: Knopf, 1949), pp. 489–532.
6. Burnham, "Turnout Problem," p. 114.
7. Stanley and Niemi, *Vital Statistics,* p. 79; actual turnout estimates were generously provided by Harold W. Stanley; see also Harold W. Stanley, *Voter Mobilization and the Politics of Race* (New York: Praeger, 1987), pp. 11–12.
8. Estimates of black voter registration are taken from David J. Garrow, *Protest at Selma* (New Haven: Yale University Press, 1978), pp. 7, 11, 19, 189.
9. Earl Black and Merle Black, *Politics and Society in the South* (Cambridge, Mass.: Harvard University Press, 1987), pp. 138–140.
10. Ibid., pp. 138–151, 292–296.
11. Key, *Southern Politics,* pp. 509–528; and Black and Black, *Politics and Society,* pp. 180–186.
12. Black and Black, *Politics and Society,* pp. 186–194.
13. The scatter plots depicting thermometer ratings of various political symbols also contain a question about religion. For this category, "Religion,"

asked in 1980, 1984, and 1988, the question was, "Do you consider religion to be an important part of your life, or not?" Respondents who said religion was an important part of their life were considered to be "warm" toward religion. Those who said it was not an important part of their life should be understood simply as "not warm" toward religion, but not necessarily hostile or cold toward religion.

14. See, for example, Jeffrey K. Hadden and Anson D. Shupe, *Televangelism, Power, and Politics on God's Frontier* (New York: Holt, 1988); and John B. Donovan, *Pat Robertson: The Authorized Biography* (New York: Macmillan, 1988).

15. Complete question wording is found in the appropriate NES codebooks for the 1980, 1984, and 1988 presidential election surveys. In instances of minor changes in question wording, we have reported the most recent version of the question.

We analyzed three racial questions, labeled on the policy scatter plots as "Minorities," "Quotas," and "Hiring." For "Minorities," asked in 1980, 1984, and 1988, the question was as follows: "Some people feel that the government in Washington should make every effort to improve the social and economic position of blacks and other minorities. Others feel that the government should not make any special effort to help minorities because they should help themselves. Where would you place yourself on this scale, or haven't you thought much about this?" After eliminating those respondents who had not given much thought to the issue, respondents who placed themselves close to the view that "government should help minorities" (positions 1, 2, or 3) were considered to be liberal, while those who placed themselves close to the view that "minorities should help themselves" (positions 5, 6, or 7) were considered to be conservative.

For "Quotas," asked in 1988, the question was, "Some people say that because of past discrimination it is sometimes necessary for colleges and universities to reserve openings for black students. Others oppose quotas because they say quotas give blacks advantages they haven't earned. What about your opinion—are you for or against quotas to admit black students?" Respondents who said they were against quotas were considered to be conservative, while those who were for quotas were liberal.

For "Hiring," asked in 1988, the question was, "Some people say that because of past discrimination, blacks should be given preference in hiring and promotion. Others say that such preference in hiring and promotion of blacks is wrong because it discriminates against whites. What about your opinion—are you for or against preferential hiring and promotion of blacks?" Respondents who said they were against such hiring and promotion were considered to be conservative, while those who were for such practices were considered to be liberal.

We analyzed four cultural questions, labeled on the policy graphs as "Death," "Prayers," "ERA," and "Women." For "Death," asked in 1988, the question was, "Do you favor or oppose the death penalty for persons convicted of murder?" Respondents who favored the death penalty were considered to be conservative, while those who opposed the death penalty were considered to be liberal.

For "Prayers," asked in 1980 and 1984, the question was, "Some people think it is all right for the public schools to start each day with a prayer. Others feel that religion does not belong in the public schools but should be taken care of by the family and the church." After eliminating respondents who were uninterested in this question, the question continued, "Which do you think—schools should be allowed to start each day with a prayer or religion does not belong in the schools?" Respondents who supported prayers in schools were considered conservative, while those who thought them inappropriate in a public school were considered liberal.

For "ERA," asked in 1980, the question was, "Do you approve or disapprove of the proposed Equal Rights Amendment to the Constitution, sometimes called the ERA Amendment?" Respondents who approved of the amendment were considered liberal, while those in opposition were considered conservative.

For "Women," asked in 1984, the question was, "Some people feel that the government in Washington should make every effort to improve the social and economic position of women. Others feel that the government should not make any special effort to help women because they should help themselves. Where would you place yourself on this scale, or haven't you thought much about this?" After eliminating those respondents who had not given the issue much thought, we classified those who believed government should help women (positions 1, 2, or 3) as liberal, and those who believed that women should help themselves (positions 5, 6, or 7) as conservative.

We analyzed four questions dealing with the provision of government services: "Services," "Taxes," "Jobs," and "Insurance." For "Services," asked in 1980, 1984, and 1988, the question was, "Some people think the government should provide fewer services, even in areas such as health and education, in order to reduce spending. Suppose these people are at one end of the scale at point 1. Other people feel it is important for the government to provide many more services even if it means an increase in spending. Suppose these people are at the other end, at point 7. And of course, some other people have opinions somewhere in between at points 2, 3, 4, 5, or 6. Where would you place yourself on this scale, or haven't you thought much about this?" After eliminating those who had not given much thought to the question, we classified those who wanted the government to provide fewer services (positions 1, 2, or 3) as conservative, while those who wanted the government to provide more services (positions 5, 6, or 7) were considered to be liberal.

For "Taxes," asked in 1980, the question was, "Do you feel you are asked to pay much more than you should in federal income taxes, somewhat more than you should, about the right amount, or less than you should?" We classified respondents who said they paid more taxes than they should, and who presumably would favor a reduction in their taxes, as conservative; respondents who said they paid about the right amount, or even less than they should, were classified as liberal.

For "Jobs," asked in 1980, 1984, and 1988, the question was, "Some people feel the government in Washington should see to it that every person has a job and a good standard of living. Others think the government should just let each person get ahead on their own. Where would you place yourself on this scale, or haven't you thought much about this?" We coded respondents who placed themselves close to the view that "the government should see to jobs and a good standard of living" (positions 1, 2, or 3) as liberal, while those who put themselves close to the view that "the government should let each person get ahead on their own" (positions 5, 6, or 7) as conservative.

For "Insurance," asked in 1988, the question was, "There is much concern about the rapid rise in medical and hospital costs. Some people feel there should be a government insurance plan which would cover all medical and hospital expenses for everyone. Others feel that all medical expenses should be paid by individuals, and through private insurance plans like Blue Cross or other company paid plans. Where would you place yourself on this scale, or haven't you thought much about this?" After excluding those who had not given the issue much thought, we classified those who placed themselves close to a "government insurance plan" (positions 1, 2, or 3) as liberal and those who put themselves close to a "private insurance plan" (places 5, 6, or 7) as conservative.

We examined five foreign policy and military security questions: "Soviets," "Communism," "Defense," "Military," and "Central America." For "Soviets," asked in 1984 and 1988, the question was, "Some people feel it is important for us to try to cooperate more with Russia, while others believe we should be much tougher in our dealings with Russia. Where would you place yourself on this scale, or haven't you thought much about this?" Respondents who placed themselves toward cooperation with Russia (positions 1, 2, or 3) were considered liberal, while those who placed themselves toward getting much tougher with Russia (positions 5, 6, or 7) were considered conservative.

For "Communism," asked in 1988, the statement was, "The United States should do everything it can to prevent the spread of Communism to any other part of the world." Respondents who agreed with the statement were considered conservative, while those who disagreed were considered liberal.

For "Defense," asked in 1980, 1984, and 1988, the question was, "Some people believe we should spend less money for defense. Others feel that defense spending should be greatly increased. Where do you place yourself on this scale, or haven't you thought much about this?" After eliminating those who have not given much thought to the question, we classified those who leaned toward greatly decreasing defense spending (positions 1, 2, or 3) as liberal, and those who leaned toward greatly increasing defense spending (positions 5, 6, or 7) as conservative.

For "Military," asked in 1988, the statement was, "The U.S. should maintain its position as the world's most powerful nation even if it means going to the brink of war." Those respondents who agreed with the statement were classified as conservative, while those who disagreed were considered liberal.

For "Central America," asked in 1984, the question was, "Some people believe that the United States should become much more involved in the internal affairs of Central American countries. Others believe that the U.S. should become much less involved in this area. Where would you place yourself on this scale, or haven't you thought much about this?" After eliminating those who had not given much thought to the topic, we classified those who thought the United States should become more involved (positions 1, 2, or 3) as conservative, and those who thought the United States should become less involved (positions 5, 6, or 7) as liberal.

16. The NES abortion question, asked in 1984 and 1988, was as follows: "There has been some discussion about abortion during recent years. Which one of the opinions . . . best agrees with your view?" The options for the respondents were: "By law, abortion should never be permitted"; "The law should permit abortion only in the case of rape, incest or when the woman's life is in danger"; "The law should permit abortion for reasons other than rape, incest or danger to the woman's life, but only after the need for the abortion has been clearly established"; or "By law, a woman should always be able to obtain an abortion as a matter of personal choice."

9. The Progressive Advantage in Democratic Primaries

1. Thomas R. Marshall, "The Impact of National Party Reform on Presidential Nomination Politics: The Case of the Southern Democrats," paper prepared for delivery at the 1978 Annual Meeting of the Southern Political Science Association, Atlanta, Georgia, November 9–11, 1978, p. 2.
2. Ibid., pp. 2, 5.
3. Ibid., p. 25; and Stephen J. Wayne, The Road to the White House, 3d ed. (New York: St. Martin's Press, 1988), pp. 90–105.
4. Joint Center for Political Studies, Blacks and the 1988 Democratic Convention (Washington, D.C.: Joint Center for Political Studies, 1988), p. 17.
5. Ibid., pp. 109–111.
6. Byron E. Shafer, Bifurcated Politics (Cambridge, Mass.: Harvard University Press, 1988), pp. 91, 75–227. There is a substantial literature on the reforms within the Democratic party. See, for example, Byron E. Shafer, Quiet Revolution (New York: Russell Sage, 1978); William Crotty, Party Reform (New York: Longman, 1983); Nelson W. Polsby, Consequences of Party Reform (New York: Oxford University Press, 1983); David E. Price,

Bringing Back the Parties (Washington, D.C.: CQ Press, 1984); and Jeanne J. Kirkpatrick, *The New Presidential Elite* (New York: Russell Sage, 1976).

7. Wayne, *Road to the White House,* p. 105; *New York Times,* August 14, 1988.

8. Wayne, *Road to the White House,* p. 91.

9. D. B. Hardeman and Donald C. Bacon, *Rayburn* (Austin: Texas Monthly Press, 1987), p. 435. Trends on primaries calculated from relevant editions of Richard M. Scammon, ed., *America Votes* (Washington, D.C.: Congressional Quarterly). For participation rules see *Congressional Quarterly Weekly Report,* March 5, 1988, 572.

10. Calculations by the authors.

11. Charles D. Hadley and Harold W. Stanley, "An Analysis of Super Tuesday: Intentions, Results, and Implications," revised paper presented at the Annual Meeting of the Midwest Political Science Association, Chicago, Illinois, April 14–16, 1988, p. 17.

12. Estimates of the distribution of white voters in the states were made on the basis of the racial composition of Democratic and Republican Super Tuesday voters in the exit polls of voters in ten southern states conducted by CBS News and the New York Times.

13. Robert W. Hooker, "Busing, Gov. Askew, and the Florida Primary," *New South,* 27 (Spring 1972), 24; Theodore H. White, *The Making of the President 1972* (New York: Atheneum, 1973), p. 94; and see Jody Carlson, *George C. Wallace and the Politics of Powerlessness* (New Brunswick, N.J.: Transaction Books, 1981), pp. 157–179.

14. White, *Making of the President 1972,* p. 95.

15. Carlson, *Wallace,* pp. 133–156.

16. White, *Making of the President 1972,* pp. 158–192.

17. Calculated from data in Congressional Quarterly, *Guide to U.S. Elections* (Washington, D.C.: Congressional Quarterly, 1975), pp. 172–173.

18. Calculations made by the authors.

19. Tip O'Neill with William Novak, *Man of the House* (New York: Random House, 1987), pp. 300–301.

20. Richard Reeves, *Convention* (New York: Harcourt Brace Jovanovich, 1977), pp. 208, 212.

21. James Wooten, *Dasher* (New York: Summit, 1978), pp. 348–349.

22. Jules Witcover, *Marathon* (New York: Viking, 1977), pp. 105–118, 132–138, 194–221; Wooten, *Dasher,* pp. 32–38; Gerald M. Pomper, "The Nominating Contests and Conventions," in Gerald M. Pomper, *The Election of 1976* (New York: McKay, 1977), pp. 10–17; and Earl Black, *Southern Governors and Civil Rights* (Cambridge, Mass.: Harvard University Press, 1976), pp. 309–344.

23. Martin Schram, *Running for President 1976* (New York: Stein and Day, 1977), pp. 6; and Witcover, *Marathon,* p. 132–138.

24. Larry M. Bartels, *Presidential Primaries and the Dynamics of Public Choice* (Princeton, N.J.: Princeton University Press, 1988), pp. 172–193; Wooten, *Dasher,* pp. 21, 115, 329; Witcover, *Marathon,* pp. 240–252; and Schram, *Running,* pp. 27–34.

25. Wooten, *Dasher*, pp. 111–114; Witcover, *Marathon*, pp. 253–260; and Schram, *Running*, pp. 75–85.

26. Wooten, *Dasher*, pp. 286–302.

27. Ibid., pp. 288–290.

28. Ibid., pp. 300–301.

29. Ibid., pp. 329–339.

30. Bartels, *Presidential Primaries*, p. 202.

31. *Raleigh News and Observer*, March 25, 1976.

32. Ibid., March 28, 1976.

33. Witcover, *Marathon*, p. 353.

34. Schram, *Running*, p. 2; and Witcover, *Marathon*, p. 351.

35. Calculated from Congressional Quarterly, *Guide to U.S. Elections*, 2d ed. (Washington, D.C.: Congressional Quarterly, 1985), p. 215; and Reeves, *Convention*, p. 179.

36. Bartels, *Presidential Primaries*, pp. 219–220.

37. Jack W. Germond and Jules Witcover, *Blue Smoke and Mirrors* (New York: Viking, 1981), pp. 48, 52.

38. Ibid., pp. 23–92.

39. Bartels, *Presidential Primaries*, pp. 219–228; Germond and Witcover, *Blue Smoke*, pp. 141–165, 191–208; and Gerald M. Pomper, "The Nominating Contests," in Marlene Michels Pomper, ed., *The Election of 1980* (Chatham, N.J.: Chatham House, 1981), pp. 22, 6–12, 20–32.

40. Germond and Witcover, *Blue Smoke*, pp. 192–195.

41. For evidence of the movement of conservative whites out of the Democratic party, see Earl Black and Merle Black, *Politics and Society in the South* (Cambridge, Mass.: Harvard University Press, 1987), pp. 249–256.

42. Gerald M. Pomper, "The Nominations," in Gerald M. Pomper with colleagues, *The Election of 1984* (Chatham, N.J.: Chatham House, 1985), pp. 6–28; and Jack W. Germond and Jules Witcover, *Wake Us When It's Over* (New York: Macmillan, 1985), pp. 175–224.

43. Germond and Witcover, *Wake Us When It's Over*, pp. 175–176; and calculations by the authors.

44. Germond and Witcover, *Wake Us When It's Over*, pp. 279–280.

45. Ibid., p. 280; and Lucius J. Barker, *Our Time Has Come* (Urbana: University of Illinois Press, 1988), pp. 211, 214.

46. Germond and Witcover, *Wake Us When It's Over*, p. 72.

47. Nelson W. Polsby, "The Democratic Nomination and the Evolution of the Party System," in Austin Ranney, ed., *The American Elections of 1984* (Durham: Duke University Press, 1985), p. 54.

48. Calculated by the authors from data in Congressional Quarterly, *Guide to U.S. Elections*, p. 220.

49. Germond and Witcover, *Wake Us When It's Over*, p. 409.

50. Ibid., pp. 409–410.

51. William D. Snider, *Helms and Hunt* (Chapel Hill: University of North Carolina Press, 1985), pp. 165, 143.

52. For thorough analyses of the 1988 Super Tuesday primaries, see Harold W. Stanley and Charles D. Hadley, "The Southern Presidential Primary: Regional Intentions with National Implications," *Publius*, 17 (Summer 1987), 83–100; and Charles S. Bullock III, "Super Tuesday," in Laurence W. Moreland, Robert P. Steed, and Tod A. Baker, eds., *The 1988 Presidential Election in the South* (New York: Praeger, 1991), pp. 3–19.

53. Stanley and Hadley, "Southern Presidential Primary."

54. Jack W. Germond and Jules Witcover, *Whose Broad Stripes and Bright Stars?* (New York: Warner, 1989), pp. 280–282, 284, 287–291.

55. Ibid., pp. 225–229, 271–272, 278–292.

56. Ibid., pp. 301–318.

57. Merle Black and Earl Black, "Don't Underestimate Bush," *New York Times*, March 13, 1988.

58. Germond and Witcover, *Whose Broad Stripes*, pp. 279–292.

59. Ibid., pp. 318–329.

60. Elizabeth Drew, *Election Journal* (New York: Morrow, 1989), pp. 221–222.

61. Germond and Witcover, *Whose Broad Stripes*, p. 354.

62. The outcomes of Democratic primaries in major statewide elections in the South have begun to reflect the numerical dominance of moderate to progressive Democrats. For an interesting discussion of the transformation of the Democratic party in one southern state, see Paul Luebke, *Tar Heel Politics* (Chapel Hill: University of North Carolina Press, 1990), pp. 156–204.

63. Thomas Byrne Edsall with Mary D. Edsall, "Race," *Atlantic Monthly*, 267 (May 1991), 69.

10. The Conservative Triumph in Republican Primaries

1. Jack W. Germond and Jules Witcover, *Whose Broad Stripes and Bright Stars?* (New York: Warner, 1989), p. 147.

2. Wayne Greenhaw, *Elephants in the Cotton Fields* (New York: Macmillan, 1982), pp. 77–169.

3. Calculated from state delegation totals in Congressional Quarterly, *Guide to U.S. Elections*, 2d ed. (Washington, D.C.: Congressional Quarterly, 1985), p. 221.

4. *Washington Post*, November 18, 1973.

5. Gerald M. Ford, *A Time to Heal* (New York: Harper & Row, 1979), p. 333.

6. David R. Runkel, ed., *Campaign for President* (Dover, Mass.: Auburn House, 1989), p. 104.

7. *Washington Post*, November 18, 1973.

8. Lou Cannon, *Reagan* (New York: G. P. Putnam's Sons, 1982), pp. 192–193.

9. Ibid., p. 194.

10. Ford, *Time to Heal*, p. 143.

11. Cannon, *Reagan*, pp. 193–194.

12. Harry S. Dent, *The Prodigal South Returns to Power* (New York: Wiley, 1978), p. 21.
13. Ford, *Time to Heal*, p. 328.
14. For these developments, see Cannon, *Reagan*, pp. 187–209; and Jules Witcover, *Marathon* (New York: Viking, 1977), pp. 35–102.
15. Witcover, *Marathon*, pp. 403, 409, 398–409.
16. Ibid., p. 411; and Cannon, *Reagan*, p. 218.
17. *Congressional Quarterly Weekly Report*, May 8, 1976, 1080; Cannon, *Reagan*, pp. 219–220; and Witcover, *Marathon*, pp. 417–432.
18. Cannon, *Reagan*, pp. 220–223; and Witcover, *Marathon*, pp. 443–471.
19. Calculated from results in Congressional Quarterly, *Guide to U.S. Elections*, p. 216.
20. Cannon, *Reagan*, pp. 227–245.
21. *Congressional Quarterly Weekly Report*, March 1, 1980, 598; and Cannon, *Reagan*, pp. 232–233, 237, 245.
22. Cannon, *Reagan*, pp. 230–240.
23. Ibid., p. 248.
24. Ibid., pp. 249–260.
25. *Congressional Quarterly Weekly Report*, March 1, 1980, 597; Gerald M. Pomper, "The Nominating Contests," in Marlene Michels Pomper, ed., *The Election of 1980* (Chatham, N.J.: Chatham House, 1981), p. 17.
26. Runkle, *Campaign for President*, p. 31.
27. Congressional Quarterly, *Guide to U.S. Elections*, pp. 429–435.
28. Ibid., p. 218.
29. Lee Atwater with Todd Brewster, "Lee Atwater's Last Campaign," *Life*, February 1991, 62; Runkle, *Campaign for President*, p. 13; and observation of one of the authors.
30. Runkle, *Campaign for President*, p. 32.
31. Ibid., pp. 104–105.
32. Ibid., p. 14; and Germond and Witcover, *Whose Broad Stripes*, p. 147.
33. Germond and Witcover, *Whose Broad Stripes*, p. 148.
34. Ibid., p. 151.
35. Runkle, *Campaign for President*, p. 34.
36. Ibid., pp. 34–35.
37. Germond and Witcover, *Whose Broad Stripes*, pp. 101–130.
38. Ibid., pp. 142–143, 130–146.
39. Ibid., pp. 151–152.
40. Ibid., pp. 146–153.
41. Elizabeth Drew, *Election Journal* (New York: Morrow, 1989), p. 145.
42. Charles D. Hadley and Harold W. Stanley, "An Analysis of Super Tuesday: Intentions, Results, and Implications," revised version of a paper presented at the annual meeting of the Midwest Political Science Association, April 14–16, 1988, Chicago, Illinois, p. 5.
43. Merle Black and Earl Black, "Don't Underestimate Bush," *New York Times*, March 13, 1988.

11. Republican Dominance after the Great Society

1. Figure 11.1 and similar tables and graphs are based on the authors' estimates of the partisan division of the white vote for the southern states, the subregions, and the region. For discussions of procedures, see Earl Black and Merle Black, *Politics and Society in the South* (Cambridge, Mass.: Harvard University Press, 1987), pp. 140–142; and Earl Black, "Competing Responses to the 'New Southern Politics': Republican and Democratic Southern Strategies, 1964–1976," in Merle Black and John Shelton Reed, eds., *Perspectives on the American South* (New York: Gordon and Breach, 1981), vol. 1, pp. 152–155.

2. Theodore H. White, *The Making of the President 1960* (New York: Atheneum, 1962), p. 203.

3. Richard M. Nixon, *The Memoirs of Richard Nixon* (New York: Grosset & Dunlap, 1978), pp. 304, 316.

4. *New York Times*, September 9, 1968; and Jules Witcover, *The Resurrection of Richard Nixon* (New York: G. P. Putnam's Sons, 1970), pp. 364–365.

5. *New York Times*, September 13, 1968.

6. Witcover, *Resurrection*, p. 403.

7. Harry S. Dent, *The Prodigal South Returns to Power* (New York: Wiley, 1978), pp. 107, 111, 114.

8. *New York Times*, October 13, 1968.

9. Ibid., September 9, 1968.

10. Ibid.

11. Ibid., September 9, 12, 1968.

12. Ibid., October 2, 1968.

13. Ibid., October 5, 1968.

14. Ibid.

15. Numan V. Bartley and Hugh D. Graham, *Southern Politics and the Second Reconstruction* (Baltimore: Johns Hopkins Press, 1975), pp. 127, 130.

16. Kevin P. Phillips, *The Emerging Republican Majority* (Garden City, N.Y.: Anchor Books, 1970), pp. 25, 287.

17. *New York Times*, September 4, 28, 1972.

18. Ibid., September 4, 1972.

19. Ibid., September 23, 1972; October 13, 1972.

20. Ibid., September 4, 1972.

21. Theodore H. White, *The Making of the President 1972* (New York: Atheneum, 1973), pp. 343–344.

22. William Schneider, "The November 4 Vote for President: What Did It Mean?" in Austin Ranney, ed., *The American Elections of 1980* (Washington, D.C.: American Enterprise Institute for Public Policy Research, 1981), p. 241.

23. Ibid., p. 212; and Jack W. Germond and Jules Witcover, *Blue Smoke and Mirrors* (New York: Viking, 1981), p. 205.

24. *New York Times*, October 4, 1980.

25. Ibid., August 4, 1980.
26. Ibid., October 16, 1980.
27. Ibid., September 2, 3, 1980.
28. Ibid., September 17, 19, 1980.
29. Ibid., September 21, 1980.
30. Ibid., October 24, 1980; and Germond and Witcover, *Blue Smoke*, p. 287.
31. *Raleigh News and Observer*, October 5, 1980.
32. *New York Times*, September 23, 1980; October 11, 23, 1980.
33. Ibid., October 31, 1980.
34. Wayne Greenhaw, *Elephants in the Cotton Fields* (New York: Macmillan, 1982), p. 140.
35. Ibid.
36. Germond and Witcover, *Blue Smoke*, p. 288.
37. *New York Times*, October 3, 1984.
38. Ibid., October 28, 1984.
39. Ibid., September 1, 1984; for analyses of the contest in the southern states, see Robert P. Steed, Laurence W. Moreland, and Tod A. Baker, eds., *The 1984 Presidential Election in the South* (New York: Praeger, 1986).
40. *New York Times*, September 14, 15, 1984.
41. *Gallup Report*, April 1988, p. 4; May 1988, p. 3; and July 1988, p. 3.
42. *Washington Post*, January 20, 1989.
43. Ibid.
44. *Washington Post National Weekly Edition*, November 7–13, 1988; *Raleigh News and Observer*, October 2, 1988; *Washington Post*, September 25, 1988; and *Tuscaloosa News*, October 25, 1988.
45. *Washington Post*, August 27, 1988.
46. *Washington Post National Weekly Edition*, August 8–14, 1988.
47. *Durham Sun*, August 30, 1988.
48. *Wilmington Sunday-Star News*, October 23, 1988.
49. Black and Black, *Politics and Society*, pp. 213–219; 232–275.
50. *New York Times*, June 18, 1988; and *Washington Post National Weekly Edition*, May 30–June 5, 1988.
51. *New York Times*, July 22, 1988.
52. Ibid., July 22, 1988; August 19, 1988.
53. Ibid., June 20, 1988; and *Washington Post*, June 19, 1988.
54. *Wall Street Journal*, July 22, 1988.
55. *Washington Post National Weekly Edition*, May 30–June 5, 1988.
56. *Christian Science Monitor*, October 25, 1988; and *New York Times*, October 28, 1988.
57. *Wilmington Sunday-Star News*, October 23, 1988; and *Raleigh News and Observer*, October 16, 1988.
58. *Washington Post National Weekly Edition*, May 30–June 5, 1988; and *New York Times*, June 20, 1988.
59. See, for example, John Shelton Reed, *The Enduring South* (Chapel Hill: University of North Carolina Press, 1986).
60. *New York Times*, September 18, 1988.

61. *Atlanta Constitution,* August 18, 1988; and *Southern Political Report,* September 13, 1988.

62. *Raleigh News and Observer,* October 2, 1988; and *Washington Post National Weekly Edition,* October 24–30, 1988.

63. *Atlanta Journal/Atlanta Constitution,* October 9, 1988; and *Raleigh News and Observer,* September 21, 1988. For analyses of the contest in the southern states, see Laurence W. Moreland, Robert P. Steed, and Tod A. Baker, eds., *The 1988 Presidential Election in the South* (New York: Praeger, 1991).

12. The Democratic Interlude

1. Jules Witcover, *Marathon* (New York: Viking, 1977), pp. 40–44; and Gerald R. Ford, *A Time to Heal* (New York: Harper & Row, 1979), pp. 428–429.

2. Witcover, *Marathon,* p. 530; *New York Times,* September 7, 1976; and Gerald M. Pomper, "The Presidential Election," in Marlene M. Pomper, ed., *The Election of 1976* (New York: McKay, 1977), p. 66.

3. Witcover, *Marathon,* p. 520.

4. Ibid.

5. Kandy Stroud, *How Jimmy Won* (New York: Morrow, 1977), p. 421; and Witcover, *Marathon,* pp. 632–636.

6. Stroud, *How Jimmy Won,* p. 420.

7. *New York Times,* September 11, 1976.

8. Martin Schram, *Running for President 1976* (New York: Stein and Day, 1977), p. 275; and Stroud, *How Jimmy Won,* pp. 346–347.

9. Schram, *Running for President,* p. 332. Italics removed from script of advertisement.

10. Stroud, *How Jimmy Won,* p. 329.

11. *New York Times,* September 12, 14, 1976.

12. Ibid., September 18, 1976. The Mississippi senators endorsed Carter but did not share his enthusiasm for the civil rights revolution. "'I never voted for a civil rights bill in my life,' said Senator Stennis. 'Neither did I,' said Senator Eastland." As Stennis explained to a *New York Times* reporter, "Let me just say one thing about this integration. I'm against it, always have been and always will be, but it's a fact. I'm not a fool. It's a fact. It's there." Ibid.

13. Ibid., September 20, 1976.

14. Ford, *Time to Heal,* pp. 411–412.

15. *New York Times,* September 1, 1976; and Witcover, *Marathon,* p. 535.

16. *New York Times,* September 26–28, 1976.

17. Jack Bass and Walter DeVries, *The Transformation of Southern Politics* (New York: Basic Books, 1976), p. 12; and Earl Black and Merle Black, *Politics and Society in the South* (Cambridge, Mass.: Harvard University Press, 1987), pp. 286–288.

18. For Lyndon Johnson's withering appraisal of McGovern's prospects of

carrying Texas, see Bobby Baker with Larry L. King, *Wheeling and Dealing* (New York: Norton, 1978), p. 266.

13. As the South Goes

1. For an excellent analysis of regional variations in partisan officeholding, see Charles S. Bullock III, "Regional Realignment from an Officeholding Perspective," *Journal of Politics*, 50 (August 1988), 553–574.
2. Jules Witcover, *Marathon* (New York: Viking, 1977), p. 520.
3. V. O. Key, Jr., *The Responsible Electorate* (Cambridge, Mass.: Harvard University Press, 1966), p. 30.
4. Thomas Byrne Edsall with Mary D. Edsall, "Race," *Atlantic Monthly*, 267 (May 1991), 53, 86.
5. The importance of white moderates as a swing group in the South has been emphasized by Edward G. Carmines and Harold W. Stanley, "Ideological Realignment in the Contemporary South," in Robert P. Steed, Laurence W. Moreland, and Tod A. Baker, eds., *The Disappearing South? Studies in Regional Change and Continuity* (Tuscaloosa: University of Alabama Press, 1990), p. 33.
6. *Atlanta Journal/Atlanta Constitution*, June 22, 1991.
7. Ibid.
8. California's role in the electoral college strategy of Republicans is stressed by George Rabinowitz and Stuart Elaine Macdonald, "The Power of the States in American Presidential Elections," *American Political Science Review*, 80 (March 1986), 79–80.
9. *Atlanta Journal/Atlanta Constitution*, June 21, 22, 1991.
10. For interesting analyses of recent political trends in the southern states, see Laurence W. Moreland, Robert P. Steed, and Tod A. Baker, eds., *The 1988 Presidential Election in the South* (New York: Praeger, 1991); Robert P. Steed, Laurence W. Moreland, and Tod A. Baker, eds., *The 1984 Presidential Election in the South* (New York: Praeger, 1986); and Robert H. Swansbrough and David M. Brodsky, eds., *The South's New Politics: Realignment and Dealignment* (Columbia: University of South Carolina Press, 1988).

Index